Essentials of Psychological Assessment Series

Series Editors, Alan S. Kaufman and Nadeen L. Kaufman

Essentials of WAIS-III Assessment
by Alan S. Kaufman and Elizabeth O. Lichtenberger

Essentials of Millon Inventories Assessment
by Stephen N. Strack

Essentials of CAS Assessment
by Jack A. Naglieri

Essentials of Forensic Psychological Assessment
by Marc J. Ackerman

Essentials of Bayley Scales of Infant Development–II Assessment
by Maureen M. Black and Kathleen Matula

Essentials of Myers-Briggs Type Indicator® Assessment
by Naomi Quenk

Essentials of WISC-III and WPPSI-R Assessment
by Alan S. Kaufman and Elizabeth O. Lichtenberger

Essentials of Rorschach® Assessment
by Tara Rose, Nancy Kaser-Boyd, and Michael P. Maloney

Essentials of Career Interest Assessment
by Jeffery P. Prince and Lisa J. Heiser

Essentials of Cross-Battery Assessment
by Dawn P. Flanagan and Samuel O. Ortiz

Essentials of Cognitive Assessment with KAIT and Other Kaufman Measures
by Elizabeth O. Lichtenberger, Debra Broadbooks, and Alan S. Kaufman

Essentials of Nonverbal Assessment
by Steve McCallum, Bruce Bracken, and John Wasserman

Essentials of MMPI-2™ Assessment
by David S. Nichols

Essentials of NEPSY® Assessment
by Sally Kemp, Marit Korkman, and Ursula Kirk

Essentials

of NEPSY® Assessment

Sally L. Kemp

Marit Korkman

Ursula Kirk

John Wiley & Sons, Inc.

NEW YORK · CHICHESTER · WEINHEIM · BRISBANE · SINGAPORE · TORONTO

Copyright © 2001 by John Wiley & Sons, Inc. All rights reserved.
Published simultaneously in Canada.

NEPSY is a registered trademark of The Psychological Corporation.

This publication is designed to provide accurate and authoritative information in regard to the subject matter covered. It is sold with the understanding that the publisher is not engaged in rendering professional services. If legal, accounting, medical, psychological or any other expert assistance is required, the services of a competent professional person should be sought.

Designations used by companies to distinguish their products are often claimed as trademarks. In all instances where John Wiley & Sons, Inc. is aware of a claim, the product names appear in initial capital or all capital letters. Readers, however, should contact the appropriate companies for more complete information regarding trademarks and registration.

Library of Congress Cataloging-in-Publication Data:
Kemp, Sally.
    Essentials of NEPSY assessment / Sally Kemp, Marit Korkman, and Ursula Kirk.
      p. cm. — (Essentials of psychological assessment series)
    Includes bibliographical references.
    ISBN 0-471-32690-9 (pbk. : alk. paper)
    1. NEPSY (Neuropsychology)   2. Neuropsychological tests for children.   3. Brain-damaged children—Psychological testing.   4. Developmentally disabled children—Psychological testing.   5. Developmental disabilitiies—Diagnosis.   I. Korkman, Marit.   II. Kirk, Ursula. III. Title.   IV. Series.

RJ486.6 .K46 2001
618.92´8075—dc21

00-068496

10 9 8 7 6 5 4 3 2 1

This volume is dedicated to all of the children who struggle with
neurological, developmental, and learning disorders,
to the parents who give them constant support,
and to the professionals who seek constantly new ways to help them.

—SALLY KEMP, URSULA KIRK, MARIT KORKMAN

CONTENTS

Series Preface   vii

One   Overview   1

Two   How to Administer the NEPSY   29

Three   How to Score the NEPSY   87

Four   How to Interpret the NEPSY   104

Five   Domain and Subtest Analysis   153

Six   Clinical Applications of the NEPSY   191

Seven   Illustrative Case Reports   224

Appendix A   NEPSY Data Worksheet   289

References   294

Index   308

Acknowledgments   317

About the Author   317

SERIES PREFACE

I n the *Essentials of Psychological Assessment* series, our goal is to provide the reader with books that will deliver key practical information in the most efficient and accessible style. The series features instruments in a variety of domains, such as cognition, personality, education, and neuropsychology. For the experienced clinician, books in the series offer a concise yet thorough way to master utilization of the continuously evolving supply of new and revised instruments, as well as a convenient method for keeping up to date on the tried-and-true measures. The novice will find here a prioritized assembly of all the information and techniques that must be at one's fingertips to begin the complicated process of individual psychological diagnosis.

Wherever feasible, visual shortcuts to highlight key points are utilized alongside systematic, step-by-step guidelines. Chapters are focused and succinct. Topics are targeted for an easy understanding of the essentials of administration, scoring, interpretation, and clinical application. Theory and research are continually woven into the fabric of each book, but always to enhance clinical inference, never to sidetrack or overwhelm. We have long been advocates of "intelligent" testing—the notion that a profile of test scores is meaningless unless it is brought to life by the clinical observations and astute detective work of knowledgeable examiners. Test profiles must be used to make a difference in the child's or adult's life, or why bother to test? We want this series to help our readers become the best intelligent testers they can be.

This volume has been prepared to introduce individuals new to NEPSY administration, scoring, and interpretation to the *NEPSY Developmental Neuropsychological Assessment* (Korkman, Kirk, & Kemp, 1998). Such individuals might be graduate students or seasoned diagnosticians who are just beginning to work with the instrument. For this reason, the book approaches NEPSY at a basic level, walking the reader through the process of preparation, tips on administration, modifications for certain populations, scoring, and providing detailed help in interpretation both at the psychometric and the clinical levels. Along the way, numerous inset boxes provide rapid reference to important information and frequent cautions against pitfalls. Finally, excerpts from reports, as well as two full reports, are presented. It is our hope that it can serve as a guide book to consult on specific questions concerning assessment and interpretation. The most important message this book is meant to convey, however, is that the child's ultimate good is paramount. This can only be achieved by being exquisitely aware throughout the evaluative process of the need to take into account all information available from the assessment, from exhaustive record review, and from interviews of key people in the child's life. The purpose of any evaluation is to develop recommendations for interventions that will enhance the child's ability to fulfill his or her own potential, both now and in the future. This can only be accomplished by comprehensive review and integration of the genetic, medical, psychosocial, educational, and family histories and the environmental forces impacting the child's life, together with sensitive observations of how the child performed and the results of the child's performance. It is our hope that this guide will elucidate the complexities of this process.

Alan S. Kaufman, PhD, and Nadeen L. Kaufman, EdD, Series Editors
Yale University School of Medicine

One

NEPSY, *A Developmental Neuropsychological Assessment* (Korkman, Kirk, & Kemp, 1998) is a new neuropsychological instrument composed of 27 subtests designed specifically for children ages 3 to 12. It assesses five domains: Attention/Executive Functions, Language, Sensorimotor, Visuospatial, and Memory and Learning. NEPSY is based on the clinical methods of Luria and on more recent traditions of child neuropsychology. NEPSY offers the advantage of being able to assess a child across functions and modalities. All of the subtests were normed on a large sample of children balanced for age, gender, and parent education level according to the 1995 United States census. Therefore, differences in the child's test performance should reflect true discrepancies, because all subtests are standardized on the same population.

HISTORY AND DEVELOPMENT

Twenty years ago, the scarcity of neuropsychological instruments for children led Marit Korkman, a pediatric neuropsychologist from Finland, to develop *NEPS* (Korkman, 1980), a brief assessment for children 5.0 to 6.11 years old. Various aspects of attention, language, sensorimotor functions, visuospatial functions, and memory and learning were each assessed with two to five tasks similar in content to the tasks in Luria's assessment (Christensen, 1975). These were scaled as 0 to 1 or 0 to 2 in order to preserve Luria's approach. No sum scores were calculated. Although the method proved most useful, the narrow age range was problematic, as was the pass/fail criterion, which was built on the medical model (Korkman, in press).

The NEPS was revised psychometrically by adding more items so that the results could be expressed in total scores. These were converted to z-scores (mean = 0 ± 1) based on age norms. During this revision new subtests were added, derived from tests which had proven useful in pediatric neuropsychology (e.g., Benton, Hamsher, Varney, & Spreen, 1983; Boehm, 1986; Reitan, 1979;

Venger & Holmomskaya, 1978). To complement the test, the shortened versions of the Token Test (De Renzi & Faglioni, 1978), the Motor Free Visual Perception Test (Colarusso & Hammill, 1972) and the Developmental Test of Visual-Motor Integration (Beery, 1983) were used in their original forms and standardized along with NEPSY. Norms were collected for children 4.0 to 7.11 years old. Later norms were extended from ages 3.6 to 9.5. The assessment was called *NEPS-U* in Finnish and *NEPSY* in English (Korkman, 1988a, 1988b, 1988c). The Swedish NEPSY for children aged 4.0 to 7.11 was published in 1990 (Korkman, 1990), and the Danish version for the same age range was published in 1993 (Korkman, 1993).

In the spring of 1987, the decision was made to develop the present American NEPSY, while keeping in mind international needs. It was also planned to expand the age range, from ages 4.0 to 7.11 to ages 2 to 12. We began to collaborate on the present NEPSY, incorporating revisions and new subtests which were based on traditions and views central to contemporary neuropsychological traditions of assessment. To accommodate the development of new material for the expanded age range and to allow for the multicultural populations the test would be designed to serve, an extended period of development and standardization was needed.

During the pilot phase (1987–1989), the original NEPSY subtests were adapted and revised for 3- to 10-year-old children. New items were added, new subtests were developed, and some subtests based on the work of others, such as Fingertip Tapping and Phonemic Fluency (Denckla, 1973; Benton et al., 1983) were included. A pilot version of NEPSY with 41 subtests was administered to 160 children in New York, New Jersey, Connecticut, and Pennsylvania beginning in the fall of 1987. The sample was randomly selected from urban and suburban settings and was stratified for age (3, 5, 7, and 10 years), gender, and educational and socioeconomic backgrounds. Piloting was completed simultaneously in Finland.

By the spring of 1988, when the pilot data were reviewed, some subtests were eliminated, others were modified, and new subtests were developed based on the pilot studies, ongoing literature review, and clinical experiences with NEPSY in Finland and Sweden. Using new items and new subtests, more pilot studies were conducted in the United States and Finland prior to the American tryout. A bias review was undertaken by the Psychological Corporation with very favorable results. Only a few adjustments had to be made on the basis of that information before the tryout phase (1990–1994) began.

The tryout version of NEPSY was composed of 52 subtests. Under the auspices of the Psychological Corporation, it was administered nationwide in 1991 to 1992 to 300 children, 2 to 12 years of age. Due to rapid development in children between 2.0 and 4.0 years of age, participants were grouped at 6-month intervals in those age bands. The sample was also stratified by race/ethnicity, gender, geographical region, and parent education, as a reliable indicator of socioeconomic status. A second bias review was undertaken with a few modifications or deletions of items being made in an effort to keep NEPSY as bias-free as possible.

In the fall of 1992, after a thorough review of the tryout data, subtests with poor reliabilities, including those for 2-year-olds, were eliminated, and floor and ceiling problems were identified and addressed. Psychometric properties were reviewed, and scoring procedures were reviewed and modified. Additional tryouts of the revised and new subtests were completed in the United States and Finland from 1992 to 1994. Standardization of the Finnish edition of the expanded NEPSY (Korkman, Kirk, & Kemp, 1997) began at the end of this period, providing data to guide the American tryout. Subsequently, the items and subtests for standardization of the present NEPSY were selected.

The Psychological Corporation conducted the standardization and validation phase of the present NEPSY from 1994 to 1996. The standardization version of NEPSY consisted of 38 subtests. The standardization sample was 1,000 children (100 at each age level) between the ages of 3.0 and 12.11 years, stratified for race/ethnicity, gender, parent education, and geographical region. Oversampling of minority groups began. Five hundred of the children were part of the bias oversample and validity cases. Validation studies were conducted with clinical populations. When the standardization phase was complete, the final selection of subtests and items was made for each of the five domains. Core and Expanded subtests were selected. Two subtests, Picture Recognition and Memory for Pictures, were eliminated due to poor psychometric properties and high production costs. Orientation and Handedness were reframed as informal supplementary screenings. Components of several subtests were combined, but supplemental scores that preserved the unique information in each component (i.e., immediate; delayed) were included. Base rates for quantified Qualitative Observations were computed.

NEPSY, A Developmental Neuropsychological Assessment was published in January 1998 (Korkman, Kirk, & Kemp, 1998). Just prior to its publication, a corresponding version of NEPSY was published in Finland (Korkman, Kirk, & Kemp, 1997). A revised version was also published in Sweden (Korkman, Kirk, & Kemp, in press). The history of NEPSY publication is shown in Rapid Reference 1.1.

≡≡Rapid Reference 1.1

The History of NEPSY

	Scandinavia			United States			
Year	Age Range (years)	Country of Publication	Author(s)	Year	Age Range (years)	Phase of Development (U.S.)	Author(s)
1980	5.0–6.11	Finland	Korkman				
1988	3.6–9.5	Finland	Korkman	1987–89	2.0–12.11	Pilot Phase	Korkman, Kirk, & Kemp
1990	4.0–7.11	Sweden	Korkman	1990–94	2.0–12.11	Tryout	Korkman, Kirk, & Kemp
1993	4.0–7.11	Denmark	Korkman	1994–96	3.0–12.11	Standardization	Korkman, Kirk, & Kemp
1997	3.0–12.11	Finland	Korkman, Kirk, & Kemp	1998	3.0–12.11	Publication	Korkman, Kirk, & Kemp
2000	3.0–12.11	Sweden	Korkman, Kirk, & Kemp				

THEORETICAL FOUNDATIONS

The theory of A. R. Luria has been a cornerstone of neuropsychology for nearly 40 years (Luria, 1962/1980). Luria conceptualized four interconnected levels of brain/behavior relationships and neurocognitive disorders that the clinician needs to know: the structure of the brain, the functional organization based on structure, syndromes and impairments arising in brain disorders, and clinical methods of assessment (Korkman, 1999).

At the structural and functional levels, Luria's concepts are based on his view of the brain as three functional units or "blocks." Block I is responsible for the basic physiological functions that support life, such as respiration and heartbeat, and for the arousal of attention that is necessary for cognitive functioning. These basic functions of Block I are subserved by the brainstem, diencephalon, and medial regions of each hemisphere. Block II refers to the posterior cortex: the occipital, parietal, and temporal lobes. These areas are purported to subserve the primary intake of information, the processing of that information, and the association of it with other information and experience. It is in this block that visual, auditory, and sensory information is received, processed, and associated across and within these modalities. Block III is purported to regulate the executive functions of planning, strategizing, and monitoring performance needed for efficient problem solving through rich connections to all areas of the brain. Block III regulates the use of information processed in Block II and is affected by, and modulates, the basic attentional/arousal function subserved by Block I (see Rapid Reference 1.2).

Working with adults, Luria also delineated brain regions that are interactively responsible for specific functions (e.g., in adults, motor programming of speech is dependent on left precentral and premotor neural systems, Broca's

---

≡ Rapid Reference 1.2

Luria's Functional Blocks of the Brain

Block I: Basic physiological functions (brain stem, diencephalon, and mesial regions of each hemisphere)
• respiration, heartbeat, etc.
• arousal of attention

Block II: Primary intake of visual, auditory, and sensory information (posterior cortex: occipital, parietal, and temporal lobes)
• processing of information
• associations of that information and experience across modalities

Block III: Regulation of executive functions of planning, strategizing, and monitoring performance for problem-solving (frontal lobes)
• use of information from Block II
• affected by and modulates attention/arousal function of Block I

area). He viewed the brain as a "functional mosaic," the parts of which interact in different combinations to subserve cognitive processing (Luria, 1963, 1973). One area never functions without input from other areas; thus, integration is a key principle of brain function in the Lurian views.

Cognitive functions, such as attention and executive functions, language, sensory perception, motor function, visuospatial abilities, and learning and memory are complex capacities in the Lurian tradition. They are composed of flexible and interactive subcomponents that are mediated by equally flexible, interactive, neural networks (Luria, 1962/1980). In other words, multiple brain systems contribute to and mediate complex cognitive functions. Multiple brain regions, for instance, interact to mediate attentional processes (Barkley, 1996; Mirsky, 1996). The executive functions subserved by Block III regulate the basic attentional functions of Block I in sustaining optimal levels of arousal and vigilance and in the search for, selection of, and attention to relevant details from a broad array of information (Korkman, Kirk, & Kemp, 1998). For example, the executive function of inhibition makes it possible for a child to resist or inhibit the impulse to respond to salient, but irrelevant, features of a task (Denckla, 1996; Levin et al., 1991; Pennington, Groisser, & Welsh, 1993). Response inhibition allows the child to sustain focused attention throughout the period needed for task performance. (See Rapid Reference 1.3.)

When considering clinical methods and the levels of impairment in neurocognitive functioning, Lurian theory proposes that impairment in one subcomponent of a function will also affect other complex cognitive

≡ Rapid Reference 1.3

Luria's Concept of Interactive Brain Function

- Multiple brain regions interact to mediate complex capacities.
- Complex capacities are composed of flexible, interactive subcomponents.
- Subcomponents are mediated by flexible, interactive neural networks.

≡ Rapid Reference 1.4

Levels of Impairment in Neurocognitive Functioning

Impairment in one subcomponent of a function will also affect other complex cognitive functions to which that subcomponent contributes.

An early-occurring anomaly or event may well affect the chain of development in a basic subcomponent that occurs subsequent to impairment.

functions to which that subcomponent contributes. This is an especially important factor to consider in children, because an early-occurring anomaly or event may well affect the chain of development in a basic subcomponent that occurs subsequent to impairment. (See Rapid Reference 1.4.)

The Lurian approach bases its diagnostic principles on identifying the *primary deficit* underlying impairments of complex functions. For example, a deficiency in auditory decoding may underlie an aphasia. The latter is referred to as a *secondary deficit* (Korkman, 1995, 1999). Both impaired performance and qualitative observations are necessary to detect and distinguish between primary and secondary deficits (Korkman, Kirk, & Kemp, 1998; Luria, 1962/1980). (See Rapid Reference 1.5.)

≡ Rapid Reference 1.5

Primary and Secondary Deficits

Primary Deficit: a deficit underlying impaired performance in one functional domain (e.g., visuospatial deficit); several primary deficits can be present in different domains

Secondary Deficit: a deficit in another functional domain arising from the primary deficit (e.g., visuospatial deficit causing a deficit in visual-motor integration for two- and three-dimensional constructions; a deficit in the comprehension of instructions based on visuospatial words; a deficit in mathematics)

At the level of clinical methods, Luria formulated explicit principles for an indirect, comprehensive review and evaluation of disorders of complex functions, which assesses subcomponents of these functions with carefully focused tests (Christensen, 1984). In accordance with this approach, NEPSY is composed of subtests that assess, as far as is possible, basic subcomponents of a complex capacity within a functional domain, as well as subtests that are designed to assess complex subcomponents that require contributions from several functional domains.

PURPOSES OF NEUROPSYCHOLOGICAL ASSESSMENT OF CHILDREN

For the child with brain damage that is either congenital (e.g., cerebral palsy, hydrocephalus, epilepsy) or acquired (e.g., traumatic brain injury, bacterial meningitis, tumor), neuropsychological assessment is valuable is assessing the effects of damage on brain function. It also evaluates the degree to which damage affects the capacity to process information in a functional domain, and, as a result, the development of competency in other domains (Christensen, 1984; Fischer & Rose,

1994; Levine, 1987; Luria, 1962/1980). Long-term follow-up for these children is as essential as the initial evaluation, because cognitive functioning may change with age (Casey, Rourke, & Picard, 1991; Morris, Blashfield, & Satz, 1996; Olson, Sampson, Barr, Streissguth, & Bookstein, 1992). The clinician needs to follow recovery of function in order to identify improved functioning, as well as persistent deficits, and to adapt interventions to changing needs (Korkman, Kirk, & Kemp, 1998).

Patterns of deficiencies in children with receptive and/or expressive language disorders and developmental disorders such as Autistic Disorders, Nonverbal Learning Disabilities, and Williams Syndrome, to name a few, can also be detected with neuropsychological assessment, thus assisting in diagnosis and intervention planning. Further, subtle deficiencies in children with less severe developmental disorders such as dyslexia, Attention-Deficit/Hyperactivity Disorder (ADHD), or graphomotor problems can be detected. Understanding these deficiencies facilitates the development of behavioral, educational, and cognitive interventions.

CAUTION

Inferences about Brain Pathology

Focal damage is more common in adults, whereas diffuse or multifocal damage is more common in children.

Lateralized or localized damage and neuropsychological findings in children are not usually evident in children with developmental disorders or early neurological insult.

Even with documented lateralized brain damage, the test profiles of children with left damage and with right damage do not differ.

Inferences concerning underlying brain pathology should be drawn with extreme caution, only by neuropsychologists who are trained in brain-behavior relationships.

CAUTIONS AGAINST LOCALIZING

The "working brain," as Luria (1973) termed it, is a very important Lurian concept. This concept is built on the notion that a highly interactive network of multiple brain systems contributes to and mediates complex cognitive functions. The development of more sophisticated imaging techniques, beginning with regional cerebral blood flow (rCBF) studies, through positron emission topography (PET) studies, to the more recent functional magnetic resonance imaging (fMRI) techniques, have demonstrated that many different brain regions are, indeed, activated simultaneously during complex cognitive activities.

Many factors must be kept in mind when assessing children and adults: age at time of event, neural plasticity, recovery of function, et cetera. Children and adults differ in that focal damage is more common in adults, whereas diffuse or multifocal damage is more common in children. For example, Multifocal and diffuse brain abnormalities are typical in very low birth-weight infants (Robertson & Finer, 1993). Such multifocal, diffuse damage also occurs in postasphyxial damage (Truwit, Barkovich, Koch, & Ferreiro, 1992), following exposure to teratogens (Miller, 1986; West & Pierce, 1986), in fetal alcohol exposure (Conry, 1990; Done & Rourke, 1995), and even in developmental disorders such as autism (Gillberg, Bjure, Uvebrandt, & Gillberg, 1993). In addition, because children are developing organisms, damage at a particular moment in time can affect both current and future neurocognitive development.

Although there is some evidence of lateralized or localized damage correlating with neuropsychological findings in children (Duane, 1991; Galaburda et al., 1985; Levin et al., 1994), for the most part, such relationships are not usually evident in children with developmental disorders or early neurological insult. Remarkably, even in children with verified lateralized brain damage, the test profiles of those with left damage and with right damage do not differ consistently (Aram & Ekelman, 1988; Korkman & von Wendt, 1995; Vargha-Khadem & Polkey, 1992). For these reasons, inferences concerning underlying brain pathology should be drawn with extreme caution, and only neuropsychologists who are trained in brain/behavior relationships in children should make such inferences, and even then with great caution. Those who are not trained in neuropsychology can still make extensive use of NEPSY by interpreting it at the cognitive processing level in order to develop modifications and interventions for children in the classroom.

PURPOSES OF NEPSY

NEPSY was developed with four interrelated purposes in mind: (a) to create a reliable and valid instrument sensitive to subtle deficiencies across and within the five functional domains that can interfere with learning in preschool and school-age children, (b) to contribute to understanding the effects of congenital or acquired brain damage, (c) to use in long-term follow-up of children with acquired or congenital brain damage or dysfunction, and (d) to study neuropsychological development in preschool and school-age children, as shown in Rapid Reference 1.6.

≣ *Rapid Reference 1.6*

Four Purposes of NEPSY

- To be sensitive to the subtle deficiencies across and within the five functional domains and help to formulate interventions
- To aid understanding of the effects of congenital or acquired brain damage so interventions can be planned
- To use in long-term follow-up of children with acquired or congenital brain damage or dysfunction
- To study neuropsychological development in preschool and school age children

≣ *Rapid Reference 1.7*

The NEPSY Model

- NEPSY has five domains: Attention/Executive Functions, Language, Sensorimotor, Visuospatial, and Memory and Learning.
- Each domain is composed of Core and Expanded Subtests.
- The Core Subtests (mean = 10±3) for each domain yield a Core Domain Score (mean = 100±15) for that domain.
- Subtest scores may be further divided into Supplemental Scores to allow further analysis of performance on the component parts of the subtest.
- Qualitative Observations at the subtest level can be quantified to provide further diagnostic information.

THE NEPSY MODEL

The NEPSY subtests are organized into five domains. Each domain includes Core and Expanded subtests from which clinicians can select additional individual subtests to answer specific referral questions. Thus, in a logical, step-down model, the Expanded Subtests are administered when deficits are revealed in the initial Core Assessment. The Core and Expanded Assessments may be administered in one session. Subtest scores provide a window to a specific function within a domain. The Core Subtest scores also contribute to the composite Core Domain Scores. Supplemental Scores allow for identifying different contributions to the performance (e.g., time vs. accuracy) in order to clarify the child's functioning. Qualitative Observations recorded at the subtest level can be compared to the responses and behavior of normally developing age-mates on the same task. Both Supplemental Scores and Qualitative Observations allow for elucidating the "how" of the child's performance. (See Rapid Reference 1.7.)

It is important to be aware that within the NEPSY model, the Core Assessments for ages 3–4 and ages 5–12 of the Core Domain Subtest differ somewhat. Therefore, the same Core Domain may reflect somewhat different functions between the two age groups.

CAUTION

NEPSY Subtests Differ for Age Ranges

Children 3 to 4 years of age take a different selection of subtests within each Core Domain than do the 5- to 12-year-olds.

Domain	Ages 3–4 only	Ages 5–12 only	Ages 3–4 and 5–12
Attention/ Executive	Statue*	Auditory Atten- tion/Response Set (AARS)	Visual Attention (VA)
Language	Body Part Naming	Tower, Speeded Naming	Comprehension of Instructions
Sensorimotor	N/A	Fingertip Tapping	Phonological Pro- cessing, VP, Imitating Hand Positions
Visuomotor	Block Construction*	Arrows	Design Copying (DC)
Memory/ Learning	Sentence Repetition*	Memory for Faces, Memory for Names	Narrative Memory

*Use expanded subtests for ages 5–12

STRENGTHS OF THE NEPSY

1. A Large, Fully Representative Standardization Sample

Unlike many neuropsychological instruments developed prior to NEPSY, a large, fully representative sample of American children from 3 to 12 years of age was used to norm NEPSY. The authors used a stratified random sampling plan to ensure that representative proportions of children from each demographic group are included in the standardization sample. The standardization sample comprises 1,000 children in each of 10 age groups, 50 males and 50 females in each group. Children from four major geographic regions specified in the 1995 Census Bureau Report were selected to participate in the standardization sample in accordance with the proportions of children living in each region. The sample was stratified according to the following parent education levels (a) 11th grade or less, (b) high school graduate or equivalent to three years of college, and (c) four or more years of college. In each age group 3 to 12, Caucasians, African Americans, Hispanics, and other racial or ethnic groups were included in the same proportion as they are found in the United States population according to

=*Rapid Reference 1.8*

Standardization Sample

- Unlike most neuropsychological instruments, NEPSY was standardized using
  —A stratified random sampling plan to ensure that representative proportions of American children ages 3 to 12 years from each demographic group were included in the standardization sample.
  —A standardization sample of 1,000 children in each of 10 age groups with 50 boys and 50 girls to a group.
  —Children from four major geographic regions specified in the 1995 Census Bureau Report in accordance with the proportions of children living in each region.
- Stratified parent education levels:
  —11th grade or less.
  —high school graduate or equivalent to three years of college.
  —four or more years of college.
- The correct racial or ethnic proportions were maintained for Caucasians, African Americans, Hispanics, and other racial and ethnic groups in the United States according to the 1995 census, not only within each age group, but also within each gender, geographic region, and parent education level.
- Any children with diagnosed neurological, psychological, developmental or learning disabilities were excluded (Korkman, Kirk, & Kemp, 1998).

the 1995 census. The racial or ethnic proportions were maintained, not only within each age group, but also within each gender, geographic region, and parent education level. Children with diagnosed neurological, psychological, developmental, or learning disabilities were excluded (Korkman, Kirk, & Kemp, 1998). This meticulous standardization process helped to insure that the norms were based on a representative sample of children in the United States. (See Rapid Reference 1.8.)

This is very important when the clinician is assessing a child whose disadvantaged background or racial experience might influence performance. A large representative sample insures that performance is not being compared only to that of white, middle-class children. The clinician might assume that a child is impaired when he or she actually has not had the same experiences as children from an advantaged background who may comprise an unrepresentative norm group. Reynolds (1997) has noted that too many of our neuropsychological data are based on impaired individuals. Because only normally developing children were included in this standardization sample, it allows for the assessment of pre-morbidly high-functioning individuals (e.g., IQs of 130) who suffer general cerebral trauma, but lose only 20 to 25 IQ points or less. Unless they were compared to a normally developing standardization group, they could appear normal and go untreated or even lose services (Reynolds, 1997). A fully representative standardization sample was a departure for pediatric neuropsychological assessments, and one that the authors feel ultimately will strengthen the field.

2. Over-Sampling of Minority Groups and Bias Review

NEPSY received two bias reviews in order to remove any language or stimuli that might be inadvertently offensive to any group, and a few modifications were made on this basis. Further, over-sampling of 300 children was included for minority groups.

3. Qualified Examiners Collected Standardization Data

Approximately 200 well-qualified examiners were selected to participate in the NEPSY standardization across the United States. Regional training workshops were conducted by the authors or by a member of The Psychological Corporation Development Team.

4. All Subtests Normed on the Same Standardization Sample

A major disadvantage of fashioning a neuropsychological assessment from numerous, brief instruments drawn from different sources is that many of them were normed on small, disparate groups of children. In these circumstances it is difficult to tell whether the between-test differences observed in performance are real differences in an individual child's functioning or merely reflect differences in the standardization sample composition. When the two normative groups are not equally representative, it is impossible to know reliably that a function assessed on a test with one norm group is a weakness for a child when it is compared to a function assessed on a second test with a different normative group. When the clinician sees that differences in a child's performance are evident on various subtests of the NEPSY, he or she can feel more confident that these reflect actual intra-individual differences, because the subtests were all normed on the same standardization sample.

5. Developmental Trends Can Be Observed

Although normative data on tests of a single function or circumscribed group of functions may reflect performance differences across age groups, they cannot reflect developmental differences in one complex, cognitive capacity that may affect development in another (Fischer & Rose, 1994). Because all capacities assessed on NEPSY were normed on the same group, the clinician can assess developmental differences, not only within a function, but across functions. Therefore, a great advantage of using NEPSY in research is the ability to observe developmental differences among different functional areas across age groups. In the normally developing child, one can see how some areas develop along the same trajectory and others show different developmental trajectories. The clinician can compare these developmental trajectories evident in normally developing children to differences in children with delays or deficits. It is important to note, however, that NEPSY subtests differ somewhat between the Core Assessment for ages 3 to 4 and the Core Assessment for ages 5–12.

6. Flexibility

Another advantage to NEPSY is its great flexibility (Kaplan, 1998). It permits assessment at a number of different levels in varying permutations, while retaining the unifying factor of a common normative group, no matter which combination of subtests is used. NEPSY permits a Core Assessment, a brief, overall view of five complex cognitive domains: Attention/Executive Functions, Language, Sensorimotor, Visuospatial, Memory and Learning. It also allows for an in-depth Full Assessment with all subtests, Core and Expanded.

Furthermore, it is possible to do an Expanded Assessment that allows a comprehensive look within a particular domain. After the clinician has administered the Core, and he or she sees that a particular function (language, for instance) shows significant subtest discrepancies, the clinician may administer all of the Expanded subtests within that domain in order to delineate further how pervasive the deficits may be. Finally, NEPSY allows for a Selective Assessment across domains after administering the Core. These may be suggested by performance on the Core, the referral question, or information in the child's history or other records. The clinician may wish to select subtests across domains that he or she knows from the research may elucidate symptoms of a particular disorder hypothesized to be the root of the child's problem. Because of the flexibility of NEPSY, a client-centered investigation using subtests selected to

Because of the flexibility of NEPSY, a client-centered investigation using subtests selected to address a specific referral question is possible (Kaplan, 1998).

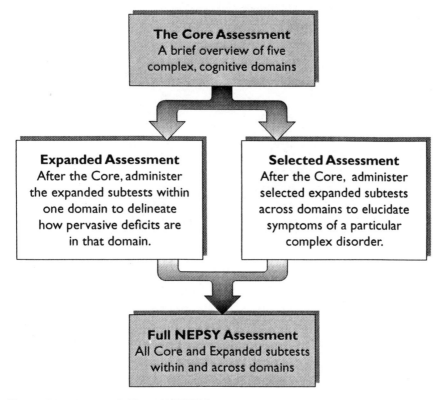

The Core Assessment
A brief overview of five complex, cognitive domains

Expanded Assessment
After the Core, administer the expanded subtests within one domain to delineate how pervasive deficits are in that domain.

Selected Assessment
After the Core, administer selected expanded subtests across domains to elucidate symptoms of a particular complex disorder.

Full NEPSY Assessment
All Core and Expanded subtests within and across domains

Figure 1.1 The Flexibility of NEPSY

address a specific referral question (Kaplan, 1998) is possible, as shown in Figure 1.1.

7. Standard Scores

The presence of standard scores is unusual on a neuropsychological assessment and raises all sorts of statistical difficulties, because the instrument that is designed to assess children who are impaired must be standardized on normally developing children. For example, a normally developing child at age 8 may easily do a task that the examiner knows from clinical experience an impaired 8-

year-old will not be able to perform. Therefore, the normally developing 8-year-old may ceiling on the task, making it impossible to derive a standard score, because the scores in the standardization sample are not normally distributed across age groups. Nonetheless, because children are developing, and development varies so much within any particular age group, the authors felt that it was important to have a standardized metric to take this into account. A cut score, which has been traditional in neuropsychology, cannot do this.

Raw scores cannot be compared or assessed directly for a variety of reasons, the most potent being the lack of comparability of the raw score distributions among the tasks of the battery and for any one task across age (Reynolds, 1997).

All subtests in NEPSY that are normally distributed have a scaled score with a mean of 10±3. All Core subtests and many Expanded subtests have scaled scores. Core Domain Scores have a mean of 100±15. Because Subtest Scaled Scores and Core Domain Scores are each expressed in comparable metrics across functions and modalities, a summary of strengths and weaknesses, as well as discrepancies, can be presented in a performance profile (Korkman, Kirk, & Kemp, 1998). The use of these standardized scores helps to solve one of the most difficult current problems of neuropsychological assessment, that of using different brief instruments normed on different groups. Furthermore, because children are functioning within the educational arena, parents and teachers are used to this type of standard score and can understand its function. However, there is some distance to go before solving the scaling problems inherent in trying to develop a standardized pediatric neuropsychological instrument.

Reliability coefficients for NEPSY were calculated for each age separately. Split-half, test-retest, and generalizability procedures were employed, depending on the nature of the subtest. Average reliabilities for ages 3 to 4 for Core Domain Scores are Attention/Executive Function, .70; Language, .90; Sensorimotor, .88; Visuospatial, .88; Memory and Learning, .91. With the exception of two subtests, the subtest reliabilities for ages 3 to 4 range from .74 (Body Part Naming) to .91 (Sentence Repetition). The two subtests at ages 3 to 4 with poor reliabilities are Verbal Fluency (.59) and Statue (.50). Given the developmental variability in attention for very young children, the low reliability for Statue and its effect on the Attention/Executive Core Domain Score is not surprising. During early childhood, the ability to attend to a task is controlled primarily by the reticular activation system (RAS) of the brain. Prefrontal control of the arousal unit of the brain develops over time (Langus & Miller, 1992). At ages 5 to 12, average reliabilities for Core Domain Scores are Attention/Executive Function, .82; Language, .87; Sensorimotor, .79; Visuospatial, .83; Memory and Learning, .87. With the exception of two subtests, the subtest reliabilities for ages 5 to 12 range from .71 (VA; Fingertip Tapping) to .91 (Phonological Processing; Sentence Repetition). The two subtests at ages 5 to 12 with low reliabilities were Design Fluency (.59) and VP (.68), both influenced by graphomotor control that is well-developed in most normally developing children in the standardization sample. See Rapid Reference 1.9 for a summary of reliabilities.

8. Dissociation of Subcomponents of Deficits Possible When Comparing Subtest Performance

It is possible with NEPSY to dissociate components contributing to poor performance in several ways. At the subtest performance level, the clinician can assess attentional problems in the visual and in the auditory modalities. The examiner can assess deficits in phonological awareness by a simple task of recognition of speech sound segments within a word, a task requiring repetition of a nonsense word and a task which requires conceptualizing a sound pattern and manipulating that pattern to form a new word. The naming of body parts can assess a naming deficit in young children. Additionally, rapid naming can be assessed (SN). The clinician can also assess memory and learning of names, which may be related to a naming deficit, not to a memory deficit per se. Fluency can be assessed verbally (Verbal Fluency) and nonverbally (Design Fluency). The Manual Motor Sequences and Oromotor Sequences subtests allow the clinician to observe deficits in motor programming in two different ways (sequences on the Fingertip Tapping subtest also assesses motor programming. See the discussion of SS that follows). Block Design and Design Copying (DC) provide a means to assess constructional apraxia on two-dimensional and three-dimensional construction tasks. Likewise, visuospatial deficits can be dissociated from deficits in graphomotor precision on DC by comparing performance on Arrows and Route Finding, which are nonmotor visuospatial tasks, with performance on VP, a task requiring graphomotor control. The clinician can compare poor performances at the integrative level for visuospatial input and motor output to Imitating Hand Positions, which does not require the use of a pencil, and DC, which does. Fingertip Tapping and Finger Discrimination provide brief comparison of motor and sensory systems. Memory for Faces and Memory for Names provide comparison of two differ

≡Rapid Reference 1.9

Reliabilities of Core Domain Scores and Core Subtest Scores

	Average r^2	
Core Domains and Subtests	**Ages 3–4**	**Ages 5–12**
Attention/Executive Function	.70	.82
Tower		.82
Auditory Attention and Response Set		.81
Visual Attention	.76	.71
Statue	.50	
Design Fluency		.59
Language	.90	.87
Body Part Naming	.74	
Phonological Processing	.83	.91
Speeded Naming		.74
Comprehension of Instructions	.89	.73
Repetition of Nonsense Words		.80
Verbal Fluency	.59	.74
Sensorimotor	.88	.79
Fingertip Tapping		.71
Imitating Hand Positions	.89	.82
Visuomotor Precision	.81	.68
Visuospatial	.88	.83
Design Copying	.86	.79
Arrows		.78
Block Construction	.80	.72
Memory and Learning	.91	.87
Memory for Faces		.76
Memory for Names		.89
Narrative Memory	.85	.77
Sentence Repetition	.91	.81
List Learning		.91

Note: Reliability coefficients for NEPSY were calculated for each age separately. Split-half, test-retests, and generalizability procedures were employed, depending on the nature of the subtest.

ent, important aspects of social functioning in children. The clinician can compare auditory short-term memory (Sentence Repetition) to recall of a quantity of details in a structured verbal narrative (Narrative Memory), to verbal learning over trials with short-delay and long-delay recall (List Learning). Thus, NEPSY provides a way to make comparisons between and among subtest performances in order to define more clearly the primary deficit related to the child's performance difficulties.

9. Supplemental Scores (SS)

Another important advantage to NEPSY is the inclusion of SS that provide a further means to tease apart a more global score in order to see what individual component may have adversely affected performance. For instance, the SN Total Score is a global score derived from a speed and accuracy table. However, because of the SS, each of these components can be considered separately. The clinician can see whether the child named accurately but had a problem with rapid access, or whether the child's accuracy in naming was the component affecting performance. Likewise, the clinician can observe whether the child's ability to focus attention was poor on a task of simple, selective auditory attention, a task of complex, shifting auditory attention, or whether he or she performed poorly on both tasks. Further, the clinician can note Omission Errors (OEs) and Commission Errors (CEs) on each auditory and visual attention task and across both simple and complex auditory and visual attention. These are but a few of the comparisons possible with SS on NEPSY.

10. Qualitative Observations (QO)

Closely related to the SS as an adjunctive means of analyzing functioning more diagnostically are the QOs. They provide a way of quantifying the qualitative observations of a child's performance that have traditionally been so important in process-approach assessment (Kaplan, 1988).

> The emphasis in U.S. psychology has been on the psychometric approach, so only recently have developmental neuropsychologists begun to collect data on the qualitative aspects of performance in both normal and abnormal development and attempted to relate these findings to neurologic models of brain development and to cognitive development. (Reynolds, 1997)

On NEPSY the clinician can tally the number of times a child makes a Rule Violation on Tower, for instance, and compare it to base-rate for age. This allows the clinician to take into account the child's development. Was it unusual, for example, for a child of 7 years to make five Rule Violations? Some QOs allow the clinician to examine a behavior across functions, as well. The presence of Recruitment, for instance, can be noted on SN, Verbal Fluency, and Manual Motor Sequences. This allows the clinician to see if the child is recruiting other systems into a task only on a motor task, only on a task that involves the access to or production of language, or on both.

11. Child-Friendly Tasks and Materials

Many pediatric neuropsychological instruments are renormed adult instruments meant to assess acquired brain damage and usually do not have materials specifically designed for children. It has been suggested that instruments meant to assess acquired brain damage in adults may not be suitable for assessing developmental disorders in children (Hynd & Willis, 1987; Kirk, 1983, 1985). The NEPSY subtests and colorful materials have been designed specifically to appeal to children. Because the child is engaged by the task and the materials, he or she will perform better. Although it is never possible to remove boredom and lack of attention completely from the testing situation, they will not be such confounding factors as they might be for a child performing a task meant for an adult. Furthermore, the subtests administration order provides a variety of different tasks in succession to help avoid boredom.

12. Ease of Administration

Materials needed, Start Points, Discontinue Rules, and Reverse Rules are consistently indicated with easy-to-spot icons in the *Manual* and Stimulus Book. The Stimulus Book, which is on an easel for ease of administration, contains the examiner script for the majority of tests. The Manual provides clear drawings when guidance is needed for hand positions, motor sequences, and so forth, and miniature drawings and text guidance are in the Record Form. Most tests can be administered from the Record Form and Stimulus Book. The Record Form is well-designed with plenty of space to record notes and miniature diagrams to record block constructions, sequence of responses on Comprehension of Instructions, and so forth. The record form provides reminders for time on immediate memory trials to ensure the delayed trial is administered at the specified time. All paper pencil items are grouped in a Response Booklet. Those assessing only preschoolers do not need to purchase Record

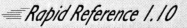

≡ Rapid Reference 1.10

Strengths of NEPSY

- A large, fully representative standardization sample
- Bias review and over-sampling of minority groups
- 200 qualified examiners collected standardization data
- All subtests normed on the same standardization sample
- Developmental trajectories can be observed
- Flexibility
- Standard scores
- Dissociation of subcomponents of deficits possible when comparing subtest performance
- Supplemental Scores (SS)
- Qualitative Observations (QO)
- Child-friendly tasks and materials
- Ease of Administration

Forms for ages 5 to 12. Rapid Reference 1.10 summarizes the strengths of the NEPSY.

WEAKNESSES OF THE NEPSY

1. Subtests Not Highly Correlated with Core Domain Scores

The NEPSY was based on theory and traditions of neuropsychological assessment rather than on factor analysis. Factor structure inherently suggests that all of the subtests contributing to a particular factor are highly correlated. Therefore, they measure one construct. Neuropsychological functions are not that simple. Complex cognitive functions require contributions from different domains to a greater or lesser degree.

The subtests included in the Core Assessment were chosen based on theory because the combination of those few subtests was most apt to allow brief screening for different acquired and developmental disorders according to current research. For instance, the authors felt it was important to include memory assessments for both names and faces in the brief Memory and Learning Core Domain, because both are significantly important for screening for different types of disorders. Autistic children do not perform well on Memory for Faces, but learn names in a rote manner. Dyslexic children, on the other hand, may perform poorly on Memory for Names due to naming problems, but often have no trouble with Memory for Faces. The two subtests do not correlate, however.

Likewise, Memory for Faces is not correlated with Narrative Memory, but the authors felt the latter measure was an important subtest to include in the brief screening of memory function provided by the Memory and Learning Domain. It allows the examiner to observe the child's ability to recall large quantities of language, including essential details, that are required daily in school. Furthermore, it allows the clinician to determine whether the child is able to recall language details spontaneously or whether he or she must have cues in order to access the details from memory. This has direct implications for instruction. The child who has problems accessing information from memory will perform better on multiple choice tests on which cues are provided by the choices. In addition, Narrative Memory can provide evidence that the structure of the story aids recall for children with attentional problems and certain language disorders. Not including Memory for Faces in the Memory and Learning Domain, and instead including a memory test such as Sentence Repetition, would have caused the subtests within the domain to correlate much more highly. Essentially, however, only one modality would have been measured—verbal memory.

The disadvantage of having moderate and a few low correlations among the two–three subtests within a Core Domain of NEPSY is that if there is significant intradomain variance, the Core Domain Score will not reflect that area of functioning overall in a reliable way. Although that is true of all global scores, such as IQs, it is a principle to which clinicians far too rarely adhere. For example, the verbal subtests on the WISC-III may show significant intrascale discrepancies. The frequencies of those discrepancies may be significant, but the Verbal IQ will be incorrectly reported as reflecting overall verbal ability.

The Core Domain Scores of NEPSY are not meant to reflect a functional area overall. Because the domains were theoretically derived, they are meant to assess *diverse* aspects of a functional area which, based on the research, should be capable of screening for dysfunction on the basis of limited testing. The global Core Domain Scores are reliable (See Rapid Reference Box 5.2). As with most global scores, however, the authors feel that they do not provide the most valuable information for understanding intra-individual strengths and weaknesses. The individual differences are best defined by inspection and reporting of variations in subtest performance where the discrepancies and frequencies of those discrepancies are significant. Beyond the Core Assessment, NEPSY provides Expanded Subtests for further diagnostic testing in areas of concern. NEPSY does not, however, measure all possible constructs. It is very important to interpret findings on NEPSY in the context of results obtained from cognitive and achievement testing, medical, developmental, educational, and psychosocial histories, and the clinician's behavioral observations.

2. Complex Recording and Administration Procedures

Two subtests, AARS and Tower are somewhat difficult to record as the child performs. In both cases, it is just a matter of acquiring the skill. On Tower, the clinician does not actually have to record the child's moves, as long as he or she keeps track of the number of moves. AARS must be recorded, but the secret is to record the color the child touches beside the word on the Record Form that the clinician hears on the tape. The clinician should not try to make any judgement about correctness at that time and should not attempt to score as he or she goes. A little practice will help the clinician relax and score with ease. The hand movements for Manual Motor Sequences also take practice. Sitting so that the drawings in the *Manual* are visible and practicing the movements repetitively with the drawings in the NEPSY Manual (pp. 159–164) will help the clinician master them. The Record Form has written descriptions of the movements to aid administration.

3. Complex Scoring and Different Types of Scores

It is true that the NEPSY is time-consuming to score when the clinician wishes to glean all of the rich diagnostic information available in Expanded Subtests, SS and QOs. There is an intermediate scoring step for three subtests that have an accuracy and a speed component. The speed and accuracy raw scores are used to look up a derived speed/accuracy score. The latter is then used to locate the Total Score in the look-up tables. There is, however, a NEPSY Scoring Assistant (Psychological Corporation, 2000) available that makes scoring very simple. It also provides graphs and tables that can be imported into the child's report. NEPSY includes not only standard scores, but smoothed percentile ranks for selected Expanded Subtests and Cumulative Percentages for SS, and QOs. Percentile ranks and cumulative percentages were calculated for subtests on which the distribution was highly skewed or attenuated due to floor or ceiling problems. This occurs, for the most part, when the clinician is attempting to standardize neuropsychological functions which develop early (e.g., motor skills) or are not a problem in normally developing children (e.g., omission errors on attention tests). Unlike tests that will be given to normally developing children, such as cognitive or achievement tests, neuropsychological tests are designed to evaluate children who are impaired in various ways. It is important to include items for assessment of these impairments even when the clinician is aware that the normally developing children who form the standardization population will be able to perform the task well. This fact causes scaling problems, but to exclude necessary areas of assessment because they cannot generate scaled scores seemed unethical. Therefore, the solution appeared to be percentile rank ranges and cumulative percentages. Actually, 21 of the 27 subtests have scaled scores. All of the Core subtests and six of the Expanded subtests are scaled. The remainder of the Expanded subtests have smoothed percentile ranks. Three of the subtests have Supplemental Scaled Scores and the rest of the SS and all of the QOs as base rates of occurrence (percentage of the standardization sample demonstrating the behavior). Percentile ranks and cumulative percentages use consistent descriptors for performance level (i.e., *At Expected Level*, etc.). On the Domain Analyses page of the Record Form, the graphs have been constructed to allow visual comparison across all types of scores.

4. No Visual Memory Subtest

Memory for Pictures and Picture Recognition, which relied on viewing the final picture on the Memory for Pictures Subtest, were dropped after standardization due to high production costs and their poor psychometric properties. Just before standardization, we changed the picture stimulus from a series of incomplete line drawings that progressed to full drawings of the objects, and substituted computer-generated degraded photographs, progressing to fully visible photographs of the objects. Although they were piloted on a limited basis, it was not sufficient, to produce a reliable subtest. Further, production costs were high.

5. No "Crack-Back" *Manual* with Dividers

We have received feedback from various examiners concerning the paperback *Manual*. It does not make into an easel, as would a "crack-back" manual, and it does not have dividers, as do a number of test manuals. This was an economic decision. A "crack-back" manual adds a significant amount to the cost of a test, and in this day of rapidly rising prices for test kits, the authors wanted very much to keep the cost of NEPSY within reason. The *Manual* does have a special binding, however, which allows the clinician to open it and press it flat without breaking the back. Once the clinician has learned the test administration well, however, he or she will find very little need for the *Manual* during testing, as most instructions are in the Stimulus Book, on the Record Form, or both. The problem of dividers has been addressed with printed side tabs. If holding the manual horizontally, one can see blue printing visible on the edge of pages in certain sections. The thick blue section is the Administration and Scoring Directions. Toward the back of the book are thinner blue sections that indicate the appendices, starting with the marker for Appendix A at the top of p. 269. The markers continue in descending positions for each appendix down to the marker for Appendix D at the bottom of p. 343.

The markers start again at the top of p. 361 with Appendix E and again move progressively down to Appendix H on p. 491. Where applicable, there are top tabs of blue to indicate ages as well. Although the NEPSY *Manual* is not the more expensive version, significant effort was made to help clinicians navigate the manual easily. Rapid Reference 1.11 summarizes the weaknesses of NEPSY.

≡Rapid Reference 1.11

Weaknesses of NEPSY

- Subtests not highly correlated with Core Domain Scores
- Complex Recording or Administration Procedures
- Complex Scoring and Different Types of Scores
- No visual memory subtest
- No "crack-back" manual with dividers

SUMMARY

Although NEPSY has some weaknesses, as do most assessments, it also has significant strengths. It is an attempt to link the best of clinical, process-approach, neuropsychological assessment with psychometrics, without losing too much of value on either front. This is an enormous challenge and one which the authors intend to continue to accept. The next chapter presents a comprehensive discussion of how to administer

≡Rapid Reference 1.12

The Publisher of NEPSY

NEPSY—A Developmental Neuropsychological Assessment. Copyright 1998 by The Psychological Corporation 555 Academic Court San Antonio, TX 78204 www.PsychCorp.com

NEPSY. It includes a general discussion of good assessment practice, instructions on how to modify NEPSY for special populations, and comprehensive subtest-by-subtest rules for administration.

COMPREHENSIVE REFERENCES

The manual of *NEPSY, A Developmental Neuropsychological Assessment* (Korkman, Kirk, & Kemp, 1998) and the references for this guide provide comprehensive lists of references on NEPSY. The *Manual* also reviews studies performed with NEPSY thus far. The *Manual* further reviews the development of the test and contains descriptions of each subtest, the Core Domains, and standardization, reliability, and validity. Rapid Reference 1.12 gives publication information.

⚓ TEST YOURSELF ⚓

Fill in the blanks.

1. NEPSY assesses children in what age range? _____

2. Upon what theory is NEPSY based? _____

3. The theory upon which the NEPSY is based proposes that impairment in one subcomponent of a function is likely to affect _____ to which that subcomponent contributes.

4. When many brief instruments are drawn from different sources and their norm groups are different, it is difficult to tell whether differences in performance merely reflect differences in the _____ _____.

5. Because all capacities assessed on NEPSY have been normed on the same group, _____ trends can be assessed, both within and across a function.

6. NEPSY permits assessment at a number of different levels. A _____ is a brief overview of functioning across domains. That might be followed by a _____ _____ across domains or an _____ _____ within a particular domain.

7. The flexibility of NEPSY permits a _____ _____ investigation (Kaplan, 1998).

8. Core Domain Scores on NEPSY have a mean of _____, and scaled scores have a mean of _____.

9. SS allow _____ of subcomponents of deficits.

10. A brief but thorough assessment of neuropsychological functions can be obtained through a _____ _____.

11. Match the Block to the appropriate function.

Block I ____ (a) Subserves the primary intake of information, the processing of that information, and the association of it with other information and experience.

Block II ____ (b) Regulates the executive functions of planning, strategizing, and monitoring performance that are needed for problem solving.

Block III ____ (c) Is responsible for the basic physiological functions that support life, and for the arousal of attention.

12. List the five domains of the 27 NEPSY subtests.

(a) _____

(b) _____

(c) _____

(d) _____

(e) _____

13. NEPSY is an appropriate instrument for assessing localized brain damage. True or False?

14. Secondary deficits are so named because they are not as important as primary deficits. True or False?

15. The NEPSY standardization sample was 500 children drawn from four geographical regions. True or False?

16. The NEPSY standardization sample included children of three parent-education levels. True or False?

17. There were 50 males and 50 females to an age group in the standardization sample. True or False?

18. The 1992 Census Bureau Report was used to determine inclusion of the proportion of racial or ethnic groups in the standardization sample that was found in the U.S. population. True or False?

19. A stratified random sampling plan was used. True or False?

20. The performance of a high-ability child with a mild generalized cerebral trauma is best assessed by comparing performance to other children with mild brain injury. True or False?

21. A bias review insures that a test maintains its restricted cultural approach. True or False?

For questions 22–25, pick the correct letter from the selection below.

22. It is unusual for a pediatric neuropsychological assessment to have _____.

23. With two exceptions, the average subtest reliabilities at ages 3 to 4 range from _____.

(continued)

24. With two exceptions, the average subtest reliabilities at age 5 to 12 range from _____.

25. Global scores do not reflect an overall function if there are significant discrepancies between the _____.

(a) subtest scores

(b) .74–.91

(c) standard scores

(d) .79–.90

(e) .71–.91

Answers: 1. Ages 3 to 12; 2. Lurian; 3. Any function; 4. In norm groups; 5. Developmental; 6. Core Assessment, Selective Assessment, Expanded Assessment; 7. Client-centered; 8. 100, 10; 9. dissociation; 10. Core Assessment; 11. Block I: c, Block II: a, Block III: b; 12. a. Attention/Executive Functions, b. Language, c. Sensorimotor, d. Visuospatial, e. Memory and Learning; 13. False; 14. False; 15. False; 16. True; 17. True; 18. False; 19. True; 20. False; 21. False; 22. c; 23. b; 24. e; 25. a

Two

HOW TO ADMINISTER THE NEPSY

One of the strengths of a standardized neuropsychological assessment for children is that it provides scores that represent a child's performance compared to other, normally developing children of the same age. In order to obtain results that are comparable to the national norms, however, the clinician must carefully follow the administration and scoring procedures that were used in standardization, without becoming robot-like in the presentation. The experience must be enjoyable for the child, so appropriate testing conditions are essential to good performance. By attending to what might seem to be superfluous details, the clinician can obtain precise and reliable information. It is a delicate balance.

APPROPRIATE TESTING CONDITIONS

Physical Environment

It is important in any type of assessment to be sure that the physical setting is conducive to testing: quiet, well-ventilated, and well-lit. The temperature of the room should not be too hot or too cold, or the child may not be able to concentrate. The testing area should have a table with a smooth surface and of appropriate height for the child to be comfortable. If a low table is not available for testing young children, the clinician may wish to acquire a booster chair to place on a chair of regular height. It is also nice to have a footstool or wooden box available for a child whose feet do not touch the floor. Providing a footrest helps to keep a child from becoming too fidgety because his or her feet are dangling without support. Chairs should be straight-backed, but padded enough to be comfortable throughout the testing session. Arms on the chairs help to contain younger children and provide elbow rests for the clinician. There needs to be ample room for test materials. A clipboard facilitates writing responses without exposing the Record Form to the child. For most tests, the clinician should be seated across the table from the child, as this facilitates observation. Watching the child perform the task and recording, not only the Qualitative Observations (QOs) provided on NEPSY, but also the clinician's observations and impressions are integral parts of a thorough neuropsychological evaluation.

For sensorimotor subtests, the clinician must sit across the table from the child in order to demonstrate the movements and positions and to observe the child from the correct orientation. However, on a few subtests (Body Part Naming, Arrows, Block Construction, and Route Finding) the clinician may feel better able to administer the subtest seated beside or at right angles to the child. This may facilitate observation of the child's response on the easel, the orientation of the materials, or the clinician's ability to point to the stimuli.

DON'T FORGET

Your Observations are a Part of a Neuropsychological Evaluation

Watch how the child performs the task. For example:

- How was it accomplished?
- What strategies were used?
- Did the child verbally mediate the task?

Record the listed Qualitative Observations for each subtest.

Also, record *your own* observations and impressions.

DON'T FORGET

Examiner Position on Certain Tests

On Sensorimotor subtests the examiner *should* sit across the table from the child

- to demonstrate the movements and/or positions.
- to observe the child in the correct orientation.

On subtests that use the Stimulus Booklet, the examiner may sit beside or at right angles to the child

- to facilitate observation.
- to ensure correct orientation of materials.
- to point to the stimuli more easily.

Test Materials

Only the test materials being used should be visible on the table during the testing. Other materials may be distracting or cause anxiety for a child who worries about being able to accomplish a task. The clinician may want to have the materials on a chair nearby or on the floor by the chair. Either is permissible, as long as the materials are out of the child's view. The NEPSY Stimulus Book easel should be placed so it is readily visible to both child and examiner. Again, it is very important that the clinician sits where he or she is able to observe the child performing the tasks. The NEPSY kit contains all materials needed except the clipboard, stopwatch, and any extra paper desired for taking notes. Be sure that the pencils (red and #2 standard) provided with the kit are sharpened. For young children, use the thick, primary pencil and the thick crayon that are provided.

Establishing Rapport

It is important to establish rapport with the child before testing begins. The examiner should greet the accompanying adult in a friendly, relaxed manner so the child can be reassured about the way the examiner relates to people. The examiner should then greet the child, offering his or her hand for a handshake. If the child is shy about shaking hands, do not force it. However, shaking hands with the child often makes him or her feel that this process is going to be a partnership and that he or she has an important role to play. When the child is young, get down to her or his level and chat for a few minutes about a toy the child brought to the testing or an article of clothing. The clinician should explain that he or she will be doing all kinds of activities with the child. When an adult refers to the clinician as "doctor," or when the evaluation takes place in a hospital or medical center, the clinician should reassure the child that he or she will not be giving shots or doing anything to hurt the child. Older children need to be reassured that they will not be receiving grades on their performance.

When a young child or a child with a developmental delay has trouble separating from the parent, the clinician should invite the parent to walk back to the testing room with the clinician and the child. The clinician should reassure the child that the parent will know exactly where she or he is, and, perhaps, have the parent leave an article (a scarf, a book, etc.) with the child for security. Do not prolong the process. When the mother, father, or both have gone, the examiner may need to play with the child for awhile

DON'T FORGET
....

Establishing Rapport

- Establish rapport with the child *before* testing begins.
- Greet the accompanying adult in a friendly, relaxed manner.
- Greet the child, offering your hand for a handshake. (Don't force it if the child is shy.)
- If the child is young, stoop down to her or his level and chat for a few minutes about a toy the child brought or an article of clothing.
- Explain that you will be doing all kinds of activities together.
- Reassure the child that you will be doing nothing to hurt him or her.
- Reassure older children that they will not be receiving grades on their performance.

to help him or her feel comfortable before testing is initiated. Occasionally, with a small child or a child with developmental disorders, the parent needs to be present for the testing. When this is the case, talk to the parent prior to the testing about not prompting the child. Most children, however, will perform better if the parent is not present.

Maintaining Rapport

The clinician should introduce the test to the child by talking about the many different activities the child will be doing with the clinician. Explain that each task will be easy at first, and then the items may get hard. The examiner should reassure the child that when the items get hard, he or she just needs to do his or her best. Explain to the child that some children find some tasks easy and others hard. This can help reassure the child that he or she is not the only one who finds some items difficult. When items become difficult, the examiner can validate the child's feelings by acknowledging, "Sometimes these get hard," or "That one was tough; let's try a different one."

In general, it is best to praise effort rather than achievement. "You are really working hard!" or "You really kept at that problem until it was solved!" It is fine to use stickers or small treats as reinforcers for small children and for older children with cognitive impairments. Older children without developmental delay may find reinforcers "babyish." As subtest materials are being changed for new ones, small talk will help keep the child at ease.

DON'T FORGET

Validate the Child's Feelings

When items get difficult, validate the child's feelings.

- "Sometimes these are hard."
- "That one was tough; let's try a different one."

DON'T FORGET

Praise Effort, Not Achievement

- "You are really working hard!"
- "You really kept at that problem until it was solved!"

Taking Breaks

The examiner should watch for signs of fatigue such as squirminess, asking how long it will be, stretching, or the child putting his or her head down on the table. Take a break as soon as possible when any of these signs is observed. It is advisable to have juice and crackers or a similar snack available for the child during the break. If possible, relocate to a playroom or office where some toys are kept or take a short walk with the child. Be sure to ask if the child would like to use the bathroom. The clinician should try to provide a change of scene and position before returning to work.

During the administration of NEPSY, however, it is *very important* to take breaks where they will not spoil a delayed memory test. Good times to take breaks are after Delayed Memory for Faces but before Memory for Names (Learning Trials); and after Delayed Memory for Names but before the Expanded Subtest List Learning, if it is to be administered. If a short break is taken between any two of these subtests, be sure to factor the time into the 30 min between the immediate and delayed administration. If at all possible, do not break for the day when an immediate memory test has already been administered. If the examiner must break for the day at such a point, he or she can still use the Supplemental Scores (SS) for the immediate memory trial but cannot compute the Total Score for that subtest or the Memory and Learning Core Domain Score. For instance, in the case of Memory for Faces, this scenario would leave only the SS for Immediate Memory for Faces, and the clinician would not be able to compute the Memory for Faces Total Score, which requires both immediate and delayed trials; nor the Memory and Learning Domain Score. This latter fact will affect the clinician's ability to make comparisons among Core Domain Scores.

When the delayed memory section of a subtest is the next one to be administered, and a full 30 min has not passed, the examiner should take a break. The time elapsed should be as close as possible to 30 min±5 min before the clinician administers the delayed memory section. This is not likely to happen with Memory for Names or Memory for Faces. When the clinician is administering only a few expanded subtests and using List Learning, he or she should be sure to

---

CAUTION

Breaks That Will Not Spoil Delayed Memory Tests

- You may take a break during a Core administration *after* Delayed Memory for Faces (and before Memory for Names).

- You may take a break during a Full administration *after* Delayed Memory for Names (and before List Learning).

- It is not recommended, but, if necessary, you may take breaks between the immediate and delayed portions of the Faces, Names, or List Learning subtests *if:*
  —the break is less than 30 min.
  —you take the break in lieu of the usual intervening subtests.

C A U T I O N

....

Delayed Memory for Lists

If you are administering only a few expanded subtests that include List Learning:

- Be sure to give List Learning first.
- Then give the Expanded Subtests you had planned.
- Check the time as you go along.
- If you still need more time to make up 30 min, take a break.

give List Learning first. Then he or the clinician should give the few planned Expanded Subtests, checking the time during the exam. If the clinician still needs more time to make up 30 min, he or she should give the child a break.

TESTING CONSIDERATIONS

NEPSY is a very flexible instrument, but it is important to select carefully the type of assessment to be administered. The assessment needs to address the referral question, the needs of the child, time constraints, and the setting in which the assessment takes place. The first consideration must be the child's age, because NEPSY subtests vary somewhat for 3- to 4-year-olds and 5- to 12-year-olds. Second, the goal of the evaluation will influence which type of NEPSY assessment the clinician selects.

A Core Assessment, which has an administration time of approximately 1 to 1.5 hr, provides an overview of the child's neuropsychological functions. It is composed of the two to three Core Subtests for each domain. The Core should always be administered as the basis of an Expanded or a Selective Assessment. An Expanded Assessment allows the clinician to administer additional subtests within a domain beyond the Core subtests to probe a specific area of concern (i.e., a specific language impairment) more thoroughly. An Expanded Assessment will take from 1.5 to 2 hr to administer, including the Core as will a Selective Assessment.

A Selective Assessment allows the clinician to evaluate a complex disorder (e.g., dyslexia, graphomotor problems) by selecting subtests across domains that target symptom clusters associated with the disorder in question. For example, suppose that the clinician formulated an hypothesis of dyslexia from the referral question, comprehensive history form, and parent/child interviews. In order to test this hypothesis, the clinician might then include in the Selective Assessment the following subtests in addition to the Core Subtests: Repetition of Nonsense Words (phonological processing), Verbal Fluency (expressive language), and Oromotor Sequences (oromotor programming) from the Language Domain, Route Finding (directionality) from the Visuospatial Domain; and the verbal memory tasks, Sentence Repetition and List Learning, from the Memory and Learning Domain. If the hypothesis of dyslexia developed during the administration of the Core, the clinician might want to move on to a selective Assessment using the above subtests. In either case, the data derived from the selected subtests would then be integrated with information from the child's performance on the Core: phonological processing skills (Phonological Processing), speed of access to labels (Speeded Naming–Time), language deficits (Comprehension of Instructions, Speeded Naming–accuracy, Memory for Names, and Narrative Memory), problems with reversals (Speeded Naming–Reversed Sequences), visuospatial ability (Arrows, Design Copying), fine motor coordination (Fingertip Tapping), and attention/executive functions (Tower, Visual Attention, Auditory Attention). The clinician would then inspect the data derived from the child's performance for the presence of the diagnostic behavioral cluster associated with dyslexia. In addition, the clinician would inspect the child's reading decoding and spelling results on an individual achievement test to see if they reflect the impaired subcomponents of the reading/spelling process. With this type of targeted assessment, the examiner can feel confident that he or she has thoroughly addressed the child's problem and that it will be possible to use the data to formulate helpful interventions and modifications for the child. In order to select appropriate subtests across domains and to interpret results on any type of NEPSY assessment, however, the clinician needs to have a thorough knowledge of the current research. Continued self-education is, therefore, an essential part of being a competent and effective pediatric neuropsychologist.

The final option for a NEPSY administration, as Rapid Reference 2.1 shows, is a Full Assessment, the administration of all Core and Expanded subtests across domains. This assessment provides an in-depth neuropsychological evaluation to assess the effects of brain damage or dysfunction, developmental disorders, low birthweight, exposure to teratogens, and so forth. It takes from 2 to 3 hr to administer all 27 subtests, depending on the child and the examiner's expertise. If the assessment needs to be spread over time, the Core can be administered in one session to provide a baseline, and then, in the second session, all of the Expanded subtests can be administered. If a child is medically fragile, the assessment can be broken into multiple sessions, keeping in mind the need to administer (if possible) both the immediate and delayed memory subtests.

ASSESSING CHILDREN WITH SPECIAL NEEDS

The NEPSY can be used to evaluate children with special needs of many kinds. The NEPSY Manual presents the performance of children with ADHD, Learning Disability (LD), Autistic Disorder, Developmental Language Disorder, Fetal Al-

Rapid Reference 2.1

Types of NEPSY Assessments

Core Assessment
- Provides an overview of the child's neuropsychological functions.
- Three Core Subtests for each domain, except Visuospatial (two).
- Administration time is 1–1.5 hr.

Expanded Assessment
- Provides a means of investigating more thoroughly a specific area of concern (i.e., language).
- After the Core, additional subtests within a domain are administered.
- Administration time is 1.5–2 hr.

Selective Assessment
- Provides a means of investigating a complex disorder (i.e., dyslexia).
- After the Core, additional subtests across domains that target impaired subcomponents of a complex function are administered.
- Selection of subtests is determined by your knowledge of the current research on the complex disorder.
- Administration time is 1.5–2 hr.

Full Assessment
- Provides a thorough neuropsychological evaluation to assess the effects of brain damage or dysfunction, developmental disorders, low birthweight, exposure to teratogens, etc.
- All 27 Core and Expanded subtests across domains are administered.
- The Core can be administered in one session to provide a baseline; Expanded Subtests can be administered in a second session.
- If a child is medically fragile, the assessment can be broken into multiple sessions, allowing for the administration of the immediate and delayed memory subtests.
- Administration time is 2–3 hr.

cohol Syndrome, Hearing Impairment, and Traumatic Brain Injury. In most cases children with special needs can take the NEPSY subtests as they are presented, but there may be exceptions. Whenever standardized administration is modified, the clinician must be sure to mark the Record Form as *Modified Administration,* and interpret the results with caution. If major modifications to standardized subtest administration are made, the use of norms may be invalidated, and the clinician may not be able to compute the Core Domain Score to which that subtest would contribute. Nonetheless, the clinician will gain valuable diagnostic information about how the child performs such a task. Following are subtests that can be used for certain populations, followed by directions for modified administrations of selected subtests.

The Child Who Is Blind

Administration of the NEPSY for this child is limited to (a) Attention/Executive Domain: Statue, Knock and Tap; (b) Language Domain: Phonological Processing (Part B only), Verbal Fluency, Oromotor Sequences, Body Part Naming, and Repetition of Nonsense Words; (c) Sensorimotor Domain: Fingertip Tapping, Finger Discrimination; and (d) Memory and Learning: List Learning, Narrative Memory, and Sentence Repetition. (See Rapid Reference 2.2.) Modifications to administration of specific tests appear below:

- *Fingertip Tapping.* This can be assessed by allowing the child to feel the position of the examiner's hand and a demonstration of the tapping. After the child understands the task, he or she can be assessed according to the regular directions. After completing the tapping part of the subtest, sequencing is demonstrated in the same way, with the child feeling the examiner's hand as the demonstration takes place. Again, when the child understands the task, the clinician can perform regular administration.
- *Body Part Naming.* This test can be administered using a large doll with well-defined features or the examiner's body. The examiner should place the child's forefinger on the part to be named. By using the examiner's body or a doll, the child does not receive sensory feedback that might cue the naming as the child would if his or her own body were touched. If both of the above methods have been tried, and if the child cannot name the body part, the examiner can then touch the part of the child's body to be named with the eraser end of a pencil. Norms should be interpreted very cautiously, and they should not be used to compute the Language Domain Score for the younger child. The clinician should use the 2 pt. (doll; examiner's body)/1 pt. (body) scoring but interpret scores with caution.
- *Knock and Tap.* This test is also administered by allowing the child to feel

---

CAUTION

Modifying Standardized Administration

- Mark the Record Form as *Modified Administration.* Note the modifications made.
- Interpret results with caution.
- If major modifications are made to standardized subtest administration, the use of norms may be invalidated.
- Do not use such modified subtests to compute Core Domain Scores.

≡*Rapid Reference 2.2*

**Assessing the Child Who
Is Blind**

Administration of the NEPSY for this child is limited to the following subtests some with modifications:

- *Attention/Executive Domain:* Statue, Knock and Tap
- *Language Domain:* Phonological Processing (Part B only), Verbal Fluency, Oromotor Sequences, Repetition of Nonsense Words and Body Part Naming
- *Sensorimotor Domain:* Fingertip Tapping, Finger Discrimination
- *Memory and Learning:* List Learning, Narrative Memory, and Sentence Repetition

the hand position as the examiner demonstrates. The child should be asked to listen to the difference between the sound of the knock and the sound of the tap. The examiner must knock and tap with force to be sure the child can make the auditory discrimination between the two. The ability to discriminate between the knock and the tap should be determined before beginning. When the child cannot discriminate between the sounds of the two movements, the clinician might try clapping and tapping, which might be discerned more easily. If the auditory discrimination cannot be made between the sounds of the two movements, the clinician should not administer the subtest.

The Child Who Is Hearing Impaired

The NEPSY *Manual* presents means and standard deviations for hearing impaired children ($n = 32$) who were a part of the validity studies for NEPSY (NEPSY *Manual,* p. 232). Therefore, these can be used as guidelines in evaluating the hearing-impaired child. Because the sample was small, only cautious comparison can be made to the average performance of other hearing-impaired children of a specific age who were of low-average intelligence or better, used American Sign Language and were free of a range of disorders (NEPSY *Manual,* p. 231). The clinician should determine before the evaluation which sign system is used by the child: American Sign Language or Exact English. If you are certified to do so, the clinician may administer NEPSY using one of these systems, but should not attempt this unless he or she is fluent. Otherwise, a certified interpreter should be used to translate the directions and the child's response. The child must be a proficient signer for his or her age in order to have NEPSY administered in sign. This is especially true for subtests requiring rapid response in sign, such as Speeded Naming and Verbal Fluency. If the child is proficient in understanding signed directions, but cannot sign rapidly, the clinician should not administer the latter two subtests. Also, the clinician needs to be very aware of regional colloquialisms in sign or of adapted sign used by the child. It is best to have an interpreter or teacher who knows the child well interpret for her or him. The clinician may present printed directions if the child reads well. Although a few subtests need modified administration, all except Phonological Processing and Repetition of Nonsense Words can be administered in sign. See Rapid Reference 2.3 for a summary of administration guidelines.

- *Statue.* This test can be administered by substituting auditory distracters for tactile ones: blowing on the neck with a straw, stroking the arm with a feather, touching the other arm with the eraser of a pencil, and touching the neck with a soft fabric (e.g., velvet, velour). Norms can be used as a guideline only for age appropriate-response.
- *Auditory Attention and Response Set (AARS).* This test can be administered with significant preparation, not as an auditory attention test, but as a test of response inhibition, shift of set, and of visual attention to sign. It takes preparation to do this, however, and the clinician will need to videotape the presentation. (This modified administration was developed with the help of participants in a NEPSY training workshop at the North Carolina School for the Deaf, Greensboro, NC.)

Practice signing the words printed on the Record Form for Parts A (Auditory Attention [AA]) and B (Response Set [RS]) at a rate of one per second. It is useful to have someone time you to be sure you maintain that rate. Using a digital clock or timer to set your pace will help. Once you feel you are maintaining your pace consistently, videotape the visual equivalent of the audiotape, including directions and a 10 s pause between the end of AA and the directions for RS. However, at the beginning of each section, you need to include the two samples that the examiner usually reads. These can be shown to the child during the teaching phase. Once the videotape is made, you have a permanent tool for modifying this test.

Prior to taping, you need to make a poster board strip approximately 7.5 cm wide and 66 cm long on which you glue, equidistant and centered, 5 cm squares of construction paper in the following primary colors and sequence: black, red, blue, yellow, black, red, blue, yellow. Tape the strip to the video monitor at the bottom of the screen, so that the interpreter on the tape is clearly visible just above it. The child needs to be able to watch the signing and touch the correct color with a minimum of movement of the eyes from the monitor to the squares. Practice this with the child, using the samples and the directions in the *Manual.*

When the child understands the task, administer the test according to

≡ *Rapid Reference 2.3*

Assessing the Child Who Is Hearing Impaired

- If proficient, administer subtests using sign language or use an interpreter familiar with the child's sign.
- Phonological Processing and Repetition of Nonsense Words are the only subtests that *cannot* be administered.
- Data for the hearing-impaired validity group are presented in the NEPSY *Manual* (p. 232).
- Modified administration procedures are detailed in text.
- Norms *do not* apply to
  —Modified Auditory Attention and Response Set.
  —Statue (with tactile distractors).

the directions given in the *Manual*. Record the color (y = *yellow*, etc.) when the child touches the square. A spontaneous correction before the next sign counts as correct. Score the test as presented in the *Manual*, but it is best to interpret this subtest clinically, noting patterns of omission and commission errors. Also, on Part B, watch for difficulty with vigilance in responding to *blue*, and difficulty inhibiting the well-learned response to *red* in Part A and shifting set to a *yellow* response on Part B. If you use the norms in the *Manual*, do so with great caution. You may wish to develop your own norms for the hearing-impaired child using this modified administration.

Children with Autistic Disorders

These children vary enormously in language delay, attention, hyperactivity, stereotypical behaviors, and degree of perseveration. For this reason, it is wise to prepare ahead of time by asking the parent or caregiver on which objects or topics the child is apt to perseverate (e.g., cars, dinosaurs, etc.). The clinician can then remove this type of toy from the area, and can avoid the topic in conversation and be prepared to redirect the child if he or she brings it up. If the child is not too perseverative, his or her special object may be used as a reinforcer. The clinician should ask about reinforcers that work for the child, as well as anything that is apt to be very upsetting to him or her. Children with autism are frequently hypersensitive to certain noises, textures, light, touch, and other stimuli, so try to remove or minimize such distractions. Ascertain from the parents if joint compression, deep pressure, or spinning in a chair is soothing to the child. It may be helpful for the child to wear a weighted vest, if he or she has one. A characteristic of children with autism is that they do not tolerate change well. It is beneficial to familiarize the child with both the examiner and the location of the testing before any evaluation is undertaken.

Assessing the Child with Autism

- Prepare ahead of time by finding out the objects or topics on which the child is apt to perseverate (e.g., cars, dinosaurs, etc.).
- Remove any related toys from the area, thereby avoiding the topic in conversation. Be prepared to redirect the child if he or she brings it up.
- If the child is not too perseverative, you may use his or her special object as a reinforcer.
- Be aware of sensory integration issues and possible reactions to certain noises, textures, light touch, etc.
- Ascertain from the parents if deep pressure (joint compression, wearing a weighted vest) or vestibular stimulation (swinging, jumping, or spinning in a chair) is soothing to the child.
- Children with autism do not tolerate change well. Allow time to establish rapport.
- If possible, allow the child to become familiarized with both the examiner and the location of the test before the evaluation.
- It may be helpful to have a caregiver present during testing.
- Be very aware of poor eye contact and reinforce good eye contact with the prompt, "Eyes to eyes," or, "Good looking" before you begin giving oral directions.
- Use simplified speech as you would with a language-impaired child.
- You may have to direct the child to look at each aspect of the materials.

It may be helpful to have a caregiver present during testing. The clinician needs to be very aware of poor eye contact and should reinforce good eye contact with the prompt the parents use. When they do not have one, the clinician should prompt, "Eyes to eyes," before talking. The clinician should use simple, direct language, as with a language-impaired child, and may have to direct the child to look at each aspect of the materials before a response is given. The examiner should attempt all subtests. The clinician should also administer a nonverbal cognitive assessment, instead of a verbally-based measure. (See Rapid Reference 2.4.)

Children with Motor Deficits

Use the standardized administration for children with milder motor difficulties, following the guidelines presented in Rapid Reference 2.5. When the child does not finish within the time limits, the clinician should just record the time and the child's results. The clinician should test the limits, however, by allowing the child to finish. In this way, the clinician can see that the child can do the task, but not quickly. The examiner should provide a primary pencil (one is included in the NEPSY kit) or a pencil with a gripper. For any child who has motor problems, the clinician should administer the motor subtests because this is the area of interest. The child with significant quadriplegia is an exception. The presence of hemiplegia, hemiparesis, or any other condition that limits or precludes the use of one or both hands often have difficulty with testing due to the need to handle materials. Children with hemiparesis should be assessed on both sides, however, in order to demonstrate differences in motor control. Below are modifications that can be made for children with limited motor control; all results should be interpreted with caution.

- *Auditory Attention and Response Set.* For a child who can point, the tokens for Auditory Attention (AA) can be arranged randomly for color, but in linear order, on the table in front of the child. When the child hears the word *red* he or she can point to the red token. The *R* is recorded when the child points to the token. For the Auditory Response Set the same method is used for responding and recording as in the AA modified administration, but the child points to *yellow* when *red* is heard, and so forth.
- *Tower.* Put an adhesive label on each peg with the appropriate number 1 to 3 from shortest to tallest. The child can then tell the examiner or, better still, someone assisting, where to move the balls by using the numbers (e.g., "Move *red* to number three"). If the child tells the examiner to make a move that is a rule violation (e.g., putting the yellow ball on the table, so he or she can get the red ball on the peg where the yellow ball is), the examiner should wait until the child has given the instruction completely and then inform him or her that it is a rule violation and cannot be carried out. Mark the Rule Violation box. The examiner may have to dispense with the time limits but should be able to get a clinical feel for the level of the child's executive functions.
- *Comprehension of Instructions.* A child who can point should be able to do this task, as long as the easel is placed as close to the child as is needed to facilitate response. It may work best to have the NEPSY Stimulus Book placed flat on the table with the answer sheet covered. If the child does not have a pointing response, but knows his or her numbers, each shape can be numbered with a small removable adhesive label. The child can then instruct the examiner where to point by number ("Point to number two, number four, and then to number 5").
- *Block Construction.* The child can point to the location in which he or she

≡ Rapid Reference 2.5

Assessing the Child Who Has Motor Deficits

- Administer the motor subtests to any child with motor problems except the child with quadriplegia.
- Provide a primary pencil or a pencil with a gripper.
- For children with milder motor difficulties, you may wish to use the standardized administration with the following modifications:
  —If the child is not finished within the time limits, do not stop him or her; just record the time and the child's results, which will be scored.
  —Allow the child to finish to see if he or she can do the task without time constraints.
- Children with hemiplegia, hemiparesis, or any other condition that limits or precludes the use of one or both hands often have difficulty with testing due to the need to handle materials. Modifications may be needed.
- Children with hemiparesis should be assessed on both sides in order to document differences in motor control.

would like the block placed. The examiner can place the block for the child.

- *Design Fluency*. This subtest can be performed with the child pointing to the dots to be connected and the examiner making the pencil marks. The clinician may have to forego time limits.

Children with Language Impairment

Whether a language deficit is developmental or acquired, the clinician should administer language subtests in order to document the deficit. The clinician should keep directions as simple and as direct as possible on all subtests. For instance, on Visuomotor Precision, the clinician might abbreviate instructions to: "Draw line fast" (demonstrating); "No hitting sides" (showing track sides); "No turning paper" (shaking head *no* and demonstrating turning paper); and "Ready, go!" The clinician should use the teaching examples three times, if needed. Record verbal responses and utterances heard during testing to analyze for semantic, syntactic, and other language errors later. Children with language impairment can be expected to perform poorly both on language subtests and on verbal memory subtests: Memory for Names, Narrative Memory, List Learning, and Sentence Repetition. When assessing cognition for these children, the examiner also needs to include a nonverbal assessment. Rapid Reference 2.6 summarizes assessment guidelines.

≡ Rapid Reference 2.6

Assessing the Child Who Is Language Impaired

• Whether a language deficit is developmental or acquired, the language subtests should be administered in order to document the deficit.
• Keep directions as simple and as direct as possible on all subtests.
• Be sure to use teaching examples up to three times as needed.
• Record responses to analyze for semantic and syntactic errors later.
• Language-impaired children can be expected to perform poorly on verbal memory subtests (Memory for Names, Narrative Memory, List Learning, and Sentence Repetition).
• When assessing cognition include a nonverbal assessment.

Children with Attentional Problems

The child with attentional problems, whether these are due to Attention Deficit Hyperactivity Disorder (ADHD), Autistic Disorder, Traumatic Brain Injury (TBI), and so forth, should be evaluated in multiple, short testing sessions, if possible. The child should also be evaluated in a plain room with no extraneous stimuli. When the referral question is to confirm the presence of ADHD, an attentional problem, or any learning disability or disorder, the child should not be evaluated while on medication. When the child receives medication and the referral question is not to confirm ADHD or an attentional problem, but rather to determine how the child is functioning with treatment, NEPSY should be administered while the child is on medication. (See Rapid Reference 2.7.)

≡ Rapid Reference 2.7

Assessing the Child With Attentional Problems

• A child's attentional problems may be due to ADHD, Autistic Disorder, TBI, depression, etc.
• The child may need to be evaluated in multiple, short, testing sessions.
• The child may also need to be evaluated in a small room with no extraneous stimuli.
• If the child has previously been diagnosed ADHD and the referral question is to confirm the presence of ADHD the child should be evaluated while *off medications* so the diagnosis can be confirmed.
• If the child receives medication and the referral question is not to confirm ADHD or an attentional problem, but rather to determine how the child is functioning with treatment, NEPSY should be administered while the child is *on medication.*

ADMINISTRATION CONSIDERATIONS

Examiner Practice for Certain Tests

There are certain tests that are difficult to administer, although the majority of the 27 subtests on NEPSY are not. The following subtests need extended practice before the clinician attempts to administer them: Auditory Attention and Response Set (AARS), Tower, Imitating Hand Positions (IHP), and Manual Motor Series (MMS). It is recommended that the clinician practice these at least twice with normally developing children and five times with children who have various impairments before administering the test for clinical purposes. Detailed administration directions for each of them can be found in the manual. In particular, the *Manual* designates specific hands and fingers for MMS and IHP and the order of movement for MMS.

Start and Discontinue Rules

Some of the subtests on NEPSY are given to all children. Other subtests have start rules that allow testing time to be shortened for most older children, but reversal rules that allow the clinician to go back to earlier items for children unable to succeed at their age level. Most NEPSY subtests have discontinue rules. Icons are provided on the Record Form to remind the examiner of these points. (See Rapid Reference 2.8.)

Recording Responses

There are specific subtests where the recording of responses is essential, while on others, the clinician can record information that will allow error analysis later. For instance, on Verbal Fluency the clinician must write down the child's words, because the number of words he or she produces in each category is the variable being

CAUTION

Subtests Requiring Examiner Practice

- Auditory Attention and Response Set
- Tower
- Imitating Hand Positions
- Manual Motor Sequences

≡ *Rapid Reference 2.8*

Subtest Administration Rules

- Start points, reversal rules, and discontinue points are in the NEPSY *Manual*, pp. 60–65.
- Example of rules are in the NEPSY *Manual*, pp. 65–68.
- A summary of each subtest's rules can be found in the Subtest-by-Subtest Rules of Administration section later in this chapter.

≡≡≡*Rapid Reference 2.9*

Optional Recording and Error Analysis

• Any erroneous response, on any subtest, should be recorded because it has potentially valuable interpretative information.

• Specific subtest error analysis:
  —Comprehension of Instructions (Number responses on miniature to look at linguistic understanding vs. attention and recall errors.)
  —List Learning (Number the child's responses in order of recall to determine strategy.)
  —Verbal Fluency (Record in squares for 15 sec. periods to look at distribution of responses, quality of responses.)

measured. On List Learning it is possible to score just 1 or 0 if the word is recalled or not recalled, but valuable diagnostic information is lost when the clinician does not number the responses or record the words in the order of recall. When the clinician numbers or records the words, he or she can inspect the record later to see if the child was clustering to aid memory recall. The clinician can also see if the child is using semantic clustering (boat, water, fish) or phonemic clustering (window, water, winter). The former is more efficient than the latter. The clinician can also see if there is a primacy (most words recalled from the first of the list) or recency effect (most words recalled from the last part of the list).(See Rapid Reference 2.9.)

Recording behavioral observations, both formally (when QOs are designated on a subtest) and informally (when the clinician observes interesting aspects of the child's behavior), is necessary for the neuropsychological evaluation. These observations often provide essential diagnostic information about how a child is, or is not, able to perform a function. For QOs the clinician can compare the child's behavior to base rates in the standardization and clinical sample. Rapid Reference 2.10 lists subtests with quantifiable qualitative observations.

Timing

Many of the NEPSY subtests are untimed. A general timing guideline of 10 s/item serves to keep the pace from slowing to the point that the child loses interest and to avoid causing a child distress when he or she cannot do an item or is unwilling to perform. The clinician should validate the child's feelings by making a comment such as, "That was kind of hard; let's try another one," or, "Sometimes the tricky ones are frustrating; let's try a different one." The Record Form and the Stimulus Book show a stopwatch icon as a reminder for the timed subtests. Timing guidelines are provided in the subtest directions. The clinician

≡ Rapid Reference 2.10

Subtests with Quantifiable Qualitative Observations

- Tower
- Auditory Attention and Response Set
- Visual Attention
- Body Part Naming
- Phonological Processing
- Speeded Naming
- Comprehension of Instructions
- Repetition of Nonsense Words
- Verbal Fluency
- Oromotor Sequences
- Fingertip Tapping
- Imitating Hand Positions
- Visuomotor Precision
- Manual Motor Sequences
- Design Copying
- Arrows
- Block Constructions
- Sentence Repetition
- List Learning

should record the time rounded to the nearest second. If a child is actively engaged in a task, and you wish to test the limits, record the time when the time limit has expired and the child's response up to that time. Then allow the child to complete the task without saying anything about the time's being over. Record the additional elapsed time-to-solution for qualitative analysis later. If the child has had additional time and still is not approaching solution, record the time you stopped her or him and the status of the child's response at the time you terminated the task.

Prompting, Querying, Self-Corrections, and Item Repetition

As a general rule, prompting ("Keep going," or "Let's give it another try") is permitted on NEPSY in order to ensure the child's best performance. The clinician should note the prompt ("Tell me more") with *P*. Some subtests have specific directions for prompting that appear in the *Manual,* Stimulus Book, and Record Form and to which the examiner should adhere. Self-corrections are allowed on NEPSY *when they are made before the next item is administered.* The clinician should record *SC* beside the item and write in the correct response. If repetitions are not allowed on a subtest, this will be designated in the *Manual* and Stimulus Book. The clinician should note *R* or *Rep* on the Record Form. On Phonological Processing, Comprehension of Instructions, and Sentence Repetition, asking for repetition is recorded as a Qualitative Observation to be compared to base rates for age in the standardization population.

Teaching the Task

NEPSY provides teaching items on most subtests. Directions for these are in both the *Manual* and the Stimulus Book. Unless otherwise specified, the teaching items are presented once, but the child may practice as much as needed to be sure he or she understands the task before the subtest actually begins. If a task actually has to be modified from the standardized directions or format due to the child's disability, the clinician should note the modifications and the reasons for them on the Record Form. The child's performance should be evaluated clinically, and the norms should be used as guidelines and interpreted cautiously.

SUBTEST-BY-SUBTEST RULES OF ADMINISTRATION

The NEPSY *Manual* provides detailed rules for subtest administration. Examiners who are new to NEPSY will want to spend time studying it in depth. This section of the administration chapter, however, provides important tips for competent administration of each of the subtests. For examiners who have already learned the NEPSY, it can serve as a guide to refresh the memory on important details of subtest administration. The tests are presented in order of administration. In addition to the QOs noted on the Record Form, the clinician will also want to record his or her own observations. Together these can provide interpretive insights into a particular subtest or can reveal patterns across domains that may be critical to the interpretive process. This section presents rules of administration and key behaviors to observe.

1. Body Part Naming (Language Domain; Core): Ages 3 to 4

This is a naming task for young children, summarized in Rapid Reference 2.11. The child is asked to name nine body parts from a picture of a child (2 points). If the part cannot be named from the picture, the child can name it on his or her body (1 point).

≡Rapid Reference 2.11

Body Part Naming Summary

Start Rule	Reverse Rule	Discontinue Rule	Timing Rule
Item 1	None	Four consecutive scores of 0	Not timed

Rules and Tips
Start Rule: Item 1 for all.
Discontinue Rule: Four consecutive scores of 0.

- If the child cannot name the body part from the initial question, "What is this called?" repeat the question, pointing to the corresponding part on the child's own body.
- Do *not* touch the child's body, as this provides kinesthetic feedback and changes the task.
- If the child is confused when you point to his or her nose or ears because these body parts cannot be seen, it is permissible to point to yours.
- If a general part is named rather than a specific part (e.g., head instead of nose), query, "What part of the head?" Place a *Q* on the Record Form to indicate your query.

Behaviors to Observe
- Poor articulation. Record this QO.
- Frustration due to poor language skills?
- Poor eye contact and lack of relatedness.
- Lack of body schema. A human figure drawing may lack integration.

2. Design Copying (Visuospatial Domain; Core): Ages 3 to 12

This subtest is an untimed two-dimensional constructional task that requires the integration of visuospatial analysis and graphomotor skills. Rapid Reference 2.12 summarizes this test. The child reproduces paper-and-pencil copies of geometric designs of increasing complexity.

Rules and Tips
Start Points: Ages 3 to 6, Item 1; Ages 7 to 12, Item 4.
Reversal Rule: If a child 7 to 12 does not complete Item 4 correctly, reverse to Item 1 and proceed forward.

≡Rapid Reference 2.12

Design Copying Summary

Start Rule	Reverse Rule	Discontinue Rule	Timing Rule
Ages 3–6, Item 1	If a child aged 7–12 does not complete Item 4 correctly, reverse to Item 1 and proceed forward	Four consecutive . scores of 0	Not timed
Ages 7–12, Item 4			

Discontinue Rule: Four consecutive scores of 0.

- The first item for 3- to 4-year-olds is imitative. Draw a line beside the horizontal line in the top box. The child draws a horizontal line below it in the empty box. From then on he or she copies independently.
- Do not allow the child to turn the paper or erase.
- Check to be sure that the child has not skipped a page of designs before moving to the next task.
- Appendix H presents scoring rules and examples, or the Design Copying (DC) items can be scored directly with guidelines on the *NEPSY Scoring Assistant* (Psychological Corporation, 2000).

Behaviors to Observe
- Pencil Grip. Record this QO. Pictures of the pencil grips are in the *Manual* (pp. 87–88).
- Overflow around the mouth or involuntary tongue movements as the child copies.
- Impulsivity or copying quickly without paying attention to errors.

3. Phonological Processing (Language Domain; Core): Ages 3 to 12

This subtest (summarized in Rapid Reference 2.13) assesses phonemic awareness, an essential underlying process in reading decoding and spelling. On the first section, Word Segment Recognition, the examiner pronounces three words that are represented by pictures. A segment of one of the words is then pronounced, and the child identifies the correct picture that represents the word from which the segment came. Part B, Phonological Processing, assesses phonological segmentation at the level of letter sounds (phonemes) and word segments (syllables). The examiner asks the child to create a new word by omitting a syllable or phoneme or substituting one phoneme or sound for another.

Part A: Word Segment Recognition—Stimulus Book
Rules and Tips
Start Points: Part A—Ages 3 to 6, Item 1; Ages 7 to 8, Item 7.
Reversal Rule: If a child aged 7 to 8 does not complete Items 7 and 8 correctly, reverse until the child passes two consecutive items, then continue forward.
Discontinue Rule: Five consecutive scores of 0.

- Children ages 3 to 4 stop after Item 14 even if discontinue rule is not met.
- Pronounce the words in a conversational tone at a moderate rate while pointing to each of the pictures. Pause. Then say the cue. *Do not repeat cue on Part A.*

Behaviors to Observe
- Asking for repetition. Record this QO.
- Impulsivity of choice, without looking at all three pictures. Were you able to redirect the child to look at all three pictures?

Part B: Phonological Segmentation—Record Form or Manual
Rules and Tips
Start Points: Ages 9 to 12, Item 15.
Reversal Rule: If Items 15 and 16 are failed, reverse until the child passes two consecutive items, then continue.
Discontinue Rule: Five consecutive errors.

- You may repeat each item only once on Part B.
- Pronounce the words in a conversational tone at a moderate rate.
- There are additional teaching items in the *Manual* if the child needs more practice after attempting the teaching items on the Record Form. Supply the correct answer on the teaching items to clarify the task. Teaching Example 1 is given before Items 15 to 25 and Teaching Example 2 before Items 26 to 36.
- The sounds are represented by the letter inside slash marks (/b/). *Do NOT attach a vowel sound to the consonant. It is /mm/, not /muh/.* Do not say the name of the letter. The letters in consonant blends are sounded together: /bl/, not /buh//luh/.
- Give credit for "in" or "ing" on Item 19.

Rapid Reference 2.13

Phonological Processing Summary

Start Rule	Reverse Rule	Discontinue Rule	Timing Rule
Part A Ages 3–6, Item 1 Ages 7–8, Item 7 *Part B* Ages 9–12, Item 15	If a child aged 7–8 does not complete Items 7 and 8 correctly, reverse until two consecutive items are passed, then continue forward. If Items 15 and 16 are failed, reverse until two consecutive items are passed, then continue.	Five consecutive scores of 0 *Children ages 3–4 stop after Item 14 even if discontinue rule is not met.*	Not timed

- The word segments for Items 26 to 36 are pronounced as they are in the word. ("Say 'changing.' Now say it again, but change the '/ang/' [pronounced '/anj/'] to '/omp/.'")

Behaviors to Observe

- Asking for repetitions. Record this QO.
- Incorrect sequencing of sounds; confusion in trying to formulate the new sequence.
- Frustration in trying to perform the task.
- Success on Part A, which has picture reinforcement, but failure on Part B due to distractibility without pictorial reinforcement.
- Difficulty with working memory on the longer items (33 to 36) but success prior to that.

4. Memory for Faces (Memory and Learning Domain; Core): Ages 5 to 12

This is a test of immediate and delayed facial recognition after a brief exposure. The child states the gender of each photo in a 5 s exposure. The child then identifies the faces seen from arrays of three faces. The clinician performs a delayed memory trial thirty minutes later. (See Rapid Reference 2.14.)

Rules and Tips

Start Point: Item 1 of the Learning Items. Item 1 on the Delay.

Time Guideline: Present each photo plate for 5 s. Delay trial is 30 min ± 5 min later.

Discontinue Rule: Administer every item.

Supplemental Scores: Separate scores for Memory for Faces and Delayed Memory for Faces.

- On the Learning Trials continue to expose the picture if 5 s have not elapsed when the child identifies the child's gender.
- Enter the time the Immediate Recall Trial ends on the Record Form to be sure you complete the Delay Trial as close to 30 min later as possible.
- If you are administering NEPSY sequentially, and you are about to begin the Arrows subtest, check the time you completed Immediate Memory for Faces. If you are close to the 30 min delay, alter the sequence of test administration and administer Delayed Memory for Faces. The clinician should alter the sequence of administration only before a delayed memory test in order to meet the 30 min interval between the immediate and delayed portions of a subtest.
- If at all possible, do *not* break for the day between the immediate and delayed memory trials, or you cannot administer the delay. You can still get an immediate memory score, but you cannot compute the Memory Domain Score.
- Be sure to use the separate photo plates provided for Delayed Memory for Faces because new distractors are provided in the Delayed Memory for Faces.

Behaviors to Observe

- Discomfort with looking at the faces, or averting his or her eyes after looking at them. Does this correlate with poor or fleeting eye contact with you or others?
- Impulsivity in glancing very quickly at the faces, wanting to move on before the 5 s exposure was complete, as opposed to reflecting on them in a focused manner.
- Performing better on Delayed Recall than Immediate Recall, suggesting slowed processing and consolidation.

Rapid Reference 2.14

Memory for Faces Summary

Start Rule	Reverse Rule	Discontinue Rule	Timing Rule
Item I of the Learning Items	No reverse rule	Administer every item.	Present each photo plate for 5 s.
Item I on the Delay			Delay trial is 30 min ±5 min later.

5. Tower (Attention/Executive Functions Domain; Core): Ages 5 to 12

This subtest assesses planning, strategizing, and monitoring performance in rule-based nonverbal problem solving by arranging colored balls on pegs to match a picture stimulus in a certain number of moves and within time limits.

Rules and Tips

Start Point: Teaching Example. Begin Subtest with Item 3.

Reversal Rule: If the child does not complete Items 3 and 4 correctly, administer Item 1 before continuing with Item 5.

Time Limits: Items 1 to 4, 30 s per item; Items 5 to 20, 45 s per item.

Discontinue Rule: Four consecutive scores of 0.

- It is essential that the child understands the teaching task and the rules. Be sure to demonstrate the rules and be certain the child thoroughly comprehends them.
- If you begin with the squirrel story for a younger child, continue with those labels, calling the balls "squirrels" and the pegs "trees."
- Follow the sequence of responses printed on the Record Form. Most children use one of these. If the child takes off on a different sequence half way through, you can begin recording from that point. Some examiners find that it is easier to record the moves from the beginning of the sequence.
- You do not need to record the ball color and peg number sequence, although this is recommended for error analysis, but you *must* keep track of the number of moves. This can be done with hash marks or by keeping count on the fingers of your left hand under the table. When the child finishes, the configuration of the balls may be the same as the pic-

ture, and the child may have completed the task within the time limits; but if you have not counted the moves, you will not know if the solution is correct.

- During the Teaching, caution against using two hands. It is allowed, but when a child starts moving the balls quickly, he or she is apt to have two balls off the pegs at once, and that is a rule violation.

- If the child asks how many moves have been made, do *not* supply that information. Monitoring the number of moves being made is an important executive function being tested.

- If the child drops a ball and it rolls off the table, stop the stopwatch, retrieve the ball and resume timing where you stopped it.

- Do not let a child start over.

- On the two items that can be solved in fewer moves but must be solved in six moves, a solution with five moves is incorrect. Part of what you are testing is whether the child can inhibit the easier response to plan the more difficult response. If the child has completed the task in five moves and then realizes six moves should have been made, he or she may try to move a ball to a different peg and then back to the same position. This would not be correct, because then seven moves would have been made (one to move to the other peg, and one to come back to the same spot). Record the behavior.

- If the child makes a Rule Violation, stop the child, and restate the rule while replacing the balls where they were when the child broke the rule. Do not stop the stopwatch. If the child realizes halfway through an item that it is incorrect, and he or she cannot fix it in the requisite number of moves, the item can be terminated. However, if a child is very invested in completing a task and time is up, or he or she will not be able to solve it, but does not realize it, you can let him or her continue. Score 0, however. This is a long subtest, so do not test the limits too often. If the child completes the task correctly after the time limit, record "correct after time." Self-corrections are allowed if the child's hand is still on the ball when he or she self-corrects.

Behaviors to Observe
- Rule Violations. Record each of these QOs in the box on the Record Form page for Tower.

- Impulsivity that causes failure because the child does not plan a solution. Is there a strategy in the way the child approaches the task or does she or he use trial and error?

Rapid Reference 2.15

Tower Summary

Start Rule	Reverse Rule	Discontinue Rule	Timing Rule
Teaching Example. Begin subtest with Item 3.	If the child does not complete Items 3 and 4 correctly, administer Item 1 before continuing with Item 5.	Four consecutive scores of 0	Items 1–4, 30 s/item Items 5–20, 45 s/item

- Does verbal mediation help the child solve the items or is there tangential talking which distracts the child?
- Does the child recall the rules, but still tries to make an illegal move, or does he or she seem to have forgotten the rules? Does the child continue to make the same errors, even when the rule has been restated after a Rule Violation? This would suggest that the child does not learn efficiently from feedback.
- Frustration is present but not oppositional behavior. Does the child make self-deprecating remarks when he or she fails an item? (See Rapid Reference 2.15.)

6. Auditory Attention and Response Set (Attention/Executive Dysfunction; Core): Ages 5–12

This assessment has two parts, Part A: Auditory Attention (AA) and Part B: Response Set (RS). The clinician must give both parts. The first section establishes the set, which will be switched in the second. AA measures simple, selective auditory attention to rapidly presented auditory stimuli. RS assesses complex auditory attention and the ability to shift and maintain a new and complex set involving both contrasting and matching stimuli (Korkman, Kirk, & Kemp, 1998, pp. 101).

Rules and Tips
Start Point: Teaching Example for Part A.
Discontinue Rule: Administer both parts. Do not discontinue.
Supplemental Scores: Separate scores for AA, and for RS; for Omission Errors (AA and RS separately), and for Commission Errors (AA and RS separately).

- To facilitate recording, hold the Record Form up on a clipboard. Place yourself so you can see the child's hand, see the words on the form, and record without having to move your head. On the form, follow the words you hear with your pencil. If the child's hand starts to move when the target word is heard, it will probably be a 2 point response if the correct color is touched. Watch only the child's hand and record when the token is *touched*. Do not attempt to score during the test.

- Practice this test extensively before administering.
- Present the Teaching Example for each section three times, if necessary, to be sure the child understands the task before you begin the test.
- Spread the tokens out so the child does not have to dig through them, but instruct him or her not to hover over them with his or her hands or to sort them into colors. Demonstrate these prohibited actions during the teaching. Practice keeping the hands on the edge of the table during the Teaching. When the child hovers or starts to sort colors during the test, simply gesture for the child to stop or if necessary move the child's hand back to the edge of the table. Do not talk because the next word on the tape will not be heard if you do.
- Although the child is told not to try to correct mistakes because of the speed of the tape, spontaneous corrections can be credited, if the correct square is touched before the next item is administered. If you have already recorded the first color, be sure to cross it out or erase and write the correct color.
- Everyone must get a 0 or 2 point credit on the last item of AA, because it is "red" and there are no squares beyond it to record a 1 point response. Therefore, the fairest thing is to credit 2 points if the child touches a red square. If a red square is not touched that is an omission and receives a "0."
- If the child picks up two squares inadvertently and puts them in the box, do not score a commission error.
- Do not allow the child to take a token out of the box again to change an answer after the next word has been pronounced.

Behaviors to Observe

- Frustration or anxiety because the RS task is complex and fast, requiring efficient attention/executive functions and temporal processing. If the task is clearly too difficult, discontinue this section. You can still get a score for AA.
- Salient behaviors (focused attention, anxious or frustrated expressions or remarks, oppositional responses) which may occur differently on the two portions of the test. This is a window to the types of complex, rapid tasks that may be causing similar behavioral responses in the classroom.

≡Rapid Reference 2.16

Auditory Attention/Response Set Summary

Start Rule	Reverse Rule	Discontinue Rule	Timing Rule
Teaching Example for Part A	No reverse rule	Administer both parts. Do not discontinue.	Present teaching items at 1 word/s.

- Boredom, impulsivity, and slips in attention. These are easier to record on the first repetitive task. Some children will perform better on the second task because they find it more challenging, which engages the attention. (See Rapid Reference 2.16.)

7. Speeded Naming (Language Domain; Core): Ages 5 to 12

This subtest assesses rapid access to and production of language labels for circles and squares of different sizes and colors. Rapid Reference 2.17 summarizes the administration rules.

Rules and Tips
Start Point: Teaching Example.
Discontinue Rule: Discontinue after 300 s.
Time Guidelines: Maximum time is 300 s.
Supplemental Scores: Time and Accuracy.

- The Teaching Example can be performed three times, if needed.
- If the child cannot demonstrate mastery of colors and shapes consistently, do not put him or her under the strain of trying to name them rapidly. If you want a measure of naming, revert to Body Part Naming, though in general it is given only to 3- to 4-year-olds.
- During the Teaching, correct the use of *box* for *square*, because that is an error. Also, encourage the use of *big* and *little*, not *large* and *small*, though the latter two are not errors if they occur on the test.
- Reversed sequences are not errors (*yellow-big-circle*), but if the child makes more than two, check the box.
- If the child makes an error (misnames a shape or omits a label), stop, correct, have the child say it correctly, but do not turn off the stopwatch.

≡Rapid Reference 2.17

Speeded Naming Summary

Start Rule	Reverse Rule	Discontinue Rule	Timing Rule
Teaching Examples	No reverse rule	Discontinue after 300 s.	Maximum time is 300 s.

Behaviors to Observe
- Recruiting the body into the effort of accessing labels and increasing voice volume. Record these QOs.
- Very slow, labored performance or impulsively fast performance, resulting in errors.
- Misnaming, even at an average pace.
- Frustration with being timed.
- Good naming skills during the Teaching Example, when speed is not required, but poor rapid naming performance.

8. Arrows (Visuospatial Domain; Core): Ages 5 to 12

This subtest assesses the judgement of line and angle orientation. The child chooses which two of eight arrows would go straight to the center of a target. (See Rapid Reference 2.18.)

Rules and Tips
Start Point: Teaching Example.
Discontinue Rule: Four consecutive scores of 0.

- After the Teaching Example do not let the child trace the arrows path to the target.
- If the child is impulsive or inattentive, direct his or her attention to each of the targets before allowing a choice to be made.
- During the Teaching be sure the child learns that the targets do not have to be adjacent or in number sequence.
- When the child chooses only one arrow, remember to prompt for a second arrow (and record *P*).

Behaviors to Observe
- Impulsivity.
- Making significantly more errors on one side of the stimulus plate than the other. Record Visual Field Errors on the Record Form as QOs.

≡Rapid Reference 2.18

Arrows Summary

Start Rule	Reverse Rule	Discontinue Rule	Timing Rule
Teaching Example	No reverse rule	Four consecutive scores of 0	No time limit

9. Memory for Names (Memory and Learning Domain; Core): Ages 5 to 12

This is an evaluation of name learning with immediate and delayed recall trials. The children learn the names of line drawings of eight children (only six names for 5-year-olds) across three trials with recall after each trial. Thirty min later the child is asked to recall the names again. Rapid Reference 2.19 presents a summary of administration rules.

Rules and Tips
Start Point: Teaching Presentation.
Time Guideline: 10 s exposure for each drawing.
Discontinue Rule: Administer all items.
Supplemental Scores: Separate scores for Learning Trials (Immediate) and Delayed Memory for Names.

- Remember to remove the cards for Sam and Maria before administering the test to a 5-year-old.
- Administer the Teaching Presentation with the cards in sequential order. After administration shuffle the cards out of the child's view for each learning trial. Do *not* expose the names on the backs of the cards.
- Order the cards face down out of the child's view starting with Item #8. The numbers and names are up with Item 1 being on top. Hold the cards in your palm so the pictures are face down and are not exposed as you pull each card sequentially from the top of the deck in your hand.
- Place the cards face up on top of the pile so that face of the previous card is covered.
- If the child misnames a picture, give the correct name, have the child repeat it, and proceed.
- Note the time the Learning Trials finish on your Record Form, so you can time the Delayed Memory for Faces as close to 30 min as possible. If you administer the tests sequentially, the Delayed Memory for Faces will fol-

≡ Rapid Reference 2.19

Memory for Names Summary

Start Rule	Reverse Rule	Discontinue Rule	Timing Rule
Teaching Presentation	No reverse rule	Administer every item.	10 s exposure for each drawing

low Narrative Memory (NM). Check the time before you begin to administer NM. If you need to do the delay trial before NM in order to administer it as close to 30 min as possible, you can alter the sequence to do so.
- Shuffle the cards for the Delayed Memory for Names subtest and administer as before.
- Diminutives (Joey for Joe) and Stable Misarticulations (Tham for Sam) are correct.

Behaviors to Observe
- Recalling the correct names but incorrectly pairing them with the faces, suggesting a problem in paired associates learning.
- Perseverating on the same few names or little learning across Learning Trials.
- Frustration in trying to remember the names, but inability to do so efficiently.
- Performing significantly better on the Learning Trials than on the Delay, suggesting memory decay.
- Performing significantly better on Delay than on Learning Trials due to slowed processing and delayed consolidation of the information.
- Impulsivity. The child looks quickly and briefly at the stimulus cards and may not attend to the name, so he or she fails to encode the information.

10. Fingertip Tapping (Sensorimotor Domain; Core): Ages 5 to 12

This subtest assesses finger dexterity, fine motor speed, and motor programming for preferred and nonpreferred hands.

Rules and Tips
Start Point: Teaching Example for Items 1 to 2.
Time Limit: 60 s for repetitions (Items 1 to 2); 90 s for sequences (Items 3 to 4).

Discontinue Rule: Administer every item.

Supplemental Scores: Separate Scores for Repetitions and Sequences for both hands together; Repetitions and Sequential Tapping taken together for each hand.

- If you have difficulty with fine motor movements for any reason, you may wish to ask a colleague to administer the test or to train an assistant to administer the test while you observe.
- During the Teaching Example for Sequential Fingertapping, be sure the child understands the sequence goes from the index finger to the little finger. Do *not* allow the child to reverse the sequence from little finger to index finger. Each sequence begins with the index finger. If the child reverses the sequence during the test, it is an error.
- Do both hands for Repetitive Fingertapping (FT), then both hands for Sequential FT. Be sure the other hand is resting on the table in plain view, so you can observe associated movements.
- If the child taps with straight fingers, taps with sides of fingers, or does not open the fingers about 2.5 cm, it is an error. Missequencing (missing a finger or tapping the fingers out of order) is also an error (on Sequential FT). Stop the child, demonstrate the correct position, saying, "Do it like this," while continuing to time; have the child do it correctly and then continue on.
- The scores are Time for 32 *Correct* Taps, (not necessarily consecutive correct taps) and Time for 8 *Correct* Sequences; again, they do not have to be consecutive. Stop when 60 s have elapsed, however.
- When you have had to stop the child three times for the same type of error, and he or she slips immediately back into the incorrect finger movement or missequencing, do not stop any more for that error. It is likely that the child is unable to hold the correct finger posture. This is diagnostic in itself. Count any of those same movements as errors and continue to correct any others that may arise. By the time the child has been stopped and corrected three times, the 60 s time limit will be nearly up.
- Even if the child is hemiplegic or has hemiparesis, assess both hands to demonstrate differences if possible. (See Rapid Reference 2.20.)

Behaviors to Observe

- Posturing? Mirroring? Overflow? Incorrect Hand Position? Visual Guidance? Rate Change? Operational definitions for these QOs are contained in the *Manual* (p. 118). Record on the Record Form when observed. Rate change is seen in dyspraxic individuals who have problems with motor programming. Posturing, mirroring, and overflow are seen

≡ Rapid Reference 2.20

Fingertip Tapping Summary

Start Rule	Reverse Rule	Discontinue Rule	Timing Rule
Teaching Example for Items 1–2	No reverse rule	Administer every item.	60 s for repetitions (Items 1–2) 90 s for sequences (Items 3–4)

in individuals with ADHD, learning disabilities, and other developmental disorders. They reflect the diffuse, mild, neurological dysfunction these individuals have.

- Associated movements co-occur with an awkward pencil grip and poor graphomotor skills on the Visuomotor Precision subtest. Were they observed at other times in the evaluation? (See Rapid Reference 2.20.)

11. Visual Attention (Attention/Executive Function Domain; Core): All Ages

This subtest assesses the speed and accuracy with which a child is able to focus selectively on and maintain attention to visual target within an array. For the 3- to 4-year-olds the first task is a simple selective attention task on which the child quickly locates and marks pictures of a bunny from many different pictures in a linear array. The 3- to 4-year-olds also receive the simple search task which is the first item for 5- to 12-year-olds. On this task, the child is required to carry out a search for pictures of a target cat embedded in a random array of many different pictures. The final task is only given to the 5- to 12-year-olds. It is a complex visual attention task which has two target faces. Other faces that match either of these two targets in every aspect of their facial features are to be located in a linear array of faces. Many of the faces in the array differ in only one tiny feature, such as the eyebrows.

Rules and Tips

Start Points: Ages 3 to 4 Bunnies and Cats; Ages 5 to 12 Cats and Faces.
Discontinue Rule: Administer both items for the child's age group.
Time Limit: 180 s/item.
Supplemental Scores: Separate scores for each item (Bunnies, Cats, and Faces). For each item: Omission Errors, Commission Errors, Time.

- For the Cat search task, you may want to make an informal search path on the facing page of the Record Form where there is a blank spot. Just make an *S* in the equivalent location where the child starts and then make a pencil track following her or his movements with a number for each target the child locates. Put an *E* in an equivalent location to the child's ending spot. You can see later the strategy the child used in locating target.
- The linear array, is administered like Coding on the WISC-III. The child is not allowed to skip around but must proceed line by line looking for both faces at the same time. Do not allow the child to go back and look for more items when he or she reaches the last item.
- On the random array, (Cats) the child can continue to search until he or she puts down the pencil, says he or she is finished, or the Time Limits are up.
- Be sure the child has a red pencil or crayon as it will make it easier to score. The scoring template will locate the targets for you quickly.

Behaviors to Observe
- Off-Task Behavior. Record this QO on Visual Attention.
- Marking pictures before you have given the directions. An impulsive child will try to do this.
- Using verbal mediation to complete the task more efficiently. Observe whether talking is tangential and distracting.
- Some children who have difficulty with auditory attention perform better on this type of visual attention cancellation task because the pictures are salient and provide an anchor for attention. Compare to see whether this type of difference is present.
- Searching in an organized or random way. (See Rapid Reference 2.21.)

≡ Rapid Reference 2.21

Visual Attention Summary

Start Rule	Reverse Rule	Discontinue Rule	Timing Rule
Ages 3–4, Bunnies and Cats	No reverse rule	Administer both items for the child's age group.	180 s/item
Ages 5–12, Cats and Faces			

12. Comprehension of Instructions (Language Domain; Core): Ages 5 to 12

This is a verbal comprehension task that requires the child to respond to oral directions related to a visual stimulus plate. The colored plate is visible when the child is given the directions. The first 13 items are related to a picture stimulus of bunnies in various permutations of size, color, and feelings. The child listens to the instructions and then carries them out. (Find a bunny that is big, and blue, and happy.) Items 14 to 28 relate to a colored plate of circles and crosses. Oral directions include linguistic clues that must be understood in order to carry out the action. For instance, "Point to a yellow circle, but first point to a blue one." The instructions include words in sequential order, words that override that order, negatives, locative words, and visual-spatial words. See Rapid Reference 2.22 for a summary.

Rules and Tips

Start Points: Ages 3 to 6, Item 1; Ages 7 to 12, Items: Prerequisite Items for Items 14 to 28.

Reversal Rule: If a child aged 7 to 12 fails either Prerequisite item, start with Item 1 and continue forward. If a child aged 7 to 12 fails Item 14 or 15, reverse until two consecutive items are passed, then continue forward.

Discontinue Rule: Four consecutive scores of 0.

- Do *not* repeat any items, but be sure to tally any requests for repetition.
- It may be easiest to sit beside the child to administer this test.
- Read directions at a normal rate of speech. Do not stress particular words.
- For items 22 and 27 the word *row* may be interpreted as either *row* or *column*. Young children often confuse the two terms, because in school, desks aligned front to back are often called rows.
- On the miniatures of the picture stimulus provided on the record form, you can number the shapes in the order the child executes the instructions for error analysis later. The sequence of the actions must be in the correct order.

Behaviors to Observe

- Asking for Repetition. This is a QO. Tally and record for both parts of CI.
- Impulsive responding, which may start before you have completed the instruction.
- Appearing confused by the language and becoming more confused as the quantity increases.

≡Rapid Reference 2.22

Comprehension of Instructions Summary

Start Rule	Reverse Rule	Discontinue Rule	Timing Rule
Ages 3–6, Item 1	If a child aged 7–12 fails either Prerequisite Item, start with Item 1 and continue foward.	Four consecutive scores of 0	No time limit
Ages 7–12, Prerequisite Items for Items 14–28	If a child aged 7–12 fails Item 14 or 15, reverse until two consecutive items are passed, then continue forward.		

- Appearing to have a working memory problem. He or she does well on the first items, but cannot remember the whole instruction on the longer items while carrying out the action.
- Having more problems on one type of instruction than another (e.g., negation, visual-spatial terms).

13. Imitating Hand Positions (Sensorimotor Domain; Core): Ages 3 to 12

This subtest assesses the ability to imitate static hand/finger positions by integrating visuospatial analysis, motor programming, and kinesthetic feedback from positions.

Rules and Tips

Start Points: Ages 3 to 4, Item 1 (Preferred Hand [PH]), Item 13 (Nonpreferred Hand [NPH]); Ages 5 to 12, Item 3 (Preferred Hand), Item 15 (Nonpreferred Hand).

Reversal Rule: for Ages 5 to 12 only: If Items 3 and 4 are failed, administer Items 1 and 2 before continuing with PH items; if Items 15 and 16 are failed, administer 15 and 16 before continuing with NPH items.

Discontinue Rule: three consecutive scores of 0 on Items 1 to 12 (PH); three consecutive scores of 0 on Items 13 to 24 (NPH).

Time Limit: 20 s for each position.

Supplemental Scores: Separate scores for PH and NPH.

- If the child is right-handed, administer Items 1 to 12 with your right hand, if left-handed use your left. For the NPH items (13 to 24), use the hand that corresponds to the child's NPH.
- The hand position is formed under the table and brought into view. Do not let the child see you forming the hand position as this changes the task.
- Hold the hand position in full view for the full 20 s, so the child can analyze it. If the child forms the hand position quickly, you can move on to the next item.
- The last two items are meant to be difficult. If the child is unable to perform them, reassure him or her.
- If you are dyspraxic or cannot perform the items for any other reason, you may want to train an assistant or ask a colleague to administer this test.
- There are diagrams and written instructions in the manual to help you practice the positions.

Behaviors to Observe
- Differences in the two hands.
- Using the Mirror Hand (echopraxia) and using the Other Hand to Help. Record these QOs in the box provided on the Record Form.
- Forming the hand position quickly and never check with the model. An impulsive or very young child may do this.
- Studying the model from every angle, but forming the position inaccurately, using the wrong fingers, or reversing the fingers used (index and middle instead of ring and little fingers). This suggests a visuospatial deficit.
- Getting visual cues that tells the child that the position is wrong when he or she forms an incorrect position. The child may or may not be able to fix it, but indicates that it is incorrect.
- Difficulties with motor coordination or programming. Can the child sequence the fingers into the position fluidly or is motor control poor? (See Rapid Reference 2.23.)

14. Visuomotor Precision (Sensorimotor Domain; Core): Ages 3 to 12

This subtest assesses graphomotor speed and accuracy. The preferred hand is used to draw a line inside a winding track. Two tracks of increasing complexity are executed.

Rapid Reference 2.23

Summary of Imitating Hand Positions

Start Rule	Reverse Rule	Discontinue Rule	Timing Rule
Ages 3–4, Item 1 (Preferred Hand [PH]), Item 13 (Nonpreferred Hand [NPH]) Ages 5–12, Item 3 (PH), Item 15 (NPH)	For Ages 5–12 only: If Items 3 and 4 are failed, administer Items 1 and 2 before continuing with PH items. If Items 15 and 16 are failed, administer 15 and 16 before continuing with NPH items.	Three consecutive scores of 0 on Items 1–12 (PH) Three consecutive scores of 0 on Items 13–24 (NPH)	20 s for each position

Rules and Tips

Start Points: Ages 3 to 4, Train task, then Car; Ages 5 to 12, Car task, then Motorcycle.

Time Limits: 180 s/item.

Supplemental Scores: Separate scores available for time and errors for each track.

- Do not allow the child to use a crayon. A primary, thick-barreled pencil is good for younger children. Use a pencil without an eraser.
- Time discreetly, so you do not convey the idea that time is more important than accuracy.
- Do not allow the child to turn the paper as he or she draws.

Behaviors to Observe

- Pencil Grip. This is a QO. The manual contains examples of different grips.
- Impulsively fast response without attention to accuracy, or fast and accurate. Supplemental Scores will reveal this.
- Slow performance, but good graphomotor control, or slow performance and numerous errors due to poor graphomotor control.
- Anxiety about being fast enough. (Often wants to know if his or her time was good.)
- Associated movements when drawing rapidly, especially around the mouth or of the tongue. (See Rapid Reference 2.24.)

≡ Rapid Reference 2.24

Visuomotor Precision Summary

Start Rule	Reverse Rule	Discontinue Rule	Timing Rule
Ages 3–4, Train task, then Car	No reverse rule	Administer both items for each child's age group.	180 s/item
Ages 5–12, Car task, then Motorcycle			

5. Narrative Memory (Language Domain; Core): Ages 3 to 12

This is a measure of story memory with Free Recall and Cued Recall (questioning for additional details after the story has been retold). Rapid Reference 2.25 summarizes the administration rules.

Rules and Tips

Start Point: Story for all ages.
Discontinue Rule: Administer every item.
Supplemental Scores: Separate scores for Free Recall and Cued Recall.

- If the child has difficulty getting started, provide help by saying, "How did the story start?" or for a young child, "Once upon a time . . ."
- If the child stops before the end of the story, prompt with, "Then what happened?" or, "Tell me more." Do *not* prompt more than three times.
- The child's response should have the essential information. It does not have to be verbatim.
- If a detail is provided in Free Recall (FR), do not ask the Cued Recall (CR) questions for those items.
- If the child has not yet been questioned on that detail and produces the detail spontaneously on Cued Recall (CR), give credit for it in Free Recall.

Behaviors to Observe

- Remembering only the beginning or the end of the story.
- Performing poorly on verbal memory tasks. This suggests a child with a language delay.
- Failing to recall many details in FR, but recalling well with cueing. This suggests an accessing or expressive problem. The information is there,

≡Rapid Reference 2.25

Narrative Memory Summary

Start Rule	Reverse Rule	Discontinue Rule	Timing Rule
Story for all ages	No reverse rule	Administer every item.	No time limit

but the child cannot access it or cannot organize the narration. This may occur developmentally in young children.

- Failing to recall efficiently on either the FR or the CR trials. This suggests that the child did not encode the information as it was being presented. Attention? Language delay?

16. Block Construction (Visuospatial Domain; Core): Ages 3 to 4; Expanded: Ages 5 to 12

This subtest, (see Rapid Reference 2.26), is a three-dimensional construction task requiring visuospatial analysis integrated with motoric output.

Rules and Tips
Start Points: Ages 3 to 4, Item 3; Ages 5 to 12, Item 6.
Reversal Rule: If the child aged 3 to 4 does not complete Items 3 and 4 correctly, administer Items 1 and 2 before continuing in sequence. If the child aged 5 to 12 does not complete Items 6 and 7 correctly, reverse until two consecutive items are passed, then continue in sequence.
Discontinue Rule: Five consecutive scores of 0. .
Time Limits: Items 1 to 7, 30 s/item; Items 8 to 13, 60 s/item.

- For Items 1 to 5, build a model and place it at the child's midline. Present the number of blocks required (in parentheses in the stimulus book) at the child's midline between the model and the child.
- Begin timing when you finish the instruction. Stop timing when the child indicates he or she is finished or the time limit is reached.
- Using notations to record imperfect performance permits error analysis later. Mark X on blocks incorrectly positioned, mark O on blocks omitted; and make a check mark on each block rotated 45 deg or more.

≡ *Rapid Reference 2.26*

Block Construction Summary

Start Rule	Reverse Rule	Discontinue Rule	Timing Rule
Ages 3–4, Item 3 Ages 5–12, Item 6	If the child aged 3–4 does not complete Items 3 and 4 correctly, administer Items 1 and 2 before continuing in sequence. If the child aged 5–12 does not complete Items 6 and 7 correctly, reverse until two consecutive items are passed, then continue in sequence.	Five consecutive scores of 0	Items 1–7, 30 s/item Items 8–13, 60 s/item

Behaviors to Observe

- A Rotation of the entire structure 45 deg or more relative to the edge of the table. This is a QO. Tally in the box on the record form. (For Items 8 to 13, it is also a failure.)
- Thinking there are not enough blocks because the child has broken the configuration of the construction or has not allowed for open spaces.
- Performing well from the three-dimensional model but failing to transition to the two-dimensional stimulus.
- Impulsively recreating the construction. Does the child reflect on the model or stimulus picture before beginning his or her construction?
- Overly precise and obsessive about perfectly lining up each block with the others and perhaps running out of time because he or she keeps adjusting blocks. Such children take longer to complete each item.

17. Sentence Repetition (Memory and Learning Domain; Core): Ages 3 to 4; Expanded: Ages 5 to 12

This subtest assesses auditory short-term memory for language with sentences of increasing length and complexity.

Rules and Tips

Start Points: Ages 3 to 6, Item 1; Ages 5 to 12, Item 5.

Reversal Rule: If the child aged 7 to 12 does not achieve 2 point responses on Items 5 and 6 (verbatim), administer Items 1 to 4 before continuing forward in sequence.

Discontinue Rule: Four consecutive scores of 0.

- Present the sentences in normal conversational tone, not too quickly and not too slowly.
- Do not repeat.
- Do not emphasize or stress any particular part of the sentence.
- Reassure the child that the sentences are getting hard when he or she begins to experience failure.
- Mark errors in the sentence for scoring later. For changes in word order, each word moved is an error.

Behaviors to Observe

- Asking for Repetition. This is a QO on this subtest, though *you may not repeat* the sentences. Tally any such requests, however, in the box on the Record Form.
- Closing his or her eyes or lowering the head in order to shut out distractions when the sentences are being repeated.
- Off-Task Behavior. Record this as a QO. Tally instances in the box on the Record Form. Does the child continue to look out the window, wiggle, squirm, and fiddle with materials when you are administering the sentences? Does this distractibility affect recall?
- Working memory deficits causing problems. The child's recall may be fine at first, but he or she may make more errors as the sentences become longer and more complex.
- Tilting his or her head toward you or turning an ear to you, as if he or she were not hearing well.
- Recalling just the first of the sentence (primacy) or just the last part (recency). (See Rapid Reference 2.27.)

18. Statue (Attention/Executive Functions Domain; Core): Ages 3 to 4; Expanded: Ages 5 to 12

This subtest measures motor persistence and the ability to inhibit motor response.

Rules and Tips

Start Point and Discontinue: All ages take the entire subtest.

≡ Rapid Reference 2.27

Sentence Repetition Summary

Start Rule	Reverse Rule	Discontinue Rule	Timing Rule
Ages 3–6, Item 1 Ages 5–12, Item 5	If the child aged 7–12 does not achieve 2 point responses on Items 5 and 6 (verbatim), administer Items 1–4 before continuing forward in sequence.	Four consecutive scores of 0	No time limit

- A child who is very anxious or is subject to Post-Traumatic Stress Disorder (PTSD) should not be given this subtest unless he or she knows the examiner very well, because the child must close his or her eyes in front of a stranger.
- Model the position (see *Manual,* p. 142) for the child, and assist the child into the position, if needed.
- Children 3 to 5 years of age may rest the free hand on a table to aid balance.
- Each time the child opens his or her eyes, moves, or vocalizes, remind, "Eyes closed," "Stay still," or "No noises," as appropriate.
- If the child stops trying to complete the task and is unwilling to re-engage, note the time and score the remaining 5 s intervals as zeroes.

Behaviors to Observe

- Becoming anxious with his or her eyes closed. This is rare, but it may happen. If so, discontinue the subtest.
- Distracted constantly and responding impulsively.
- More distracted by the sounds or by silence?
- Swaying noticeably when the eyes are closed and ceasing to get visual input to judge his or her position in space. (See Rapid Reference 2.28.)

≡ Rapid Reference 2.28

Statue Subtest Summary

Start Rule	Reverse Rule	Discontinue Rule	Timing Rule
All ages take the entire subtest.	No reverse rule	No discontinue rule	75 s for entire subtest.

19. List Learning (Memory and Learning Domain; Expanded): Ages 7 to 12

This is a subtest of verbal learning and supraspan memory. It includes assessment of immediate and delayed recall, rate of learning, and the role of interference in prior and new learning. Retention of words after interference is also assessed. Rapid Reference 2.29 summarizes the administration rules.

Rules and Tips

Start Point: Item 1.

Time: Read the lists at 1 word/min.

Discontinue Rule: Administer every trial. Discontinue a trial when the child cannot produce any more words.

Supplemental Scores: Learning Effect (Trial 1–Trial 5); Interference Effect (Trial 5–Trial 7); Delay Effect (Trial 5–Delay Trial); Learning Curve plotted on graph.

- Read the list over many times to yourself so you will recognize the words easily as you administer the test.
- Be sure the child does not see the list, even upside down. Do not emphasize any words or clusters as you read the words.
- Number the child's responses so you can analyze clustering (semantic: boat, water, fish; phonemic: water, window, winter), primacy (remembering the beginning of the list), recency (remembering only the end of the list), and so forth. Record any words not on the list.
- Check a word each time it is recalled more than once (perseveration).
- Be sure the delayed recall trial is administered as close to 30 min ± 5 min as is possible. If all of the expanded tests are not being given, you will need to plan this out ahead of time.
- Do not read the list on the recall trials.

Behavior to Observe

- Appearing to be focused on the list as it is being administered.
- Closing his or her eyes or putting his or her head down when listening to the words in order to shut out distractions.
- Any anxiety or frustration that appears to impede the child's performance.
- Appearing to use clustering techniques or trying to recall the words in order, though it is not necessary.
- Repetitions. These are tallied as QOs on this subtest. Repetitions are perseverations on words that the child has already said. Novel intrusions are also tallied. These are words that are not on either list but are recalled

≡ Rapid Reference 2.29

List Learning Summary

Start Rule	Reverse Rule	Discontinue Rule	Timing Rule
Item I	No reverse rule	Administer every trial. Discontinue a trial when the child cannot produce any more words.	Read the lists at I word/s.

as if they were. Finally, interference intrusions are recorded and tallied. These are words from one list that are recalled in the other.

- Recalling only the first of the sentence (primacy) or only the last part (recency).

20. Design Fluency (Attention/Executive Functions Domain; Expanded): Ages 5 to 12

This subtest is designed to assess nonverbal fluency and executive functions through the ability to generate as many unique designs as possible using two or more straight lines on a structured array and on a random array. (See Rapid Reference 2.30.)

Rules and Tips
Start Point: Structured Array.
Time Limit: 60 s/array.
Discontinue Rule: Administer both arrays.
Supplemental Scores: Structured Array and Random Array.

- Only unique designs count. All lines must be straight. Two or more dots must be connected.
- Erasures are not allowed. Use a pencil without an eraser. Be sure the pencil is sharp and that there is an extra.
- Be sure the arrows on the Random Array are pointing toward you and away from the child. This correctly orients the Random Array.

Behaviors to Observe
- Anxiety, especially in children who have done poorly on Visuomotor Precision or Design Copying. Graphomotor skills may affect performance.

≡Rapid Reference 2.30

Design Fluency Summary

Start Rule	Reverse Rule	Discontinue Rule	Timing Rule
Structured Array Teaching Presentation	No reverse rule	Administer both arrays.	60 s/array

- Appearing to forget the rules or needing to make unique designs.
- Creating a plan before starting. Is the child impulsive? Does he or she monitor his or her work to catch errors?
- Very conscious of time.
- Does the child use strategies (e.g., varying designs in a systematic fashion)? Is performance better on the structured or random array.

21. Repetition of Nonsense Words (Language Domain; Expanded): Ages 5 to 12

This subtest is an additional subtest of phonological awareness. It measures decoding of the word presented on the audio-tape and the ability to encode it and reproduce it orally. The child is credited for each correct syllable produced. Rapid Reference 2.31 describes this subtest's administration rules.

Rules and Tips
Start Point: Item 1.
Discontinue Rule: Four consecutive scores of 0.

- Be sure the levels are set on the tape recorder and that the test tone is passed. If not, it may startle the child. Be sure the child can hear clearly and comfortably.
- If you have administered the Auditory Attention and Response Set Test, the tape will already be cued.
- You need record only incorrect syllables; this will save time and still allow you to score the number of correct syllables.
- Do not talk over the tape or the child will not hear the next word.
- Self-corrections are allowed if they are made before the next word is presented.

≡ Rapid Reference 2.31

Summary of Repetition of Nonsense Words

Start Rule	Reverse Rule	Discontinue Rule	Timing Rule
Item I	No reverse rule	Four consecutive scores of 0	No time limit

Behaviors to Observe
- Stable Misarticulations. These are consistent mispronunciations and are QOs on this subtest (/*th*/ = /*f*/). Mark the presence of stable misarticulations on the Record Form.
- Tipping his or her head or ear toward the sound source.
- Frustration with trying to reproduce the words.
- Producing the correct syllables in the wrong order.
- Do results on this subtest compare in level of performance to those on Phonological Processing?

22. Route Finding (Visuospatial Processing Domain; Expanded): Ages 5 to 12

This subtest measures visual-spatial relations and directionality. It also assesses the ability to transfer a route from a simple schematic map to a more complex one. The child traces the direct route to a house on a simple schematic diagram and then, without tracing the route, must locate that same house on a more complex schematic map of other streets and houses. Rapid Reference 2.32 summarizes the administration rules.

Rules and Tips
Start Point: Teaching Example.
Discontinue Rule: Five consecutive Scores of 0.

- This is the only test that is presented vertically in the stimulus book, which is flat on the table.
- It is wise to affix clear, acrylic sheets over the pages, because the child will be using his or her finger to trace the simple path. Eventually an uncovered page will become soiled. Also, the spot where the finger has touched the larger map will become marked.
- Repeat the teaching as necessary so the child understands the task before you begin.

≡*Rapid Reference 2.32*

Summary of Route Finding

Start Rule	Reverse Rule	Discontinue Rule	Timing Rule
Teaching Example	No reverse rule	Five consecutive scores of 0	No time limit

- If you have trouble with directionality, you may wish to turn the Record Form upside down so it is in the same orientation with the stimulus book.

Behaviors to Observe
- Attempting to turn his or her head to see the stimulus from another angle or tries to turn the stimulus book. (This is not allowed.)
- Reflecting on the task before tracing and making his or her choice.
- Some children with good visual-spatial abilities will not trace the simple route first, but will point directly at the correct target house. This is permissible. But for the very impulsive child who is incorrect, you should remind the child to trace the simple route before making his or her choice.

23. Verbal Fluency (Language Domain; Expanded): All Ages

This subtest, summarized in Rapid Reference 2.33, assesses the ability to generate words within specific semantic and phonemic categories.

Rules and Tips
Start Point: Ages 3 to 6, Items 1 and 2 (Semantic only); Ages 7 to 12, Items 1 to 4 (Semantic and Phonemic).
Discontinue Rule: Administer all items for age.
Time Limit: 60 s/item.
Supplemental Scores: Separate scores for Animals, Food/Drink, Semantic and Phonemic categories.

- Remember that children under 7 do *not* take the Phonemic Fluency section.
- Record responses in the correct 15 s division on the Record Form. Do not try to judge correctness as the child is producing words. Record everything. It will be useful for error analysis.
- Begin timing immediately after saying, "Go." Keep timing for the full 60 s period.

≡ Rapid Reference 2.33

Verbal Fluency Summary

Start Rule	Reverse Rule	Discontinue Rule	Timing Rule
Ages 3–6, Items 1 and 2 (Semantic only)	No reverse rule	Administer all items for age.	60 s/item
Ages 7–12, Items 1–4 (Semantic and Phonemic)			

- If the child stops, prompt with, "Tell me some more," or "What other _____ can you think of?" or, on Phonemic Fluency, "Tell me some more words which begin with _____."

Behaviors to Observe
- Body movement or Increasing Voice Volume in conjunction with the production of words (recruiting other systems into the task). This is a Qualitative Observation and should be checked for presence on the Record Form.
- Producing everything within the first 30 s and very little afterwards. Is there is a long period of silence and then the child begins producing words in the last 30 s, or is there a steady production of the words throughout the one minute period?
- Looking at objects around the room to cue her- or himself for words. Does this occur more on the Semantic than the Phonemic categories, vice versa, or on both?
- Does the child's performance on the Phonemic section compare to the level of performance on Phonological Processing or with Repetition of Nonsense Words?

24. Manual Motor Sequences (Sensorimotor Domain; Expanded): All Ages

This subtest assesses the ability to imitate a series of rhythmic hand movement sequences (motor programming) using one or both hands.

Rules and Tips

Start Points: Ages 3 to 7, Item 1; Ages 8 to 12, Item 3.

Reversal Rule: For the child 8 to 12, if all five sequences on Item 3 are incorrect, administer Items 1 and 2.

Time Guideline: Maintain a presentation rhythm slightly faster than 1 movement/s. For items 9, 11, and 12, demonstrate at 1/s then 2 movements/s.

Discontinue Rule: Four consecutive scores of 0 (the child does not produce at least one correct sequence on four consecutive items).

- If you are dyspraxic or for any other reason cannot perform the items, you may want to train an assistant or to ask a colleague to administer this test.
- You need to practice this test sufficiently before you administer it. There are diagrams and written instructions in the *Manual* (pp. 189–164) to help you, but on some diagrams both hands are depicted when only one changes position. Circle that hand in red.
- Train the movements before each NEPSY evaluation. When you administer the test, perform the sequence two to three times on your lap and then bring it up onto the table in the child's view.
- Use the hand directly across the table from the child's preferred hand for Preferred Items and vice versa for Nonpreferred Items. (If the child is right-handed you use your left hand.) If necessary, point to the hand the child should use.
- Tap gently, because the child will probably be more forceful than you are. You do not want the child to have red knuckles at the end of the test.
- Encourage the child to keep the movements going by gesturing in rhythm with each movement.
- Count sequences silently. Stop the child after five sequences.
- If the child makes an error in the first or second sequence, demonstrate again and restart the test.
- Mark an *X* on an incorrect or missed sequence (hesitation as long as it would take to produce a sequence).

Behaviors to Observe

- Lack of fluid movement in the hands, jerky movements with hesitations.
- Inattentiveness when the movements are being demonstrated, causing poor performance later.
- There are a number of QOs for this test. Tally Changes in Rate (variable speed or starting quickly and slowing down) on the Record Form. Also

≡ Rapid Reference 2.34

Manual Motor Series Summary

Start Rule	Reverse Rule	Discontinue Rule	Timing Rule
Ages 3–7, Item 1 Ages 8–12, Item 3	For the child aged 8–12, if all five sequences on Item 3 are not correct, Administer Items 1 and 2.	Four consecutive scores of 0. (The child does not produce at least one correct sequence on four consecutive items.)	Maintain a presentation rhythm slightly faster than 1 movement/s. For items 9, 11, and 12, demonstrate at 1/s then 2 movements/s.

check the presence of: Overflow (associated movements in another part of the body, in this case the mouth), Perseveration (movements continue for three or more sequences after the child is told to stop), Loss of Asymmetrical Movement (when the sequence involves different movements for the each hand, the child begins doing the same movement with each hand), Body Movement (recruiting the whole body into the production of the hand movements), Forceful Tapping on the Table (also recruitment—the tapping becomes louder and louder with the effort of producing the rhythmic movement sequence). (See Rapid Reference 2.34.)

25. Oromotor Sequences (Language Domain; Expanded): All Ages

This is an assessment of oromotor programming, the ability to repeat articulatory sequences. Rapid Reference 2.35 provides a summary of administration rules.

Rules and Tips
Start Points: Ages 3 to 7, Teaching Example, then Item 1.
Reversal Rule: If a child 8 to 12 does not repeat Item 4 correctly five times, administer Items 1 to 3 before continuing on in sequence.
Time Guideline: Present Items 1 to 8 at a rate of 1 sequence/s. Items 9 to 14 should be presented at 1 sequence/2 s.
Discontinue Rule: Four consecutive scores of 0 (does not produce at least one sequence on four consecutive items).

≡ Rapid Reference 2.35

Oromotor Sequences Summary

Start Rule	Reverse Rule	Discontinue Rule	Timing Rule
Ages 3–7, Teaching Example, then Item 1 Ages 8–12, Teaching Example, then Item 4	If a child aged 8–12 does not repeat Item 4 correctly five times, administer Items 1–3 before continuing on in sequence.	Four consecutive scores of 0. (The child does not produce at least one sequence on four consecutive items.)	Present Items 1–8 at a rate of 1 sequence/s. Items 9–14 should be presented at 1 sequence/2s.

- Motioning with your hand will help the child continue the sequences until all five are completed.
- Count silently as the child completes the sequences.
- If a child has very poor oromotor control, you need to administer the subtest to document the disability, but reassure the child about how difficult it is and do not rush him or her.

Behaviors to Observe

- Oromotor Hypotonia (poor tone in oromotor musculature—the mouth may appear lax) and Stable Misarticulations. Record these QOs by checking the box on the Record Form. Change in Rate is also a QO. Tally the occurrences.
- Difficulty in coordinating the musculature of the mouth due to oromotor hypotonia or oromotor dyspraxia.
- Intelligibility of speech.
- Difficulty controlling saliva at the edges of the mouth.
- No speech impairment, but poor performance on this subtest.
- Frustration or anxiety.

26. Finger Discrimination (Sensorimotor Domain; Expanded): Ages 5 to 12

This subtest, summarized in Rapid Reference 2.36, assesses tactile perception of light touch on the fingers and the ability to identify the fingers touched.

≡Rapid Reference 2.36

Finger Discrimination Summary

Start Rule	Reverse Rule	Discontinue Rule	Timing Rule
Teaching Examples	No reverse rule	Administer every item	No time limit

Rules and Tips
Start Point: Teaching Examples.
Discontinue Rule: Administer every item.

- There is a shield available in the kit, so the child cannot see the fingers being touched. Raise the shield and have the child point to the fingers touched. Do not have the child raise the fingers (young children cannot and others are not able to) or name them. This is a different task.
- Use your index finger to touch the child's finger once between the first and second joints. Do *not* brush down the finger or press hard. Practice this on an adult or older child who can give you feedback about the lightness of the touch—not too light, but not too hard. It should be easily perceived by the average person with the eyes closed.
- Also practice double simultaneous touch. Be sure both touches are equal, if using one hand. *Do not indicate in advance which two fingers will be touched.*
- Do all Preferred Hand items before doing Nonpreferred.
- Record these types of errors.

Behaviors to Observe
- Not perceiving single touch or perceiving it on a different finger.
- Perceiving only one of the double simultaneous touches with the other being suppressed.
- Trying to see over the shield. Ask the child to sit back and relax. Be sure you have spent enough time on the teaching example so the child understands what is happening.

27. Knock and Tap (Attention/Executive Function Domain; Expanded): Ages 5 to 12

This is an assessment of self-regulation and motor inhibition. It requires the child to maintain a cognitive set involving suppressing motor actions while producing conflicting motor responses. Rapid Reference 2.37 summarizes the administration rules.

≋Rapid Reference 2.37

Knock and Tap Summary

Start Rule	Reverse Rule	Discontinue Rule	Timing Rule
Teaching example	No reverse rule	Four consecutive scores of 0	Present each item at a rate of 1 motor cue/2s.

Rules and Tips
Start Point: Teaching example.
Time Guideline: Present each item at a rate of 1 motor cue/2 s.
Discontinue Rule: Four consecutive scores of 0.

- This is not a speed test. Respond as soon as the child responds, keeping a continuous flow, but do not make the child feel that he or she must do the test as quickly as possible. However, *do not wait more than 5 s.*
- Instruct the child to use his or her preferred hand.
- Administer with your nonpreferred hand so you can track responses. Recording only the incorrect ones is easier.
- Do not hit the table too forcefully, as the child will probably knock harder than you. You do not want the child to end up with red knuckles.
- For each set of items (Items 1 to 15; Items 16 to 30), present the teaching three times if necessary.

Behaviors to Observe
- Imitating the examiner's movement, because he or she cannot seem to inhibit the response (echopraxia).
- Pausing to make a conscious decision about his or her response (hesitations).
- Frequent self-corrections.
- Good performance on the first section but weak on the second. The child cannot seem to shift to the new set and inhibit the well-routinized routine of tapping to your knock.

CONCLUSION

It is very important to practice administering the NEPSY. No one, no matter how experienced, is ready to administer a test without practicing it. If possible, the clinician should locate an experienced NEPSY examiner who can observe and give feedback. The more background knowledge the clinician acquires in neuropsychology, the richer his or her observations will be, the more connections will be made in interpreting results, and the more accurately will he or she delineate strengths and weaknesses in children's neuropsychological functioning.

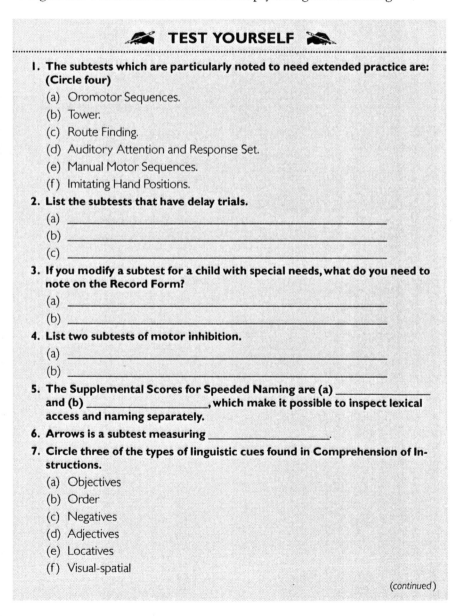

🐟 TEST YOURSELF 🐟

1. **The subtests which are particularly noted to need extended practice are: (Circle four)**
   (a) Oromotor Sequences.
   (b) Tower.
   (c) Route Finding.
   (d) Auditory Attention and Response Set.
   (e) Manual Motor Sequences.
   (f) Imitating Hand Positions.

2. **List the subtests that have delay trials.**
   (a) _____
   (b) _____
   (c) _____

3. **If you modify a subtest for a child with special needs, what do you need to note on the Record Form?**
   (a) _____
   (b) _____

4. **List two subtests of motor inhibition.**
   (a) _____
   (b) _____

5. **The Supplemental Scores for Speeded Naming are (a) _____ and (b) _____, which make it possible to inspect lexical access and naming separately.**

6. **Arrows is a subtest measuring _____.**

7. **Circle three of the types of linguistic cues found in Comprehension of Instructions.**
   (a) Objectives
   (b) Order
   (c) Negatives
   (d) Adjectives
   (e) Locatives
   (f) Visual-spatial

(continued)

8. The Supplemental Scores on Narrative Memory are (a) _____ and (b) _____.

9. The two subtests that measure two-dimensional and three-dimensional constructions are (a) _____ and (b) _____.

10. A subtest that should not be administered to young children who are very cautious or have PTSD is _____.

11. Two subtests which assess phonological processing are (a) _____ and (b) _____.

12. Qualitative Observations that can be compared to base rates are recorded with checkmarks or tally marks to indicate (a) _____ of the occurence or (b) _____ of the occurrences.

13. Extra diagnostic information without additional testing is provided by (a) _____ and (b) _____.

14. Name two precautions that should be taken when you are going to assess a child with autism.

    (a) _____.

    (b) _____.

15. When evaluating a child with hemiparesis, do you assess both hands?

    (a) Yes

    (b) No

Answers: 1. b, d, e, f; 2. a. Memory for Faces, b. Memory for Names, c. List learning; 3. Modified Administration; 4. Statue, Knock & Tap; 5. Time, Accuracy; 6. Judgement of line and angle orientation; 7. c, e, f; 8. Free recall, Cued recall; 9. Design Copying, Block Construction; 10. Statue; 11. Phonological Processing, Repetition of Nonsense Words; 12. Presence; number; 13. Supplemental Scores, Qualitative Observations; 14. Any two of the following: Find out about stereotypical interests, Find out about sensory issues, Allow time for child to become accustomed, to you and the surroundings, Have caregiver available if needed during testing; 15. a

Three

HOW TO SCORE THE NEPSY

coring an assessment with care is essential. Important decisions about a child's life may be made at least partially on the strength of your scoring. It is essential, therefore, that you are precise about each number recorded. A computer scoring program for NEPSY is available through The Psychological Corporation, which provides graphed scores and a print-out that can be imported into the Test Results section of your report. Nonetheless, even if a scoring program is available, it is wise to score NEPSY by hand initially, so you are aware how the scores are derived. Always check your scoring carefully because there are many scores on NEPSY a fact that may increase the possibility of error. This chapter will introduce the clinician, step by step, to the process of scoring. You will learn how to compute raw scores, record them, and how to locate the appropriate tables for converting. Conversion into scaled scores, cumulative percentiles, cumulative percentages, and domain scores will be discussed. Finally, you will be shown how to record and graph all scores: Core and Expanded Subtest Scores, Core Domain Scores, Supplemental Scores, and Qualitative Observations.

Immediately following the administration of NEPSY and before the child leaves, be sure to take time to look over the Record Form to check that all desired subtests have been administered and all demographic information has been recorded. Give the child a break while you perform this check. In this way, if anything is missing, there may still be time to administer a subtest you meant to give or to obtain missing information before the parent or caregiver and the child depart.

Prior to looking up a score, it is essential that you compute the correct age for the child. Always double-check the birth date with the parent or caregiver before testing and check your computation twice. If you have made an error on the age, all scores, not to mention interpretations, will be incorrect. Before you begin to score, check that all items below the start point or basal have been credited and that all parts of a Total Score (i.e., immediate and delayed) have been entered.

CAUTION

Double-Check Birth Date and Age Computation

Example:	Yr.	Mo.	Day
		19	
	98	2̶0̶	43
Date of Testing:	9̶9̶	8̶	1̶3̶
Date of Birth:	93	10	20
	5	9	23

CAUTION

Before You Begin to Score

Credit points below the Start Point on the following subtests:

- Design Copying
- Phonological Processing
- Comprehension of Instructions
- Imitating Hand Position
- Block Construction
- Sentence Repetition
- Verbal Fluency
- Manual Motor Sequences
- Oromotor Sequences

Total the immediate and delayed parts of the memory subtests:

- Memory for Faces
- Memory for Names
- List Learning

STEP-BY-STEP SCORING

STEP 1: Compute Raw Test Scores, Raw Supplemental Scores, and Raw Qualitative Observations

The clinician should obtain these scores for all Core and Expanded Subtests except Visual Attention, Auditory Attention and Response Set, Speeded Naming, Design Copying, and Visuomotor Precision. (The latter subtests have more complex scoring rules, so the clinician should delay scoring them until he or she has scored the subtests with more straightforward scoring.) Rapid Reference 3.1 lists subtests with complex scoring rules.

When only the Core Subtests are administered, subtest raw and scaled scores are entered under Core Analyses on the front of the Record Form. Core Domain Scores are also computed and graphed there. In addition, Core Subtest Scores (both raw and scaled) in each domain are entered on the second page of the Record Form, the Domain Analyses page. The scaled scores are graphed there as well.

When Expanded Subtests are administered in an Expanded or Selective Assessment, raw and scaled scores are entered, and scaled scores are also graphed on the Domain Analyses page. The raw scores for some Expanded Subtests are converted to Smoothed Percentiles or Cumulative Percentile Ranges rather than to scaled scores. These scores are entered under the appropriate domain, and the performance level (i.e., *Above Expected Level*) is checked on the bar to the right of the scaled score. In this way, all subtest scores are aligned so that a visual comparison can be made. (See Rapid Reference 3.2.)

While working with the raw scores, the clinician should enter on the Supplemental Score page of the Record Form (facing the Domain Analyses page) those raw scores for which he or she wants a Supplemental Score (SS). For example, while recording the Fingertip Tapping total raw score, the clinician also records the raw scores for Preferred and Nonpreferred Hand and for Repetitions (repetitive finger tapping) and Sequences. In this way, the clinician does not have to go back to those subtest pages again, thus saving time. Rapid Reference 3.3 lists those subtests with SS.

Qualitative Observations (QOs) should now be entered for each subtest scored. During the testing, the clinician checked the presence of these behaviors or tallied them, depending on the observation. These values or checks should now be entered on the back page of the Record Form.

≡ *Rapid Reference 3.1*

Subtests with Complex Scoring Rules

- Visuomotor Precision
- Visual Attention
- Speeded Naming
- Design Copying
- Auditory Attention and Response Set

≡ *Rapid Reference 3.2*

Recording Subtest Scores for Core and Expanded Subtests

- Record Total Scores for Core Subtests (a) on the *front* of the Record Form, and (b) on p. 2, Domain Analysis.
- Record Total Scores for Expanded Subtests on Domain Analysis page.

STEP 2: Score Subtests with Complex Scoring

As mentioned before, the tests are Visuomotor Precision (VP), Visual Attention (VA), Speeded Naming (SN), Design Copying (DC), and Auditory Attention and Response Set (AARS). Rapid Reference 3.4 tells how to convert to Total Raw Scores.

The *Visuomotor Precision (VP)* subtest is scored for both speed and precision.

- *Time* was recorded for each track when the child completed the task. The Time raw scores for each track are added to obtain the Total Time Raw Score.

≡Rapid Reference 3.3

Subtests with Supplemental Scores

- Memory for Faces
- Auditory Attention and Response Set
- Speeded Naming
- Memory for Names
- Fingertip Tapping
- Visual Attention
- Imitating Hand Positions
- Visuomotor Precision
- Narrative Memory
- List Learning
- Design Fluency
- Verbal Fluency

≡Rapid Reference 3.4

Converting to Total Raw Score

To convert the Time Score and the Accuracy or Error Score into the Total Raw Score:

- Use Appendix A. (NEPSY *Manual*, pp. 269–271)
- This total raw score is used to find the scaled score.

- *Errors* for each track are scored next. For each instance in which the pencil line strays across an outside edge of the track, an error is counted. There must be white space between the child's line and the outside edge of the track. A good rule of thumb is that if you can place a pencil point between the two lines, the mark is an error. If the child's mark remains outside the outer edge of the track for more than one segment, each segment counts as an error. Number consecutively each segment in which an error occurs. In this way the last number recorded in a segment will be the total number of errors for that track. Do this for both tracks. Figure 3.1 tracks errors in visuomotor precision.
- The *VP Total Time Raw Score* and *Total Error Raw Score* are entered on the subtest page for later conversion.
- For *Supplemental Scores (SSs)*. Errors and Time for each track are recorded.
- *Pencil Grip* is entered on the Qualitative Observations (QO) page.

The *Visual Attention (VA)* subtest is scored for

- *Time* (which you recorded when the child completed the test).
- *Commission Errors (CEs)*—pictures outside the designated boxes that were marked incorrectly—are totaled for each array. Enter that figure in the box for each array on the subtest page.
- *Omission Errors (OEs)*—target pictures that were not marked and

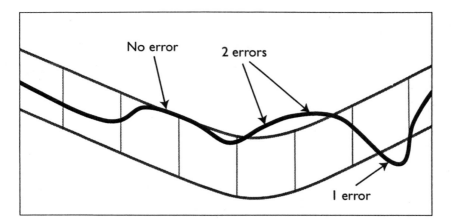

Figure 3.1 Errors on Visuomotor Precision

should have been—are determined for each array by subtracting the Total Number Correct under *Targets* from 20 (the total number of targets). Write this figure for each array at the bottom of the subtest page. (The VA Scoring Template is oriented at the designated point on the VA picture stimuli in the Response Booklet as instructed on the template, depending on whether you are scoring the Bunnies, Cat, or Face stimuli.)

- *Total Correct* for each array is computed (targets that were marked and appeared in the boxes on the template). Enter under *Targets* on the subtest page.
- On the *SS* page enter the Time, CE, and OE Raw Scores for each array under VA (e.g., Cats—Time).
- The *Accuracy Score* for each array equals *Targets minus CEs*. Enter this score on the Record Form for each of the two parts of the Visual Attention Test (Bunnies and Cats, or Cats and Faces), depending on age.
- *Sum the two VA Accuracy Scores and sum the two Time Scores,* and enter in the appropriate boxes on the subtest page. Hold for conversion.
- *QOs for Off-Task Behavior* are tallied and entered on the QO page.

The *Speeded Naming (SN)* subtest is scored for time and accuracy.

- *Time* was recorded when the child took the test.
- *Accuracy* (total correct) is recorded on the subtest page and held for conversion.
- *Supplemental Scores* are recorded on the SS page for Time and Accuracy separately.

- *Qualitative Observations* are recorded on the QO page for
  —Reversed Sequences: presence of more than two.
  —Recruitment: presence of behavior with effort of rapid naming.
  Oral/Verbal Recruitment notes increases in Voice Volume. *Motor Recruitment* notes Body movement.
- *Time and Accuracy/Error Totals* for speeded subtests should now be computed.
- *Total Raw Scores Conversions* for these subtests will be obtained in the appropriate raw score conversion table and are summarized in Rapid Reference 3.5. For instance, for SN, locate the child's time in the left-hand column and locate the Number Correct across the top. These two values intersect at the child's subtest raw score. Enter the raw score from the conversion table in the subtest raw score box on the Core Analyses page (front page) and on the Domain Analyses page (second page). The subtests that use a score conversion table are:
  —SN: Time; Total Correct (Table A.1, p. 269 in the *Manual*)

—VA: Time; Total Correct minus CEs (Table A.2, p. 270 in the *Manual*)

—VP: Time; Total Errors (Table A.3 in the *Manual*). There are separate tables on this page for ages 3 to 4 and 5 to 12. Be certain that you are in the right age section of the table.

For *Design Copying (DC)*, use the DC scoring template to score each design in the Response Booklet. Refer to Appendix F (pp. 367–407) in the *Manual* for examples and scoring criteria. (See Rapid Reference 3.6.)

- *Total the points* for each design and enter on the subtest page.
- *Total the item scores* for the DC Total Score. Enter this raw score on the subtest page and on the Core Analyses and Domain Analyses pages of the Record Form.

≡*Rapid Reference 3.5*

Subtests Using a Score Conversion Table

- Speeded Naming
- Visual Attention
- Visuomotor Precision

CAUTION

Table A.3 of the NEPSY *Manual*

Make certain that when you do the raw score conversion for Visuomotor Precision, you are using the correct part of the table.
- Upper Section is for ages 3.0–4.11.
- Lower Section is for ages 5.0–12.11.

- *QOs* for Hand Tremor and Pencil Grip should be entered on the back page of the Record Form. (Consult pp. 87–88 in the *Manual* for examples of pencil grips.)

The *Auditory Attention and Response Set (AARS)* subtest is made up of two sections. In the Auditory Attention (AA) section, look for all of the *R*s that occurred within the three shaded spaces (3 s) for each target word "*RED.*" Circle *2* if you have written *R* next to the target word. Score *1* if *R* is written in either of the next two shaded spaces. Rapid Reference 3.7 describes recording and scoring the AARS.

- *CEs:* If *R* is written outside the shaded spaces or if any other color is designated, circle "e" for a CE.
- *OEs:* If there is a "RED" to which there is no response, circle the word "RED" as an OE.
- *Evaluating Overlapping Sets:* If two targets have overlapping shaded areas, evaluate from the top of that sequence to score the first response. In other words, if the response to the first "RED" falls in the third shaded space (3 s) after the target word "RED" and a second "RED" occurs there, assume that the *R* response you have recorded is the child's response to the first "RED" and not the second. Therefore, it receives 1 point (see Fig. 3.2). If you have recorded a second *R* in the next space, it would be scored as the child's response to the second "RED" and would, therefore, receive 1 point.
- *CEs in Overlapping Sets:* If the *R* response is outside the shaded area for the second RED, or if it is another color within or without the shaded area, it is scored "e."
- *OEs in Overlapping Sets:* If there is no response to the second "RED," circle that target word to designate an OE. Total all.
- *The Points Earned Box:* Enter the total of the 1's and 2's here.
- *The CE Box:* Put the total number of "e"s here.
- *The Part A Total Raw Score (AA):* Compute by subtracting CEs from Points Earned. Enter on the subtest page.
- *SSs:* Enter the following on the SS page:
  —AA Total Score (raw)
  —OE Score (raw)
  —The CE Score (raw)

Recording and Scoring Auditory Attention and Response Set

During each section of the test, record every response and score later.

I. *Auditory Attention*
  A. Scoring
    1. Any *R* in a shaded area receives either 1 or 2 points depending on *when* the child responded.
      a. If *R* is noted beside the target word "RED," then score 2 points.
      b. If *R* is noted beside either of the next two words, then score 1 point.
    2. Commission Errors:
      a. Any *R* outside shaded areas is scored an "e" (for Commission Error).
      b. Any other response at any point during the subtest is an "e"
      c. Omission error: circle any target word for which no response is made.
  B. Sum all points earned. Sum all "e" responses and subtract this from the points to obtain Part A Total Score.
  C. Sum all omissions (circled words) for the supplemental score.

II. *Auditory Response Set*
  A. Scoring
    1. Any *R,Y,* or *B* in a shaded area receives either 1 or 2 points depending on *when* the child responded.
      a. Score 2 points if:
        i. *R* is beside the target word *yellow.*
        ii. *Y* is beside the target word *red.*
        iii. *B* is beside the target word *blue.*
      b. Score 1 point if the correct response (*R* for *yellow,Y* for *red,* or *B* for *blue*) is noted beside either of the following two words (in the shaded area).
      c. Score Commission Errors "e" if:
        i. Any *R* or *Y* is noted next to the matching color word.
        ii. Any *R,Y,* or *B* is noted outside of shaded areas.
        iii. Any other response at any point during the subtest is an "e."
      d. Omission errors: circle any target word for which no response is made.
  B. Sum all points earned. Sum all "e" responses and subtract this from the points to obtain Part B Total Score.
  C. Sum all omissions (circled words) for the supplemental score.
  D. Sum Parts A and B for the subtest Total Score.

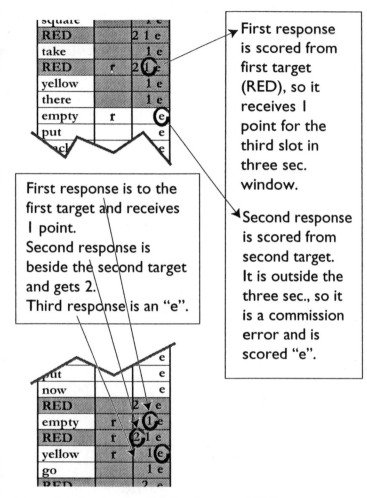

First response is scored from first target (RED), so it receives 1 point for the third slot in three sec. window.

Second response is scored from second target. It is outside the three sec., so it is a commission error and is scored "e".

First response is to the first target and receives 1 point.
Second response is beside the second target and gets 2.
Third response is an "e".

Figure 3.2 Scoring Overlapping Sets on AARS

The *Response Set (RS)* is scored in the same way but there should be an *R (red)* in response to the target word "YELLOW," a *Y (yellow)* in response to the target word "RED," and a *B (blue)* in response to the word "BLUE." These correct responses are scored 2 or 1 just as they are on the AA.

- *CEs:* Correct responses that occur outside the shaded 3 s area or any other colors in any location are scored as CEs.
- *OEs:* If no response occurs, the target word (i.e., "RED," "YELLOW,"

or "BLUE") is circled to indicate an OE. Tally the scores and enter them on the Record Form in the same way you did for AA.

- *SSs:* Also fill in the raw scores for the SS in the same way as on AA.

To obtain the Total Score for the AARS, add the Part A Total Score for the AA section to the Part B Total Score for the AR section. Enter this raw score on the front page of the Record Form next to *Auditory Attention and Response Set.* For the AARS Supplementary Scores, enter the raw scores for Time and Accuracy on the SS page. Enter QOs for AARS on the QO page.

- Recruitment:
  - —Body Movement
  - —Increasing Voice Volume
  - —Reversed Sequences (more than two)
- *Off-Task Behavior for both sections* is entered on the QO page under the Off-Task heading next to *Auditory Attention and Response Set.*

STEP 3: Compute Core and Expanded Total Scores

Appendix A (pp. 269–302) of the NEPSY *Manual* contains all of the subtest-level scaled score tables arranged by age for both Core and Expanded Scaled Subtests, as well as the standard Core Domain Scores. It also contains Test Ages (pp. 303–304). For each year of age, the tables are divided into 6-month intervals on facing pages (e.g., 11.0–11.5; 11.6–11.11). Be sure you are in the correct section for the 6-month interval.

To determine *Core and Expanded Subtest Scaled Scores,* the clinician should locate the appropriate age band in Table A.4 (pp. 272–302 in the *Manual*). He or she should locate each subtest within a domain going down the columns in the white (Core Subtests) or blue (Expanded Subtest) sections, then locate the child's raw score in the subtest column. The scaled score for that subtest will be located in both the first white column on the left and the last on the right, under the heading *Scaled Scores.* The clinician enters the Core Subtest Scaled Scores in the appropriate box on the front of the Record Form and on the Domain Analyses page, and the Expanded Subtest Scaled Scores on the Domain Analyses page.

Expanded Subtest Cumulative Percentage Scores are entered on the appropriate domain graph on the Domain Analyses page. The scaled scores and percentages are aligned, so that a visual comparison can be made whether the score is scaled or a cumulative percentage. These subtest level graphs can be a very helpful visual aid in reporting results to a child's parent. As a precaution, when administering any Expanded Subtests after the Core, the clinician may want to jot down on the front page of the Record Form the names of the Expanded Subtests used with the child. In this way, if NEPSY is not scored right away, and the clinician has administered only a few Expanded Subtests toward the back of the Record Form, he or she will not forget to score them when scoring the Core Subtests.

The *Expanded Subtests with Smoothed Percentile Rank Scores* are found in the *Manual*'s Table A.5, page 292. These subtests are arranged by domain going down the page.

> ## CAUTION
>
> ### Note Expanded Subtests on Front Page of Record Form
>
> When you administer only a few of the Expanded Subtests for an Expanded or Selective Assessment, write the names of the subtests in the margin on the front page of the Record Form. They are not computed in the Core Domain Scores, so you might forget to score them otherwise.

The clinician should perform the following steps: (a) Locate the subtest being scored and then find the child's age in years across the top of the page. (b) Go down the age column to the appropriate test and find the raw score ranges. (c) Locate the raw score range within which the child's performance falls, and move to the far left-hand column along that horizontal plane to find the percentile ranges. (d) To record the score, turn to the Domain Analyses page and locate the columns on the right-hand side of the domain graph where the percentile ranks for the subtest you are scoring appear. Darken or make an X on the square in the appropriate percentile-rank band for the child's performance. (e) Graph the Core and Expanded Subtest Scaled Scores and the Expanded Subtest Smoothed Percentile Ranks on the Domain Analyses page.

The *Domain Analyses* page on the inside front cover of the Record Form is where the clinician enters the subtest raw scores, scaled scores, and cumulative percentages for Core and Expanded Subtests in each domain.

STEP 4: Compute Core Domain Scores

Core Domain Scores are located on pages 293 to 302 of Appendix A in the *Manual*. The clinician should be cautious in looking up Core Domain Scores because there are only a few pages for these scores. They are divided into age groups of 3.0 to 4.11 years and 5.0 to 12.11 years, with one page for each Core Domain for that age group. It is easy to mistakenly locate scores on the 3.0 to 4.11 Language Domain page instead of on the 5.0 to 12.11 Language Domain page. Therefore, if the Core Domain Score appears inflated, the clinician should check carefully that he or she is working in the correct section for age.

The *Sums of Scaled Scores* are obtained by adding the subtest Scaled Scores in each do-

C A U T I O N

Double-Check Core Domain Scores

The Core Domain Scores are found in Appendix A of the Manual (pp. 293–302).

• Two sections by age: 3.0–4.11 and 5.0–12.11.

• One page for each of the five Core Domain Scores in each section.

• It is easy to get into the wrong section.

If a child's Core Domain Scores seem inflated, check the age scores carefully.

≡Rapid Reference 3.8

What Is a Confidence Interval?

A confidence interval accounts for error inherent in any standard or scaled score, such as a Core Domain Score. The level of confidence (usually 95%) represents the probability ($p < .05$) that a child's true score lies within the range created by the standard error of measurement. It reminds us that a score is not infallible; there is error inherent in any score. For example:

• There is a 95% likelihood that Johnny's true Language Core Domain Score falls in the range of 88–107.

• His confidence interval would cover the percentile range from 20 (percentile for 88) to 68 (percentile for 107).

main. Entering the sum in the appropriate box at the bottom of the column gives the raw score for each domain.

Core Domain Scores are found in Manual Table A.6 with their associated Percentile Ranks and Confidence Intervals. (See Rapid Reference 3.8 for an explanation of Confidence Intervals.) There is a separate page for each Domain within the age bands 3.0 to 4.11 and 5.0 to 12.11. The clinician should locate the obtained Sums of Scaled Scores for the appropriate domain in the left-hand column. The Core Domain Score, Percentile and Confidence Intervals appear in the adjacent columns to the right. The clinician should enter these scores on the front of the Record Form in the appropriate boxes underneath the previously recorded Sums of Scaled Scores. To the left of the Confidence Interval boxes, the clinician should enter the chosen level of confidence, 90% or 95%, in the blank space (____%) shaded in blue. Core Domain Scores for Ages 3.0 to 4.11 are located on pages 293 to 297; Core Domain Scores for ages 5.0 to 12.11 appear on pages 298 to 302.

A Scoring Example is found in Manual Table A.6. In the Language Domain at ages 3.0 to 4.11, the Sums of Scaled Scores obtained is 30. On page 294, skimming down the left-hand column to 30, one sees in the adjacent columns to the right a Core Domain Score of 100, Percentile Rank of 50, and a 95% Confidence Interval of 92 to 108. (A 90% Confidence Interval is also available.)

- The *Core Domain Scores Graph* on the front of the Record Form is where one plots Domain Scores.
- The *Domain Analyses* page on the inside front cover of the Record Form is where one enters the subtest raw scores and scaled scores for core and expanded subtests in the domain.

STEP 5: Look up SSs and QO Scores

Supplemental Scores are located in the *Manual*'s Appendix C (pp. 319–342). Pages 340 to 342 of Appendix C are SS means and standard deviations. The Supplemental Scaled Scores appear on pages 319 to 326 with each of those pages divided into 6-month intervals. For instance, the scores for ages 6.0 to 6.5 appear on the top half of the page, and scores for ages 6.6 to 6.11 appear on the bottom half of the same page. So, again, the clinician must be sure he or she has the correct table for the child's age level. SS expressed in percentile ranks are found categorized by domain on pages 327 to 339 and are recorded on the third page of the Record Form. These scores break down more global information to provide a more diagnostic view of the child's performance. (See Rapid Reference 3.9.)

Supplemental Scaled Scores appear in Table C.1 by age (pp. 319–326 in the *Manual*). On the appropriate page for the age level, the clinician should locate the raw score obtained for one subcomponent of the subtest (i.e., Immediate Memory for Faces) within the ranges presented under the name of the section of the test being scored. The adjacent Scaled Score column is printed in blue at the extreme left, and the Scaled Score that is equivalent to the raw score is on the extreme right. The clinician should enter the Scaled Score in the appropriate box on the SS page of the Record Form.

Supplemental Scores that appear as Cumulative Percentages of the standardization sample are found in *Manual* Table C.2, pages 327 to 339 under each do-

=== Rapid Reference 3.9

Appendix C of the NEPSY *Manual*

Supplemental Scores break down global scores to provide more specific diagnostic information.

All SS are located in Appendix C of the NEPSY *Manual* by age and domain.

- SS means and standard deviations are found on pp. 340–342.
- Supplemental Scaled Scores are found on pp. 319–326. (Each page divided into 6-month intervals. So check scores carefully.)
- SS as Cumulative Percentages are found on pp. 327–339.

≡ *Rapid Reference 3.10*

....

Classification Levels for Percentile Ranks and Cumulative Percentage

>75%	Above Expected Level
26–75%	At Expected Level
11–25%	Slightly Below Expected Level
3–10%	Below Expected Level
≤2%	Well Below Expected Level

main and subtest. After locating the subtest component to be scored under the appropriate domain and subtest, the clinician should scan across the *Age in Years* line at the top of the table and locate the child's age. Going down the column beneath the correct age, the clinician should locate the range in which the raw score for that subcomponent fell. The clinician should then locate the correct percentile range in the column on the far left of the table. That percentile is entered next to the raw score on the SS page and the qualitative descriptor is written to the right of the cumulative percentile. Rapid Reference 3.10 shows these classification levels.

QOs on NEPSY encompass the "how" of a child's test performance, problem solution, or both. Although recording the QOs is optional, the examiner is encouraged to do so. These observations, which can be quantified on NEPSY, can enrich the diagnostic picture immeasurably. In the best process-approach tradition (Kaplan, 1988), the examiner is encouraged to write down any other observations he or she might make during the testing. For example, the clinician might see the child respond impulsively on a certain subtest or develop an effective problem-solving strategy on another. Noting these behaviors provides more information about the child's functioning.

- *Quantified QOs:* These are QOs for which designated space is provided on the Record Form. Some of them (i.e., Asks for Repetition, Off-Task Behaviors) are tallied each time you see an instance during testing; for others, the presence or absence of the observation is recorded (i.e., Stable Misarticulation, Oromotor Hypotonia). After the assessment, appropriate.
  —Tallied QOs: Each time a designated behavior is observed, a tally mark is placed in the designated box. These marks are added and transferred to the outside back page of the Record Form.
  —The QOs recorded as presence or absence: These observations are recorded with a check mark in the correct box.
- *Categories of QO:* For ease of interpretation later, QOs are grouped in categories that include: Attention/Executive Behaviors; Rate Change; Visual Behaviors; Pencil Grip; and Oral/Verbal Behaviors and Motor Behaviors, both of which include Recruitment. These are shown in Rapid Reference 3.11.

Rapid Reference 3.11

Categories of Qualitative Observations

Attention/Executive Behaviors
Off-task Behaviors
- Auditory Response Set
- Visual Attention
- Sentence Repetition

Asks for Repetition
- Phonological Processing
- Comprehension of Instructions
- Sentence Repetition

Miscellaneous Attention/Executive Behaviors
- Rule Violations (Tower)
- Repetitions (List Learning Trials 1–7)
- Novel Intrusions (List Learning Trials 1–7)
- Interference Intrusions (List Learning Trials 1–7)

Rate Change
- Fingertip Tapping (FTT)
- Manual Motor Sequences
- Oromotor Sequences

Visual Behaviors
- Right Visual Field Errors (Arrows)
- Left Visual Field Errors (Arrows)
- Rotation (Block Construction)

Oral/Verbal Behaviors
- Reversed Sequences (Speeded Naming)
- Misarticulation (Repetition of Nonsense Words, Oromotor Sequences)

Recruitment
- Voice Volume (Speeded Naming; Verbal Fluency)

Pencil Grip: Mature/ Intermediate/Immature
- Design Copying
- Visuomotor Precision

Motor Behaviors
- Tremor (Design Copying)
- Motor Difficulty (Tower)
- Visual Guidance (FTT)
- Incorrect Position (FTT)
- Posturing (FTT)
- Mirroring (FTT)
- Mirror Hand (Imitating Hand Positions)
- Other Hand Helps (Imitating Hand Positions)
- Overflow (FTT, Manual Motor Sequences)
- Perseveration (Manual Motor Sequences)
- Loss of Asymmetry (Manual Motor Sequences)
- Oromotor Hypotonia (Oromotor Sequences), Field Errors (Arrows)

Recruitment
- Body Movement
- With word production (Speeded Naming)
- With effort (Verbal Fluency, Manual Motor Sequences)
- Forceful Tapping (Manual Motor Sequences)

Rapid Reference 3.12

Appendix D of the NEPSY *Manual*

Means, standard deviations, and cumulative percentages of Qualitative Observations for the standardization population are found in Appendix D (pp. 343–360) of the NEPSY *Manual*. Comparisons can be made to

- the performance of normally developing children of the same age in the standardization population.
- children with particular disorders (e.g., ADHD, Autistic Disorder, etc.) in the validity groups.

Example: You can determine whether Off-Task Behavior occurs more in 8-year-old Wendy than in other normally developing 8-year-olds in the standardization sample. You may also wish to know if the level of Wendy's Off-Task Behavior correlates with that of ADHD children in the validity sample.

- *Cumulative Percentages of QOs:* These values for the standardization population are found in Appendix D (pp. 343–360) of the NEPSY *Manual*. The cumulative percentage for a particular behavior is entered into the appropriate box next to the raw score or check mark (i.e., *At Expected Level, Above Expected Level*). If the clinician wishes to make comparisons to the performance of other children who have a particular disorder, cumulative percentages are available for validity groups as well. For instance, a clinician would want to know if Off-Task Behavior occurred more in the 8-year-old he or she was testing than in other 8-year-olds in the standardization sample, but may also wish to know if the level of the child's Off-Task Behavior correlated with that of ADHD children in the validity sample. Along with cumulative percentages, means and standard deviations are also available in Appendix D of the *Manual*. Rapid Reference 3.12 summarizes Appendix D.

〰 TEST YOURSELF 〰

1. **The subtests that are more difficult to score than most or that require the use of a template are (check all that apply):**

   (a) _____ Memory for Names.

   (b) _____ Finger Tapping.

   (c) _____ Phonological Processing.

   (d) _____ Design Copying.

   (e) _____ Visual Attention.

   (f) _____ Auditory Attention and Response Set (AARS).

   (g) _____ Arrows.

   (h) _____ Speeded Naming.

Fill in the Blanks

2. **A Commission Error on AARS would be a _____ token or any other _____ token being picked up when *red* is the target, or the touching of any token to pick up outside the ____-s window.**

3. **Supplemental Scores for Narrative Memory are _____ and _____.**

4. **A pencil mark went outside the track in VMP and came back into the track in the next segment would count as _____ errors.**

5. **The _____ confidence interval is recommended when one is computing statistical differences.**

6. **A performance that occurred in more than 75% of the standardization sample would be described as being _____ _____ _____ according to the NEPSY *Manual*.**

7. **Supplemental Scores can be expressed as _____ _____ or _____ _____ .**

Matching

8. _____ **A scaled score of 4**   a. Design Copying

9. _____ **Appendix D**   b. Above Expected Level

10. _____ **A scaled score of 14**   c. Cumulative Percentages for Qualitative Observation

11. _____ **Supplemental Scores**   d. Below Expected Level

12. _____ **Appendix C**   e. Core and Expanded Scores

13. _____ **Appendix F**   f. At Expected Level

14. _____ **Domain Analyses Page**   g. Supplemental Scores

15. _____ **26–75%**   h. Visuomotor Precision

Answers: 1. d, e, f, h; 2. red, color, 3; 3. Error; 4. 2; 5. .95; 6. above expected level; 7. scaled scores, cumulative percentages; 8. d; 9. c; 10. b; 11. h; 12. g; 13. a; 14. e; 15. f

Four

HOW TO INTERPRET NEPSY

This chapter presents a systematic method of interpreting NEPSY. Goals of interpretation of NEPSY and some general principles of interpretation at two levels will be discussed. This will be followed by a discussion of interdomain differences at the Core Domain Level and intradomain differences at the subtest level, as well as the meaning of such differences. Supplemental Scores and the quantifying of Qualitative Observations as a means of teasing apart a problem will be presented. Finally, the chapter will discuss the integration of results and patterns of findings that Bernstein and Waber (1990) have termed "diagnostic behavioral clusters." These diagnostic behavioral clusters are not necessarily domain or content specific, but they must be consistent with current knowledge of brain function in children and the nature of acquired or developmental disorders. The careful integration of all findings is essential in identifying subtle deficiencies that may interfere with learning (Korkman et al., 1998).

GOALS OF INTERPRETATION

The First Goal of Interpretation is to consider the child's neurocognitive development comprehensively. The Second Goal of Interpretation is to identify impairments, as well as the child's strengths and weaknesses, and wherever possible to analyze the child's impairments (Korkman, Kirk, & Kemp, 1998). The Third Goal of Interpretation is to analyze presenting problems in detail with an eye to integrating results with all developmental, neurobiological, medical, educational, and environmental information about the child in order to formulate recommendations for compensatory methods, remediation techniques and/or treatment options.

Implementation of the Goals of Interpretation

In order to meet the above goals, the clinician will implement two levels of interpretation. The first level involves looking at the child in terms of psychometric comparisons, but interpreting the data in terms of the child's needs. The second level involves inspecting the results derived from the first level in a more clinical manner to analyze further the child's pattern of strengths and weaknesses and, if possible, to identify and analyze any impairments for specific disorders. Both levels lead to a final step of integrating the results with all other developmental, neurobiological, medical, educational, and environmental information, so that meaningful recommendations and treatment plans can be formulated.

Interpretation at the Psychometric Level accomplishes the first goal of considering the child's neurocognitive development comprehensively. The clinician develops a comprehensive overview of the child's neurocognitive development through the NEPSY test profile and assesses the child's strengths and weaknesses. This level of interpretation may be an end in itself or the first step in the next level of interpretation. The purpose of any evaluation in the final analysis is to provide a basis for rehabilitation and remediation plans. The results at this level of interpretation are interpreted for "behavior-behavior relationships" (Taylor & Fletcher, 1990). For example, the clinician might discuss a child's reading disability in terms of his poor performance on the Phonological Processing subtest in comparison to other children his age. Interpretation at the psychometric level is carried out in three steps: (a) describing the child's performance in comparison to the normally developing child of his or her age, (b) looking at the child's performance in terms of his or her own functioning, and (c) relating these results to observed areas of difficulty in learning or in everyday life.

First, examine psychometrically the profile of Core Domain Scores, scaled scores, percentile ranks, and cumulative percentages derived from the assessment in terms of how the child functions in comparison to the normally developing child of his or her age in the NEPSY standardization population. The clinician compares the child's performance to the NEPSY Core Domain Test Mean of 100±15 and the NEPSY Core, Expanded, and Supplemental scaled score mean of 10±3. Comparison is also made to the classification levels for percentile ranks and cumulative percentages (≤2% well below expected level; 3–10% below expected level; 11–25% slightly below expected level; 26–75% at expected level, and >75% above expected level). Some of the qualitative behavioral observations (QOs) are quantified on NEPSY so that base rates for the normative group can be used as a reference point for interpreting a child's performance. (See Rapid Reference 4.1.)

Next, describe the child's relative strengths and weaknesses in terms of his or her own functioning in terms of Core Domain and subtest comparisons. The clinician will focus on how the child's performance of a particular task was deviant from the child's performance on other subtests within or across domains. (An in-depth discussion of these comparisons follows.) For those Core Domain Scores that are interpretable, because there is no significant interdomain subtest

Rapid Reference 4.1

Performance Levels for NEPSY Core Domain Scores, Scaled Scores, and Percentile Ranks

Core Domain Score	Scaled Score	Percentile Rank	Performance Level
147–111	19–13	99.9–76	Above Expected Level
110–91	12–9	75–26	At Expected Level
90–82	8–6	25–11	Slightly Below Expected Level
81–70	5–4	10–3	Below Expected Level
<69	3–<1	≤2	Well Below Expected Level

scatter, the clinician may also want to describe the strongest domain, the weakest and those that fell in between.

Finally, the last step in interpretation at the psychometric level is to relate the child's performance to that of age peers, to his or her own pattern of strengths and weaknesses, and to observed areas of difficulty in school and in everyday life. For instance, using behavior to behavior relationships (Taylor & Fletcher, 1990), the clinician relates the child's poor phonological processing performance to his or her performance on other NEPSY subtests, and to classroom difficulties with reading decoding and spelling.

EXAMPLE: *(One segment of a full report, not meant to imply conclusions were based on one subtest):* Ricky's significantly poor performance (PP scaled score 5) on the Phonological Processing subtest in relation to the NEPSY subtest mean for a child his age on that subtest, suggested a deficit in the phonological awareness that underlies efficient reading decoding and spelling (Brenner, 1996; Bradley, 1989; Bradley & Bryant, 1978; Tallal et al, 1993; Torgesen, Wagner & Rashotte, 1994; Scarborough, 1990). Ricky also displayed a relative weakness in phonological awareness in terms of his own average performance on NEPSY Core Subtests overall, suggesting that this is an area which is apt to cause him significant difficulty in school and everyday life in relation to his other abilities. His parents have noted, and Ricky's teachers have reported, marked struggles in reading decoding and spelling since reading instruction began last year. In particular, he has struggled with phonics. This background information lends support to the finding of a deficit in phonological awareness. (Rapid Reference 4.2 provides guidelines for interpreting results.)

Interpretation at the Clinical Level accomplishes the second goal of interpretation in which the clinician is to identify impairments, as well as the child's strengths and weaknesses, and wherever possible analyze the child's impairments (Korkman,

≡ Rapid Reference 4.2

Interpretation of the Results at the Psychometric Level; Guidelines for Describing Neurocognitive Development Comprehensively From the Test Profile

To interpret the results at the psychometric level you should focus on the broad picture.

I. Examine psychometrically the profile of Core Domain Scores, scaled scores, percentile ranks, and cumulative percentages derived from the assessment in terms of:

A. How the child functions in relation to the normally developing child of his or her age as represented by the NEPSY standardization population.

(Core Domain Mean = 100±15; scaled score mean = 10±3)

1. Describe the domains (if interpretable) in relation to the norm.

2. Describe strengths and weaknesses at the subtest level, Core and Expanded, Supplemental, and QOs, in relation to the norm.

3. Remember that strengths are as important as weaknesses.

B. Describe the child's relative strengths and weaknesses according to behavior-behavior relationships as described by:

1. Core Domain Scores (when interpretable). Which is strongest? Which is weakest? Which fell in mid-range for the child?

2. Subtest comparisons in terms of the child's own functioning within or across domains.

II. Integrate the child's results from NEPSY with behavioral observations and with family, medical, developmental, educational, and emotional history.

Kirk, & Kemp, 1998). After interpretation at the psychometric level, the clinician can proceed to the clinical level. The first step at this level aims to discover WHAT function is specifically impaired, while the second step addresses the question WHY a particular activity is so difficult for the child (Korkman, in press), and the third step answers the question, WHICH disorder based on a diagnostic behavioral cluster composed of the observed primary and secondary impairments might be present? Sometimes, however, a diagnostic behavioral cluster is not present. The clinician should then analyze the specific impairments instead. This level of the interpretation process involves three separate steps: (a) to identify specific impairments; (b) to analyze the specific impairments or the child's presenting problem and (c) to locate diagnostic behavioral clusters that point to specific disorders.

First, the clinician identifies specific impairments. To do so, the clinician must delineate some aspect of performance derived at the psychometric level on which the child tends to exhibit specific problems in a fairly consistent fashion. Such impairments may be demonstrated:

1. When one domain is impaired both in relation to the age norm and in relation to results in other domains;

   EXAMPLE: Specific impairments of this type are language impairments, attentional problems, sensorimotor problems or visuospatial impairments. Even these disorders, which may affect one domain differentially, will often show effects in other domains (e.g. a language impairment affecting verbal memory performance).

2. When two or more subtest scores, SS, or QOs within a domain or across domains indicate that a certain aspect of performance is impaired either in relation to the age norm or in relation to the child's own mean.

   EXAMPLE: An example of consistent findings across domains is when a child has poor scores on the Tower subtest and the Response Set task of the AARS subtest, and also performs poorly on the List Learning subtest due to a flat learning curve. Together, these findings indicate an executive function problem related to planning, programming and monitoring performance. Other examples might be dysnomic or semantic problems evident on the SN and the MN subtests, or motor coordination problems that may affect not only sensorimotor tasks but also the DC subtest in the Visuospatial Domain.

This step in interpretation differs from the more straightforward behavioral interpretation of findings at the psychometric level. Interpretation at this level is going to be richer if the clinician has current knowledge of patterns to look for based on familiarity with the research. Identifying specific impairments is not exactly the same thing as defining strengths and weaknesses behaviorally. The problem may be more subtle or complex than describing a behavior in relation to the norm. It often takes place through error analysis. The more neuropsychological training and expertise a clinician has, the more skillful he or she is in inferring the role of deficits. (See Rapid Reference 4.3.)

EXAMPLE: (A segment of a report only, not meant to present conclusions from a single result) Lyndsey, a 7-year-old girl, received scores Below or Well Below Expected Level on all Core Language Domain subtests. Her Core Visuospatial Domain score was At Expected Level for age. The other Core Domain Scores showed intradomain scatter, so they could not be regarded as measures of the Domains. Inspection of her Memory and Learning subtest performance revealed that Lyndsey performed poorly on Memory for Names and Narrative Memory, both verbal memory tasks. Memory for Faces was At Expected Level for age. The pattern of weaknesses in Lyndsey's performance suggests a Receptive and Expressive Language Disorder. After reviewing the scores in the Attention/Executive Functions, Sensorimotor, and Visuospatial Domain in a similar fashion, it was concluded that Lyndsey also had problems with auditory but not visual attention, and slight problems with manual motor coordination. These were especially evident on tasks that demanded executing motor series, whereas her precision on paper and pencil tasks, her favorite activities, was not a reason for great concern.

Second, impairments should be analyzed by specifying primary and secondary deficits, whenever possible. The impairments the clinician identified should be further analyzed to determine why the function was impaired.

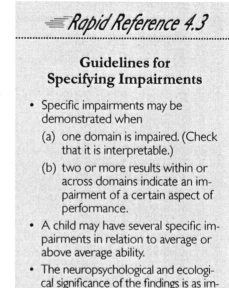

=== *Rapid Reference 4.3*

Guidelines for Specifying Impairments

- Specific impairments may be demonstrated when

  (a) one domain is impaired. (Check that it is interpretable.)

  (b) two or more results within or across domains indicate an impairment of a certain aspect of performance.

- A child may have several specific impairments in relation to average or above average ability.

- The neuropsychological and ecological significance of the findings is as important as the statistical significance.

1. Analyze separately, as far as is possible, all subcomponents that are known to be a part of the function in question. In the Lurian tradition, specific NEPSY subtests represent subcomponents of complex processes. For example, for language to be processed normally, a child needs to be able to decode words phonologically (Phonological Processing and Repetition of Nonsense Words); to comprehend syntactic and conceptual relations (Comprehension of Instructions); to hold a verbal sequence in memory long enough to process its content (Sentence Repetition); to attach verbal labels to things and concepts, and to retrieve them smoothly (SN, Memory for Names); to organize articulatory sequences (Repetition of Nonsense Words, Oromotor Sequences) and the details of a narration (Narrative Memory). In a similar way, the clinician finds represented subcomponents used in the organization of complex visuomotor performance, reading, solving arithmetical problems, and so forth (Korkman, Kirk, & Kemp, 1998).

2. Specify what particular part of the process is deficient and whether the deficit contributing to the dysfunction is primary or is secondary to another deficit. The Lurian view, upon which NEPSY is based, suggests that cognitive capacities are functional systems composed of basic and complex interactive subcomponents (Christensen, 1984; Luria, 1973,

1962/1980). Therefore, a primary deficit in one functional system could affect performance in other functional systems, causing secondary deficits. For example, the child may be unable to learn a long list of isolated words, due, not to a language disorder, but to executive dysfunction. The child cannot organize and monitor the list. Each subcomponent performs its role in the chain of subprocesses. When one of them is deficient, the whole functional system may be disturbed. On the other hand, a disorder such as dyslexia may have more than one underlying deficit.

Kaplan's (1988) view, that a process approach to assessment can provide information about a child's problem that cannot be obtained from an analysis of summary scores alone, also underlies NEPSY. Therefore, where total scores are provided, NEPSY often provides SS, so that different aspects of a global score can be considered separately (e.g. speed and accuracy) to facilitate interpreting and identifying primary and secondary deficits. For instance, the clinician can break down the Total Score for SN into SSs for Time and Accuracy to consider whether a naming deficit is evident, or whether the child was slow to access words, but did not have a naming problem, or if both problems are present. A naming deficit might also be confirmed by a poor Memory for Names performance.

After administering the appropriate subtests, the clinician should analyze the findings by determining the deficient subcomponent that causes the overt dysfunction. Because all human performance is more or less complex, every test result will depend on many capacities. For example, on the Arrows subtest in the Visuospatial Domain, the child must judge the orientation of lines and angles by pointing to the two arrows that will hit the target on each item. The child needs not only to perceive and judge the direction and orientation of the arrows correctly, but also to attend to the lengthy task and to look actively at each of the eight arrows before responding. Sometimes a poor performance on the Arrows subtest co-occurs, not with other signs of poor visuospatial perception, but with poor visual attention or executive dysfunction. The former problems would be characterized by the child's inability to focus attention on the task or to sustain attention across the task. The latter could lead to responding impulsively, because the child can not inhibit the impulse to point to the first two arrows seen. Underlying primary deficits may have to be inferred in this way, by using error analysis and looking at the pattern of findings.

Specifying primary deficits in children is complicated by the high degree of comorbidity of deficits and the widespread neural networks in the developing child. When a child suffers from several co-occurring deficits, such as an attention disorder and a language disorder, both of which can affect many types of performance, it can be difficult to specify primary and secondary weaknesses. Inattention affects language processing, but poor language processing can contribute to inattention. In these cases, it may be sufficient to provide a comprehensive description of the child's neurocognitive status. The clinician may not always be able to specify primary and secondary deficits. In such instances, one may have to describe the total test profile and identify specific impairments, but not perform an in-depth analysis of the disorders.

Third, *identify diagnostic behavioral clusters that characterize particular diagnostic groups.* Luria (1969, 1962/1980) referred to the process of "syndrome analysis," and Bernstein and Waber (1990) discuss the need to locate "diagnostic behavioral clusters." Both terms are apt for the diagnostic process of looking for specific patterns of symptoms that frequently cluster together to characterize a particular disorder. We have chosen the latter for use in this volume, however, because it is so descriptive of the process. This term refers to the process of recognizing specific patterns that usually characterize different diagnostic groups, such as in children with ADHD, dyslexia, autistic spectrum disorders, Fetal Alcohol Syndrome, Asperger's Syndrome, William's Syndrome, and so forth. Such disorders may be of neurological, genetic, or of unknown etiology. The identification process is based primarily on clinical expertise and knowledge of the literature, and, secondarily, on the pattern of the child's specific psychometric scores.

The fact that a child shows a pattern of scores similar to that seen in a disorder does not necessarily mean the child has the disorder. Unless the child's functioning is consistent with the disorder and the medical, genetic, environmental factors, and so forth that are consistent with the disorder are present, the disorder should not be identified. For instance, a girl might have a visuospatial deficit and a math learning disability, but be very sociable, maintain good eye contact, and be expressive during the evaluation. Her history reveals that she has many friends and participates successfully in several group activities. In this case, identifying Nonverbal Learning Disability would be inappropriate, because there is no evidence of social perceptual difficulties.

Sometimes, however, the parent may not report a family history of the disorder because he or she has forgotten about it, is embarrassed, or did not make the connection between the child's problem and the presence of a similar problem in a member of the extended family. These are the kind of cases in which the importance of the diagnostic interview, the depth of the clinician's knowledge of the literature, and the level of clinical insight can prove most valuable.

EXAMPLE: *(A segment of a report only. No conclusions would be drawn from a single result)* Suppose that Sonia has been referred for an evaluation of a reading problem. There is no record of any familial dyslexia or reading problem on the history form. You notice, however, that there are many misspellings on the history form that was filled out by Sonia's mother, who has a college degree. In your diagnostic interview you ask if there was anyone in the family who had a reading difficulty, and the response is negative. But when you ask if anyone had or has trouble pronouncing new words, you learn that the family playfully teases Sonia's maternal aunt for that. When you ask if anyone has trouble finding words when he or she is talking (word-finding problems), you discover that Sonia, her mother, her maternal aunt, and her maternal grandfather all have this problem. You then ask if anyone has had difficulty learning a foreign language, and even though Sonia's mother has not been able to express this on the history form, she now tells you that she had a great deal of difficulty getting her college degree because she had trouble passing French. She also reports that Sonia's older sister, who is a very good student, is really struggling with French, too, because she cannot seem to master the pronunciation or spelling. Finally, when you ask if anyone has dropped out of school early, Sonia's mother reveals that her own father left school after ninth grade, because he "just couldn't keep up." A little more gentle discussion reveals that, despite the fact that he runs a successful retail business, he has marked difficulty reading and spelling. He keeps it very secret, and his wife does all of the ordering and bookkeeping for him. Through a skillful clinical interview, you have established a family history of dyslexia.

Being able to recognize diagnostic behavioral clusters rests on the clinician's ability to gain as much training and expertise in clinical neuropsychological practice as possible, and it is one of the reasons why clinicians must stay current with the literature. As the clinician performs his or her evaluation, he or she needs to know the direction to follow to confirm the hypotheses. For instance, if the clinician suspects dyslexia, as in Sonia's case, he or she needs to know to look for phonological processing deficits and naming problems. The clinician needs to know that Sonia's results on the Phonological Processing subtest are poor and that the hypothesis of a phonological processing deficit contributing to dyslexia should be confirmed by the Repetition of Nonsense Words subtest. The clinician also knows (because he or she is current with the literature) that children with dyslexia usually have naming deficits, but may or may not have other language deficits. Further, the clinician knows that a naming deficit usually affects the child's ability to learn the names of people as well as objects and concepts, because our names are actually just labels. The clinician also knows from his or her study that reading decoding and spelling are usually more negatively impacted than reading comprehension in dyslexia, and that reading comprehension actually may be at grade level. The following is an example of a diagnostic behavioral cluster revealed in Sonia's testing.

EXAMPLE: Indeed, when you subsequently evaluated Sonia, you found performance *Well Below Expected Level* on the Phonological Processing and Repetition of Nonsense Words subtests, establishing a primary deficit in phonological analysis. SN performance was *Below Expected Level.* The SSs revealed *Borderline* speed of access as well as accuracy in naming that is *Well Below Expected Level*. Performance on Memory for Names was *Below Expected Level*, as well, including the SSs for the Learning Trials and Delay. Therefore, a primary naming deficit was identified with secondary deficit in ability to learn people's names. Difficulty with access seen on SN was confirmed when Sonia, despite performance *At Expected Level* on the Comprehension of Instructions subtest, had problems on the Free Recall Trial *(Below Expected Level)* of the Narrative Memory subtest. She was able to access story details *Above Expected Level* on the Cued Recall Trial, however. The questions provided cues for accessing the details. Her difficulties with speed of processing appeared to be more generalized than just in accessing language. On VP, her SS for Time score was *Below Expected Level*, though accuracy for graphomotor control was *At Expected Level*. Graphomotor control did not appear to be the problem, because DC was *Above Expected Level*. Further, on the VA subtest her Time score was also *Below Expected Level*, even on the simple search task. Therefore, there appeared to be a primary deficit in processing speed, which was also apparent on Sonia's WISC-III results, with a secondary deficit in speed of lexical access, which was further complicated by her primary naming deficit. Performance in all other domains was compatible with that of the general population and in terms of Sonia's own performance within or across domains. There were weaknesses revealed by SSs on VP, VA, and Narrative Memory in other domains, but the total scores were *At Expected Level*. Academic achievement testing revealed reading decoding and spelling discrepancies with predicted achievement based on her ability level, though reading comprehension was average and within the range of her ability as measured by the WISC-III. Familial history was present, and Sonia was reported to have marked struggles in mastering phonics and learning to read. She often experienced word-finding problems, and these were noted during her evaluation in her frequent use of "thing" when she could not access a word. The diagnostic behavioral cluster for dyslexia was present.

If a diagnostic behavioral cluster is not present, the clinician should identify and analyze primary and secondary deficits. If this is not possible, the clinician should identify neurocognitive strengths and weaknesses. The clinician should not attempt the diagnosis of disorders for which he or she has no neuropsychological training or background. Rapid Reference 4.4 provides steps for interpretation at the clinical level.

Pediatric Neuropsychologists May Interpret by Neuroanatomic Axes

It is important that the clinician be very aware of the ethical considerations of making interpretations based on the depth and specificity of his or her training and knowledge of current research. Localizing brain dysfunction in a child, by neuropsychological means, is problematic (see pp. 115–116). There are times, however, when the pediatric neuropsychologist may interpret results at the clinical level by making reference to functional organization of the brain in children in general terms, using the three primary neuroanatomic axes of the brain: left/right hemisphere; anterior/posterior; and cortical/subcortical, without assuming that there is any focal brain lesion or focal dysfunction (Bernstein & Waber, 1990). That is, it is common to think of neuropsychological processes in terms of frontal

Rapid Reference 4.4

Interpretation at the Clinical Level

The three steps of the interpretation process at this level are:
- to identify specific impairments.
- to analyze specific impairments.
  —Analyze separately, as far as possible, the subcomponents known to be a part of that function.
  —Specify and discuss what part of the process is deficient.
  —Specify and discuss primary and secondary deficits.
- Identify diagnostic behavioral clusters that characterize particular diagnostic groups.
  —Look for a diagnostic behavioral cluster to describe a disorder.
  —Just because a cluster of symptoms is present does not necessarily mean a disorder is present.
- Interpret by neuroanatomic axes.
  —Left/right; anterior/posterior.
  —No assumption of any focal brain lesion or focal dysfunction.

CAUTION

Appropriate Training is Essential

It is essential to acquire appropriate training in pediatric neuropsychology and to keep yourself current with the literature in order to perform pediatric neuropsychological assessments. Otherwise, interpretation of NEPSY should be confined to a comprehensive description of neurocognitive strengths and weaknesses in behavior to behavior terms at the psychometric level.

lobe functions, posterior brain processes, and left and right hemisphere functions, without presupposing any direct relationship between test findings and underlying brain dysfunction. In these cases, the neuropsychologist's training and knowledge of current research form an integral part of the interpretation. This type of interpretation is not a necessary step in applying the NEPSY and should be undertaken only by those with specialized training in pediatric neuropsychology.

THE CHALLENGE OF INTERPRETING CHILD VERSUS ADULT NEUROPSYCHOLOGICAL TEST RESULTS

Traditionally, one aim of neuropsychological assessment was to localize brain damage or dysfunction by specifying which part of the brain, judging from neuropsychological evidence, seemed to be dysfunctional. With the advent of neuroimaging techniques, this aim is no longer essential in clinical neuropsychology. Without enormous expertise or, in very special circumstances, it is not advisable to attempt to localize brain dysfunctions on the basis of neuropsychological findings in children with or without neuroimaging. The following points outline certain aspects of interpreting neuropsychological performance in children that make it a special challenge in comparison to the interpretation of performance in the adult population.

1. *Widespread and diffusely distributed neural networks.* Children may have more widespread and diffusely distributed networks of neural processes that underlie cognitive functions than adults have. There is also a high degree of neural redundancy in childhood. During development, neural substrates are organized and crystallized, increasing efficiency, but decreasing redundancy and plasticity, as neural circuits become committed to specific functions.

2. *Functional organization of the young brain may be modified.* Evidence from children with lateralized brain damage shows that the ongoing functional organization of the brain may be modified following early brain damage; therefore, in the young child functional organization may not be predictable.

3. *Diffuse damage or dysfunction.* Children tend to have diffuse or multifocal brain dysfunction (Korkman, 1999). In the adult, because development is complete, a lesion in one area will cause predictable, circumscribed

CAUTION

Cautions against Localizing Brain Functions in Children

Inferences about underlying brain pathology in children should be avoided.

- Focal damage is more common in adults; diffuse or multifocal damage or dysfunction is more common in children. The original lesion may adversely affect functions of developing neural pathways, causing diffuse damage.
- Children are still developing; therefore, damage at a particular time can affect *current* and *future* neurocognitive development.
- Profiles of children with verified, lateralized brain damage do not differ consistently. Children have a high degree of neural redundancy. Functional organization of the brain may be modified following early brain damage.
- Age at the time of the event, neural plasticity, and recovery of function can all contribute to a changing developmental picture.

deficits. Because children are still developing, a deficit in one area may cause subtle, diffuse dysfunction in multiple areas due to subsequent development affect by the original lesion.

Integration of the Results with All Other Information About the Child

This goal is intimately connected to all diagnostic conclusions. The clinician integrates the results of the evaluation with all other developmental, neurobiological, medical, educational and environmental information about the child. He or she analyzes presenting problems and the child's situation in detail with an eye to providing recommendations for compensatory methods, remediation techniques, or treatment options. The entire assessment is geared toward providing help and advice to those involved in the intervention and education of the child. The following is an example of recommendations drawn up following Sonia's evaluation.

EXAMPLE: Following Sonia's evaluation, the clinician recommends that she work with a reading specialist on a multisensory, phonological approach to decoding. He or she recommends that Sonia's weekly spelling list be modified to 10 rather than 20 words. Further, the clinician suggests that Sonia have a multiple choice spelling test with no dictation sentences, because children with dyslexia have marked difficulty spelling in context. Another recommendation was that spelling in context not be penalized. Sonia and the teacher would draw up a list of five words that she uses often and misspells frequently. These would be the only words circled for correction. When she begins to spell one of the words correctly on a regular basis, another frequently misspelled common word would be added to the list. The list would be circulated to all of her teachers, so that she can use the same system, no matter what the subject. Mother and Dad were shown several multisensory methods that Sonia could use for studying spelling. Word-processing instruction was to begin for Sonia immediately, so she could learn to use the computer for any written expression. Because Sonia's school started foreign language study in the third grade, the clinician recommended that this be delayed for Sonia until her reading is fluent. If she wants to study a foreign language then, Spanish would be recommended because of its simple phonetic structure. Latin would be an alternative, because it builds word analysis and vocabulary skills in English due to the great number of Latin roots, prefixes, and suffixes in English. Talking Books to be ordered through the Library of Congress are also recommended for Sonia. In this way she could "read" books that other children were reading but she could not yet handle. She could read the book along with the tape, however. The clinician also recommended these for her social studies and science books, as these texts are particularly difficult content reading. Further recommendation was made that Sonia have drill and practice with the Dolch Sight Words in order to give her a ready sight vocabulary for reading. Her teachers were asked not to make her read aloud in front of classmates. Software programs were recommended for help with reading decoding and spelling both at school and at home. Because Sonia was comfortable reading to her mother, she was to read for 10 min each night with her. Her parents were asked to read to her nightly from a book of her choice. Sonia loved ballet, so it was recommended that Sonia's mother consult the children's librarian at the public library about simple books that Sonia could read on that topic. Sonia's parents were given a bibliography of books which would help them understand dyslexia and another list of books which they could read to Sonia to help her learn about famous people who had overcome dyslexia. (See Rapid Reference 4.5.)

STEP-BY-STEP INTERPRETATION OF NEPSY

During the scoring procedures addressed in Chapter 3, the clinician recorded the subtest scores, Core Domain Scores, their percentiles, and confidence intervals on the Record Form. These latter values account for the standard error of measurement and establish a range within which the "true" score can be expected to fall with a certain level of confidence (usually 95%). The Supplemental Scaled Scores and those that appear as cumulative percentages were recorded, along with their descriptors. Finally, on the Record Form, the clinician also recorded QOs, their cumulative percentages, and descriptors, along with frequencies in the standardization sample, where applicable. Much of this information will now be transferred to the NEPSY Data Worksheet in Appendix A of this volume, which will help facilitate interpretation of the test data. (See Rapid Reference 4.6.)

This section focuses on psychometric scores. However, the clinician should remember that this is just one level in the interpretative process. After psychometric discrepancies have been considered, and strengths and weak-

═Rapid Reference 4.5

Goals of Interpretation

1. Consider the child's neurocognitive development comprehensively.

2. Identify and, where possible, analyze impairments.

3. Integrate all information obtained from a developmental, neurobiological, medical, educational, and environmental perspective. Analyze presenting problems and the child's situation to provide recommendations for compensatory methods, remediation techniques, and treatment options.

• This goal is intimately connected to all diagnostic conclusions.

• Intervention for and education of the child is paramount to the outcome of assessment.

═Rapid Reference 4.6

NEPSY Data Worksheet in Appendix A

Appendix A (p. 289) of this volume contains the NEPSY Data Worksheet (reproducible), which will help you

• Organize and integrate the child's test results

• Make decisions concerning significant deficits in the child's functioning

• Identify the primary and secondary deficits

• Facilitate interpretation and formulation of recommendations

nesses defined in a comprehensive overview of neurocognitive status, the subsequent steps of identifying and analyzing primary and secondary deficits, identifying diagnostic behavioral clusters, and interpreting the findings still lie ahead. Therefore, the clinician should keep in mind any preliminary hypotheses he or she may have derived from the review of the records, diagnostic interview with the parents and the child, and the assessment itself. The clinician should continue to formulate and refine hypotheses when working with the psychometric test results. Then, as the clinician begins the next levels of interpretation, he or she will have a clearer view of where the primary and secondary deficits may lie, what diagnostic behavioral clusters should be considered, and what the disorder or dysfunction may be. The clinician should also remember that interpretation of performance depends on knowledge of current research concerning the deficit or deficits that may underlie learning disabilities, neurodevelopmental disorders, and acquired neurological dysfunction to which the diagnostic behavioral clusters may point (Korkman, Kirk, & Kemp, 1998). Ultimately, all of the levels of interpretation will provide a basis for formulating rehabilitation and remediation plans.

STEP 1: Enter Psychometric Test Data on the NEPSY Data Worksheet

Transfer the following results to the NEPSY Data Worksheet: the Core Domain Scores, their percentiles, the confidence interval for each of the five domains, and the Core Subtest Scaled Scores. As the clinician performs these steps, he or she needs to consider any hypotheses concerning deficits that may have been formulated during testing.

STEP 2: Examine Psychometric Differences in Scaled Scores on NEPSY and Determine Whether Core Domain Scores are Interpretable

Variability within and across domains is important for understanding neurocognitive strengths and weaknesses for a child. Considering strengths through which the child can feel success and that may be avenues for remediation or rehabilitation is just as important as identifying weaknesses. There are a number of ways to make these clinical judgements on NEPSY. Because the clinician has to consider subtest level differences to decide whether or not the Core Domain Scores can be used to determine the child's overall functioning for each domain, and because much of the diagnostic information on NEPSY lies at the subtest level, we will consider psychometric interpretation of subtests first.

   Subtest-level comparisons. When scoring, the clinician may find that some of the child's scores are out of line with the others. There are six ways (outlined in

≡ Rapid Reference 4.7

Six Methods of Comparison at the Subtest Level

From Appendix B of the NEPSY *Manual* (pp. 310–315), choose only the comparison(s) you feel are pertinent for interpreting the child's functioning. You can compare

1. Core Subtest Scaled Score(s) to the child's mean for all *Core* Subtests *within the Core Domain*.
2. *Core* and *Expanded* Subtest Scaled Scores to the average of all *Core and Expanded* Subtest Scaled Scores *within a Domain*.
3. *Core* Subtest Scaled Score to the average of all *Core* Subtest Scaled Scores *across Domains*.
4. *Core and Expanded* Subtest Scaled Scores compared to the child's mean for all *Core and Expanded* Subtests *across Domains*.
5. *Two Core* and *Expanded* Subtest Scaled Scores or *two Supplemental* Scaled Scores using *pairwise contrasts*.
6. *Core Subtest Scaled Scores* or *Core Subtest Scaled Score mean* to the NEPSY *Core Subtest mean* (10±15) for children his or her age in the standardization population.

Rapid Reference 4.7) to make psychometric comparisons at the subtest level. These will help elucidate the child's strengths and weaknesses. In line with preliminary observations the clinician may want to select several methods that fit the child's referral question and performance best. For example, the clinician might decide to compare Jan's NEPSY Core Subtest Scaled Scores to the NEPSY Core Subtest Scaled Score mean (10±3) based on normative information. For example, if the clinician compares Jan's SN Scaled Score of 5 to the NEPSY subtest mean of 10, he or she would be comparing Jan's performance in lexical access to that of normally developing children her age. Differences at the subtest level are computed using tables in Appendix B in the NEPSY *Manual* (pp. 305–319).

Within-Domain Subtest Differences

Within-domain differences are important not only for establishing the child's strengths and weaknesses, but also for establishing whether a Core Domain Score can be interpreted as reflecting the child's overall functioning in that domain. If there are no significant discrepancies among the Core Domain subtests, then the clinician can assume, overall, that the child's skills in that domain are developed fairly evenly. When there are significant differences in the child's intradomain performance, however, as reflected by the Core Subtest Scaled Scores, then the Core Domain Score may not be interpretable. Two methods of subtest-level compar-

CAUTION

Appendix B Difference Tables: Be Sure to Check Age Levels

Appendix B (pp. 305–318) of the NEPSY *Manual* contains all of the difference and frequency tables for scaled score and Core Domain Score comparisons.

Tables are arranged in two age groups: Ages 3 to 4 and 5 to 12. Some of the tables have data for 3- to 4-year-olds on the upper half of the page and the data for 5- to 12-year-olds on the lower half. Therefore, be sure to check age levels twice when you are scoring.

isons help the clinician make this determination. Because the Core Domain Score is a global score, without the following steps, it may mask discrepancies within the domain.

1. Compare Differences Between Core Subtest Scaled Scores within a Domain and the Child's Personal Mean for Core Subtest Scores in That Domain

This is a way to look at the child's functioning on a particular subtest in relation to overall functioning within that domain, as well as a way to look at intradomain variability. For this approach, the clinician should use Table B.3 on pages 310 to 311 in the NEPSY *Manual.* The clinician should be sure he or she is on the right page for the age level.

First, compute the child's mean and find the difference for the Core Domain subtests. If there are three subtests in a Core Domain, as there are for all domains for ages 5 to 12, except Visuospatial, the clinician should average the Core Subtest Scaled Scores and round off the mean. The clinician should do this for all domains except Visuospatial. All of the domains on the Core NEPSY for ages 3 to 4, except for the Language Domain, have only two subtests. In these cases, the clinician should subtract one subtest scaled score within the domain from the other. Begin with the Attention/Executive Grid for the appropriate age level (Appendix A) and enter the child's Attention/Executive Core Subtest Scaled Score mean in the second column headed *Subtest Mean.* Do this for each domain. For children 3 to 4 years of age, find the difference and enter it in the *Difference* column. The clinician should do this for each domain.

For Ages 5 to 12, subtract the child's Core Subtest mean from each of the Core Subtest Scaled Scores. Enter the difference in the *Difference* column. For the Visuospatial Domain for Ages 5 to 12, enter the difference between the two Visuospatial Core Subtest Scaled Scores in the *Difference* column, as well.

Compare the child's difference to the difference required for significance at the .05 level. The resulting value is then compared to the difference required for significance in the standardization population. In Table B.3 (ages 3–4, p. 310; ages 5–12, p. 311), this difference is shown in the blue-shaded column to the right of the subtest under the chosen significance level. It is best to use the .05 significance level, because the .15 level is not stringent enough for diagnostic purposes. The clinician should write the number required for significance at the .05 level on the NEPSY Data Worksheet in the column headed *Required for Sig. (.05)* for each of the Attention/Executive Core Subtests on the Attention/Executive Domain grid. If the child's difference is equal to or greater than the difference for the standardization sample, it is statistically significant at the .05 level. Put another way, there is a 95% likelihood that this difference did not occur by chance. (See Rapid Reference 4.8.)

EXAMPLE: Suppose that the Attention/Executive Core Subtest mean for Shellie (8 years of age) is 10, the average of her Tower and VA scaled scores of 12 and her AARS score of 6. Turning to Table B.3 for Ages 5 to 12, the clinician would see in the blue *Significance Level* column at the .05 level, that to reach significance, a difference of 2.69 (3.0 rounded) would be needed between the Tower Scaled Score (12) and Shellie's Attention/Executive mean of 10. In the *Difference* column there is a 2 (the difference between the Tower Score and her Attention/Executive Domain Core Subtest mean). Therefore, Shellie's Tower performance would not show a significant difference from her mean subtest performance for the Attention/Executive Domain. The same would be true of her VA scaled score, which would need to show a 2.98 (3.0) difference with her Attention/Executive Domain Core Subtest mean to be a significant difference. Finally the AARS score of 6 would be considered. Table B.3 indicates that a 2.69 (3.0) difference is required for significance. There is a –4 point difference between Shellie's AARS Scaled Score and her Attention/Executive Domain Core Subtest mean; therefore the difference is significant. In order to indicate this, the clinician put an asterisk (*) beside the 4 in the *Difference* column. The next question is whether this level of difference occurs with a low enough frequency to be considered outside the range of normal variation.

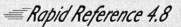

Rapid Reference 4.8

Is A Significant Difference Different Enough?

A statistically significant discrepancy in two values may occur too frequently in normally developing children to be considered abnormal.

- The extreme 15% of the general population, or one standard deviation from the mean (e.g., for the NEPSY mean of 100±15, a Core Domain Score of 85 or lower), can be considered outside normal variation (Kaufman & Lictenberger, 1999).

Appendix B in the NEPSY *Manual* provides cumulative percentages of 25, 10, 5, 2, and 1 for frequency in the standardization population.

- Use a cumulative percentage of 10 or lower from the difference table in Appendix B as a stringent marker of low frequency for a statistically significant difference.
- A frequency of 25% means that one quarter of the children that age exhibited the behavior, so it would not be a significant-enough difference to be outside the range of normal variation.

Determine whether a significant difference is different enough. In other words, although the discrepancy between the two values is statistically different and not merely a chance occurrence, does it occur too frequently in normally developing children to be considered abnormal? (Kaufman & Lictenberger, 1999). According to Kaufman and Lichtenberger the extreme 15% of the normal population, which corresponds to one standard deviation from the mean, can be considered outside normal variation. The frequency with which a difference occurs in the normal population (represented by the standardization sample) is found in Table B.3 in the *Cumulative Percentage* columns of the *Manual*. The extreme 10%, 5%, 2%, and 1% values are presented in the table, along with the 25% frequency level. A difference at the 25% level would occur in one quarter of the children at any given age and would not be considered unusual. The clinician would need to select the 10% column or one of lower frequency, according to his or her clinical judgement. Looking at the significant difference which occurs in the extreme 10% of the normal population, the clinician would see a value of 4 (3.67 rounded), which is the value of Shellie's difference. Additionally, he or she would note that a difference of 4 (4.33 rounded) is seen in the 5% frequency column. Therefore, the difference Shellie shows in her performance on AARS in relation to her overall performance on Attention/Executive subtests occurs in only the extreme 5 to 10% of the normal population of children across ages 5 to 12. Therefore, it is an unusual result and a significant weakness within Shellie's Attention/Executive Domain. In the *S-W* column for AARS the clinician should enter *W* to indicate Shellie's personal weakness in this area.

EXAMPLE: In your report you might interpret these results in the following way *(This is an excerpt only, not meant to imply conclusions drawn from a single finding)*. Shellie's ability to plan, strategize, and monitor her performance according to rules on a visual, nonverbal problem-solving task was *At Expected Level* for her age. Visual attention was also *At Expected Level* on both a simple, visual-search task and a complex, selective visual-attention task. She appeared to be able to "anchor" her attention with the salient pictures on the VA subtest of NEPSY. Shellie's Attention/Executive Core Domain Score was within the average range. It did not, however, reflect Shellie's overall functioning in this domain, because her scores on the AARS Subtest were *Below Expected Level* and a significant weakness in terms of her own performance on other Attention/Executive Domain tasks. Therefore, the average Attention/Executive Core Domain Score cannot be interpreted. Shellie displayed a significant weakness on two auditory tasks. One task was a pure selective auditory attention (listening for a target word, *red,* and putting a red token in the box). The second part of the task required auditory attention for complex auditory stimuli, as well as executive functions to shift set and maintain an alternating auditory set, while still being vigilant for a constant target word. Shellie's performance was *Below Expected Level* on both parts of the AARS Subtest, according to her Supplemental Scores for AA and for RS which were *Below Expected Level.* These results suggest poor auditory attention skills and executive dysfunction in shifting, maintaining and alternating auditory set. There is a 95% likelihood that only 5 to 10% of the general population

Shellie's age would score at this low level. Her significant weakness in this area can be expected to adversely impact her performance in the classroom, especially when a quantity of auditory information is presented without any visual reinforcement. Visual materials might help anchor Shellie's attention. (*The clinician would then go on to integrate the rest of Shellie's test results with these findings in order to see if auditory attention is a primary deficit or possibly a secondary deficit due to a receptive language disorder or hearing loss, and so forth.*)

Computer scoring of within-domain differences. The *NEPSY Scoring Assistant,* (The Psychological Corporation, 2000) computes the Core Subtest differences within Core Domains for the clinician, designating whether the subtest score represents a strength *(S)* or a weakness *(W)* within the Core Domain on the printout. The clinician needs to designate the .05 significance level and the *Comparisons Within Domains* command before the scores are computed. Also, for a Full NEPSY Assessment, including Core and Expanded Subtests, the scoring program computes the strengths and weaknesses across all of these subtests. Because the Expanded Subtests are not used in the computation of the Core Domain Scores, the clinician will need to use Table B.3 or B.7 of the *Manual* to analyze intradomain variability for the Core Scaled Scores only, as shown in Rapid Reference 4.9. Then the clinician will know whether the Core Domain Score can be interpreted as reflecting overall functioning within that domain.

2. Compare Differences Between Two Subtest Scaled Scores Within a Domain Required for Statistical Significance Using Pair-Wise Comparison

The clinician can use Table B.7 (pp. 316–318) in the *Manual* to determine significant intradomain differences by doing a pair-wise comparison of subtests within a domain. For instance, in the previous example of Shellie, the clinician might have chosen to do a pair-wise comparison between performance on the auditory attention task (AARS subtest) versus the visual attention task (VA subtest) of NEPSY. This comparison may provide evidence that the attention problem is more specific to the auditory than to the visual modality. Further,

=== *Rapid Reference 4.9*

Computer Scoring for NEPSY

The *NEPSY Scoring Assistant* (The Psychological Corporation, 2000) will compute

• The Core Subtest Scaled Score differences within and across domains in a Core Assessment.

• The Core and Expanded Scaled Score differences within and across domains in a Full Assessment.

• The *Scoring Assistant* will not compute a Selective or Expanded Assessment. Compute for the Core and then score by hand the extra Expanded subtests.

such pair-wise comparisons can add information to the previous comparisons made between the child's score on one Core Domain Subtest Scaled Score to the child's Core Domain Subtest Scaled Score mean. Both types of comparisons will help determine whether a particular Core Domain Score can be interpreted. (Two subtest scaled scores can be compared across domains as well.)

Find the difference between the two subtests. Enter this value in the Difference column for each of the subtests.

Locate the value required to reveal a statistical difference between two subtests within a domain in Table B.7 in the NEPSY Manual (pp. 316 for ages 3–4; pp. 317–318 for ages 5–12). The clinician should be very careful that he or she is on the correct page for the child's age level. The clinician will want to use the values in the white area of the table that represent differences significant at the more stringent .05 level, rather than those that appear above the diagonal in the blue-shaded area. The .05 significance level represents a 95% probability that the difference in the scores does not reflect a chance occurrence. The values in the blue area of Table B.7 represent scores required for significance at the .15 level (85% likelihood that the difference does not occur by chance). The .15 level allows for too much error.

The clinician should enter the value required for a significant difference between the two subtests in the *Required for Significance* column for the two subtests (same number in each). If the value in the *Difference* column is equal to or greater than the value in the *Required for Significance* column, then there is a significant difference at the .05 level between the two subtests. On the Core Domain Grid of the NEPSY Data Worksheet, the clinician will show this difference in the *Difference* column.

EXAMPLE: Suppose the examiner wants to know if there is a statistically significant difference between 10-year-old Lyndsey's VA Subtest Score of 10 and her AARS of 5. He or she locate VA on Table B.7 for Ages 5 to 12 (p. 317) and then move horizontally two columns to the right to the column "AARS." Here the examiner sees the value required for a significant difference between VA and AARS (4.11). Because the difference between VA and AARS (5) is equal to or greater than 4.11, the difference is significant. Therefore, on the Attention/Executive Grid of the NEPSY Data Worksheet, the examiner enters *4. I I* in the *Needed for Significance* column in the row for the VA Subtest and *AARS* in the column headed *Domain Subtest Discrepancies*, indicating that there is a significant discrepancy between VA and AARS. Likewise, the examiner enters *4. I I* in the AARS row of the *Needed for Significance* column and *VA* in the *Domain Subtest Discrepancies* column. Each pair of Core Subtest Scores is then checked and recorded in this way. Frequencies are not given for these comparisons because the total number of pair-wise comparisons for which to provide frequencies would be very large and unwieldy.

The clinician may wish to continue a pair-wise comparison of any Expanded subtests given in addition to the Core subtests but should not enter them on the Core Domain Grid, because Expanded subtests are not used in computing the Core Domain Score. He or she should use the designated area on the NEPSY Data Worksheet to enter Expanded Subtest results. The clinician does not have to make comparisons for all subtests. Because there are only two to three subtests in a domain, a significant difference between a single pair of Core subtests will cause the Core Domain Score to be uninterpretable. It will not reflect the child's functioning overall in that domain. Therefore, when "eyeballing" the results, the clinician should select the pair of scores that has the greatest discrepancy and consult Appendix B to see whether that apparent discrepancy is significant.

When you have already used the Core Domain Grid for the comparison between a Core Domain Subtest scaled score and the Core Domain Subtest scaled score mean, you can do your pairwise comparisons and enter only the name of the test with which there is a discrepancy in the Difference *and leave out the rest of the entries.* Either of the methods can be used alone, however, to reveal significant intradomain discrepancies in scores that preclude the interpretation of that Core Domain Score.

Enter percentiles and performance levels for Subtest Scaled Scores. The percentiles of subtest scaled scores help determine performance level. If Susie earned a scaled score of 10 on the Comprehension of Instructions subtest, her score has a percentile rank of 50. (NEPSY subtest mean=10 ± 15.) This percentile falls within the range of the 26th to 75th percentile; therefore, Susie's performance would be *At Expected Level* for age. The clinician should enter the classifications (performance levels) for the scaled scores on the NEPSY Data Worksheet in Appendix A.

3. Compare the Difference Between a Core and/or Expanded Subtest Scaled Score to the Average of All Core and Expanded Subtest Scaled Scores Within a Domain

This is a way to look at the child's functioning on a particular task in relation to a broader range of functioning within a particular domain across Core and Expanded subtests. This comparison cannot be used to determine the interpretability of a Core Domain Score, however, because it includes Expanded Subtest

Scores which are not included in the computation of the Core Domain Scores. Table B.4 (pp. 312–313) in the Manual is used for this comparison.

Across Domain Subtest Differences

At the subtest level comparisons can also be made across domains to look at neurocognitive development and patterns of functioning across modalities.

1. Compare the Core Subtest Scaled Score to the NEPSY Subtest Scaled Score mean.

The child's single subtest score is compared to the average performance on NEPSY (mean=10±3) of a child that age in the standardization population. This is the comparison that is used for the overview of general neurocognitive development in interpretation at the psychometric level. As seen in Rapid Reference Box 4.9, a score of 9 to 12 suggests performance *At Expected Level* for a child of that age (26th to 75th percentile). A score of 13 or above suggests performance *Above Expected Level* (>75th percentile), and a score of 8 or 7 suggests *Borderline (Slightly Below Expected Level)* performance (11th to 25th percentile). A weakness in terms of in the general population of any age as represented by the standardization sample appears at a score of 6, 5, or 4, which is *Below Expected Level* (3rd to 10th percentile). A score of 3, 2, or 1 is *Well Below Expected Level* (<2nd percentile). The NEPSY age norm Table A.4 (pp. 272–291) in the manual is used for this comparison.

This method compares the child's performance to that of the normative sample on which NEPSY was standardized (NEPSY mean=10±3). For instance, if Pippas performance achieved a scaled score of 14 on the Narrative Memory Subtest, which would be more than +1 standard deviation from the subtest mean for the normative sample her age, her performance level would be *Above Expected Level* for age. In terms of the general population, Pippa's performance would be interpreted as a significant strength. Conversely, if Sasha achieved a scaled score of 4 significant at the .15 confidence level, the clinician might wish to report that Sasha's visuospatial integration for paper/pencil copying of geometric figures was borderline.

EXAMPLE: *(This is a segment of a report only. It is not meant to represent a full discussion of test results.)* Sasha's performance in making pencil lines through winding tracks quickly and accurately on the VP Subtest of NEPSY was *Below Expected Level* for age in terms of the normative group. It was not, however, a relative weakness for Sasha in terms of his personal subtest mean (8.5) on the NEPSY Core across domains. SS for the VP subtest revealed slow performance and poor graphomotor control in comparison to age-mates. Written work will be difficult for Sasha, especially if it must be accomplished under time constraints. Additionally, his visuospatial analysis integrated with his ability to use paper and pencil to copy geometric figures was *Below Expected Level* for age. It was not a relative weakness, but was borderline, in terms of Sasha's own functioning on the NEPSY Core. Therefore, Sasha may experience some difficulty in copying from the board or his book to a paper. On the Imitating Hand Positions Subtest, Sasha was required to imitate the examiner's hand positions by integrating visual-spatial analysis, kinesthetic feedback from positions, and motor programming to perform this task. His performance was not only significantly weak in comparison to the mean performance of children his age in the standardization sample, but his performance was also a relative weakness in terms of his personal NEPSY Core Subtest mean.

Overall, it can be seen that Sasha's performance on these three subtests was poor in comparison to the general population of his age. In terms of his own functioning, however, it is notable that the more complex the task, the more his performance declined. While all three tasks required fine motor coordination, VP showed the least need for visuo-spatial analysis and executive functions and required simple graphomotor control for speed and accuracy. DC also required graphomotor control, but it further required a significant amount of visuospatial analysis. It is also interesting to note that DC is untimed (unlike VP) so speed does not appear to be the significant factor in Sasha's declining performance on a graphomotor task, at least in terms of his own ability. The task that required the integration of the greatest number of functions, (motor programming, visuospatial analysis, and kinesthetic feedback) was the one on which Sasha showed the weakest performance of the three tasks. His performance was weak even in terms of his own ability. It would appear that Sasha has difficulty with integrative functions that require motor output, and the more complex the task, the more difficult is the task for Sasha.

2. Compare a single Subtest Scaled Score to the average of all Core Subtest and Expanded Scaled scores across Domains.
If a Full NEPSY has been administered, the clinician may wish to compare a subtest to the subtest mean for all of the Core and Expanded subtests in NEPSY (Table B.5) (pp. 314–315 in the manual). The subtest mean is computed just as in the previous comparison, but the Expanded Subtest Scaled Scores are be included in the computation. Using the previous example of Sasha's performance, the interpretation might be revised as follows:

EXAMPLE *(a segment of the report only; no conclusions would be drawn on the basis of one subtest):* Sasha's performance was not only significantly weak in comparison to the mean performance of children his age in the standardization sample, but it also represented a relative weakness in terms of his own functioning based on his mean subtest performance across all domains on the Full NEPSY.

Table B.6 (p. 315) allows comparison of a single subtest or several subtests individually with the average of 12 Core and Expanded subtests across domains for ages 3 to 4 (top of the page). The same comparison can be made for the average of 20 Core and Expanded subtests across domains for ages 5 to 12 (bottom half of the page). For 5 to 6-year-olds, differences are computed based on the average of 19 subtests. List Learning is omitted because it is only given to children ages 7 and older.

3. Compare differences between two subtest scaled scores across domains required for statistical significance using pair-wise comparisons
This comparison is made just as it was between two subtests within a domain (see p. 129). SSs on NEPSY are consistent with the process approach (Kaplan, 1988)

to clinical neuropsychological assessment. They provide a way to interpret subcomponents of a Total Score (e.g., Speed vs. Accuracy on VP) in order to help the clinician identify the deficit contributing to poor performance more precisely. For example, the clinician might use a comparison of SSs of a specific Total Score, if he or she wishes to determine if there was a significant loss of information in the 30 min between an immediate and a delayed memory trial. The clinician might compare 10-year-old Bonnie's Supplemental Scaled Score for Immediate Memory for Faces (11) with her Supplemental Scaled Score for Delayed Memory for Faces (6) to reveal that her average Total Score for Memory for Faces (9) is misleading. Table B.7 is used to determine that the difference of 5 between the Immediate and Delayed Memory for Faces scores is significant at the .05 level.

> **EXAMPLE:** In the report the clinician might interpret these results in the following way. *(Segment of a report not meant to imply that conclusions would be drawn from one subtest):* Although Bonnie's Memory for Faces Total Score was *At Expected Level,* suggesting that she should be able to recognize faces immediately after exposure and over time, inspection of her SSs for this subtest revealed a different story. Her Immediate Memory for Faces performance was *At Expected Level,* suggesting average incidental learning and facial recognition skills, but she did not retain the information well. Thirty minutes after the Immediate Recall Trial, Bonnie's performance was *Below Expected Level* on the SS for Delayed Memory for Faces. These results suggest that Bonnie encodes the visual information in her short-term memory buffer, but does not consolidate it in long-term memory. This deficit in facial memory may relate to Bonnie's visuospatial deficits, as seen on her weak subtest performances in the Visuomotor Domain, and to her visual attention deficit revealed in the Attention/Executive Function Domain of NEPSY. Bonnie is reported to have social difficulties, and this problem may be related to her poor facial recognition skills. *(Further assessment of facial memory and visual memory is indicated in order to confirm the finding of poor facial memory and to see if she has a more generalized visual memory problem.)*

STEP 3: Interpret Domain Scores and Develop Overview of Test Profile

If the Core Domain Score is not interpretable due to discrepancies among the Core Subtest Scores within the domain, that should be reported and no further interpretation of overall functioning from the Core Domain Score should be made. This might be expressed in the following way: "Because there is significant intradomain scatter among the subtests of the Sensorimotor Core Domain, this Core Domain Score does not reflect overall functioning in the sensorimotor area and cannot be interpreted. Therefore, interpretation will be undertaken at the subtest level." If you have determined, through the decision chart on the Core Domain Grid of the NEPSY Data Worksheet, that a particular Core Domain Score may be interpreted, proceed with the following steps.

1. *Find statistical differences at the Core Domain level.* Table B.1 (p. 305) is used to find differences between Core Domain Scores required for statistical significance. Locate the child's age in the left-hand column. Place a ruler under the .05 significance level, horizontal line of values for that age. The domains to be compared (i.e., Language-Memory) are listed across the top of the table. Locate the comparisons you need to make. Follow the column down to the row for the child's age and your chosen confidence level. The value listed is the difference between those two domain scores which is required for statistical significance. Compare the difference in the child's Core Domain Scores with that value. If the difference between the two Domain Scores is greater than or equal to the value listed, then there is a statistical difference between the child's performance on the two domains being compared. Compare all domains. Then check the frequency of the difference to be sure that, despite its statistical significance, it occurs rarely enough to be considered outside normal variation. This is achieved in the following step.

2. *Determine the frequency of the Core Domain differences.* Locate the percentages of the standardization sample by obtaining various Core Domain Score discrepancies in Table B.2 on pp. 306 to 307 of the NEPSY *Manual* for ages 3.0 to 4.11 and on pp. 308 to 309 for ages 5.0 to 12.11. Locate the two domains compared at the top of the table. Scan down the far left-hand column until you locate the value of the discrepancy you obtained between those two domains. Move horizontally to the appropriate column on the right. Where the row and column intersect is the percentage of the standardization sample obtaining that discrepancy. If the frequency (percentage) in parentheses beside the appropriate discrepancy is ≤15, the difference is unusual enough to be considered significant. Make any comparisons needed in various combinations of domains. If the frequency suggests that the difference is greater than the extreme 15% of the normal population, then the difference can be viewed as abnormal (Kaufman & Lichtenberger, 1999). Note significant differences between domains by entering the abbreviations for the domains that differ in the appropriate box for each domain (i.e., if Attention/Executive differs with Memory and Learning, write "M/L" in the box by Attention/Executive and "A/E" in the box beside Memory and Learning.) Rapid Reference 4.10 shows abbreviations for core domains. If there are no differences between any Core Domain Scores, you can assume there

is little variance in the child's functioning across domains. You would interpret these subtests in your report after the discussion of Core Domain Scores.

3. *Determine through subtest discrepancies whether a Core Domain Score can be interpreted:* On the core Domain Grids of the NEPSY Data Worksheet, there is a decision chart on which the clinician circles *Yes* or *No* after determining whether a Core Domain Score can be interpreted. The clinician should do this for each Core Domain. In the examples above, the Attention/Executive Core Domain Score would not be interpreted, because significant differences were seen within the domain. If there are no significant differences, or there are some significant differences, but the frequency of such differences is too high to be outside the bounds of normal variation, then the Core Domain Score can be interpreted as reflecting the child's functioning overall in that domain. In the latter case, if, for example, the frequency was 25%, the clinician would probably want to discuss the difference as being an indicator of a possible problematic area. The frequency indicated that this difficulty occurred in 25% of the children who were the examinee's age. In other words, the child is functioning in this domain at the top of the bottom quartile for children his or her age. Subtests should always be interpreted both individually and in relation to each other, regardless of whether the Core Domain Scores can be interpreted.

≡ *Rapid Reference 4.10*

Abbreviations for Core Domains

Attention/Executive Functions	A/E
Language	L
Sensorimotor	S
Visuospatial	V
Memory and Learning	M/L

Determine the Performance Levels for the Core Domain Scores

The percentile rank of the Core Domain Score is one way to express the level at which an individual performs. For instance, if 6-year-old Johnny obtained a Language Core Domain Score of 97, the percentile rank of that score would be 42. Therefore, he performed better on the Language Domain of NEPSY than 42 out of 100 children his age in the standardization sample that represents the general population of children ages 3 to 12 in the United States. Levels of performance for the Core Domain Scores range from *Above Expected Level* (>75th percentile) to *Well Below Expected Level* (≤2nd percentile). A Language Core Domain Score of 97 is *At Expected Level* (26th to 75th percentile) because the percentile rank of 42 falls within that range. Therefore, the clinician can interpret Johnny's language functioning on NEPSY overall as being *At Expected Level* for age. Enter this classification on the NEPSY Data Worksheet.

Interpretation of the Core Domain Confidence Interval

The Core Domain confidence interval on the data worksheet is important for your discussion of test results be-

---

CAUTION

Be Careful of Conclusions Drawn from Core Domain Scores Only

- The domains represent only 2 to 3 subtests, so any significant discrepancies between subtests or between a subtest and the Core Domain mean will make the Core Domain Score uninterpretable.
- Even when Core Domain Scores reflect no intradomain and or interdomain scatter, do not interpret them alone.
- CHECK discrepancies CAREFULLY.
- Always interpret at the Subtest level, including SS and QOs.

---

cause it reminds the reader that there is error inherent in the Core Domain Score. In other words, there is a 95% chance (the level of confidence chosen) that Johnny's true Language Core Domain Score falls in the range of 88 to 107. We can see that his confidence interval covers the percentile range from 20 (percentile for 88) to 68 (percentile for 107). A percentile rank of 20 is slightly *Below Expected Level*, or *Borderline*, (11th to 25th percentile), according to the NEPSY classification system. A percentile rank of 68 is *At Expected Level* (26th to 75 percentile). Therefore, in the report, the clinician wants to report Johnny's performance level as *At Expected Level* for age, but he or she may also want to report and interpret the confidence interval. A segment of the interpretation may say, "There is a 95 percent likelihood that Johnny's true language performance on NEPSY, taking into account the standard error of measurement, falls in the range of 88 to 107. His overall language performance on NEPSY could range from slightly *Below Expected Level* to *At Expected Level* for age." This information is useful for understanding Johnny's performance at the subtest level performance within the domain.

General Overview of the Test Profile Expressed by Core Domain Scores

With those Core Domain Scores that are adequate expressions of overall functioning in their domains, you are now in a position to describe the child's general neurocognitive status. Although a lack of discrepancy within or between Core Domain Scores is unusual in assessment of children with various disorders, it can happen. This is a rare event, however, and the examiner is cautioned to be very sure that Core Domain Scores do not express any intradomain scatter before he or she interprets them. The clinician is cautioned not to describe a child's general neurocognitive status from Core Domain Scores alone, even when they reflect functioning within the domain and there is no difference among them. SSs and QOs may show differences not reflected in scaled scores, so they should be interpreted.

Nonetheless, when this is the case, the Core Domain Scores can be used to describe general neurocognitive status. Even in the rare circumstance of no within or between differences for Core Domain Scores, the clinician should discuss the Core Subtest performance. Taking such a case, let us suppose that Sam suffered a bout of viral meningitis, from which there are not usually sequelae, unlike bacterial meningitis, which can cause significant damage. He was referred for a neuropsychological evaluation by his pediatrician. Interpretation of his general neurocognitive status may be reported in the following way when all Core Domain Scores reflected Sam's functioning within the domains, and there were no significant discrepancies between the Core Domain Scores.

EXAMPLE: *(An excerpt of a report only; not meant to imply that only Core Domain Scores would be reported)* Sam, a 10-year-old boy who suffered viral meningitis for five days one month prior to this evaluation with no apparent sequelae, displayed a relatively even test profile of functioning across the five NEPSY Core Domains assessing attention and executive functions; language, sensorimotor, visuospatial functions, and memory and learning. His performance in all these domains was well within the average range for his age. Slight differences were noted between the Core Domain Score representing language, in which he received a score at the bottom of the high average range for his age (110), and that representing sensorimotor functions (94). Because the discrepancy between the two Core Domain Scores was not significant, and none of the subtest scores were *Borderline*, or *Below Expected Level*, this relative difference should be of no major concern for his performance in school and everyday life. Sam and his parents describe him as very verbal and more drawn to intellectual activities, such as books and computers, than to sports. This background information is in accordance with the pattern of performance observed in the assessment [*subtests to be discussed would be discussed here*]. Thus, his general neurocognitive status provided no evidence of any negative sequelae following his recent illness.

Examples of diagnostic conclusions representing specific instances where comparisons of test scores yield significant differences are presented below.

Interpretation of NEPSY When Core Domain Scores Show Interdomain Differences, But No Intradomain Scatter

When a comprehensive overview of the child's neurocognitive status is the aim then the child's performance in relation to the average for his or her age is the comparison of interest. Therefore, the NEPSY Core Domain Mean of 100 ± 15 and the NEPSY Core and Expanded Subtest and Supplemental Scaled Score mean of 10±3 are used for comparison. Intraindividual comparison of the performance level in the different domains is also of great interest. Such is the case, for example, when the differences between the domains is large and you want to demonstrate that the child has a specific impairment in a particular domain.

Suppose that on the NEPSY Data Worksheet you have determined that Ronnie's Language Core Domain Score is significantly lower than all other Core Domain Scores at a frequency which places the performance outside the range of normal variation. The Core Domain does not show significant intradomain scatter, so it can be interpreted. Therefore, in your report you want to discuss what this signifies. You can use the performance level descriptors based on Core Domain percentiles to describe the functional area.

EXAMPLE: *(Only a segment; not intended to imply conclusions were drawn from one finding)* Ronnie's Language Core Domain Score was *Below Expected Level* and reflected his performance on the language tasks overall on NEPSY. The Attention/Executive Function, Sensorimotor, Visuospatial, and Memory and Learning Core Domain Scores were all *At Expected Level.* There was a significant difference between Ronnie's performance on the Language Core Domain and all other domains, suggesting a significant language deficit for Ronnie in relation to his other average abilities. All subtest performance within the Language Domain were *Well Below Expected Level* (Comprehension of Instructions) or *Below Expected Level* (Phonological Processing and SN) [subtest level comparisons, SS and QOs would then be discussed]. Ronnie is in need of a thorough language assessment and treatment by a speech/language pathologist specialized in the treatment of children. Treatment should also include training, either by the speech pathologist, reading specialist, or a special education teacher, in phonological awareness in order to diminish the risk of dyslexia as formal reading instruction starts.

Interpretation of Core Domain Scores with Both Interdomain and Intradomain Differences

The example in the preceding section is more an exception than the rule for Core Domain Scores on NEPSY. More frequently than not, children have diffuse dysfunction across and within domains. If the Core Domain Grid on the NEPSY Data Worksheet has revealed significant subtest scatter within a Core Domain, you should not interpret the Core Domain Score as representing general functioning in that domain, nor discuss it as being significantly different from any other Core Domain Score. As noted previously, the Core Domain Score is a global score, and it may mask deficits within the domain, which the clinician should interpret.

EXAMPLE: If 6-year-old Julie earned a Sensorimotor Core Domain Score *At Expected Level,* but her performance on the VP within that domain was *Well Below Expected Level,* the examiner could not reliably interpret her sensorimotor functioning overall as being *At*

Expected Level. The clinician may need to discuss intradomain scatter and its implications for overall functioning within that domain. For example *(only a segment; not intended to imply conclusions were drawn from one finding),* you might say, "Julie obtained a Sensorimotor Core Domain Score *At Expected Level.* Her Core Domain Score does not reflect her sensorimotor functioning overall, however, because there was significant intradomain scatter between her poor performance on the VP subtest and the average results on the other two subtests in that domain." *(Then you would go on to discuss the Sensorimotor Core Subtests, other test findings, and pertinent recommendations.)*

STEP 4: Interpret Subtest Scores Other Than Scaled Scores

Some of the subtests on NEPSY do not have scaled scores. Because the distributions are skewed, they can not support a scaled score, so smoothed percentiles or cumulative percentiles are used instead. The skills assessed in these subtests tend to develop early in normally developing children, so most children in the standardization group were able to achieve "high" total scores. This is one difficulty in standardizing a neuropsychological assessment, because such a tool is usually used to assess children with disorders. One way to compare the performance of the child with an impairment to that of the normally developing children in the standardization sample is to use smoothed percentile ranks and percentile rank ranges.

Expanded Subtests That Have Smoothed Percentile Ranks

Some of the Expanded subtests (see Rapid Reference Box 4.11) use smoothed percentile ranks instead of scaled scores. These scores can be used to locate the child's performance relative to that of the standardization sample. This provides more useful information than the exact percentile obtained, which could be misleading when the distribution is not normal (Korkman, Kirk, & Kemp, 1998).

When you scored the Expanded subtests that had percentile rank scores, you entered those scores on the Domain Analyses Page in the columns to the right of the appropriate Domain graph. These columns show the percentile rank in alignment with the scaled scores. The performance level descriptor is printed in the column to aid you in interpreting the score. As noted earlier, the percentile rank ranges are: >75th percentile, *Above Expected Level;* 26th to 75th percentile, *At Expected Level;* 11th to 25th percentile, *Slightly Below Expected Level (Borderline);* 3rd to 10th percentile, *Below Expected Level;* ≤2nd percentile, *Well Below Expected Level.* The percentile ranks for the selected Expanded subtests should be entered on the Expanded Subtest Grid for the appropriate domain of the NEPSY Data Worksheet in Appendix A.

EXAMPLE: *(Report segment only; not meant to imply that a conclusion would be drawn from one finding)* Denise, a 3-year-old girl, attained a percentile rank at the 11th to 25th percentile on the Statue Subtest. The clinician might interpret her performance in this way, "Denise's ability to inhibit motor response in the presence of noise distracters was borderline." Inter-

≣ *Rapid Reference 4.11*

Expanded Subtests with Smoothed Percentiles—How and Why

For some subtests total raw scores are converted to percentile ranks, not scaled scores. This is necessary because

- The underlying distributions are highly skewed, because normally developing children for whom an assessment must be standardized are able to perform these tasks at an early age.
- The ability to identify the child who was functioning below normal level is crucial even though most normally developing children can accomplish the task.

Subtests that have smoothed percentile ranks are

- The Expanded Subtests—Finger Discrimination, Route Finding, Manual Motor Sequences, Oromotor Sequences, and Knock and Tap.
- Statue for 5- to 12-year-olds.

Smoothed percentile ranks are derived by inspecting the progression of scores within and across ages and eliminating minor sampling irregularities by smoothing.

Percentile ranges, rather than exact percentile values, are chosen because identification of a specific percentile value could be misleading when the underlying distribution is nonnormal. Descriptors for the percentile ranks and cumulative percentages are found in Rapid Reference Box 4.1.

---

preting the percentile rank in this example would be no different than interpreting a scaled score of 7 or 8, both of which would fall within the 11th to 25th percentile range. (A scaled score of 7 has a percentile of 16, and a scaled score of 8 has a percentile rank of 25.)

SSs with Cumulative Percentages

As discussed previously, SSs are extremely useful for interpreting subcomponents of a subtest Total Score. We have already considered SSs that have scaled scores. Now we consider SSs that have cumulative percentages for comparison to the standardization sample instead of scaled scores. (See Rapid Reference 4.12.)

Some Supplemental Scores did not support a Scaled Score because many normally developing children obtained high scores and few normally developing children obtained low scores. Therefore, scores are presented in terms of cumulative percentages that represent base rates of occurrence in the standardization sample. These scores are interpreted using the same performance level descriptors as the Expanded subtests with smoothed percentile ranks.

EXAMPLE: Suppose that you wish to know whether a child who performed poorly on VA was inattentive, impulsive, or both. You could review the SSs for omission and commission errors on each section of the VA Subtest. For example, 9-year-old Mark made one omission error on the first array (Cats), which occurred in only 11 to 25% of the stan-

Rapid Reference 4.12

Supplemental Scores that have Cumulative Percentages

Some Supplemental Scores are scaled (AA, RS, Memory for Faces and Memory for Names—Immediate, and Memory for Faces and Memory for Names—Delayed). (See NEPSY *Manual* Table C.1; pp. 319–326)

A. Problems in standardizing a neurospsychological instrument are
   - Normally developing children can do many of the tasks at an early age.
   - Assessment will be used for children with deficits.
   - Must compare performance to that of normally developing children.
   - Some Supplemental Scores do not support a scaled score because
     —The raw scores did not have a normal distribution.
     —They had ceiling or floor problems (too many normally developing children obtained high scores or too few obtained low scores).

B. Some Supplemental Scores presented as cumulative percentages, representing the pure base rates of occurrence in the standardization sample.

C. These Supplemental Scores are in Tables C.2–C3 (pp. 327–329 in the NEPSY *Manual*).

D. Attention/Executive Domain: AA and RS each Omission, Commission Errors; VA Bunny and Faces each time, Omission, Commission; Design Fluency Structured Array and Random Array.

E. Language Domain: SN Time and Accuracy; Verbal Fluency: Animals, Food/Drink; Semantic, Phonemic.

F. Sensorimotor Domain: Fingertip Tapping Repetitions and Sequences across hands; Preferred and Nonpreferred hand across tasks; Imitating Hand Positions Preferred and Nonpreferred; VP Train, Car, & Motorcycles each.

G. Memory and Learning Domain: Narrative Memory—free and cued Recall; List Learning: Learning Effect; Interference Effect, Delay Effect.

dardization sample for 9-year-olds, according to Table C.2 (p. 329 in the *Manual*). His performance level was borderline. Mark made five omission errors on the complex attention section (Faces) of the VA Subtest. This level of errors occurred in 3 to 10% of the children Mark's age in the standardization sample. Therefore, his performance level was *Below Expected Level* for age. With regard to Commission Errors (CEs), the clinician sees that Mark made no errors on the Cat array, a performance that occurred in 26 to 75% of the standardization sample. Mark made four CEs on the Face array, as did 26 to 75% of 9-year-olds in the standardization sample. Thus, CEs were *At Expected Level*. Mark's performances would be described as *Borderline* or *Slightly Below Expected Level* for Omission Errors (OEs) on the Cat array and on the Faces section. His CE rate was *At Expected Level* on both the Cat and the Faces sections of the VA Subtest.

(Report segment only; not meant to imply that a conclusion would be made from one finding.)

These results might be interpreted in the following way: Mark's attention as measured by omission errors was at a *Borderline* level on a simple visual attention task and *Below Expected level* for age on a complex attention task. This performance suggests inattention that increases with the complexity of the visual attention task. Impulsivity, as measured by commission errors, was *At Expected Level* for both simple and complex visual attention. These results suggest that on tasks requiring visual attention, Mark is likely to be inattentive, but not impulsive.

QOs That Are Compared to Base Rates

The QOs on NEPSY, like the SSs, reflect the process approach (Kaplan, 1988) of clinical neuropsychological assessment. Often observations about the manner in which a child completes a task are as important in helping the clinician reach a final diagnosis as the score the child obtains. Some of these important observations have been quantified on NEPSY to allow the clinician to compare a child's performance to age-related base rates. Although all possible QOs could not be included in or quantified for NEPSY, you are encouraged to record other observations that may be of interest. These observations may contribute to the formulation of recommendations for treatment or remediation.

When you scored the QOs, you entered them on the back page of the Record Form. Here they are grouped into categories of observations across tests, as well as combinations of specific behaviors. Cumulative percentages are provided for the normative group by age and for clinical groups.

> **EXAMPLE:** During 5-year-old Amy's assessment, the clinician noticed that she frequently asked for repetition, so she tallied these instances in the boxes provided on the Phonological Processing, Comprehension of Instructions, and Sentence Repetition subtests. Amy asked for repetitions three times each on the Phonological Processing and Comprehension of Instruction subtests. She asked for repetitions five times on the Sentence Repetition subtest. When the clinician scored Amy's NEPSY, Table D.1 (pp. 343–344), told her that three instances of asking for a repetition on the first two subtests occurred in only 3 to 10% of the 5-year-olds in the standardization sample. The descriptor the clinician wrote next to each of the scores was *Below Expected Level.* Amy's five requests for repetitions on the Sentence Repetition subtest were *Well Below Expected Level* (<2% of the standardization sample).

STEP 5: Inspect NEPSY Data Worksheet for Interpretation at the Psychometric and Clinical Levels

The process of interpretation really began as the assessment was taking place, and the clinician was testing hypotheses. As results accumulated, the clinician may have noted indications of a problem and pursued a "branching approach" (Wilson, 1992). Further subtests may have been administered within one or more domains (Expanded Assessment) or across domains (Selective Assessment) to look for suspected diagnostic behavioral clusters. The clinician may have administered a Full Assessment to test further hypotheses that evolved during the evaluation process.

By this point the clinician will have chosen the type of comparisons he or she wants to make, or the clinician may have computed all possible differences to note any interesting discrepancies. The clinician have also recorded all scores, significant discrepancies, and performance levels on the NEPSY Data Sheet (Appendix A). It is likely, therefore, that he or she will have discarded some hypotheses, and the results are beginning to converge on some specific areas of concern.

Interpretation at the Psychometric Level: Analyzing the Test Profile for Comprehensive Overview of the Child's Neurocognitive Development

At this point, you interpret NEPSY at a psychometric level to look at neurocognitive development comprehensively. You will then move on to interpret at a clinical level, identifying deficits, analyzing their contribution to dysfunction as primary or secondary, and locating diagnostic behavioral clusters, which may point to a specific disorder.

Look at the NEPSY Data Worksheet (Appendix A) that you filled in earlier to locate strengths and weaknesses for your comprehensive overview of neurocognitive development in relation to normally developing children.

Significant strengths for Core and/or Expanded Subtest Scaled Scores should be interpreted first. For psychometric interpretation, compare the child's score to the norm, that is to scaled score mean of 10 ± 3. This interval represents performance of the normally developing child at any age as reflected in the NEPSY standardization population. Core Domain Scores which are interpretable (have no intradomain scatter) can also be interpreted psychometrically. You may wish to discuss the strongest area for a child, as well as individual strengths reflected in his or her subtest performance. You should then look for the child's relative strengths. For this comparison, you compute the child's subtest mean, either within or across domains, as you chose. Be sure to describe how the child's mean was computed, however.

EXAMPLE: (A segment of a report only) (in relation to her average performance across all domains for all of the Core and Expanded Subtests on NEPSY, Mary Beth displayed a relative strength in visuomotor integration. This can be observed in her very good performance in paper/pencil copying of geometric figures on the DC subtest.) If a child's personal mean is low, there may still be areas in which he or she can feel success in terms of his or her own functioning. It is just as important to identify strengths as it is to identify weaknesses (Korkman, Kirk, & Kemp, 1998). A child's learning might well be directed through the strong area or areas, whereas remediation is addressed in weak areas. An obvious example is that in which 5-year-old Mary Beth meets the DSM-IV criteria for a Receptive and Expressive Language Disorder (Developmental Language Disorder), but has well-developed visual perceptual and visuomotor skills. Pictures, charts, models, and manipulatives can be used to teach her.

An area of strength can also provide an extracurricular area of success. For instance, in the present example, Mary Beth may enjoy and be successful with crafts, art projects, model-building, or constructional activities. Developing a successful hobby will help Mary Beth's self-esteem so that she can face better the daily challenge of coping with weak language skills. Speech and language therapy, by contrast, will focus on strengthening receptive and expressive language skills.

Significant weaknesses should be considered next. Again, for interpretation at the psychometric level, you compare performance to the NEPSY Subtest Scaled Score mean and Core Domain mean to see how a particular child's neurocognitive development compares to that of the normally developing child as represented by the NEPSY standardization sample. Do the weaknesses all fall in one domain? Are they evident across domains? You should also compute relative weaknesses in terms of the child's own ability as you did for the strengths. Obviously, it is helpful to know which weaknesses are apt to affect the child's learning. Remediation or rehabilitation should focus the most on these areas. The child's strengths may provide compensatory means for circumventing a problem. A child might have a specific deficit within one domain or a pattern of deficits across domains.

EXAMPLE 1: At this level of interpretation 10 yr. old Chris's phonological deficit would be related to his reading disorder (an excerpt of a report only). *Chris's performance on Phonological Processing and Repeating Nonwords was Below Expected Level, suggesting a phonological deficit resulting in a mild dysphonetic dyslexia. No other subtests on NEPSY, including language subtests showed significant weaknesses. Reading remediation using a multisensory, structured phonics approach would be helpful.*

EXAMPLE 2: The child's significant strengths and weaknesses are identified in relation to the general population (using the NEPSY scaled score mean of 10±3), and to the child's own functioning (personal subtest mean) in a particular domain. Suppose that Hannah, aged 8, was referred for an evaluation due to reading difficulties. On the NEPSY, she achieved a scaled score of 5 on the Phonological Processing subtest. The clinician interpreted this score in terms of the general population of Hannah's age as a significant weakness when compared to NEPSY scaled score mean of 10±3. He wanted to determine if this was a relative weakness for Hannah in terms of her Language subtests overall. During scoring, the clinician averaged the three subtests of the Language Domain (SN, 8; Comprehension of Instructions, 11; Phonological Processing, 5). He determined that her language subtest mean was 8, which is not a significant weakness in terms of the general population, because it is within 1 SD of the NEPSY Subtest mean. The clinician then compared Hannah's Phonological Processing scaled score of 5 to her Language Domain Subtest mean and found a difference of 3.0. When he inspected Table B.3 for Ages 5 to 12, he noted that a difference of 2.33 (2.0 rounded) was significant at the .05 level. The frequency of such a difference occurs in 25% of the nonclinical standardization sample, however, so it would occur too frequently in 8-year-old children to be considered outside the range of normal variation. On the other hand, Hannah's difference was 3, and the clinician noted that a difference of 3.33 (3.0 rounded) occurs in only 10% of the norm group. Therefore, Hannah's subtest difference of 3.0 indicated a significant deficit in terms of her own language functioning on NEPSY. Furthermore, her phonological processing skills were a significant weakness in terms of the general population (NEPSY scaled score mean = 10±3), because a scaled score of 5 would be approximately 1.5 SD from the mean.

A possible interpretation is written as the following *(only a segment of a report):* "Hannah displayed understanding of linguistically complex oral instructions At Expected Level for age. Her performance on the Comprehension or Instructions Subtest (63rd percentile). Therefore, receptive language skills for Hannah were at a level better than 63 out of 100 children of 8 years. On the WISC-III, her expressive vocabulary performance was in the high average range (Vocabulary, 13), and verbal abstract reasoning was average (Similarities, 11). Hannah does not appear, therefore, to be subject to a generalized language disorder that often underlies a reading disability.

Hannah's SN was slightly *Below Expected Level* for age (25th percentile), however. Inspection of her SS for SN revealed a Time Score *Slightly Below Expected Level* (11–25% of the standardization sample), and Accuracy was *Below Expected Level* for age (3–10%). Hannah's results revealed borderline speed of access and poor naming ability, causing her word-finding problems. Her weakness in the basic expressive language ability of naming was also seen in her Memory for Names performance which was *Below Expected Level.* Therefore, *Hannah did appear to have a specific dysnomia (naming deficit).*

Hannah's phonological processing skills are not only significantly poor in terms of the general population of Hannah's age, as represented by the NEPSY standardization sample, but they also appeared as a relative weakness in terms of Hannah's language performance on the NEPSY Language Domain. Phonological processing is the ability to conceptualize speech-sound patterns and to manipulate those patterns. It is the underlying process in reading decoding and spelling. Hannah displayed a significant deficit in this area (5 percentile). It would appear that Hannah's deficit in phonological processing is related to her marked difficulty in reading decoding and spelling.

Academic achievement testing with the Wechsler Individual Achievement Test (WIAT) (Psychological Corporation, 1992) revealed that performance on the Basic Reading subtest (decoding) was in the low average range (Standard Score, 80; mean = 100±15), Spelling was borderline (75), but results on the Reading Comprehension Subtest were in the average range (99). The latter result suggests that Hannah is "finessing" the meaning from passages, even though she cannot decode all the words. This profile is typical of dyslexics with good reasoning ability.

Hannah's WISC-III Full Scale IQ was 106 (66th percentile), and there was no significant discrepancy between the Verbal and Performance Scales. Therefore, Hannah's FSIQ should be a reliable indicator of the level of her cognitive functioning overall. Both reading decoding and spelling skills showed a significant discrepancy with Hannah's ability level. Therefore, Hannah's test results provided evidence of a Reading Disorder and Disorder of Written Language (spelling), and she should be referred for learning disability intervention. To address her weakness in phonological processing, intensive work in multisensory phonological analysis of words is recommended, along with training to automatize access to high frequency words and irregular spellings.

Interpretation at the Clinical Level: Specifying and Analyzing Primary and Secondary Deficits, Locating and Interpreting Diagnostic Behavioral Clusters

As noted earlier in this chapter, interpretation at the clinical level involves specifying and analyzing primary and secondary deficits, locating diagnostic behavioral clusters (patterns of symptoms that cluster together and point to a specific disorder), and discussing all of the above in the context of all the factors impacting the child. If you are a neuropsychologist, you may choose to interpret in terms of neuroanatomic axes *without assumption of focal damage or focal dysfunction*. You have inspected and interpreted the NEPSY data for differences, strengths, and weaknesses in relation to the normally developing child in the first step of interpretation at the psychometric level. As you carried out this first step you identified areas of weakness, which you will now analyze more actively.

Poor performance in one area or across domains, suggesting deficits converging on a particular function, and your background in neuropsychology and the current research should help you recognize diagnostic behavioral clusters pointing to a particular disorder. By studying the deficits observed through the test results and in your observations of the child's performance during testing, you should analyze which deficits appear to be at the root of a dysfunction (primary deficit) and which deficits appear to be the result of the primary deficit adversely affecting another function (secondary deficit). Figure 4.1 demonstrates an example of a diagnostic cluster.

Using the preceding case of Hannah, let us see how the next step in interpretation at the clinical level should proceed.

EXAMPLE: *(A segment of a report only; not meant to encompass all possible findings or conclusions)* Hannah displayed the diagnostic behavioral cluster associated with dyslexia, including a primary deficit in phonological processing, which underlies the secondary deficit in mastering phonics, and marked difficulty in spelling and in decoding words. Her reading comprehension was significantly better than reading decoding skills or spelling, which often occurs in dyslexics who have good verbal reasoning ability. She had difficulty spelling in context, a particular problem for dyslexics. Furthermore, Hannah displayed another deficit known to be comorbid with dyslexia, poor lexical access. Speed of access was *Borderline* for age, and she displayed a primary deficit in naming, a basic expressive language function. Although slowed speed of access may be a primary deficit, it may be secondary to Hannah's difficulty in naming. Her primary deficit in naming (dysnomia) contributed to two secondary deficits, her word-finding problems reported by parents and teachers, as well as observed during the evaluation, and her poor performance in learning and recalling names. Her dysnomia was also seen in her Memory for Names performance, which was *Below Expected Level*. As is true of some dyslexics, Hannah did not appear to have any language deficits other than naming. Her receptive language understanding was good on NEPSY, and expressive vocabulary was within normal limits on the WISC-III. Finally, dyslexia is a highly heritable disorder, and family history showed evidence that there is a familial reading disorder in the paternal great-grandfather and the paternal uncle. Therefore, Hannah's primary and secondary deficits, as well as comorbid deficits, comprise a diagnostic behavioral cluster consistent with dyslexia.

Recommendations should include learning disability assistance, as well as intensive work in multisensory phonological analysis of words to address her phonological processing deficit, along with training to automatize access to high-frequency words and irregular spellings due to her poor performance in lexical access. (Recommendations would actually be enumerated at length—see Ch. 7.)

However, diagnostic behavioral clusters frequently cut across domain boundaries much more comprehensively than in Hannah's case.

EXAMPLE: The clinician has just evaluated Sarah, 9 years of age, and her NEPSY performance showed a Language Core Domain Score *At Expected Level* (98). All subtests were also at that same performance level. There was a significant difference between Sarah's higher Language Core Domain Score and her lower Attention/Executive Functions, Visuospatial, and Sensorimotor Core Domain Scores. There was not a significant difference between Language and the Memory and Learning Core Domain Score. Sarah performed very poorly on the Visuospatial Domain overall (Visuospatial Core Domain Score, 57). All of the Visuospatial Core and Expanded Subtest scaled scores were *Below Expected Level* (DC; SS, 4) or *Well Below Expected Level* (Arrows; SS, 2 and Route Finding; SS, 1). The Sensorimotor Domain and Attention/Executive Function Core Domains Scores were both *Slightly Below Expected Level (Borderline)*. Within the Attention/Executive Function Domain, Sarah's performance on AARS was *At Expected Level* (SS, 9). Sarah's Supplemental Scores for AARS revealed, however, that her AA on a simple selective auditory attention task was *At Expected Level* (SS, 11), but complex auditory attention on the RS, which required shifting attention, inhibition of response to a well-learned routine, and selective attention, was *Borderline* (SS, 7). In contrast, Sarah's performance on VA was *Below Expected Level* (SS, 5) overall. Inspection of the SS for VA showed Time (to completion) Scores were *Well Below Expected Level* on both simple and complex visual attention tasks. SS for OE and CE rates were *Below Expected Level* on both arrays. There was a significant difference (.05) between Sarah's better auditory and poorer visual attention.

Sarah's executive functions as assessed by Tower were *Below Expected Level* (SS, 6). Her ability to adhere to the rules for this problem-solving task was *Below Expected Level* on the Qualitative Observation for Rule Violations. Sarah did not seem to be able to plan intermediate moves in order to get a ball to a certain destination without taking a ball off the peg and putting it on the table, so she could put another ball on that peg. She continued to commit this rule violation even when corrected. Design Fluency, an Expanded Attention/Executive Function Subtest yielded an even poorer performance (SS, 5) than Tower, possibly due, at least partially, to the visuospatial aspects of the stimuli.

Sensorimotor Subtest scores were *Slightly Below Expected Level (Borderline)* on Fingertip Tapping (SS, 8), but there was a significant difference between the SSs for Repetitions (SS, 9) and for Sequences (SS, 6) which assesses the motor programming required for sequential finger movement. The VP Subtest, an assessment of graphomotor speed and accuracy, yielded a weak performance (SS, 6), *Below Expected Level* for age. SSs for Time and Error showed Sarah's time to completion as *Below Expected Level*, and her error rate was also at that level. Therefore, graphomotor function was both slow and poorly controlled. Sarah's performance on Imitating Hand Positions was also *Below Expected Level* (SS, 6). This performance was notable for the anxiety she seemed to display in having to attend closely to the examiner's hand as she attempted to reproduce the hand positions. This necessitated a greater need to look to another person than seemed comfortable for her. She had some difficulty with the motor programming, but she frequently used the wrong fingers, as if she could not analyze the visuospatial aspects of the hand position. Some of her errors seemed to be due to her anxiety, however. Her affect had been flat up until this subtest was begun, and then she became noticeably anxious.

Finally, Sarah's Memory Core Domain Score was *At Expected Level*. She performed very well *(Above Expected Level)* on Narrative Memory (SS, 13), and her performance was *At Expected Level* on Memory for Names (9). It was interesting to note, however, that Sarah's Learning Trial Supplemental Score on Names was *Borderline* (SS, 7), but the Delayed Memory for Names Supplemental Score was *At Expected Level* (SS, 11). This suggests that it took Sarah an extended period to consolidate the information. After a 30 min delay, she was actually able to recall more names correctly than she could immediately after the three learning trials. Sarah's Memory for Faces performance was *Below Expected Level* (SS, 5). Again, the examiner observed anxiety on this subtest. Sarah would glance at the photographs of children's faces very quickly. She had to be prompted to look at each face for 5 s. SS for Immediate and Delayed Trials were equally poor (SS, 5), and she seemed anxious again when she had to look at the photos for 5 s each.

Studying Sarah's NEPSY Data Sheet and pulling together the components of this complex profile the clinician would see the following diagnostic behavioral cluster:

1. Language functioning and verbal memory *At Expected Levels* on NEPSY with a Language Core Domain Score significantly better than the Visuospatial and Sensorimotor Domain Scores.
2. Visuospatial areas, visual attention, and facial recognition were *Below Expected Levels.*
3. Motor programming, graphomotor control were *Below Expected Level* and of significant associated movements were present.
4. Executive functions were *Below Expected Level,* including the Qualitative Observation for Rule Violations.
5. Sarah's performance was also notable for the anxiety she displayed when she was asked to look at the examiner's hand during the Imitating Hand Positions Subtest and at photographs of faces on the Memory for Faces Subtest.

Because you are staying current with professional reading and research, you would recognize this sample profile as being consistent with the pattern of deficits that occur in children with Nonverbal Learning Disability (Rourke, 1988). Sarah's highly significant visuospatial deficit would be the primary deficit, while poor facial recognition and visual attention, as well as poor performance on tasks with a visuospatial component (e.g., Design Fluency) would be secondary deficits. Sarah's anxiety at being required to look at people's faces is probably secondary to the social problems reported by her parents. The social deficits in children with

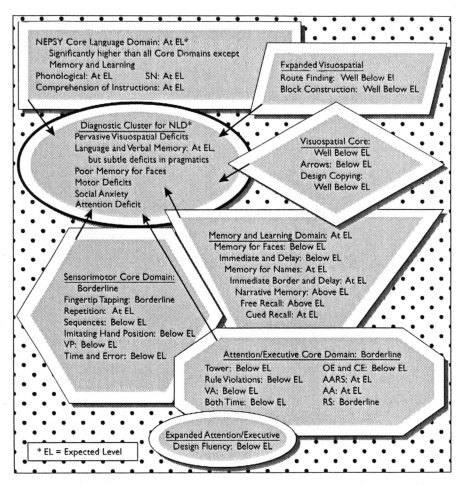

Figure 4.1 An Example of a Diagnostic Cluster for Nonverbal Learning Disability*

Nonverbal Learning Disability are thought to be secondary to the visuospatial deficit, because they do not perceive faces and nonverbal social cues well. Motor programming problems and dysexecutive function, especially when abstract reasoning or mental representation is needed, are comorbid deficits. You would not be ready to identify the diagnostic behavioral cluster as pointing to Nonverbal Learning Disability, however, until you had performed the final step in the interpretative process. This last step places Sarah's NEPSY performance in context. It fills in holes in the diagnostic picture, verifies your results, and helps you plan realistically for interventions.

STEP 6: Integrate and Verify NEPSY Interpretation with Other Assessment Results and Developmental, Neurobiological, Medical, Educational, and Environmental Information

Throughout the process of scoring, analyzing, and interpreting results, the clinician should hold the referral question in mind. She should ask herself questions about what may have caused the problem by comparing NEPSY Core and Expanded subtests, SSs, and QOs to the information available about the child. It may also be useful to refer to subtest intercorrelations to see what components may be included in the performance of different subtests (see shared abilities below). Note, however, that these may be different in the normally developing children of the standardization sample than in children with developmental or acquired disorders. By returning to the referral question or questions periodically as she undertakes the interpretative process, the clinician can be assured that she addresses it in her report.

Verification of Interpretation Within NEPSY

The process of verification which follows is dependent not only on inspecting results of other subtests within a domain for similar deficits, but also on reviewing performance *on subtests across domains that share abilities with the subtest being verified.* In this way, it is possible to review performances across Core and Expanded subtests, including SSs and QOs, to trace a diagnostic thread and corroborate the results seen on the test you are interpreting.

EXAMPLE: Suppose the clinician observed a lack of response inhibition on Knock and Tap in 11-year-old Charlie's performance on a Full NEPSY evaluation. Before interpreting it as a deficit, he would want to look at other measures where this component might have adversely affected performance.

In the Attention/Executive Domain the clinician needs to look at SSs for CEs, which represent impulsivity or a lack of response inhibition, on AARS and VA to see if they occurred at a significant level. He would want to know if a lack of response inhibition was present on the simple, on the complex, or on both tasks of these subtests. He could then compare the patterns on VA and AARS to those on the two parts of Knock and Tap. The QO for Off-Task Behavior on those two subtests might also reveal impulsive, off-task behavior. Furthermore, the clinician would want to inspect the notes he made during the Tower administration to see if Charlie worked impulsively on that subtest. He might also find that Charlie displayed impulsive responding on Design Fluency, perhaps more so on the Random Array than on the Structured Array (SSs). Statue is another subtest of inhibition of motor response, and the clinician may have administered this Expanded subtest in order to check his findings on Knock and Tap.

After reviewing other subtests within the same domain, the clinician will want to review similar results on other subtests that also require response inhibition. In the Language Domain, both Comprehension of Instructions and Phonological Processing can elicit impulsivity. Charlie may have demonstrated this by not waiting for the whole oral instruction or the whole phonological pattern before he began to respond. This fact would be present in his notes.

In the Sensorimotor Domain, the clinician may have noted impulsive responding on Imitating Hand Positions and Manual Motor Sequences. Charlie's SS for Time may be *Above Expected Level*, despite the fact that he made many errors. (Accuracy was *Below Expected Level*.) This suggests that he was impulsive and sacrificed accuracy for speed. Similarly, on DC in the Visuospatial Domain, Charlie may have executed his designs impulsively. The clinician's observational notes may reveal that he responded impulsively on Arrows, not looking at all eight arrows before making his choices. On Route Finding, the clinician may also have found impulsive responding.

In the Memory and Learning Domain, Charlie may have just glanced at the photos of children, so the clinician had to remind him to look for the full 5 s. If Sentence Repetition was administered, it may have revealed a significant level on the QO for Off-Task Behavior. Finally, Charlie's QOs for List Learning may show that he was not able to inhibit Novel Intrusions or Interference Intrusions on List Learning.

Thus, by looking within the same domain and across domains to establish a deficit pattern, the clinician can verify his interpretation of NEPSY results. Poor performance on one subtest in the absence of corroborating evidence is not sufficient to identify a dysfunction or disability (Korkman, Kirk, & Kemp, 1998). Significant findings for verification of interpretation would include:

- Performance level *Below* or *Well Below Expected Level*.
- Subtest results with scaled scores of less than 7.
- If a result is *Borderline*, it shows a significant discrepancy with other performances within or across domains.

When two or more significant findings, such as the following, point to the same deficit, then the working hypothesis can be accepted and the interpretation verified.

- two subtests performances
- a subtest performance and a qualitative observation
- a subtest performance and supplemental score

Interpretations must:

- be logical and consistent with the research investigating mechanisms of a disorder.
- have ecological validity that is related to actual events occurring in the child's life.

An interpretation can be considered *verified* provided that at least two of the following are true of the Subtest Results (which can include SSs):

- They assess the same function (e.g., other subtests of attention and/or executive function) within the same domain.
- They are not in the same domain and do not primarily assess that func-

tion, but the ability in question is required (e.g., response inhibition) and has adversely affected performance on the subtest.
- There are QOs (e.g., Rule Violations) to support the interpretation.

Verification and Integration of NEPSY Interpretation with Other Assessment Results and Developmental, Neurobiological, Medical, Educational, and Environmental Information

The final step before arriving at a diagnosis is to integrate NEPSY results with all other information available about the child in order to corroborate the findings with and verify your interpretation of them. Integrating the NEPSY results in this way helps you to understand the impact of the primary and secondary deficits on the

> ### CAUTION
>
> **Findings Must Be Logical and Consistent With Current Research Related to the Dysfunction**
>
> It is essential that your findings be logical in terms of
> - the referral question.
> - other assessment results.
> - developmental, medical, and environmental history.
>
> It is your responsibility as a neuropsychologist to keep abreast of current research in the field and to be sure that
> - your findings are consistent with that research.
> - you inform yourself in order to discuss pertinent details of research, resources, and treatment with the child's parents.

child's life, and to formulate a remediation or rehabilitation plan. This step allows you to obtain as complete a picture of the child's functioning as possible. It is essential that the assessment of risks faced by the child account not only for the neuropsychological profile, including both strengths and weaknesses, but also for the particular characteristics of the child's environment (Rourke, Fisk, & Strang, 1986).

A comprehensive neuropsychological assessment should include cognitive and achievement measures. Test results from the cognitive and achievement measures must be integrated with NEPSY performance. The comprehensive history (see NEPSY *Manual* pp. 410–417) obtained prior to the assessment is invaluable for this step of the interpretative process. The comprehensive history form and your pre-assessment interview with the parent provide information concerning family, school, and community. School records, teacher summaries, and behavioral rating scales can fill out the educational picture. This is especially important if the teacher and parent do not perceive the child's problems from the same perspective. Problems encountered in school and at home should be addressed in your neuropsychological interpretation.

A formal checklist to assess adaptive functioning can be an important adjunct to your NEPSY assessment. Multiple copies of such a checklist can be provided to parents, therapists, and teachers prior to the assessment, so that when you undertake this final interpretative integration of information, you have the data concerning the child's adaptive functioning. There are many such checklists available (Achenbach & Edelbrock, 1991; Conners, 1989). This type of checklist allows you to look at the child's emotional status, behavioral adjustment, and adaptive behavior. Children referred for neuropsychological assessment often experience difficulties in these areas. Comparing the child's neuropsychological profile and the context within which the child functions to the child's current adaptive failures increases the reliability of the forecast of the potential risks faced by the child in the future (Yeates & Taylor, 1997).

EXAMPLE: In the preceding case of Sarah, the clinician is still missing some important information until she completes this final interpretive step. Her parents' referral stated, "We are very concerned about Sarah's poor math skills. Sarah has always had problems making friends. We have always thought she was just extremely shy, but now we wonder if there is something more that is causing all of her learning and social difficulties." Therefore, there was evidence from the outset that Sarah had social problems and math difficulties, both characteristics in Nonverbal Learning Disability.

As soon as the clinician greeted Sarah in the waiting room, she noticed her flat affect and fleeting eye contact. Sarah continued to display these characteristics throughout the evaluation except when she became increasingly anxious on two subtests. When required to look at photographs of faces and study the examiner's hand position with her face in close proximity to it during the NEPSY administration, Sarah appeared anxious and uncomfortable. Teacher comments revealed, "Sarah's parents are so supportive of her, and our experience at school since kindergarten has been that they are a very warm, nurturing family. It is hard to see why Sarah has so much trouble relating to peers. Her older brother and younger sister are both very gregarious. Sarah always goes off by herself on the playground. When I try to facilitate interaction with other kids, she really does not seem to want to interact with them. She is never rude, however. She just seems uncomfortable and doesn't make eye contact well. Sarah relates better to adults." The comprehensive history and parent interview revealed concerns about Sarah's ability to relate to peers from early childhood to the present. A comment in the pediatrician's notes showed that Sarah's mother had discussed Sarah's social problems with him approximately six weeks prior to the evaluation. He questioned autism in his notes, but this was never mentioned to Sarah's mother. He did encourage an evaluation, however. Preschool records showed concern with "Sarah's extreme shyness." All of Sarah's background information revealed concerns with poor social interactions, so that piece of the puzzle fits the clinician's hypothesis of Nonverbal Learning Disability. The clinician would then want to turn to the cognitive and processing aspects of Nonverbal Learning Disability.

First, children with Nonverbal Learning Disability are known to have severe visual-spatial deficits. This was very apparent in Sarah's NEPSY results, but the clinician needs corroboration of this in everyday life. Her teacher's summary stated, "The class has begun working with maps in social studies, and Sarah seems to have a terrible time understanding maps and locating features on them. We learned about the compass points, so the children could use compass directions when discussing maps, but Sarah doesn't ever seem to remember where north is, even on a flat map. She has a terrible time reproducing tangrams when we work with geometric shapes in math. I have also noticed that she doesn't line up her digits correctly when she is copying math problems, and she has difficulty copying from the board, though that may be because of her poor handwriting." The teacher added, "I have wondered about a visual perceptual problem." The teacher and parents reported that Sarah loses her way easily. The teacher noted that it took Sarah nearly three weeks after school began to learn where her classroom was. Parents noted on the history, "Sarah seems to get turned around, so she doesn't remember which direction she needs to go." Developmental history revealed that Sarah still does not know left from right consistently. In dancing class, the teacher has noticed that Sarah is frequently using the wrong foot or going the wrong direction. Parent report and educational records from kindergarten and first grade showed that Sarah confused shapes when asked to identify them, although she knew all the names. In short, the impact of her visual-spatial deficit can certainly be verified from Sarah's background information.

Second, children with Nonverbal Learning Disability are known to have significant deficits in mathematics due to their visuospatial deficits, and concerns about math were part of her referral question. It is important, therefore, to integrate the visuospatial deficit seen on NEPSY and corroborated in her records with results from the achievement testing performed in Sarah's evaluation. Indeed, the clinician saw that Sarah showed a significant discrepancy between her math abilities and reading abilities. Therefore, her math abilities constituted a significant learning disability in terms of her cognitive ability on the cognitive assessment performed. The notes from the parent interview, the comprehensive history filled out by them prior to assessment, and the school records all revealed that Sarah qualifies for LD help in math and is receiving the same for 30 min a day in the resource room. Her parents reported that they worked with her nightly on math and noted, "She just doesn't seem to get it, no matter what we do." The LD teacher reported, "Even with individualized help, manipulatives, and Touch Math, Sarah is making little progress in math. She does best when she can work alone on the computer, but even then, she does not seem to make much progress." Therefore, additional testing, educational records, and parent and teacher report all provide evidence of a significant math disability.

Furthermore, the clinician's inspection of the achievement testing revealed reading decoding skills in the superior range, but reading comprehension in the low average range, despite Sarah's good vocabulary skills on the cognitive assessment. These results suggest that abstract reasoning was indeed a problem for her, as suggested by her NEPSY Tower results. At Sarah's level in school (fourth grade), comprehension questions are moving away from concrete facts to a more abstract, inferential level. Her teacher's comments in the educational records you requested prior to the assessment revealed that Sarah's teacher has concerns. ("Sarah has always been a strong reader, but she is experiencing increasing difficulties with reading comprehension, especially in making inferences from her reading.") School records and parent report revealed excellent initial reading skills, but a widening gap between reading decoding and comprehension in the past two years of school.

In the initial interview, the parents described Sarah's handwriting as "terrible." Her developmental history described her as "uncoordinated and somewhat clumsy." They noted, "She always seems to be bumping into things despite good eyesight." Developmental history showed that Sarah did not learn to skip or tie her shoes until age 7, and she still has difficulty riding a bike. Medical records showed delayed motor landmarks and hypotonia. This information provides evidence of the motor "clumsiness" and dysgraphia often seen in Nonverbal Learning Disability children and corroborates the findings of poor graphomotor performance seen on NEPSY.

Finally, integrating both test results and results from adaptive behavior rating scales is very important to understanding Sarah fully. These rating scales (*Achenbach Child Behavior Checklist and Teacher Report Form*, Achenbach & Edelbrock, 1991) were sent out prior to the evaluation in order to be available to the clinician when she interpreted results from your evaluation. The Teacher Report Forms from the classroom and LD teachers showed significant ratings on the scales for Withdrawal, Thought Problems, and Social. The classroom teacher rated Attention as *Significant*, while the LD teacher rated it *Borderline*. Both endorsed Anxiety as *Borderline*. The mother's and father's Child Behavior Checklists showed significant ratings on Withdrawal and Social. The mother's rating for Attention was *Significant;* the father's was *Borderline*. Both rated Anxiety as *Borderline*. All informants showed significant ratings for Internalizing behaviors. The rating scales showed good agreement on the same behavioral dimensions with the significance of the problem varying somewhat depending on setting and time spent with the child. The dimensions noted were consistent with the difficulties children with Nonverbal Learning Disability have with social interaction—appearing withdrawn and anxious in social situations. The significant ratings for Thought Problems appeared to grow out of concerns that Sarah was an enigma to those around her. She gave unusual, concrete responses, which could seem bizarre if one did not realize how concrete her thinking was. Therefore, there was a concern that she might have some type of thought disturbance that caused her to be such a loner. These behavioral ratings appeared consistent with the hypothesis of Nonverbal Learning Disability.

Attention was also noted as a concern, and it is often a problem for children with neurobiologically based developmental disorders. Sarah's NEPSY performance had been poor on complex auditory attention and both simple and complex visual attention. Additionally, she was observed losing her focus of attention during various parts of testing, not just on tasks which were difficult for her, although attentional problems increased under those circumstances. She acknowledged that "daydreaming" was a problem for her, and her teacher comments agreed with this opinion. ("Sarah often seems to slip off into her own world when she is supposed to be working.") Therefore, test results, the clinician's observations, the parent and teacher rating scales and comments all converged on an attentional component to Sarah's disorder.

At this point, then, having integrated Sarah's NEPSY performance with results from additional testing, as well as developmental, neurobiological, medical, educational, and environmental information, the clinician is ready to make her final diagnosis of a Nonverbal Learning Disability and to formulate recommendations.

⚓ TEST YOURSELF ⚓

1. An educational diagnostician can interpret NEPSY at the psychometric level. True or False?

2. Core Domain scores should always be interpreted. True or False?

3. The ultimate goal of a NEPSY assessment is to assess performance. True or False?

4. To look at a child's neurocognitive development, the clinician would use the NEPSY test and subtest means. True or False?

5. It is recommended that the clinician analyze the subcomponents contributing to a function. True or False?

6. A good clinician can always specify primary and secondary deficits. True or False?

7. Being current with the research helps clinicians to be aware of comorbid deficits. True or False?

8. An important underlying deficit in dyslexia can affect foreign language learning. True or False?

9. One of NEPSY's most important purpose is to pinpoint focal brain dysfunction very precisely. True or False?

10. The clinician should use the Core Domain mean to look at the child's relative strengths and weaknesses overall. True or False?

Fill in the Blanks:

11. The NEPSY can be interpreted at two levels: _____ and _____.

12. List the three goals of interpretation.

   (a) _____

   (b) _____

   (c) _____

13. Defining the child's strengths and weaknesses in terms of neurocognitive development would be a part of the _____ step of interpretation at the clinical level.

14. Specific impairments can be interpreted when a minimum of _____ findings are present on NEPSY.

15. The _____ and _____ are as important as the statistical significance.

(continued)

Matching: Each letter can be used only once.

16. _____ Diagnostic behavioral cluster

17. _____ Knock and Tap

18. _____ An individual with this training can interpret using neuroanatomic axes without implication of focal dysfunction or damage.

19. _____ Damage or dysfunction in children is usually _____.

20. _____ Outside normal variation ranks

(a) multifocal and diffuse

(b) Points to disorder

(c) for skewed distributions

(d) 12%

(e) neuropsychological

(f) smoothed percentile

Answers: 1. True; 2. False; 3. False; 4. True; 5. True; 6. False; 7. True; 8. True; 9. False; 10. True; 11. psychometric, clinical; 12. See Rapid Reference Box 4.5; 13. First; 14. 2; 15. neuropsychological, ecological; 16. b; 17. f; 18. e; 19. a; 20. d

Five

DOMAIN AND SUBTEST ANALYSIS

DOMAIN AND SUBTEST-BY-SUBTEST ANALYSIS

The following is an analysis of NEPSY to aid you in the interpretive process. The theoretical aspects of each domain are discussed. Each subtest is discussed in terms of functions being assessed, dysfunction(s) that cause poor performance, and questions to guide interpretation of the subtest. These questions assume that the results of each subtest are verified according to the preceding principles, after the inspection of shared abilities with other NEPSY subtests and the child's performance on them. As has been discussed, the interpretation process should include the integration of NEPSY results from additional testing, and all developmental, neurobiological, medical, educational, and environmental information.

Attention/Executive Function Domain

These subtests measure different aspects of attention and executive functions. Evidence has begun to accumulate that suggests multiple brain regions interact when mediating attentional processes (Barkley, 1996; Mirsky, 1996). Attention has to be evaluated in relation to some activity, and pure measures of attention are difficult to obtain (Korkman, Kirk, & Kemp, 1998). On NEPSY, attention is assessed in the visual and auditory modalities with simple and complex tasks in each modality.

A wide range of children with acquired and developmental disorders are apt to show attentional problems: children with Fetal Alcohol Syndrome (Nanson & Hiscock, 1990; Spohr & Steinhausen, 1987; Streissguth et al., 1986), very low birthweight (Korkman, Likanen, & Fellman, 1996; Szatmari et al., 1990), congenital hypothyroidism (Rovet & Alvarez, 1995a), shunted hydrocephalus (Fletcher et al., 1992), and leukemia treated with Central Nervous System prophylaxis (Copeland et al., 1982) among many other groups.

Executive function is a term that was first used in cognitive theory (Brown &

DeLoache, 1978; Neisser, 1967). The concept of efficient working memory was later added by Shallice (1982). In developmental neuropsychology the term "executive function" denotes the use of flexible strategies and planning (Denckla, 1996). It includes the ability to adopt, maintain, and shift cognitive set; the ability to use organized search strategies; the ability to monitor performance and correct errors; and the ability to inhibit the impulse to respond to irrelevant, but salient, interfering stimuli (Denckla, 1996; Levin et al., 1991; Pennington, 1991; Pennington, Groisser, & Welsh, 1993). It also includes the ability both to maintain awareness of task-relevant information and to manipulate it while working on a task mentally (working memory) (Baddeley, 1991, 1992; Goldman-Rakic, 1992). The executive functions interact with, direct, and modulate attentional processes. Both Mirsky and his colleagues (1991) and Welsh and her colleagues (1991) indentified a Speed and Fluency Factor consisting of performance on speeded visual cancellation and visual search tasks, motor sequencing tests, verbal fluency tests, and the WISC-III Coding subtests.

Tower (Core, Ages 5–12)

This subtest is a variant of a widely used neuropsychological test (Tower of London; Shallice, 1982). Single photon emission computed tomography (SPECT) regional cerebral blood flow (rCBF) studies suggest that performance on the Tower of London (Shallice, 1982) produces increased regional blood flow in left and right mesial frontal cortex in adults (Rezai, Andreasen, Alliger, Cohen, Swayze, & O'Leary, 1993). ADHD children had more difficulty with the Tower of London (Shallice, 1982) than did LD children (Levin et al., 1991). Children with severe frontal lobe damage also had difficulty with the Tower of London, while children with posterior damage did not (Levin et al., 1994): Fewer Tower of London problems were solved by children with shunted hydrocephalus than by children with arrested or no hydrocephalus (Fletcher et al., 1994). The NEPSY Tower, like the Tower of London, is thought to assess the executive functions: planning, strategizing, monitoring, self-regulating, and problem solving within a set of rules. Because the task involves the execution of a long sequence of moves that cannot be changed once executed, correct solution depends on how successfully the child planned the initial sequence.

Executive dysfunction causing poor performance on Tower:

- A deficit in the ability to plan performance and generate a solution
- Lack of monitoring
- Poor response inhibition
- Deficit in working memory

Secondary reasons for poor performance on Tower:

- Motor difficulty affecting the ability to manipulate the balls, thus affecting time
- Language deficits affecting the ability to understand the complex verbal directions and rules

Some questions to guide interpretation:

- Did the child seem reflective and plan before beginning the task, or begin impulsively without planning?
- Did the child monitor the performance as he or she proceeded, keeping a hand on the ball until he or she was sure of the move?
- Did the child ask how many moves he or she had made, suggesting a lack of monitoring or poor working memory?
- Did the child guide solution by verbally mediating the task?
- Despite feedback, did the child violate rules frequently because of oppositionality, impulsivity, working memory deficit, or poor cognitive capacity?
- Did the child have difficulty putting the balls on the pegs? Did it slow him or her appreciably? (Note this in the report. This is very different from poor time performance due to slowed processing. A modified presentation may be needed (see p. 41).
- Did the child become anxious or frustrated with himself or herself or with the task? Was he or she able to persist?
- Did the child seem to need a number of demonstrations or explanations of the rules due to poor language comprehension or poor cognitive ability?

Auditory Attention and Response Set (AARS) (Core, Ages 5–12)

This subtest has two parts: AA assesses simple, selective, auditory attention and RS assesses shifting attention, as well as selective attention. The two parts are administered together, however, and the second part is dependent on the first.

Korkman and Pesonen (1994) found that ADHD children were more impaired in inhibiting impulsive responses than children with LD were. They also had more difficulty developing, maintaining, and shifting set (as the child must do on the RS section than children did with LD (Kemp & Kirk, 1993; Kirk & Kelly, 1986; Milner, 1975; Pennington et al., 1993). ADHD children tend to have slow reaction time (Barkley, 1997).

Deficits in attention causing poor performance on AARS:

- Poor vigilance on relatively simple and boring auditory tasks (AA)
- Difficulty sustaining attention

- Lack of ability to shift attention (RS)
- Off-Task Behavior due to short attention span, distractibility

Executive dysfunction contributing to poor performance on AARS:
- Poor response inhibition
- Maintenance of a complex set

Secondary reasons for poor performance on AARS:
- Slowed reaction time
- Poor motor skills affecting performance on RS subtest (see modified administration, p. 41)

Some questions to guide interpretation:
- Did the child perform better on AA (simple, selective attention) or on RS (complex auditory attention), or both? (SSs for AA and RS)
- For both AA and RS check the SSs, did you observe more OEs (inattention), more CEs (impulsivity or inability to shift attention), or were both significant?
- Comparing the "Off-Task Behavior" QO to base rates for age, was the child's result *Borderline* or below?
- Did the child comment on the tape being too fast on RS because he or she could not shift quickly? (Both tasks are administered at the same speed.)
- Did performance deteriorate after initial success, suggesting inability to sustain attention?

Visual Attention (Core Subtest, Ages 3–12)
- *Linear Array (Bunnies):* Ages 3 to 4 only. The child uses selective attention to locate the target stimulus quickly in the linear array.
- *Random Array (Cats):* Ages 3 to 12. The child uses a search strategy to locate the target stimulus (cats) quickly in the random array.
- *Complex Linear Array (Faces):* Ages 5 to 12. The child marks each of two target faces wherever they occur in the linear array. The child must be vigilant to the features (eyebrows, eyes, nose, mouth, hair), because all features except one may match the target face. Target stimuli are multiple, making the task complex.

A visual continuous performance task has been demonstrated to increase regional blood flow in the left and right mesial frontal cortex on SPECT studies (Rezai et al., 1993). This increase may reflect stimulation of the midline attentional circuits. Barkley (1997) has noted the difficulty that ADHD children have in separating affect from performance. If the task interests them, they are excited by it and perform well. If they perceive it as boring initially, they cannot separate their emotional reaction of boredom and indifference from the need to attend to the task.

Deficits in attention causing poor performance on VA:
- Poor vigilance for targets on a simple task
- Inattention to complex stimuli

Executive dysfunction contributing to poor performance on VA:
- Impulsivity in choosing targets (lack of response inhibition)
- Inefficient search strategy

Secondary reasons for poor performance on VA:
- A graphomotor problem, causing the child to take longer to mark targets (the child can point to targets).
- Visual field defect causing one quadrant of the array to be neglected. This is rare and would occur on both arrays and on other tasks where stimuli in that same quadrant would be ignored. These patterns suggest a visual field defect, or an inability of the eye(s) to see in a particular visual field: right, left, upper, lower, or in the inferior or superior quadrant (Baron, Fennell, & Voeller, 1995). The child should be referred to a neurologist.

Some questions to guide interpretation:
- Were there more omission (inattention) or commission (impulsivity) errors? Were there differences in these errors on the simple and complex tasks?
- Did the child perform better on the complex task than on the simple attention task, suggesting that the child's attention was poorer on simple tasks, which he or she perceived as boring, than it was on a more complex task which he or she perceived as challenging?
- Was an inefficient, random search strategy used, or was there a logical pattern? (Draw a small search path on the Record Form as the child completes the task on the Response Form.)
- Was the child fast and accurate? Slow and accurate, suggesting slowed processing but good attention? Fast, but he or she sacrificed accuracy to finish quickly, suggesting impulsivity? Was the child slow and inaccurate, possibly suggesting more generalized cognitive impairment? Did speed differ with the task?
- Did the child have to check back to the target faces frequently, suggesting poor working memory?

- Did the child skip lines, suggesting a convergence insufficiency in which the eyes do not converge on the same point?
- Did the child make many omissions in one quadrant of the array, as if the objects were not seen? (This should happen consistently in the same location on both arrays and on other tasks with visual stimuli.)

Statue (Core, Ages 3–4; Expanded, Ages 5–12)

Statue assesses the basic motor persistence needed to maintain a position and to inhibit response to noise. Korkman and Pesonen (1994) found that ADHD children were more impaired in inhibiting impulsive responding than children with LD were.

Deficits in response inhibition and motor persistence causing poor performance on Statue:
- Inability to inhibit motor response to noise distracters
- Difficulty holding a position (motor persistence) without moving

Secondary reasons for poor performance on Statue:
- Loss of postural control (swaying, loss of balance) when the child is standing with eyes closed.
- A child with pronounced tremor or spasticity may have difficulty holding the arm in a perpendicular position. Modified administration may be used with both hands at the sides. Note on the Record Form. Movement of the limb(s) in question should not be counted.
- PTSD or extreme anxiety. These children should not be given this test.

Questions to guide interpretation:
- Did most errors (eyes opening, body movement, etc.) occur in response to the noise distracters, suggesting a lack of impulse control and inhibition?
- Did most errors occur during silent periods, but not in response to noise distracters? This may suggest the child who is vigilant, anxious, or curious and needs to see what is happening. The child should be referred to a neurologist.

CAUTION

Statue and Children with PTSD

Do not administer Statue to a child with PTSD or extreme anxiety. The child must close his or her eyes as a part of this assessment, and this may be too traumatizing in the presence of a stranger. Most young children love it, but be sensitive to the child's needs.

Expanded Attention/Executive Functions Subtests

Design Fluency (DF) (Ages 5–12)
This subtest is a measure of the executive functions of planning, monitoring, and shifting set in order to

generate unique designs rapidly. Speed and fluency is a greater factor on DF than on Tower, but rules are simpler.

In the Tower study mentioned earlier, the performance of children with ADHD only was not impaired on Design Fluency. They appeared to be able to retain the two simple rules, plan, and generate unique designs as well as normally developing children. When ADHD children also had LD, however, Design Fluency performance was impaired. These results suggest that the additive effects of ADHD and LD cause children to be even less cognitively flexible and less able to plan, monitor, and generate solutions than children with ADHD alone. Both groups were impaired on Tower, suggesting that, even when the ADHD child had no LD, the multiplicity of factors involved in the task stressed the ability to employ executive functions in planning, monitoring, and shifting set for problem solution (Korkman, Kirk, & Kemp, 1998).

A group of high-functioning autistic children was also impaired on both Design Fluency and Tower, though they were not impaired on the NEPSY attention measures. These results suggest that their deficits are more in planning, cognitive flexibility, and problem solution than in attentional areas *per se* (Korkman, Kirk, & Kemp, 1998).

Executive dysfunction causing poor performance on Design Fluency:
- A lack of planning, strategizing, and monitoring for problem solution
- A lack of cognitive flexibility to shift set and generate new designs
- A lack of response inhibition producing impulsivity

Secondary reasons for poor performance on Design Fluency:
- Language deficits causing difficulty understanding rules
- Graphomotor problems causing difficulty manipulating a pencil quickly
- Visuospatial deficits causing perceptual confusion and directional/spatial problems in generating designs

Some questions to guide interpretation:
- Did the child begin impulsively or deliberately?
- Did the child monitor performance to be sure each design was unique?
- Did he or she have difficulty shifting from one design to the next or in generating new designs, remaining stuck on a restricted number of designs?
- Did the child demonstrate poor graphomotor control, slowing performance?
- Did the child perform better on the structured or unstructured array? (Consult SSs.)

Knock and Tap (Ages 5–12)

This subtest is a classic Lurian Go-No-Go task. The first part relates to the need to inhibit motor response in a single cognitive set, while the second part requires the executive functions to break the well-routinized set, inhibit the desire to respond to the previous set, shift, and respond to a different cognitive set. The performance of ADHD children and children with TBI was impaired on Knock and Tap, while children with reading disability and language disability did not display this executive dysfunction (Korkman, Kirk, & Kemp, 1998).

Executive dysfunction deficits causing poor performance on Knock and Tap:
- Poor ability to inhibit motor response
- Inability to shift set and form a new cognitive set

A secondary reason for poor performance on Knock and Tap:
- Motor deficits

Some questions to guide interpretation:
- Was the child able to inhibit motor response on the first part of Knock and Tap (single cognitive set), or was he or she pulled to respond to the examiner's hand motion?
- On the second part, was the child able to inhibit the desire to respond to the previous set, shift, and respond to a different cognitive set? Did this happen on the RS section of AARS, too?
- Did the child's inability to make smooth motor movements have an adverse effect on performance because all of the effort went into the motor movement? (He or she may need a modified administration; see p. 41)

Language Domain

NEPSY approaches language in two ways, as an important domain of development involving many subprocesses and as an avenue to reading and conceptual, factual learning. The subtests in the Language Domain are related to different aspects of linguistic capacities associated with problems in speech and language, reading, spelling, and written language. The fact that language is key to efficient functioning in children is seen in the correlation of the Language Domain with all other domains and in language subtests with many other subtests across domains.

Oromotor programming and the ability to produce phonological sequences have proven to be necessary for normal speech and articulation (Hall & Tomblin, 1978; Rapin, Allen, & Dunn, 1992). In addition, a very important component of language is the auditory perception and analysis of the phonological composition of words and speech. Impairment in this ability may cause receptive language disorders (Rapin, Mattis, Rowan, & Golden, 1977; Tallal, Miller, & Fitch, 1993). More subtle problems with phonological processing may lead to dyslexia (Bradley & Bryant, 1978; Korkman & Peltomaa, 1993; Rack & Olson, 1993; Torgeson, Wagner, & Rashotte, 1994).

Korkman and Hakkinen-Rihu (1994) studied kindergarten children with language delays and disorders. Based on the previous Finnish NEPSY (Finnish version, Korkman, 1990) performance on language subtests (which vary slightly in format from this version), the children were classified into three groups: Global, Specific Comprehension, and Verbal Dyspraxia. The Global subtype was impaired on all language subtests. The Specific Comprehension subtype was impaired on the Token Test (DeRenzi & Faglioni, 1978), similar to the Comprehension of Instructions Subtest in the present NEPSY) and on Repeating Words and Nonwords, the Finnish analog to the present Repetition of Nonsense Words. This group showed receptive, phonological problems. The Verbal Dyspraxia group had articulation problems with poor performance on Oral Motor Series, a subtest similar to Oromotor Sequences, and on Repeating Words and Nonwords.

It was predicted that the Global and Specific Comprehension subtypes would have dyslexia-related problems at school, while the Verbal Dyspraxia subtype would not. These hypotheses were confirmed (hit rate of 80.5%) at follow-up three years later. When classifications were validated, by evaluating a somewhat more heterogeneous group of 40 children with language disorders, NEPSY performance profiles revealed the same subtypes in these children, but an additional small group emerged, the Dysnomia subtype. These children showed specific naming problems on Tokens (SN in the present NEPSY), Body Parts (Body Part Naming), and Name Learning (Memory for Names Subtest).

There is evidence (Wolf & Obregon, 1992; Korhonen, 1991; Denckla & Rudel, 1976b) that children with dyslexia display slow speed of access to language labels, that is, slow naming or semantic access. Dysnomic problems may be regarded as a language disorder as well and may occur in the context of more generalized language disorders (Korkman & Hakkinen-Rihu, 1994; Vellutino & Scanlon, 1989).

A basic assumption in the administration of the subtests in the Language Domain is that the child has auditory acuity within the normal thresholds for speech. Auditory acuity should be tested prior to NEPSY administration, if it has not been done already. Of course, the child with hearing loss may be helped by hearing aides, but modifications still may be needed (see pp. 38–40). If the child is very congested that day or has a history of chronic ear infections or fluid in the ears, the clinician may wish to hold the administration of the Language Domain Subtests, unless, in that setting, he or she can have the child's ears checked for fluid or infection prior to testing. It is also assumed that the child speaks English as his or her primary language. If not, he or she should have been in an English speaking school for five years to be assured of fluency. Otherwise, an interpreter may be needed.

Body Part Naming (Core, Ages 3–4)

This subtest assesses the most basic language function, naming. Naming is the ability to access the name, or semantic label, for an object, shape, word, and so forth when it is perceived. It is a basic component of expressive language. In this subtest the young child names the designated body parts on a drawing of a child. If the child is unable to name the body part on the picture (2 points), he or she can name it on his or her own or the examiner's body (1 point).

Language deficits causing poor performance on Body Part Naming:
- The storehouse of words (vocabulary) is narrow in scope, and there is a global language delay.
- The child cannot access semantic labels efficiently (dysnomia), even when he or she knows them and can demonstrate this receptively when you test the limits.

Secondary reasons for poor performance on Body Part Naming:
- Lack of exposure to language stimulus or to English
- Immaturity (Be careful of this term, however. It often masks early signs of a LD.)

Some questions to guide interpretation:
- Did the parents report the child having trouble remembering names of preschool classmates or having trouble learning names for colors, shapes, and so forth, despite the fact that he or she can identify the colors, shapes, suggesting dysnomia? Did the child show word-finding problems?
- Did history show or parents' report note that he or she had a language delay or did you observe such?
- Is the child's primary language English? If not, obtain an interpreter or refer to a bilingual examiner.
- Did the child seem very young in behavior and overall development, not just in language?
- Did the child come from a disadvantaged background with little exposure to language?
- Was articulation poor? (Check the QO for "Misarticulation.")
- Were other language subtests weak?

Phonological Processing (Ages 3–12)

Phonological awareness is essential to reading decoding and spelling (Bradley & Bryant, 1978; Korkman & Peltomaa, 1993; Rack & Olson, 1993). The profile seen in the diagnostic cluster of dyslexia includes poor phonological awareness (Rack & Olson, 1993) and slowed speed of access to language labels (Wolf & Obregon, 1992) manifested in reading decoding and spelling deficits. This test is comprised of two sections.

Word Segment Recognition: Part A (Core for Ages 3–4; Ages 5–8 begin with Item 7 of Part A). This task is a basic phonological task related to auditory discrimination (Kirk, Kemp & Korkman, 2000). The child identifies the word in which an orally presented segment is found by pointing to one of three word pictures.

Phonological Segmentation: Part B (Core for Ages 5–12; Ages 9 and up start with Part B). This section assesses phonological awareness, which is the ability to conceptualize a speech-sound pattern as a whole and to analyze, manipulate, and change the phonemic pattern to produce a new word.

Deficits causing poor performance on Phonological Processing:
- Part A: Inability to discriminate the sounds or to perceive the sound pattern from which the segment comes
- Part B: Inability to conceptualize a speech-sound pattern as a whole, analyze and manipulate the phonemic sequence, and reassemble the speech-sounds into a new pattern (new word)
- Inability to perform either of the above, suggesting both deficits are present

Secondary reasons for poor performance on Phonological Processing:
- Inattention or impulsivity
- Working memory deficit (dysexecutive function)

Some questions to guide interpretation:
- Did the child have difficulty picking out the word picture on Part A, suggesting difficulty discriminating sound patterns?
- Did the child have difficulty reproducing the altered sound pattern on Part B, suggesting difficulty conceptualizing the sound pattern and being able to manipulate it? Was Repetition of Nonsense Words also affected? Impaired performance here is symptomatic of dyslexia.
- If the child had an articulation problem, did it appear to be motoric with difficulty moving the musculature of the mouth and tongue (oromotor dyspraxia), or was the child unable to reproduce the sound pattern ("pahsghetti," suggesting a phonological articulation disorder)?

- Did the child's poor cognitive capacity affect performance? He or she did not understand the task?
- Did the child do well on Word Segment Recognition and on items 15 to 25, but the performance began to break down when the load was increased on items 26 to 36, suggesting a working memory problem? Did the child ask for repetitions frequently? Did this appear to be related to attentional problems, problems with working memory, or to a language deficit? Inspect attention subtests and other subtests requiring working memory.
- Did he or she start asking for repetition when the stimuli became longer or more complex, so the information could not be held in working memory? Did he or she ask for repetition early in the tests, as if he or she did not understand what was being said? This may be related to a language or more global cognitive deficit.

Speeded Naming (SN) (Core, Ages 5–12)

SN assesses rapid access to alternating language labels. Denckla and Rudel (1976a) first showed a relationship between slowed semantic retrieval and dyslexia. Wolf (1986) then demonstrated that if the stimuli were presented in alternating patterns, the task was even more sensitive to dyslexia.

Deficits in language causing poor performance on SN:
- A naming deficit (dysnomia) with or without slow access because the child must search his or her lexicon for the label
- A global language delay (Global Language subtype)

Secondary reasons for poor performance on SN:
- Slowed processing in general
- Impulsivity
- General cognitive deficit
- Visuospatial deficit

Questions to guide interpretation:
- Was the child fast and accurate? (No naming or processing deficit)
- Was the child fast and significantly inaccurate? This suggests impulsivity and a possible naming deficit or good processing speed and a naming deficit. Even with the child trying to search the lexicon, the processing does not slow enough to fall *Below Expected Level*. This pattern may be due to low cognitive capacity with the child unaware the labels are wrong, or the child may know the labels well enough to name without speed constraints, but can't name rapidly.

- Was the child slow and accurate? This suggests slowed processing in general, but no naming deficit. If there are many last minute, spontaneous corrections, this suggests a mild naming deficit for which he or she may be compensating, but it is costing her time.
- Was the child slow and inaccurate? This suggests a naming deficit and slowed access as he or she searches her lexicon.
- Did the child recruit the body into the effort, or did the voice volume increase when producing labels quickly? This suggests the need to recruit other systems into the effort of producing labels quickly.
- Did the child reverse more than two sequences? This suggests a dyslexic characteristic, especially with naming deficit.

Comprehension of Instructions (Core, Ages 5–12)

Comprehension of Instructions is a receptive language test of increasing complexity. It has two sections. In **Part A, Items 1 to 13,** the child is asked to point to rabbits of different size, color, and facial expression to demonstrate language understanding. In **Part B, Items 14–28,** the child is required to point to target shapes by color, position, and relationship to other figures in response to verbal instruction (Korkman, Kirk, & Kemp, 1998). Linguistic cues of increasing complexity present words in a sequence, words that override order, negation, locative words, and spatial words.

Children with Receptive and Expressive Language Disorder (Global Language subtype) and children with Autistic Disorder are more extreme examples of children with receptive language deficits, but more subtle problems comprehending oral language can also cause significant problems in the classroom. Verbal processing and comprehension deficits may occur without any evidence of more generalized language disorders (Korkman & Hakkinen-Rihu, 1994). Older head-injured children appear to be impaired on tasks of comprehension of complex language (Ewing-Cobbs et al., 1987).

Language deficits causing poor performance on Comprehension of Instructions:
- A specific receptive language deficit (Specific Comprehension subtype of Developmental Language Disorder; Korkman & Hakkinen-Rihu, 1994)
- A receptive language disorder as a part of an autistic disorder or other pervasive developmental disorder
- A global language delay (Global subtype)

Secondary reasons for poor performance on Comprehension of Instructions:
- A working memory deficit
- Attentional or impulsivity problems

- Visuospatial deficits having an adverse affect on visuospatial language concepts

Some questions to guide interpretation:
- Did the child have difficulty understanding and carrying out the instructions from the outset, or did it become difficult as the items became longer? (The first suggests a receptive language disorder; the second suggests a working memory deficit.)
- Did the child's inattention cause him or her not to hear all of the instructions, so he or she did not carry them out correctly?
- Was the child impulsive in responding, so he or she did not hear all of the instruction (e.g., point to the second cross in the first row, *but first* to a blue circle)?
- Did he or she ask for repetitions frequently?
- Did the child perform within normal limits on a one-word picture vocabulary test but not do well on the more complex receptive language assessed on NEPSY?
- Even on the initial instructions in Part B (14–20), did the child appear to understand the simple language, but did not pick up the linguistic cues, such as, ". . . but first . . . ?"
- Did the child recall the first part of the complex direction, but forget the second or vice versa?

Repetition of Nonsense Words (Expanded, Ages 5–12)

Repetition of Nonsense Words is another assessment of phonological processing in which the child must analyze the orally presented speech-sound pattern (a nonsense word) and reproduce that word. This ability is related to reading decoding and spelling (Rack & Olson, 1993). Children who have trouble reproducing novel speech sound patterns may also have trouble learning a foreign language. In an important functional magnetic resonance imaging (fMRI) (Shaywitz & Shaywitz, 1998) study of dyslexics, sounding out nonsense words activated Broca's area (motor speech) in the anterior cortex, while good readers used posterior areas in primary visual cortex, the angular

CAUTION

Number Responses on Comprehension of Instructions

The Comprehension of Instructions Subtest includes miniatures of the stimuli the child uses to follow the oral directions. If you number the shapes on the miniature in the order the child points to them, you will be able to analyze errors later. If you merely score 1 or 0, this analysis will not be possible.

gyrus, and the superior temporal gyrus, none of which were activated in dyslexics. The Shaywitzes have noted that greater anterior activity and less posterior activity is the "neural signature" of dyslexia. Children with a Specific Comprehension subtype of Developmental Language Disorder performed poorly on Repeating Nonwords (the Finnish equivalent subtest; Korkman, 1988a) as well as on Comprehension of Instructions.

Deficits in language causing poor performance on Repetition of Nonsense Words:
- Generalized language disorder (Global subtype; Korkman & Hakkinen-Rihu, 1994)
- Specific receptive language disorder (Specific Comprehension subtype)
- A phonological processing deficit, suggesting dyslexia

Secondary reasons for poor performance on Repetition of Nonsense Words:
- Oromotor production deficit (dyspraxia) affecting ability to reproduce words correctly (Dyspraxia subtype)
- A deficit in auditory memory span seen in the inability to remember longer words. The child reproduces the beginning of the word correctly, but forgets the end of it.
- Inattention to the oral presentation of the nonsense word

Some questions to guide interpretation:
- Did the child have difficulty articulating the words?
- Did the child produce at least part of the sound pattern?
- Were word speech sounds missequenced?
- Was the child inattentive, so he or she did not attend to the word?

Verbal Fluency (Ages 3–12)

This subtest assesses the ability to generate words in semantic categories and with phonemic constraints. Developmental trends are evident for semantic and for phonemic fluency (Korkman, Kirk & Kemp [in press]). Total Phonemic Fluency lagged behind Total Semantic Fluency by an average of 10 words produced across the age groups 7 to 12 (Kirk & Kemp, 1999). It is important to remember this difference in interpreting the results.

ADHD children have been shown to reduce verbal fluency (Koziol & Stout, 1992), which was true for the ADHD and ADHD/LD validity groups on the NEPSY (Korkman, Kirk, & Kemp, 1998). Supplemental scores revealed that the ADHD children were significantly poorer than normal controls on both phonemic and semantic conditions. Children with autism and children with hearing impairment were also impaired on Verbal Fluency in the NEPSY validity studies. Bassett and Slatter (1990) found impaired fluency in children with mild to moderate head injury. This may be reflective of lexical retrieval difficulties (Rourke, 1995). Verbal fluency was found to be associated in children with left and right frontal gray-matter and white-matter lesions, particularly in dorsilateral frontal (Levin et al., 1991).

Deficits in language causing poor performance on Verbal Fluency:
- A global language delay (Global subtype)
- An expressive language deficit
- Slow access to words causing fewer words to be produced in one minute
- A phonological processing deficit affecting Phonemic Fluency

Secondary reasons for poor performance on Verbal Fluency:
- Weak executive functions needed to initiate the task and to search across the lexicon to locate words beginning with a particular letter
- Poor general ideation due to a lack of cognitive flexibility or poor cognitive ability
- Lack of exposure to language stimulus
- Distractibility
- Oromotor dyspraxia

Questions to guide interpretation:
- Did the child perform poorly on the Semantic Fluency section only, the Phonemic Fluency section only, or both (use SS)?
- Was access to words slow or difficult overall?
- Did the child recruit the body into the effort, or did his or her voice increase in volume with the effort?
- After a short period, did the child start to look around the room at objects to cue words?
- Did the child become distracted by a word and start to talk about it, forgetting the task?
- Did the child produce the words slowly due to dyspraxia?
- Did he or she seem to have no strategy for retrieving words that began with "F" or with "S," suggesting executive dysfunction?
- Did he or she produce words that did not actually begin with the designated letter, or did he or she seem to have a very difficult time producing them because the child was unsure of the initial sound, suggesting a phonological processing deficit?

Oromotor Sequences (Ages 3–12)

On this subtest, the child is required to produce repetitive articulatory sequences. The oromotor control needed to produce smooth, intelligible articulation is key to efficient use of language. Oromotor dyspraxia is an articulation disorder due to a deficit in motor planning affecting the musculature of the mouth and tongue, as opposed to a phonological articulation disorder. Dyspraxia is characterized by inconsistent articulation errors. Oromotor hypotonia causes "lazy" diction in its mild form, and drooling, chewing, and swallowing problems in its more severe forms. The latter is seen in a more generalized neurological impairment or developmental delay. Dysarthria is muscle incoordination of the oromotor apparatus characterized by stable misarticulations along with rate changes (see QOs). The terms dysarthria and dyspraxia are often used interchangeably.

Korkman and Hakkinen-Rihu (1994) found that the Specific Verbal Dyspraxia subtype of Developmental Language Disorder showed poor performance on this subtest and on a subtest similar to Repeating Nonsense Words, but not on other language subtests. In NEPSY validation studies, children with Reading Disorders showed poor performance on Oromotor Sequences significantly more often than the normal controls. They also showed significantly more problems on Manual Motor Sequences, a possible indication of a greater incidence of dyspraxia or apraxia in this population (Korkman, Kirk, & Kemp, 1998).

Cause of poor performance on Oromotor Sequences:
- Oromotor dysfunction

Some questions to guide interpretation:
- Did the child display misarticulations that were stable (always the same sound mispronounced in the same way)? Were there rate changes present? This suggests dysarthria.
- Did the child seem to have "lazy" or slightly mumbled diction due to low muscle tone in the oromotor apparatus (oromotor hypotonia)?

Sensorimotor Domain

The Sensorimotor Domain looks at the ability to produce rapid, accurate, and co-ordinated finger and hand movements; to produce rapid, accurate, successive simple and complex sequential finger movements; and to organize and produce a series of novel rhythmic hand movement sequences. It also assesses graphomotor speed and accuracy. The assessment of tactile perception and sensory differentiation is a part of this domain, as is the assessment of kinesthetic feedback from a hand position integrated with visual-spatial analysis and motor programming.

Finger agnosia, along with difficulty with right/left discrimination, arithmetic problems, and marked reading deficits, comprise Gerstmann Syndrome (Benson & Geschwind, 1970). Children with Nonverbal Learning Disability tend to have poor tactile perception (Rourke, 1995). In the NEPSY validity studies (Korkman, Kirk, & Kemp, 1998), ADHD children showed significantly poor performance on Manual Motor Sequences, Imitating Hand Positions, and Finger Discrimination when compared to matched normal controls. Children with reading disorders showed poor performance on Manual Motor Sequences, suggesting that motor programming and the ability to sequence may be related to reading disorder. Children with Developmental Language Disorders showed impaired Fingertip Tapping and Imitating Hand Positions performance. Children with Autistic Disorders showed more generalized sensorimotor deficits on all Sensorimotor subtests except Fingertip Tapping. Of the Sensorimotor Subtests administered to the small TBI group, deficits appeared on Fingertip Tapping and VP, but not on Imitating Hand Positions, suggesting that motor speed is a problem for these children rather than the integration of kinesthetic praxis, motor programming, and visual-spatial analysis that are required for Imitating Hand Positions. The results on this latter subtest approached significance, however, and the sample was only 8, so with a larger sample the results might have been significant.

Ehlers and Gilberg (1993) have shown generalized dyspraxia in 80 percent of these individuals. Children with Tourette's Syndrome have poor fine motor coordination, as well as problems with paper/pencil tasks, while children with arithmetic disabilities also show difficulty on fine motor and visuomotor paper/pencil tasks, but they also have a more generalized visuospatial processing deficit (Brookshire, Butler, Ewing-Cobbs, & Fletcher, 1994).

In a study of very low birthweight (VLBW) children, both small for gestational age (SGA) and average for gestational age (AGA), and children who had suffered birth asphyxia (Korkman, Liikanen, & Fellman, 1996), the VLBW children in both groups and the asphyxia group showed no differences on VP or Manual Motor Movements. However, there were significant differences in the asphyxia group and both the VLBW-SGA and the VLBW-AGA on a task of finger discrimination. The asphyxia group performed like the Normal Controls. The VLBW-SGA had the poorest performance on this task. Numerous QOs appear in this domain. In a study of QOs in an ADHD group (Huckeba, Kreiman, Korkman, Kirk, & Kemp, 1998), significant differences ($p < .01$) were found in involuntary motor overflow in the mouth and tongue on the Fingertip Tapping and Manual Motor Series subtests. ADHD children used the mirror hand (echopraxia) in the Imitating Hand Positions subtest significantly more often than normal controls. The Manual Motor Series showed a number of QOs which occurred significantly more often in ADHD children than in normal controls: perseverations, loss of asymmetry, and forceful tapping. These results suggest that ADHD children display diffuse dysfunction in motor performance, particularly in motor programming. Denckla and Rudel (1976a, b; 1978) established in early landmark studies that ADHD boys were slower in performing successive and sequential finger movements than were reading disabled children, who were slower than normal controls. Winogron, Knights, and Bawden (1984) identified slowing of both Preferred and

Nonpreferred Hands on a Fingertip Tapping task in a severely head-injured group. Motor slowing is most likely to persist beyond six months only in the severely head-injured group, though it is a common finding in the initial assessment of the even mildly head-injured child.

Fingertip Tapping (Core, Ages 5–12)

This subtest assesses the child's ability to make dexterous finger movements, first tapping the forefinger against the thumb rapidly and then tapping the fingers sequentially against the thumb rapidly. SSs make it possible to look at associated movements on this assessment, as well as task differences and hand differences. The anterior corpus callosum plays an important role in suppressing bimanual overflow (Jeeves, Silver, & Milner, 1988; Preilowski, 1972).

Motor deficits causing poor performance on Fingertip Tapping:
- Deficit in fine-motor coordination
- Deficit in motor programming
- Motor slowing or generalized slow processing

Some questions to guide interpretation:
- Did the child perform better on SSs for Repetitions than on Sequences? (The latter suggests coordination; the former suggests motor programming.) Were both poor?
- Did he or she show a difference between Preferred and Nonpreferred Hand (SS)? Did they correlate with differences on Imitating Hand Positions and Finger Discrimination? Such results may signal a mild hemiparesis or inefficient processing of tactile, kinesthetic information on one or both sides of the body.
- Did the child's fingers frequently revert to an incorrect position (see QOs) despite cueing?
- Were associated movements present (QO for overflow, mirroring, posturing), suggesting diffuse motor response?
- Was time for 32 taps or eight sequences slow, but movements were accurate? Did he or she show rate-based problems on other subtests requiring speed?

Imitating Hand Positions (Core Ages 3–12)

This is a subtest of kinesthetic praxis, the ability to imitate a hand position from a model, and of tactile processing. It is a highly integrative task, which also relies on motor programming and visual-spatial analysis. In the validity studies for NEPSY, this Sensorimotor Subtest appeared as significant in the ADHD, Developmental Language

Disorder (DLD), Autistic, and Hearing-impaired groups (Korkman, Kirk, & Kemp, 1998). Premotor cortex is involved in the integration of visual information into motor performance and depends on sensory feedback (Baron, Fennel, & Voellner, 1995).

Sensorimotor deficits causing poor performance on Imitating Hand Positions:
- Motor programming
- Fine motor coordination
- Poor kinesthetic feedback from positions

Secondary reasons for poor performance on Imitating Hand Positions:
- Visuospatial deficit
- Dysexecutive function affecting inhibition of impulsive response, planning, monitoring
- Social-perceptual deficit as in Autistic Disorder, Asperger's Syndrome, Nonverbal Learning Disability

Some questions to guide interpretation:
- Did the child seem to be able to move the correct fingers easily, but could not reproduce the shape; or did he or she seem confused with the orientation or spatial relationships of the position, suggesting a visuospatial deficit?
- Did the child have difficulty moving the fingers into position (motor coordination and programming)?
- Did the child make errors with both hands? Was the difference in side in Preferred and Nonpreferred performance the same observed on Fingertip Tapping and Finger Discrimination? No difference? Prolonged ambidexterity may be a marker of a neurodevelopmental problem. Compare to age norms.
- Was sensory input on Finger Discrimination also affected in a lateralized manner?
- Did the child need to help with the other hand do to poor coordination and programming (QO)?
- Did the child seem uncomfortable with studying the examiner's hand?

Visuomotor Precision (VP) (Core, Ages 3–12)
This subtest assesses graphomotor speed and accuracy. SS provide separate scores for speed and for accuracy. Many children with developmental and acquired disorders have graphomotor deficits.

Motor deficits causing poor performance on VP:
- Graphomotor control
- Poor fine motor coordination overall

Secondary reasons for poor performance on VP:
- Dysexecutive function causing inability to inhibit impulsive response, plan ahead, estimate the difficulty of the track, and monitor on-going execution
- Convergence insufficiency, poor coordination of the two eyes to focus on one point, causing difficulty perceiving the edge of the track correctly. Compare to closure on VP.

Some questions to guide interpretation:
- Was the child's performance fast and accurate? Fast and inaccurate, suggesting impulsivity causing errors or impulsivity and poor graphomotor control? Slow and accurate, suggesting motor or generalized slowing or the awareness that he or she needed to work slowly due to poor graphomotor control? Slow and accurate suggesting good motor control or poor motor control in a child working very hard to compensate? Slow and inaccurate, suggesting motor or generalized slowing and poor graphomotor control?
- Did the child begin by previewing the tracks or did he or she rush to start with barely a glance at the tracks, suggesting impulsivity?

Manual Motor Sequences (Expanded, Ages 3–12)

This subtest assesses the ability to imitate, learn, and automatize a series of rhythmic hand movements. Apraxia refers to an inability to perform movements that is not explained by weakness, incoordination, sensory loss, or inability to understand directions (Geschwind, 1975). When the origin is developmental, it is usually referred to as generalized dyspraxia, if it is acquired, apraxia. For the purposes of this discussion, we refer to apraxia in order to avoid confusion with oromotor dyspraxia, which can occur in isolation or be part of the generalized disorder. The apraxic individual is unable to access or evoke movement representations of skilled actions that are stored in the inferior parietal lobe, usually of the dominant hemisphere (Baron et al., 1995). Although this subtest assesses apraxia at the production level, apraxia can also occur at the conceptual level.

Children with reading disorders showed poor performance on Oromotor Sequences significantly more often than normal controls in the NEPSY validation studies, and they also showed significantly more problems on Manual Motor Sequences performance. There may be a greater incidence of dyspraxia or apraxia in this group than in the general population (Korkman, Kirk, & Kemp, 1998).

Motor deficits causing poor performance on Manual Motor Sequences:
- Deficit in motor programming causing difficulty in organizing and sequencing the movements or difficulty sustaining the rhythm and sequence throughout the series

- Deficit in manual motor coordination causing a lack of fluid movement, but not affecting the sequence

Secondary reasons for poor performance on Manual Motor Sequences:
- Dysexecutive function causing difficulty with inhibiting impulsive response initiating response, and monitoring performance
- Inattention to motor sequence initially

Some questions to guide interpretation:
- Did the child have difficulty producing the motor sequence in correct order (programming)? Compare to Oromotor Sequences.
- Did the child have difficulty with fluid hand movement (coordination), but the sequences were correct?
- Was he or she inattentive when the motor sequence was demonstrated, so he or she could not reproduce it accurately?
- Were associated movements present, suggesting diffuse motor response (e.g., Overflow)?
- Did the child recruit other systems into the effort as seen in the QO for Tapping Forcefully?
- Did the child lose the asymmetry of movement on a sequence and begin to do the same movement with both hands (QO, Loss of Asymmetry)?
- Did the child perseverate on a sequence, unable to inhibit the production of movements?

Finger Discrimination (Expanded, Ages 5–12)

This subtest assesses the ability to perceive sensory (tactile) input without benefit of vision. One or two fingers are touched lightly with the child's hand shielded from view. The clinician lifts the shield, and the child points to the finger or fingers touched. Thus, this is purely a sensory perception task, rather than a naming task (in which the fingers that were touched are named by the child).

While poor performance on this test can be an indication of inefficient processing of tactile information, it can also be a developmental issue. For this reason, it is very helpful to have scores on NEPSY that compare performance to that of normally developing children of the child's age. Errors in perceiving double simultaneous touch are not uncommon before the age of 8. A child 8 or older may have a delay in efficient processing of tactile information, or, in the case of a child with a lesion, the extinction may occur in the hand contralateral to the lesion. This is not always so, however. Lenti and colleagues demonstrated that of 39 hemiplegic children and young adults, 23 showed extinction. However, only 19 manifested extinction in the hand contralateral to the damaged hemisphere.

Gerstmann Syndrome has been reported in children (Benson & Geschwind, 1970; Spellacy & Peter, 1978). It has been associated with dysfunction in the dominant parietal lobe and involves finger agnosia, dyscalculia, dysgraphia, and left/right confusion (Geschwind & Strub, 1975). Gerstmann Syndrome has been associated with poor oculomotor scanning and control (Pirozzolo & Rayner, 1978). Constructional apraxia has also sometimes been associated with Gerstmann Syndrome (Critchley, 1966), so the clinician should compare performance on DC and Block Construction to Finger Discrimination. Children with autism displayed poor finger discrimination in the NEPSY validity studies (Korkman, Kirk, & Kemp, 1998), as did children with ADHD.

Sensory deficit causing poor performance on Finger Discrimination:
- Poor tactile perception of the digits (finger agnosia)

Secondary reasons for poor performance on Finger Discrimination:
- Inattention to stimuli

Some questions to guide interpretation:
- Did errors occur when one finger was touched, when two fingers were touched simultaneously, or both? Compare to errors expected for age. Suppression may be noted on double simultaneous stimulation.
- Were errors greater, fewer, or the same between Preferred and Nonpreferred hand performance? Any relationship to differences in motor performances? To Finger Discrimination differences?

Visuospatial Domain

This domain contains two subtests of visuospatial ability, a judgement of line orientation task and a map-reading task. It also includes two subtests of the integration of visuospatial and motor skills for constructional tasks: one in two dimensions and one in three dimensions.

Significant deficits in the visuospatial area are markers for Nonverbal Learning Disability (Rourke, 1995) and Williams Syndrome (hypercalcemia) (Udwin, Yule, & Martin, 1987). Children with arithmetic disabilities have a generalized deficit in processing visual-spatial information (Brookshire et al., 1994; Fletcher, 1985; Rourke, 1989; Strang & Rourke, 1985). Children with Tourette's Syndrome demonstrate relative difficulty on visual-motor paper/pencil tasks, but not on motor-free, visual-spatial tasks (Brookshire et al., 1994). Children who have been subject to acute lymphocytic leukemia and have undergone central nervous system prophylaxis may have compromised visuospatial organization (Copeland, 1992). Those who had cranial radiation therapy as part of their treatment demonstrate significantly poorer performance on a visual-spatial analysis task than did their control counterparts.

In the NEPSY validity studies, children with reading disorders showed deficits on DC and Route Finding. Children with autism showed deficits on Arrows, Route Finding, and Block Construction. These results may be related to attentional problems in autistic children, however. The Visuospatial Domain has a moderate correlation with the Language Domain, suggesting the importance of language mediation in carrying out these tasks (Korkman, Kirk, & Kemp, 1998). A child with a deficit in this domain, but with good attention and executive abilities as well as strong language and memory skills, may compensate well for mild visuospatial problems well, whereas another child who has both language and visuospatial deficits would not be able to do so (Korkman, Kirk, & Kemp, 1998).

Design Copying (DC) (Core, Ages 3–12)

This subtest assesses integration of visuospatial input and motor output for two-dimensional construction: paper/pencil copying of geometric shapes. This subtest and the Block Design subtest can assess constructional apraxia (difficulty in two- and three-dimensional constructional tasks). Constructional tasks require the integration of visuoperceptual and visuospatial skills with coordinated motor activity. Difficulty on constructional tasks can be due to motor, visuospatial, and attention problems, or to a combination of these factors (Korkman, Kirk, & Kemp, 1998). The child with attentional problems may not attend to details or may copy impulsively. Graphomotor problems may cause difficulty because the child has problems manipulating the pencil (tool use), and, therefore, produces the design poorly or cannot produce the details within the design elements. The latter problem is due to fine motor coordination rather than an inability to perceive the spatial relationships among them. A combination of these factors, along with poor visuospatial processing, can cause the child to produce a very poor design. Careful observation during testing is needed to distinguish the extent to which poor performance on the DC may be due to one or more of these factors.

Constructional apraxia has been associated with Gerstmann's Syndrome (Critchley, 1966). Children with Tourette's Syndrome have difficulties on paper/pencil copying of geometric designs, but not in visuospatial functioning when there is no motor output (Brookshire et al., 1994). Children with Fetal Alcohol Syndrome also show impaired performance on this type of task (Mattson, Riley, Gramling, Delis, & Jones, 1998). Korkman and Pesonen (1994) found a visual-motor integration task separated ADHD children from LD children and ADHD/LD children. Although the latter group showed great inter-individual variability, the group difference was not significant. VLBW children, both SGA and AGA, tested at 5 to 9 years of age, showed significantly poor performances on a paper/pencil design copying task in relation to normal controls and a group of children who had birth asphyxia (Korkman, Liikanen, & Fellman, 1996). Visuomotor copying deficits have been observed among moderately and severely head-injured children (Fletcher & Levin, 1988). Thus, a number of acquired and developmental conditions in children appear to impair visuomotor integration.

Visuospatial deficit causing poor performance on DC:
• Deficit in integration of visuospatial input and motor output
• Deficit in visuospatial perception with graphomotor control within normal limit

Secondary reasons for poor performance on DC:
• Deficit in graphomotor control or fine motor coordination with visuospatial ability within normal limits
• Impulsivity and inattention
• Convergence insufficiency

Some questions to guide interpretation:
• Did the child's designs show directional confusion, poor spatial relations of elements, or poor line quality, reflecting poor graphomotor control? This profile suggests a visuomotor integration deficit.
• Did the child's designs show directional confusion or poor spatial relationships, but line quality and production was adequate?
• Did the child's designs show no directional confusion and adequate spatial relations of elements but line quality was heavy and poorly controlled? Was graphomotor production slow and effortful?
• Did the child take time to plan before copying a design or did he or she begin impulsively? Did he or she monitor the performance? Compare to planning on Tower and Design Fluency or other impulsive performances.

- Were the child's spatial errors only where two points intersected or was there closure between two elements with no directional confusion present and adequate graphomotor control was present? This may indicate a convergence insufficiency. Did the child skip lines on SN and in reading?

Arrows (Core, Ages 5–12)

This subtest assesses the child's ability to judge line orientation by using nonmotor, visuospatial processing to determine which two arrows would hit the target. A child who has difficulty with this subtest may have a tendency to reverse letters and numbers, may have difficulty learning math symbols, or may have difficulty acquiring sight vocabulary. He or she may have problems with mathematics and difficulty interpreting graphs and charts in any subject area.

Children with Williams Syndrome have been shown to perform poorly on judgement of line orientation tasks (Bellugi, Sabo, & Vaid, 1988). Children with shunted hydrocephalus perform more poorly on a judgement of line orientation task (Judgement of Line Orientation Test; Benton et al., 1983) than do children with arrested hydrocephalus or no hydrocephalus. On purely perceptual tasks, such as judgement of line orientation, the performance of children with meningomyelocele, meningocele, or aqueductal stenosis is found to be related to right lateral ventricle size (Fletcher et al., 1992).

A visual field cut is very rare in children, but it is very important that the clinician recognizes the condition when he or she sees it in evaluation. Be aware, however, that inattention can produce many omissions, though not usually just on one side. Through SS for Visual Field Errors on Arrows, the number of errors in the two visual fields can be compared independently to the percent seen in the standardization sample for age. The clinician should not attempt to analyze visual field errors unless he or she has presented an equal number of targets on the right and on the left. These items are reordered for item difficulty after standardization, so if the test is discontinued early, you may not have a sufficient number of targets on each side to make the judgement. A homonymous hemianopsia refers to a loss of the left or the right half of the visual field. In bitemporal hemianopsia, the temporal visual fields of both eyes are affected. Therefore, there may be consistent omission errors on both sides of the array, just as if the ends of the long arrows were not there. This defect can be seen more clearly on the Visual Attention subtest arrays, where the child would not appear to see any of the pictures on either the right or the left. Only the pictures in the center would be marked. If visual field errors are consistently noted on

Arrows, Visual Attention, Speeded Naming, and other subtests with visual stimuli, immediate referral to a neuropsychologist or neurologist is appropriate.

Visuospatial Deficit Causing Poor Performance on Arrows:
- Poor ability to judge orientation of lines and angles

Secondary Reasons for Poor Performance on Arrows:
- Inattention and impulsivity
- Visual field defect in one quadrant or in rare instances two quadrants
- Occasionally convergence insufficiency, or the inability of the two eyes to focus (converge) on one point will cause poor performance

Some questions to guide interpretation:
- Did the child attend to all of the targets well, but nonetheless, make incorrect choices, suggesting inability to judge line orientation?
- Was the child inattentive and impulsive, not looking at all eight arrows before making a choice? This suggests attentional problems.
- Did the child have problems with closure on DC? Did he or she lose his or her place or skip lines on the VA Subtest? Did he or she skip lines in reading? These signs may point to a convergence insufficiency. The clinician should refer the child to a vision professional.
- Did the child show significantly more visual field errors in one quadrant than in the others? Did this happen *consistently* in the same quadrant on VA arrays and other subtest visual full-page stimuli? (See the preceding discussion concerning visual field errors.)

Block Construction (Core, Ages 3–4; Expanded, Ages 5–12)

This is an assessment of the ability to reproduce three-dimensional block constructions from a model or diagram. A focus of the assessment is on the ability to visualize, understand, and reproduce three-dimensional spatial relations. Although it requires the integration of visuospatial skills with motor output, the child needs much less fine motor coordination to manipulate the blocks than he or she needs for pencil/paper reproductions in DC. Along with DC (two-dimensional copying), this subtest provides a means of assessing constructional apraxia. Children with visuospatial problems often have constructional problems, but it is possible for visuoperceptual skills to be intact and constructional skills to be impaired, and vice-versa.

As noted earlier, constructional apraxia can occur with Gerstmann Syndrome (Critchley, 1966). This causes the child to have marked math problems, dysgraphia, left/right confusion, and poor tactile perception on a finger discrimination task, but in children it is less diagnostic of right parietal dysfunction in children with developmental disorders than in adults (Kinsbourne & Warrington, 1963; Spellacy & Peter, 1978). The clinician should also expect deficits on Block Construction in children with arithmetic deficits, Nonverbal Learning Disabilities, and Fetal Alcohol Syndrome (Done & Rourke, 1995).

Visuospatial deficit causing poor performance on Block Construction:
- Deficit in the ability to visualize, understand, and reproduce 3-dimensional spatial relationships
- Deficit in integration of visuospatial input and motor output

Secondary causes for poor performance on Block Construction:
- Deficit in fine motor coordination without visuospatial deficit
- Inattention and impulsivity

Some questions to guide interpretation:
- Did the child perform well on Block Construction, Arrows, and Route Finding, but perform poorly on DC, suggesting a graphomotor problem, not a visuospatial problem?
- Did the child perform poorly on Block Design as well as on DC, with visuospatial errors present on both, but his or her nonmotor visuospatial subtests, Arrows and Route Finding, as well as the fine motor assessment, Fingertip Tapping, were *At Expected Level* or *Above?* This profile suggests a specific deficit in visuomotor integration causing global constructional apraxia.
- Did the child perform well on the nonmotor visuospatial tasks, Arrows and Route Finding, but poorly on Block Construction because he or she displayed awkward motor movement and did not receive time bonuses? Were Fingertip Tapping and DC performances weak with poor quality figures on DC due to poor motor control, but few spatial errors? This profile suggests fine motor coordination problems without visuospatial deficits.
- Was the child very impulsive and careless in reproducing the block constructions, causing poor performance on Block Construction and Route Finding? Did he or she have difficulty manipulating the blocks? Were similar difficulties evident on the Tower Subtest or while handling any other manipulatives? Compare performance to other motor subtests.

Route Finding (Expanded, Ages 5–12)
The Route Finding subtest assesses the child's understanding of visuospatial relationships and directionality, as well as the ability to transfer this knowledge from a simple schematic map to a more complex one. A poor performance on this subtest could be related to difficulty understanding the relative positions of objects in space or to problems with representational thinking. The child must understand that a map represents something in the real world, and that the map corresponds, in a schematic way, to the spatial relationships that exist in the real world (Korkman, Kirk, & Kemp, 1998). The child must estimate the distance from the starting point to the target house. He or she must also have a clear perception of directionality, so he or she does not confuse left and right.

Difficulty with spatial understanding may underlie math disorders. Children with math disorders, as well as children with Nonverbal Learning Disability, appear to have a generalized deficit in procession of nonverbal visual-spatial information (Rourke, 1987, 1988, 1989). While the right parietal lobe is generally purported to subserve visuospatial processing, adult frontal lobe patients do show clear impairments in the visuospatial domain when they are examined. The prefrontal cortex participates in processing representational information about the location of objects in space (Rezai et al., 1993). Neuropsychological studies of patients with Tourette's Syndrome and with Obsessive Compulsive Disorder have been found to have cognitive set shifting and visuospatial deficits, consistent with right frontal dysfunction (Bornstein, Carroll, & King, 1986). Obsessive Compulsive Disorder patients, who had significantly higher ventricular-brain ratios than normal, showed deficits on a map-reading task (Money Road Map test), as well as on the Rey Osterrith Complex Figure, and stylus maze learning (Head, Bolton, & Hymas, 1989). In the NEPSY validity studies, children with Autistic Disorder, Fetal Alcohol Syndrome, and TBI displayed poor performance on the Route Finding Subtest (Korkman, Kirk, & Kemp, 1998).

Visuospatial deficits causing poor performance on Route Finding:
- Deficits in visuospatial processing, including directionality, estimating distance, spatial relationships, and understanding of representational space

Secondary reasons for poor performance on Route Finding:
- Inattention
- Dysexecutive function causing a lack of inhibition of impulsive respond-

ing, monitoring of performance, and understanding of representational space

Some questions to guide interpretation:

• Did the child perform poorly on both Route Finding and Arrows, suggesting a visual-spatial deficit?
• Did the child turn in the correct direction but at an intersection before or after the correct one, suggesting difficulty estimating distance, a process of spatial analysis?
• Did the child seem to have difficulty comprehending that the schematic array represented a real-world situation? Children with cognitive deficits may perform poorly. Children with Autistic Disorder also have trouble with mental representations.
• Did the child respond impulsively without taking time to reflect on the location of the target house, suggesting that poor performance was related to impulsivity, rather than to visuospatial processing?

MEMORY AND LEARNING DOMAIN

Different components of verbal and nonverbal memory are assessed by the subtests in the Memory and Learning Domain: verbal memory span, immediate and delayed memory for names and for faces, free and cued recall of a narrative, and supraspan memory when a list is learned over repeated trials. Memory is a complex capacity which improves developmentally at the rate at which a child's ability to conceptualize, categorize, and make associations develops. Access to what is learned becomes more automatic as more sophisticated encoding strategies are employed (Levine, 1987). Memory is essential to a childs ability to perform and learn in other functional domains and to participate fully and effectively in life (Korkman, Kirk, & Kemp, 1998).

Memory problems in children with developmental disorders are usually secondary to deficits in attention, verbal processing, and visual perception (Delis, 1989). A specific memory problem is, therefore, rare in children with developmental disorders. Memory difficulties in children are usually modality specific. Children with language deficits and the reading difficulties that usually accompany the same, for instance, show reduced auditory memory span (Aram, Ekelman, & Nation, 1984; Korkman & Pesonen, 1994; Wilson & Risucci, 1986) which may well stem from deficiencies in language processing. Reduced memory span can compromise working memory, which the child needs for processing and comprehending extended verbal narratives (Luria, 1973; Martin, Jerger, & Breedin, 1987). Children with temporal lobe tumors show memory dysfunction (Carpentieri &

Mulhern, 1993). Children with traumatic brain injury (TBI) to the right hemisphere or with right temporal lobe epilepsy have been observed to have impaired memory for figures (McFie, 1961). Children with left temporal lobe epilepsy are more impaired on verbal short-term memory tasks than on visuospatial tasks, as are children with Down Syndrome (Camfield et al., 1984; Wang & Bellugi, 1994). Children with ADHD may have difficulty acquiring new information, despite adequate memory span (Korkman & Pesonen, 1994; Siegel & Ryan, 1989). This might be due to inadequate or inconsistent registration of information due to distractibility, superficial encoding skills, and/or attention to nonsalient or unusual details.

Memory For Faces (Core, Ages 3–12)

Immediate and Delayed Memory for Faces. Immediate memory for faces is assessed by asking the child to remember the faces in photographs that he or she sorts into two piles by gender as an attention-focusing device. The same faces embedded in arrays with two distracters are presented immediately for the Immediate Memory Trial. Thirty minutes later, again the child identifies the faces she has seen but in different arrays.

Facial memory may have a spatial component (Tzavaras, Hécaen, & LeBras, 1970) and a language component (Hamsher, Levin, & Benton, 1979). Despite numerous other visuospatial deficits, children with Williams Syndrome have average facial recognition skills (Udwin & Yule, 1991). It may be that they compensate by using verbal mediation or "talking their way through" the task, as they use when asked to do freehand drawings of objects (Bellugi, Sabo, & Vaid, 1988). Children with Asperger's Syndrome and high-functioning autism frequently have facial recognition deficits. Failure to make use of configural information in faces may lead to reduced facial perceptual capacity (Davies et al., 1994). Kracke (1994) proposed developmental/congenital prosopagnosia (the inability to recognize faces) as a core deficit in certain cases of Asperger's Syndrome.

Deficit causing poor performance on Memory for Faces:
• Deficit in Facial Recognition

Secondary reasons for poor performance on Memory for Faces:
• Inattention and impulsivity
• Poor social perception

Some questions to guide interpretation:
• Did the child perform poorly on the Immediate Memory trial, on the Delayed Memory Trial, or on both? Good performance on the Immedi-

ate Trial with significantly lower performance on Delayed Trial suggests memory decay. Significantly better performance on the Delayed Trial than the Immediate Trial suggests slowed consolidation of information due to slowed processing. Poor performance on both suggests poor encoding of facial information. (Consider Autistic Disorder or Asperger's Syndrome.) Were visuospatial deficit and math deficits present as well? (Consider Nonverbal Learning Disability.)

- Did the child attend to the faces well, or did he or she glance impulsively at the pictures?
- Did he or she appear uncomfortable looking at the faces? Was eye contact with the examiner fleeting? Did parents report poor social skills? (Consider Autistic Disorder, Asperger's Syndrome, Nonverbal Learning Disability.)

Memory for Names (Core, Ages 3–12)

Learning Trials and Delayed Memory.   This subtest assesses name learning of eight line drawings (six for 5-year-olds) of children over three trials with immediate and delayed recall (30 min after Learning Trial). Korkman and Pesonen (1994) demonstrated that name learning may be impaired in children with LD, with ADHD, and with ADHD/LD. Name learning is also impaired in a small group of children with Dysnomic Language Disorders (Korkman & Hakkinen-Rihu, 1994). In the NEPSY validation studies (Korkman, Kirk, & Kemp, 1998), children with Fetal Alcohol Syndrome, language disorders, and reading disorders performed poorly on Memory for Names, but not on Memory for Faces. Autistic children in the validation studies showed the opposite profile on these two subtests, performing poorly on Memory for Faces (revealing their social-perceptual deficits), but memorizing names successfully, albeit in a rote fashion.

Memory deficit causing poor performance on Memory for Names:
- Verbal memory deficit (brain lesion or TBI)

Language deficits causing poor performance on Memory for Names:
- Naming deficit (Dysnomic Language Disorder; Korkman, Hakkinen-Rihu, & Rhiu, 1994)
- Global language deficit (Global Language Subtype)
- Expressive Language Disorder

Secondary reasons for poor performance on Memory for Names:
- Inattention and impulsivity
- Difficulty accessing words (slowed processing)
- Poor learning over three trials indicating signs of executive functions

Some questions to guide interpretation:

- Did the child recall significantly more names on the Learning Trial than on Delay, suggesting memory decay? More names on the Delay than on the Learning Trials, suggesting slowed consolidation? Poor performance on both, suggesting naming deficit or global language disorder? Was accuracy on SN also poor? Was performance poor on all language subtests?
- Did the pattern of learning from trial to trial show a learning curve that built with each trial, or did the child learn the names on the last trial? The names may not be retained because learning wasn't consolidated.
- Is poor performance on Memory for Names due to a general difficulty in accessing information from memory or to a more specific difficulty in accessing names? Compare to Narrative Memory, List Learning, SN Supplemental Score for Time.

Narrative Memory (Core, Ages 3–12)

This subtest assesses narrative memory with free recall and cued recall. The child listens to a story and then retells it. In the cued recall condition, the examiner asks the child questions to elicit details that were not reported in free recall. Recalling an oral narrative requires attention, planning, organizing, sequencing, semantic and syntactic language skills, and the ability to encode, store, and retrieve names and content (Davenport, Yingling, Fein, Galin, & Johnstone, 1986). Information that is produced on free recall provides evidence that the child can encode and access it. Information that is not produced on free recall, but is accessed on cued recall, indicates that it was encoded and that the problem is one of access. When information cannot be accessed on free or cued recall, it is likely that it was never encoded (Delis, 1989). Poor encoding can be due to poor language comprehension, memory span (too much information at once), the rate of presentation (especially if processing is slow), and lack of familiarity with the subject. Encoding can also be affected by inattention, distractibility, anxiety, lack of interest, and motivation. Auditory memory span may be related to language processing deficits (Aram, Ekelman, & Nation, 1984; Korkman & Pesonen, 1994).

Memory deficit causing poor performance on Narrative Memory:
- Verbal memory deficit (due to brain lesion or TBI)

Language deficits causing poor performance on Narrative Memory:
- Global language deficit
- Receptive language deficit
- Expressive language deficit

Secondary reasons for poor performance on Narrative Memory:
- Inattention and impulsivity
- Dysexecutive function adversely affecting organizing and sequencing information
- Anxiety
- Slow processing
- Memory span (probably related to language processing deficits)

Some questions to guide interpretation:
- Did the child perform poorly on free recall, but significantly better on cued recall, suggesting an accessing problem or a dysexecutive problem, or did he perform poorly on both, suggesting information was not encoded? Children with slowed processing or naming deficits may have trouble accessing information. Children with attentional deficits, language comprehension deficits, global language problems, or low cognitive ability may have problems encoding information.
- Did the child seem to have difficulty understanding the story, possibly due to receptive language problems? Difficulty using expressive language to retell the story?
- Did the child attend well as the story was being told?
- Was the story recalled in sequence or as random details, suggesting dysexecutive function?

Sentence Repetition (Core, Ages 3–4; Expanded, Ages 5–12)

Poor performance on Sentence Repetition, a test of auditory short-term memory, could be due to a reduced memory span, to the length of the sentences, to the linguistic complexity of the sentences, or to inattention. A reduced memory span could affect the amount of information the child can hold in working memory. The following questions may be helpful for interpreting a child's performance. A child with ADHD is particularly susceptible to auditory short-term memory deficits because he or she tends to be distractible (Goodyear & Hynd, 1992) and impulsive (Barkley, Grodzinsky, & DuPaul, 1992), yet the child's memory span may be adequate (Korkman & Pesonen, 1994). Children with left temporal lobe epilepsy and with Down syndrome are more impaired on verbal than visuospatial short-term memory. Children with language and reading disorders may have a limited auditory memory span (Aram et al., 1984, Korkman & Pesonen, 1994) due, possibly, to language processing problems.

Memory deficit causing poor performance on Sentence Repetition:
- Verbal memory deficit (due to BBI, closed Head Injury)

Language deficits causing poor performance on Sentence Repetition:
- Global Language Disorder
- Receptive Language Disorder
- Expressive Language Disorder

Secondary deficits causing poor performance on Sentence Repetition:
- Inattention and impulsivity
- Dysexecutive function adversely affecting organizing and sequencing information
- Memory span (probably related to language processing deficits)

Some questions to guide interpretation:
- Was the child's difficulty related to the amount of verbatim information to be recalled, in other words, the length of the sentences (span)? This may be related to a language deficit. Did the child omit or substitute words but retain the gist of the sentence, suggesting a working memory deficit? Did the child perform poorly on other subtests when the stimuli required more working memory due to length (Comprehension of Instructions; Phonological Processing)?
- Did errors occur at the end of the sentences but not at the beginning (Primacy effect on recall), or did errors occur at the beginning of the sentences but not at the end (Recency effect on recall)? Compare to List Learning.
- Was the QO for Asks for Repetition significant?

List Learning (Expanded, Ages 7–12)

This is a complex task that assesses supraspan memory, or the ability to learn and recall long lists. Traditionally, it is assessed by learning a list over five trials. The clinician then administers an interference trial and then the child must recall the first list. The clinician administers a 30 min delay trial to assess retention and recall of information over time. NEPSY follows this traditional neuropsychological format. This task requires attention and effort, planning and organization, as well as monitoring of performance to avoid repeating words, adding extraneous words, and reporting words from the wrong list. This is an excellent subtest for observing a child's learning curve, retention, and recall. Children with ADHD can have great difficulty on list-learning tasks that require organized, structured, rehearsal strategies (Douglas & Benezra, 1990). Fay and colleagues (1994) found that children with TBI are impaired on immediate memory for lists (after the interference trial). These investigators felt this might be due to cognitive impairment rather than memory, per se. Yeates, Blumenstein, Patterson, and Delis (1995), however, found that children with TBI are more impaired on delay trials than on immediate trials, suggesting their problems may be related more to memory than cognitive level.

Memory deficit causing poor performance on List Learning:
• Verbal memory deficit

Secondary deficits causing poor performance on List Learning:
• Dysexecutive function
• Inattention, distractibility
• Language deficit
• Anxiety
• Memory Span
• Slow Processing

Some questions to guide interpretation:
• How many words did the child recall in total over the five trials (Total Score)? How did the child's performance compare to the performances of children of his or her age in the standardization sample?
• What was the difference between the child's first recall and recall on Trial 5, the last learning trial? Inspect the SS for Learning Effect (Trial 1–Trial 5).
• Did the learning curve build gradually over trials, or did the child show an unusual pattern of learning? (Inspect the graph for the learning curve on the SS page of the Record Form and compare each trial to the mean for the child of his or her age in the normative group.)
• Did the child retain the expected number of words after the introduction of the Interference Trial (Inspect Trial 7)?
• Were words from List A (Trial 6) reported on the recall of List B (Trial 7)? These results suggest an inability to inhibit words from the old list interfering with the new information. Inspect the SS for Intrusions.
• Did the child perseverate on the same word? Inspect the SS for Repetitions (Total Trial 1–7).
• Did words that were not on any list intrude on recall (i.e., "school" is recalled because of its associate with "teacher" and "pupil")? This suggests inability to inhibit associated words from intruding on information being learned. Inspect SS for Novel Intrusions.
• Did the child retain the expected number of words after the 30 min de-

lay? Was memory decay (a significant decline in words recalled) present between the Immediate and Delayed trials? Did the child recall significantly more words on Delay than Immediate, suggesting slowed processing and consolidation of the information?

- Did the child show a primacy effect (remembering more words from the beginning than the end of the list), or a recency effect (remembering more words from the end than the beginning of the list)? Primacy is the more efficient of the two. Primacy and Recency together is the most efficient.

- Did the child cluster words to facilitate recall, or did he or she recall words haphazardly? If the child clusters words did he or she use semantic clustering (grouping by words that can be associated such as water, boat, fish) or phonemic clustering (grouping by initial sound such as winter, water, window)? Semantic clustering is the most efficient.

- Did the child recall fewer words than expected after the introduction of the Interference List (Retroactive Interference)? This suggests that the new information caused loss of the old. Did the child recall fewer words on the Interference Trial than on the first trial (Proactive Interference)? This suggests that the information the child has already learned interferes with new learning.

- Was the child attentive when stimuli were administered? If so, at the beginning of the subtest only, or could he or she sustain attention across all trials? Did the child cover his or her eyes or focus on the wall or floor as a compensation to try to minimize external stimuli?

INTERPRETATIVE REPORT OF NEPSY RESULTS

Having now interpreted the NEPSY results and having verified your interpretations in the manner prescribed, the clinician is ready to compose his or her report. It is recommended that, if possible, a cognitive assessment and achievement testing be included in the evaluation. After the clinician has discussed the child's history and test observations, he or she presents all scores, along with a description of the functions assessed by that subtest in the Test Results section. This part of the report can be compiled by the *NEPSY Scoring Assistant,* (The Psychological Corporation, 2000). The clinician is then ready to present the clinical impressions. The clinician should discuss subtest results grouped by domain first, being sure to include discussions of the QOs and SS. The clinician then pulls together the "threads"observed across NEPSY. Finally, he or she weaves those threads into the diagnostic behavioral clusters that point to a particular hypothesis or disorder. The clinician needs to be sure to discuss primary and secondary deficits.

The results of the cognitive assessment should be discussed first, then the results of NEPSY, and finally the results of the achievement testing. The clinician integrates and interprets results by domains or functional areas across all assessments administered. Finally, the clinician will discuss primary and secondary deficits and the diagnostic behavioral clusters observed. In order to attain ecologically relevant outcomes, this discussion must place the child in the environmental context of family and school. The discussion must answer the referral question, but it may also present additional findings.

The final step in composing the report is very important: formulating recommendations. Recommendations need to address referrals for any medical needs, as well as any psychological or occupational/physical therapies required. Recommendations also must address cognitive rehabilitation, remediation, or compensatory methods for each of the deficits or disorders you have discussed. Keeping in mind the information acquired from the questions used in guiding interpretation, the QOs from NEPSY, observations about how the child performed tasks, and the SSs that teased apart problem areas, the clinician must consider how the child may be taught to accomplish a task or to compensate for the impairments standing in his or her way. The clinician must combine this information, with his or her knowledge of the current research and numerous available resources (Bos & Van Reusen, 1991; Bryan & Lee, 1990; Byrne & Fielding-Barnsley 1993; Ellis & Lenz, 1991; Gaskins et al., 1988; Gray & Dean, 1989; Iverson & Tummer, 1993; Olson, Folz, & Wise, 1986; Rourke, Fiske, & Strang, 1986; Semrud-Clikeman & Hynd, 1991; Shapiro, 1989; Teeter, 1989; Teeter & Semrud-Clikeman, 1998; Walker, Holmes, Todis, & Horton, 1988; Walker et al., 1988; Wise & Olson, 1991; Wise et al., 1989) to formulate useable, practical, age-appropriate recommendations. Examples of actual reports are found in Chapter 7. First, however, a discussion of clinical applications of NEPSY with special populations will be considered in Chapter 6.

Six

CLINICAL APPLICATIONS OF THE NEPSY

APPLICATIONS OF NEPSY DERIVED FROM STUDIES OF DISORDERS

Children with virtually all types of developmental problems may be assessed with NEPSY. Because the brain organizes all behavior, an evaluation that assesses the various brain processes underlying complex behavior is, in principle, applicable to all situations where disordered development is of concern. The problem often lies in time constraints: How can the clinician, with a restricted amount of time, direct his or her efforts in the most efficient way and choose among the wide variety of NEPSY subtests as well as other instruments? The best way to answer this question is for the clinician to review what types of findings he or she may expect in various disorders, that is, what aspects he or she may want to evaluate. Experience naturally comes with assessing children with many types of disorders. However, it is also possible to build on the experience of others.

This chapter discusses the applications and findings of the NEPSY Developmental Neuropsychological Assessment (Korkman, Kirk, & Kemp, 1998) in various developmental and acquired disorders. The focus is on test results that are characteristic of different diagnostic groups. This review serves as a guide to help clinicians recognize patterns of results (diagnostic behavioral clusters) that are characteristic of different types of disorders. The review does not encompass all possible disorders, but considers some syndromes that are representative of types of disorders, both developmental and acquired, in which the NEPSY has been shown to provide helpful diagnostic information. Obviously, no two children with a disorder will produce identical results on an assessment. What follows is a discussion of patterns that have been observed in group studies where individual variations are collapsed into the mean performance of groups of children with particular disorders. The NEPSY validity studies are presented as the basis of the review of performance patterns observed in particular disorders, as a guide for selecting Expanded subtests beyond the NEPSY

Core for various disorders, and as illustrations of the type of children who may benefit from assessment.

APPLICATION OF THE NEPSY IN DIAGNOSING ADHD

Attention Deficit Hyperactivity Disorder (ADHD) is a disorder that can cause significant inattention, distractibility, impulsivity, and sometimes hyperactivity in children at home and at school. The *DSM-IV* (American Psychiatric Association, 1994) recognizes three subtypes of ADHD: Predominately Inattentive Type, Hyperactive/Impulsive Type, and Combined Type. Children diagnosed with this disorder are at high risk for significant school problems, substance abuse, and poor occupational outcomes in adulthood (Mannuzza, Klein, Bessler, Malloy, & La-Padula, 1993). They are also at risk, not only for comorbid learning disabilities and language disorders (Stanford & Hynd, 1994), but also for Oppositional Defiant Disorder, Conduct Disorder, affective and anxiety disorders (Biederman, Newcorn, & Sprich, 1991), and Antisocial Disorder in adulthood (Mannuzza et al., 1993). Therefore, early diagnosis and treatment is essential.

Inconsistent and mixed neuropsychological test results have been obtained in children with ADHD. They are frequently impaired on tasks that require selective or sustained attention, as well as executive functions (Korkman, Kemp, & Kirk, 1998). Executive functions such as planning and strategizing, carrying out an organized search (Welsh, Pennington, & Groisser, 1991), maintaining and shifting set (Kemp & Kirk, 1993; Kirk & Kelly, 1986), and impulse control (Barkley, Grodzinsky, & DuPaul, 1992, Korkman & Peltomaa, 1991) are implicated. Children with ADHD are also distractible (Goodyear & Hynd, 1992) and show inconsistent attention on tasks that require sustained, selective attention (Kinsbourne, 1990). Barkley (1997) has recently developed a model in which the primary deficit is response inhibition, and the secondary deficits are poor working memory, inadequate internalizing of speech, an inability to separate affect from content in order to arouse attention and motivation, and an inability to reconstitute information. Poor motor performance can be a comorbid disorder in ADHD, but it can also be adversely affected by poor executive control, according to Barkley (1997).

A sample of 51 children (mean age 8.7±1.4) who met the *DSM-IV* criteria for ADHD and were free of other psychiatric or neurological diagnoses, had normal or corrected vision, normal hearing, and IQs equal to or greater than 80, were evaluated with NEPSY. The sample included 28 Combined Type, 15 Predominately Inattentive Type, and 8 who met the criteria for ADHD, but type was unspecified. The performance of the clinical ADHD group on the Full NEPSY for ages 5 to

12 was compared to that of matched normal controls (NCs) was drawn from the NEPSY standardization sample. They were matched for age, sex, ethnicity, and parent education.

Huckeba, Kreiman, Korkman, Kirk, and Kemp [(2000) manuscript in preparation] examined the QOs and SS of NEPSY performance in children with ADHD and in nonclinical controls. The nonclinical controls were matched to the above ADHD sample ($N = 51$) in the same manner that was employed in the NEPSY validity study of ADHD. The discussion that follows is based on information derived from these two studies. The information about Core Domain Scores and NEPSY subtests is based on the NEPSY validity studies (Korkman, Kirk, and Kemp, 1998), and the data from SS and QOs were derived from the Huckeba and colleagues study.

The performance of the children with ADHD differed from that of the nonclinical controls on the Attention/Executive Domain overall (Attention/Executive Core Domain Score $p < .0002$). On Tower, a subtest of planning, strategizing, and monitoring performance for problem solution, they solved fewer problems correctly (Total Score, $p < .022$) and made more Rule Violations ($p < .001$). They also demonstrated more Motor Difficulty ($p < .03$), having trouble placing balls on the pegs or dropping them.

Performance on AARS differed ($p < .005$) between the two groups for the AA Subtest overall, and the children with ADHD showed more Off-Task Behaviors ($p < .03$) during the performance of AARS than did the normal controls. The groups did not differ on the simple, selective AA, which requires selective auditory attention and the ability to establish and maintain a set. They differed in performance on the RS section. In relation to the normal controls, the ADHD group demonstrated less ability ($p < .001$) on this complex auditory attention task, to change the auditory set established on AA and adopt a new set, utilizing working memory and response inhibition, as well as selective attention. The SS for RS revealed that the ADHD group was more impulsive (CEs, $p < .001$) and inattentive (OEs, $p < .001$) than the NCs.

Children with ADHD frequently have comorbid motor findings. Barkley's (1997) model of ADHD also posits poor motor function in these children due to a lack of executive control. The ADHD and NC groups differed ($p < .014$) in performance on Statue, a subtest of motor persistence and response inhibition in which children are required to stand quietly with their eyes shut and hands at their sides when confronted with noise distracters. The ADHD children's performance on Knock and Tap, a go-no-go motor inhibition task differed ($p < .017$) from that of the normal controls.

The ADHD group and NCs did not differ in performance on the VA subtest

(Total Score) or on any of the QOs or SS dimensions derived from that test (simple task [Cats], versus complex task [Faces], Time, OEs, CEs). Nor were there differences on the Design Fluency subtest, which assesses executive functions. The very salient, static pictures of objects and faces on VA, as well as the design arrays on Design Fluency may have been an anchor for attention. This may explain why the ADHD group performed as well as they did. There were, of course, individual differences in the performance of ADHD children on VA. Children with Combined Type and Hyperactive Impulsive Type ADHD are apt to perform poorly on this subtest than are normal controls. Children with visual-perceptual problems may also perform poorly on this test.

Thus, the results from NEPSY suggest that children with ADHD demonstrate executive dysfunctions in planning, strategizing, and monitoring performance; adopting, maintaining and changing set; failure to inhibit automatic responses on complex, rather than inattention on simple tasks, or secondary working memory deficits. These results are consistent with Barkley's (1997) model.

Although this sample of children with ADHD did not have identified learning disabilities, their performance was significantly poorer than NCs on the Language Core Domain Score ($p < .002$) overall. The ADHD sample showed deficits, as compared to NCs, in the phonological processes which underlie reading decoding and spelling (Phonological Processing, $p < .003$; Repetition of Nonsense Words, $p < .001$). On these tasks, the children with ADHD had difficulty perceiving a word segment and identifying the word from which it came, listening to a speech-sound pattern (a word) and then deleting or changing a segment or phoneme in order to create a new word, and repeating nonsense words (a novel speech-sound pattern). Furthermore, they had problems comprehending linguistically complex oral instructions (Comprehension of Instructions, $p < .002$), rapidly producing words within a category (Verbal Fluency, $p < .01$), and producing oromotor sequences (Oromotor Sequences, $p < .001$). The ADHD group demonstrated motor programming and sequencing deficits, not only on Oromotor Sequences, but also on Manual Motor Sequences, again suggesting the comorbid motor deficits that are often evident in children with ADHD, as well as possible executive dyscontrol affecting motor programming.

The ADHD group also differed from the NCs on the SS for Verbal Fluency, producing fewer words in categories on both the Semantic trials ($p < .042$) and the Phonemic trials ($p < .040$). They did not ask for repetition more often than the NCs ($p < .118$) on Phonological Processing, when perhaps they should have (one repetition is allowed per item on Part B).

There were no differences ($p < .548$) between the ADHD and NC groups on SN, suggesting that ADHD per se did not affect performance on this task. Because SN has a visual stimulus plate, it may also anchor the attention more than the Verbal Fluency task where the child must produce words spontaneously from the internal verbal store.

Children with ADHD appeared to be subject to secondary memory deficits that affected their performance on the harder items of the Phonological Processing, Rapid Naming, and Comprehension of Instructions subtests. Furthermore, the inability to attend to oral directions on Comprehension of Instructions could have affected the understanding of them. Performance on Verbal Fluency also may have been affected by executive dysfunction especially on the Phonemic Fluency section. They might have difficulty developing a strategy for producing as many words as possible or might have difficulty accessing words. This would be particularly true on the Phonemic section of Verbal Fluency, where the child might be unable to perform an efficient search of his or her lexicon for a word beginning with a particular sound.

Children with ADHD obtained lower Sensorimotor Core Domain Scores ($p <$ .005) than the NCs, which suggests the comorbid motor dysfunction often seen in ADHD. Barkley also posits executive dyscontrol of motor function (1997). Subtest differences between the children with ADHD and NCs were observed in their poor performance on Imitating Hand Positions ($p < .003$), a highly integrative task requiring visuospatial analysis, motor programming, and kinesthetic feedback. They were unable to produce sequences of hand movements requiring motor programming as well as the NCs on Manual Motor Sequences ($p < .001$). Children with ADHD displayed poor Finger Discrimination for the Preferred hand ($p < .002$), a brief assessment of tactile localization. The children with ADHD performed as well as the NCs on the Fingertip Tapping subtest ($p < .190$). There were, however, significant differences ($p < .01$) observed on the QO for Overflow in Fingertip Tapping performance between the ADHD sample and NC group, suggesting an increased amount of associated movements in the children with ADHD. A significant amount of involuntary movement around the mouth or in the tongue was observed when fine motor movement was being performed. Differences were also observed in the amount of Overflow ($p < .01$) on Manual Motor Sequencing as well as in the number of perseverations ($p < .01$), the presence of recruitment in Forceful Tapping ($p < .001$), and in the Loss of Asymmetry when the two hands executed different movements in the sequence ($p < .001$). Further, the ADHD sample demonstrated echopraxia (switching to the hand contralateral to the clinician's) more often than the NC group by using the Mirror Hand ($p < .001$) on Imitating Hand Position.

According to the model posited by Barkley (1997), Imitating Hand Position may have been adversely affected in children with ADHD due to two factors: their difficulty with motor programming due to executive dysfunction and their inability to reconstitute information. Manual Motor Sequence performance would be adversely affected in children with ADHD by the executive dyscontrol of motor programming. Tactile perception differed on the Preferred hand performance, but not on the Nonpreferred hand as compared to NCs (Finger Discrimination—Nonpreferred Hand, $p < .07$).

The two groups did not differ on the VP Total Score ($p < .159$), but SS revealed that although the children with ADHD worked as quickly on both tracks ($p < .219$; $p < .077$, respectively) as the NCs, they made significantly more errors (drawing the line outside the track) on both the wider, winding track ($p < .016$) and the narrower, more convoluted track ($p < .017$). This has marked implications for the classroom. The children with ADHD may be impulsive and rush through their work, regardless of the need to be accurate. On the other hand, they may have learned to sacrifice accuracy for speed in order to complete a pencil/paper task in the same amount of time allowed for age-mates.

The Visuospatial Core Domain Score was significantly lower ($p < .04$) for the children with ADHD than it was for NCs. Although the groups did not differ on the individual subtests, the children with ADHD scored somewhat lower than NCs, which affected the global score. The significant Core Domain Score difference is an artifact of measurement due to the additive nature of the small differences in performance on its component parts.

Memory and Learning Core Domain Scores for the children with ADHD were significantly lower ($p < .03$) than those of NCs. They recalled significantly fewer details of a narrative both spontaneously and with cues (Narrative Memory, $p < .051$) than the NC group. Recall was also poorer on an auditory short-term memory task (Sentence Repetition, $p < .039$). They learned fewer words over trials than NCs and recalled fewer of them, both in immediate recall after interference and after a 30 min delay (List learning, $p < .001$). The groups did not differ on the QOs for free recall versus cued recall on Narrative Memory or on Asks for Repetition on Sentence Repetition. Off-Task Behavior was more frequent on Sentence Repetition ($p < .011$) in the ADHD sample than in the NCs, however, suggesting that lower scores on this task may have been due to distractibility or to poor attention affecting auditory short-term memory.

On the List Learning supraspan verbal memory task, the ADHD sample did not differ from NCs on Repetitions (perseverations) ($p < .455$) or Interference Intrusions (from List A, Trial 5 to List B Recall or from List B to Immediate Recall of List A) ($p < .117$). They were, however, subject to more Novel Intrusions ($p < .009$) (words recalled that were not on any list) than the NCs. The children with ADHD did not seem to be able to inhibit the intrusion of other unassociated words into their recall of the list words. They did not differ on Memory for Names

≡Rapid Reference 6.1

Group differences between the ADHD Sample and NCs in the NEPSY validity studies on the Memory and Learning Domain

The performance of children with ADHD differed from the performance of NCs in the NEPSY validity studies on Memory and Learning Core Domain Score ($p < .03$) performance overall.

* Narrative Memory: ($p < .051$)—retrieval of significantly fewer details spontaneously.
* Sentence Repetition: ($p < .039$)—poorer auditory short-term memory.
  —QOs for Off-Task Behavior on Sentence Repetition ($p < .011$)—more distractible.
* List Learning: ($p < .001$)—fewer words learned over 5 trials.
  —SS for Novel Intrusions ($p < .009$)—retrieval of more words not on any list, suggesting inability to inhibit extraneous words in recall.

and Memory for Faces ($p < .188; p < .201$, respectively). These results suggest that the social problems of children with ADHD may be more related to their impulsive behaviors (lack of response inhibition) than to problems with dysnomia or imperception of facial cues. Moreover, all three of the subtests on which the children with ADHD performed poorly required auditory short-term memory, and there were no visual "anchors" for their attention on these tasks. On both the Memory for Names and Memory for Faces subtests, there were visual stimuli to anchor attention. (See Rapid Reference 6.1.)

In undertaking an assessment to rule out Attention Deficit Hyperactivity Disorder, it is important to consider the wide-ranging deficits that such children can demonstrate. In the light of the above results, it is clear that, at the minimum, the clinician should administer a Selective Assessment, including a Core NEPSY along with the Expanded subtests across domains on which children with ADHD differed as compared to NCs (as shown in Rapid Reference 6.2). Beyond the Core, the Expanded subtests that yielded significant differences in performance for children with ADHD when compared to NCs were Statue, an assessment of the ability to inhibit motor response to noise distracters (it is an Attention/Executive Domain Core Subtest for ages 3 to 4, but can be administered effectively to children from 5 up to about 10 years of age. Though it may seem very "young," clinicians can give it to children ages 11 to 12); Knock and Tap, a Lurian go-no-go task of motor inhibition; Repetition of Nonsense Words, a phonological processing task which requires auditory attention and working memory; Verbal Fluency, an assessment of word production within semantic and phonemic categories; Finger Discrimination, an evaluation of tactile discrimination; Sentence Repetition, an as-

===*Rapid Reference 6.2*

Selective Assessment for ADHD Diagnosis Based on NEPSY Validity Studies

NEPSY Core plus the following Expanded subtests across domains which showed differences in performance between the ADHD and NC groups:

Attention/Executive Domain
- Knock and Tap
- Statue*

Language Domain
- Repetition of Nonsense Words
- Verbal Fluency
- Oromotor Sequences

Sensorimotor Domain
- Manual Motor Sequences
- Finger Discrimination

Memory and Learning Domain
- Sentence Repetition*
- List learning**

*Core for ages 3–4   ** Starts at age 7.0

===*Rapid Reference 6.3*

Deficits of Children with ADHD Observed on NEPSY Validity Group Performance That May Aid Diagnosis*

Inattention
- Auditory inattention (AARS, RS Totals, and RS Omissions)

Executive Dysfunction
- Lack of planning, strategizing, and monitoring performance for problem solution (Tower; Rule Violations)
- Difficulty adopting, monitoring, and changing an established set (AARS Total, RS Total)
- Difficulty inhibiting responses and secondary effects on complex auditory attention (Off-Task, CEs on RS; Total for Narrative Memory, Sentence Repetitions, List Learning, Novel Intrusions, Knock/Tap Statue, Loss of Asymmetry on Manual Motor Mirror Hand on IMH)
- A lack of executive control of motor programming
- Inefficient search strategy (Verbal Fluency, Phonemic Trial of Verbal Fluency)
- Secondary working memory deficits in holding and manipulating information on-line (AARS Total, RS Total, Long items on Phonological Processing, CI, Repetitions of Nonsense Words)

Comorbid sensorimotor deficits
- Fine motor coordination, graphomotor control; Motor Difficulty on Tower, Overflow on Fingertip Tapping and Manual Motor Sequences, Errors on VP, Finger Discrimination/PH.

(*All ADHD children may not show this specific pattern, but the areas of inattention, executive dysfunction, and comorbid sensorimotor deficits, children usually display.)

sessment of auditory short-term memory; and List Learning, a supraspan learning and memory task. It is very important that clinicians include all SS and QOs in the analysis, because a great deal of diagnostic information can be gleaned from them.

Specifically, the NEPSY validity studies and the Huckeba and colleagues study (submitted for publication) would point to the following problems for children with ADHD:

Because the performance of children with ADHD can vary, all of these factors may not be present in every child who has ADHD. It is very important to have parents and teachers complete adaptive behavior scales pertinent to ADHD. In order to get a broad picture of functioning in children with ADHD, the clinician may also administer a cognitive assessment, another continuous performance measure, and achievement tests. These can be reviewed for patterns of deficits that corroborate or disconfirm NEPSY hypotheses. In other assessments, the clinician should look for evidence of auditory short-term memory deficits, dysgraphia, working memory problems, inattention, impulsivity, and distractibility, as well as executive dysfunction. Observational notes, results of a classroom observation (if possible), and the comprehensive history covering all educational, medical, developmental, and psychoemotional factors should be combined with the NEPSY results. Together these measures should yield enough information to confirm or discard the diagnosis of ADHD reliably, according to the *DSM-IV* criteria. (See Rapid Reference 6.4.)

≡Rapid Reference 6.4

Additional Measures Recommended For Comprehensive ADHD Evaluation

Because LD is often comorbid with ADHD, and because these children can have significant academic problems, it is wise to administer a comprehensive evaluation. In this way, parents, teachers, and the child will have a full picture of strengths and weaknesses. This makes possible the formulation of appropriate recommendations for remediation, compensations, and modifications for school and home. Recommended additional measures to be integrated with NEPSY results are

- A cognitive assessment.
- A second continuous performance measure to confirm any positive results from NEPSY.
- An achievement test.
- Adaptive behavior scales pertinent to ADHD filled out by parents and teachers.
- Your observational notes from testing.
- Results of a classroom observation, if possible.
- The comprehensive history covering all educational, medical, developmental, and psychoemotional factors.

APPLICATION OF THE NEPSY IN DIAGNOSING A LEARNING DISABILITY

Specific learning disabilities in reading, mathematics, and written expression make up 2 to 10% of the disorders in child development (Korkman, Kirk, & Kemp, 1998). The child must display a significant discrepancy between intellectual functioning and academic achievement (American Psychiatric Association, 1994) for a deficit to be considered a learning disability. Studies by Rourke (1975; Rourke & Finlayson, 1978) indicated that neuropsychological instruments could be used to distinguish children with reading disabilities from those without a reading problem.

Phonological awareness is related to reading achievement (Berninger, 1996; Bradley, 1989; Tallal et al., 1993; Scarborough, 1990). Phonological processing deficits as assessed on tasks of phoneme segmentation (Hurford, Schauf, Bunce, Blaich, & Moore, 1994), initial phoneme discrimination, and auditory conceptualization (Felton, 1992) have been identified as causes of reading disability, in particular dysphonetic dyslexia. Lexical access (Felton & Brown, 1991), as measured by rapid color and letter naming (Blachman, 1984; Denckla & Rudel, 1976a; Korkman & Hakkinen-Rihu, 1994), naming of alternating stimuli (Wolf, 1986), name learning (Korkman & Hakkinen-Rihu, 1994), and word naming time (Denckla & Rudel, 1976b, Stanovich, 1981) have also been identified as stable predictors of reading ability and disability (Torgeson et al., 1994). Doehring (1985) and Hynd & Hynd (1984) also implicated visual-perceptual deficits in the processing of the visuospatial and neurolinguistic aspects of reading. More recently Stein (1994) posited a theory that right parietal dysfunction in vergence control affects reading due to convergence insufficiency. He demonstrated that patching the master eye only during reading would stimulate vergence and improve reading. Lovegrove (1994) has demonstrated experimental evidence of a deficit in rapid visual processing of transient stimuli in reading disabilities. Because this study is experimental in nature, it remains unclear as to what extent this factor contributes to reading disabilities.

Bishop (1992) reported a motor programming deficit in reading-disabled children. It is not uncommon to find children diagnosed as reading disabled who also exhibit some characteristic signs of ADHD (Halperin, Gittelman, Klein, & Rudel, 1984; Shaywitz & Shaywitz, 1988). Pennington (1991) noted that inattention, distractibility, and impulsivity may arise in dyslexics as a reaction to their academic difficulties, rather than from a neurological base. Pennington and his colleagues (1991) studied children with ADHD, with reading disabilities (RD), and with both. They found that the ADHD group had more executive dysfunction, and the dyslexic group had more indicators of phonological processing problems. The children with both conditions performed like the dyslexic group, leading to the conclusion that dyslexia was the primary deficit. It is also possible that some children have both, as comorbid disorders.

Dyslexia is a particular reading disability in which neuronal anomalies (ectopic neurons and dysplasia with abnormally placed neurons and disorganized cortical layering) in the left hemisphere have been demonstrated consistently in postmortem examination of brain (Drake, 1968; Galaburda & Kemper, 1979; Galaburda & Eidelberg, 1982; Galaburda et al., 1985). It is important to be able to recognize the profile of the dyslexic child, which usually includes

- phonological processing deficits on Phonological Processing or Repetition of Nonsense Words.
- poor lexical access on SN; may also have a naming deficit on Memory for Names.
- on a standardized individual achievement test, a significant discrepancy between cognitive ability and performance on reading decoding and spelling subtests; frequently better reading comprehension than decoding and spelling performance.

In addition, dyslexics usually have

- Language deficits, even if it is as subtle as a naming deficit alone (SN, Memory for Names). However, they may have a receptive or expressive language disorder.
- A family history of reading or spelling problems or diagnosed dyslexia.
- A history of difficulty rhyming, keeping time with music, mastering phonics and reading decoding or spelling.

They may or may not

- Have difficulty with visuospatial skills (Arrows, Route Finding, DC).
- Continue to make letter and number reversal errors after 8 years of age when reversals should have disappeared developmentally.

Mathematics disabilities often coexist with language, spatial, attentional, and psychomotor disabilities (McCarthy & Warrington, 1990). Strang and Rourke (1985) note that dyscalculia has often been thought of as a language-based disorder, or at the very least, one involving verbal memory deficits. Subtypes of arithmetic disorders have included (a) deficits in comprehension and, infrequently, in retrieval of numbers (as opposed to deficits in calculation), spatial deficits, memory deficits, and retrieval deficits for operations and math facts, speed of pro-

The Dyslexic Profile

All children with dyslexia may not show all of these deficits, but deficits in the areas of phonological processing, lexical access, language, and deficits in reading decoding and spelling are characteristic.

- Deficits include Phonological processing difficulties on Phonological Processing or Repetition of Names subtests.
- Poor lexical access on SN; may also have a naming deficit on Memory for Names.
- A significant discrepancy between cognitive ability and performance on reading decoding and spelling achievement tests; frequently better reading comprehension than decoding and spelling performance.

In addition, dyslexics usually have

- Language deficits, even if as subtle as a naming deficit alone (SN/Memory for Names), but they may have a receptive or expressive language disorder.
- A family history of reading and spelling problems or diagnosed dyslexia.
- A history of difficulty with rhyming, keeping time with music, mastering phonics, and initial reading.

They may or may not

- Have deficits in visuospatial skills (Arrows, Route Finding, DC).
- Continue to make reversals errors with letters and numbers after the 8th year, when reversals should have disappeared developmentally.

cessing and problem-solving (McCarthy & Warrington, 1990); (b) difficulties in math due to reading deficits and inexperience with the material (as opposed to deficits in spatial organization), visual detail deficits, graphomotor control deficits, memory deficits, judgement/reasoning deficits, and a tendency to perseverate, as well as problems understanding procedure (Rourke, 1993), and (c) deficits in memory storage and retrieval deficits on nonverbal tasks (Fletcher, 1985).

Written language disabilities are closely aligned with spelling and reading disabilities but can be manifested uniquely (James & Selz, 1997). Writing has been described as a process whose end product may be constrained by visual memory and retrieval of letters, motor control, and visual-motor integration, linguistic (ability to write sentences and paragraphs), and cognitive factors (e.g., planning and revising; Berninger, Mizokawa, & Bragg, 1991). Difficulty with paper/pencil copying of geometric figures (Beery, 1983) was found to correlate with spelling achievement at the end of kindergarten and first grade (Berninger et al., 1991). Berninger and her colleagues (1991) also found that the ability to copy the alphabet correctly in 1 min correlated with writing difficulties in grades two through nine. At the end of kindergarten, the ability of normally developing children to print the lowercase alphabet correctly in sequence correlated significantly with their spelling achievement at the end of first grade (DeBruyn, Smith, and Berninger, 1985).

When NEPSY is used to diagnose a learning disability, it should be combined with a cognitive assessment, achievement testing, and, of course, information from the comprehensive history (developmental, medical, educational, family, etc.), as well as additional summaries of functioning gathered from the child's teachers, records of any previous assessments, and copies of standardized testing. The following is a discussion of findings on NEPSY associated with reading disability in the validity studies. NEPSY can also address the diagnosis of other learning disabilities. In doing so, however, it is important to keep current with the research, so that diagnostic behavioral clusters and new diagnostic factors will be recognized.

Thirty-six children diagnosed with reading disabilities (RD), according to the State Department of Education or Special Education criteria for the child's home state, were assessed in the NEPSY validity study. These children were free of psychiatric or neurological diagnoses (including ADHD), had normal or corrected vision, normal hearing, and IQ greater than or equal to 80. The normal control (NC) sample was derived from the NEPSY standardization group and matched on age, sex, race, ethnicity, and parent education (Korkman, Kirk, & Kemp, 1998). Analysis of QOs and SSs on NEPSY for the RD sample also revealed some differences in performance when compared to the NC group.

The clinical sample of children with RD did not differ from the NCs on the Attention/Executive Function Core Domain Score ($p < .167$). At the subtest level the RD group did not differ from the NCs in planning, strategizing, and monitoring performance for problem solution (Tower, $p < .324$). Nor did they differ in the ability to complete a visual search for a target object on a random array of common objects or on the more complex visual attention section of the subtest, requiring location of all the faces with multiple features identical to two target faces in a linear array of many faces (VA, $p < .869$). Results on the executive rule-bound task of generating as many unique designs as possible on structured and random 5-dot arrays also produced no difference in performance between the two groups (Design Fluency, $p < .484$). Performance also did not differ on a task requiring the inhibition of motor response to match the examiner's hand movement when an alternate response was required (Knock and Tap, $p < .621$). The performance of RD children, however, differed significantly on an auditory attention task that required selective auditory attention, as well as the adoption and changing of an auditory set, utilizing working memory (AARS: $p < .012$) and on a task requiring inhibition of motor responses to noise distracters Statue ($p < .008$). Interestingly, the SSs for the RD sample showed a significant difference ($p < .001$) in performance on the AA section, a simple, selective auditory attention task, rather than on the complex auditory set-shifting task (RS), which characterized the ADHD sample. Despite the lack of difference on the QOs for Omission, Commission, or Off-Task Behaviors in this domain, there was evidence for inattention (AA) and lack of response inhibition (Statue). The RD group made Rule Violations significantly more often ($p < .002$) on Tower than NCs, possibly due to mild inattention or executive dysfunction to working memory problems related to the amount of language that had to be processed in order to understand them.

In a sample of children with reading disabilities, the clinician would expect to find deficits in the Language Domain on NEPSY, because reading deficits are often considered language-based disorders (James & Selz, 1997). Indeed, the Language Core Domain Score was significantly lower ($p < .001$) for the RD sample than for the sample of NCs. Furthermore, their performance differed from that of the NCs at the subtest level on Phonological Processing, a task requiring the conceptualization of speech-sound patterns (words) and manipulation of them to produce new patterns; on SN, a task which assesses rapid lexical access, and on Oromotor Sequences, a task requiring the production of articulatory sequences ($p < .001$ for all subtests). They did not differ on Repetition of Nonsense Words, another task of phonological processing ($p < .060$). The Phonological Processing task requires the child not only to be able to conceptualize the speech-sound pattern, but to manipulate it in order to create a new pattern. On RN the child must conceptualize a novel sound pattern and reproduce it without having to manipulate it. Furthermore, a child receives 1 point credit for each correct syllable he or she reproduces, so the nonsense word can be partially correct and still receive some credit.

More children with reading disabilities demonstrated more Stable Misarticulations on RN ($p < .04$) than the NC group. They also displayed a change in the rate of production on Oromotor Sequences more often than did the NCs (QO for Rate Change, $p < .001$). These results, along with the significant difference in the Oromotor Sequences Subtest Scaled Score, suggest that children with RD are more apt to have stable articulation problems than are children who are good readers. The QOs Asks for Repetition revealed that the RD sample asked for an item to be repeated on Phonological Processing more often ($p < .04$) than did the NC group. These results suggest that the poor readers were unsure about the phonological pattern being presented due to deficits in phonological processing or in working memory, but unlike the ADHD group who did not ask for repetitions on Section B of Phonological Processing when they could have, the RD group attempted to help themselves by asking for a repetition. As noted above, poor phonological awareness is related to reading disabilities (Berninger, 1996; Tallal,

1993), as are naming problems (Blachman, 1984; Denckla & Rudel, 1976a, b; Korkman & Hakkinen-Rihu, 1994; Stanovich, 1981; Wolf, 1986). Therefore, deficits on Phonological Processing and Speeded Naming would be expected in an RD sample. It is of interest that 42% of the RD sample scored more than −1 SD from the mean on Speeded Naming, whereas only 11% of the NC group scored at that level. When contributions to the Total Score for Speeded Naming were analyzed using the SS for Time ($p < .220$) and Accuracy in Naming ($p < .08$), differences in the performance of the RD and NC groups were not evident. These results suggest that both speed in accessing names and the accuracy of the names accessed are related to reading, and that many more children with reading disabilities scored −1 SD from the mean on Speeded Naming overall, thus negatively impacting the SN Total Score. Frequently in individual cases, the SS for Time or for Accuracy (naming correctly) are poor.

Although the groups did not differ in performance on Verbal Fluency ($p < .075$), they did differ on the "Animals" Trial of Semantic Fluency (.032). These results suggest subtle semantic language differences between children with and without reading problems. Performance on the Phonemic Trial did not differ ($p < .075$). This may be because the phonemic trial is difficult for most young children, irrespective of reading ability. The performance of poor readers did not differ ($p < .190$) from the performance of NCs in understanding linguistically complex oral directions as they progressed in difficulty (Comprehension of Instructions). These results would suggest that, as a group, this sample of poor readers did not have receptive language deficits. Many children with reading deficits have generalized language disorders, though some have a narrow language deficit in one or two areas (e.g., naming, semantics), and others have no language deficit.

The Sensorimotor Core Domain Score did not differ ($p < .357$) for the RD sample as compared to the same score for the NC sample. In this domain, performance differed ($p < .024$) between good and poor readers only on the Manual Motor Sequences subtest, which required motor programming of hand movements sequences. The RD group also showed differences on Oromotor Sequences ($p < .001$) in the Language Domain, which suggests that children with reading disabilities may have generalized motor programming difficulties or dyspraxia. On the other hand, they had no difficulty with fine motor coordination (Fingertip Tapping), graphomotor speed and accuracy (VP), the ability to imitate a hand position (Imitating Hand Position), and tactile perception (Finger Discrimination).

The performance of children with RD and the performance of children in the NC did not differ ($p < .203$) on the Visuospatial Core Domain Score. At the subtest level, differences in performance between the two groups occurred on an untimed Core Subtest of visuospatial analysis and visuomotor integration (DC, $p <$

.040) and on an Expanded Subtest of visuospatial analysis and directionality in locating a target house on a schematic map. (Route Finding, $p < .016$). These results are consistent with the visuospatial deficits noted by some investigators (Cermak & Murray, 1991; Eden et al., 1996; Wimmer & Frith, 1997). The RD group performed as well as the NC group, however, in judging line orientation (Arrows, $p < .874$) and in reproducing a 3-dimensional construction (Block Design, $p < .881$). It is notable that the QO for Tremor occurred more frequently ($p < .010$) on DC in the RD group than in the NC group. Along with the poor performance of the RD group in producing oromotor and manual motor sequences, the presence of tremor in this group implicates motor dysfunction in children who are poor readers. On an individual basis, however, not all poor readers have visuospatial or visuomotor deficits.

Memory deficits are modality specific in most developmental disorders (Delis, 1989). For children with reading disorders, verbal memory is usually poor. This was evident in the RD sample as compared to the NC sample. The two groups differed significantly ($p < .001$) on the Memory and Learning Core Domain Score. At the subtest level, the children with RD demonstrated poor performance in learning and recalling names (Memory for Names, $p < .001$); in using auditory short-term memory to recall progressively longer sentences (Sentence Repetition, $p < .001$); and in the ability to recall a story, both spontaneously and when subsequently cued with questions about the missing details (Narrative Memory, $p < .002$).

At the SS level, Narrative Memory Free Recall differed ($p < .012$) for children with RD when compared to children in the NC sample. These results indicate that children with RD cannot retell spontaneously a long story immediately after hearing it, but they can recall story details as well as the NC group when cued with questions (Cued Recall Trial for Narrative Memory, $p < .082$). Therefore, the problem for children with reading problems appears to be one of accessing language, not failing to encode the information in memory. An SS difference was also observed on the RD group's immediate ($p < .001$) and delayed recall of names ($p < .008$). Children with RD learned fewer names than the NCs on the learning trials for Memory for Names, suggesting that the naming problems evident in poor readers can extend to learning and retaining names of other children. This deficit can have adverse social implications. Fortunately, the children with RD recalled faces on the Immediate and Delay Trials as well as the NC group (Memory for Faces, $p < .717$).

Based on the results of the NEPSY validity study of children with RD and on the subsequent analysis of the SS and the QOs, the following deficits may be evident in the NEPSY performance of a child with reading problems. Not all children with RD will show all of these deficits, however.

The clinical sample of the NEPSY validity studies was a group of children with mixed reading disabilities (See Rapid Reference 6.6), so it is very important to note

≡Rapid Reference 6.6

Deficits of Children With RD Observed on NEPSY Validity Group Performance That May Aid Diagnosis of Reading Disabilities*

All children with RD may not show this specific pattern, but these children generally display deficits in the areas of language skills, phonological processing, verbal memory, and lexical access. Other areas may or may not be present.

Speech and Language Deficits

- Poor semantic skills. Poor readers may have a generalized language disorder, a narrower receptive (i.e., comprehension) or expressive language disorder (i.e., semantic; naming), or no language disorder. (Semantic Trial of Verbal Fluency)
- Poor lexical access (SN)
- Phonological processing deficit (Phonological Processing Total & Asks for Repetition on PP)
- Articulation problems (Oromotor Sequencing; Stable Misarticulation on Repetition of Names)

Secondary Verbal Memory Deficits (due to language deficits)

- Deficit in name learning and recall (Memory for Names)
- Inability to recall story details spontaneously (Narrative Memory Total and Free Recall)
- Auditory short-term memory possibly secondary to language deficit (Sentence Repetition)

Mild Attentional Problems

- Auditory attention deficit possibly secondary to language deficit (AA of AARS)

Executive Dysfunction*

- Working memory deficit, possibly secondary to language deficit (Rule Violations on Tower)
- Difficulty inhibiting motor response to noise distracters (Statue)
- Poor executive control of motor programming (Oromotor Sequencing, Manual Motor Sequencing)

Visuospatial Deficits

- Visuospatial analysis and directionality, visuomotor integration (Route Finding)

Comorbid Motor Deficits

- Dyspraxia—oromotor and manual motor (Oromotor Sequencing, Manual Motor Sequencing)

*This RD sample did not include children diagnosed with ADHD. Children with RD may have ADHD, however. Conversely, difficulties in processing language may cause attentional problems.

that individual children may or may not have visuospatial deficits, attentional problems with simple or complex attention problems, comorbid dysarthria, or executive dysfunction. Most will have some language difficulties, even if subtle, as well as problems with rapid lexical access and phonological processing deficits. Depending on the amount of language deficit, children may also display verbal memory and working memory problems. Rapid Reference 6.5 gives a profile of deficits common in children with dyslexia.

In order to obtain a full diagnostic picture of a child's reading disability, NEPSY test results need to be integrated with results on assessments of academic and cognitive functioning, as well as with information from the comprehensive history and reports of the child's functioning in school and at home. ADHD can often co-occur with learning disabilities. Therefore, after administering the NEPSY Core, the clinician may want to combine the NEPSY Expanded subtests recommended for ADHD assessment with those recommended for R.D. assessment. In that way the child will be tested for both disorders. (See Rapid Reference 6.7.)

Because this section could only deal with one example of a NEPSY assessment of a learning disability, refer to Table 3.2 in the NEPSY *Manual* (pp. 48–49). This table provides recommendations for choosing subtests for Expanded and Selective Assessments by disability.

≡*Rapid Reference 6.7*

Selective Assessment For Diagnosis of a Reading Disability Based on NEPSY Validity Studies

Administer **the NEPSY Core Assessment** plus the following Expanded subtests across domains which showed differences in performance between the RD and NC groups:

Attention/Executive Domain
• Statue

Language Domain
• All Expanded Subtests

Visuospatial Domain
• Route Finding

Sensorimotor Domain
• Manual Motor Sequences

Memory and Learning Domain
• Sentence Repetition*

*Core for ages 3–4.

APPLICATION OF THE NEPSY IN DIAGNOSING AUTISTIC DISORDER

Although NEPSY can be used to assess children with a variety of developmental disorders, we have chosen Autistic Disorder as a representative example. Autistic Disorder is a Pervasive Developmental Disorder that is characterized primarily by marked deficiencies in social interaction and behavior (Fein, Pennington, Markowitz, Braverman, & Waterhouse, 1986), significant communication deficits, restricted behaviors, and stereotypical interests (American Psychiatric Association, 1994). It occurs in approximately 4 to 5 births per 10,000 (Spreen, Risser, & Edgell, 1995) and often includes intellectual functioning in the deficient range, which is strongly related to prognosis (Spreen et al., 1995). High-functioning children with autism are considered to be those individuals with IQs greater than or equal to 70, but there is significant heterogeneity in the degree and nature of cognitive dysfunction in individuals with autism. Neuropsychological evaluations of children and adults with high-functioning autism (HFA) have yielded the following results: deficits in complex memory, language, and learning tasks, as well as relatively intact simple and complex attention and associative memory (Minshew, Goldstein, Muenz, & Payton, 1992); generally intact list learning performance, but increased number of intrusions as compared to NCs (Minshew & Goldstein, 1993); intact auditory processing (Lincoln, Dickstein, Courchesne, Elmasian, & Tallal, 1992); poor motor imitation abilities (Jones & Prior, 1985); impaired executive functioning; and deficits in source and temporal-order aspects of memory, but not in recognition memory (Bennetto, Pennington, & Rogers, 1996). Minshew & Goldstein (1993) noted that the relationship between autism and memory dysfunction remains uncertain and appears to occur intermittently, suggesting a possible subgroup.

The NEPSY validity group of 23 children with HFA (IQ < 80) met the *DSM-IV* criteria for Autistic Disorder. Group members had no other neurological complications not associated with autism, no psychiatric diagnoses, and no learning disabilities. They had normal auditory acuity and normal or corrected visual acuity. Their performance on NEPSY was compared to that of matched NCs from the standardization population.

As a group, the children with HFA differed from NCs on the Attention/Executive Core Domain Scores ($p < .005$). Because there was significant intradomain scatter, the Core Domain Score did not reflect the overall attentional behaviors and executive functioning of this group, however. Subtest analysis of the domain revealed poor performance was due to executive dysfunction only, not to attentional problems *per se*. In relation to the NC group, the children with HFA performed poorly on two executive function measures, the Tower Core Subtest ($p <$

.005), and the Design Fluency Expanded Subtest (p < .001). Both of these subtests require rule-guided behavior, the understanding of multiple rules, planning, strategizing, and monitoring performance for problem solving. Design Fluency also measures nonverbal fluency and mental visualization of unique designs. Children with HFA have difficulty with forward planning and mental visualization. The groups did not differ in performance on Knock and Tap, a straightforward, motor inhibition, "go-no-go" task (p < .063). The children with HFA appeared to be able to learn the task in a stimulus-response manner as it was demonstrated ("When I knock, you tap."). They did not have difficulty on the other Core subtests of attention as compared to NCs (AARS, p < .772; VA, p < .086).

Similarly, the Language Core Domain Score did not differentiate (p < .081) between the HFA and NC groups, but significant intratest scatter was evident. Therefore, the Language Core Domain Score did not reflect overall language function for the HFA group. The autistic group was able to perform phonological tasks on a Core subtest (Phonological Processing, p < .100) and a Supplementary subtest (Repetition of Nonsense Words, p < .407) as well as the NC group. These results support the findings of Scheuffgen (1998) that children with HFA, despite poorer verbal intelligence and semantic knowledge than normal controls, do not differ in phonological skills. As a group, the children with HFA could also access names for multiple, alternating visual stimuli on SN (p < .639) and produce articulatory sequences (Oromotor Sequences, p < .194) as well as NCs. The children with HFA differed from NCs, however, on a Core subtest that assesses receptive language. It requires understanding linguistically complex oral directions as they progress in difficulty (Comprehension of Instructions, p < .045). In an oral instruction such as *Point to a blue circle, but first, point to a yellow cross,* the children with HFA did not seem to understand that the linguistic construction *but first* changes the order in which to point to the two objects. They also had difficulty understanding linguistic constructions that included negatives such as *Point to a shape that is not a circle and is not yellow and black.* Furthermore, on an expressive language, verbal fluency task, the children with Autistic Disorder produced fewer words in categories (Verbal Fluency, p < .002) than NCs. These results would suggest that as a group, the children with HFA are capable of phonological processing and rapid lexical access, but their receptive and expressive language is impaired. It should be noted that the children in this study were required to have an IQ of >80, and that they may not be representative of autistic children in general, who often have severe language and communication problems.

The HFA and NC groups did not differ on the Sensorimotor Core Domain

Score ($p < .109$), but this global score masked significant scatter among subtests. Performance of simple finger tapping and more complex hand movement sequences did not differ for the HFA and NC groups (Fingertip Tapping, $p < .622$). However, on a subtest that involved integrating visual-spatial information, using motor programming, and using kinesthetic feedback from position to imitate the examiner's hand position (Imitating Hand Positions, $p < .007$), the children with HFA performed poorly in relation to the NCs. The interpersonal aspects of Imitating Hand Positions and the difficulty children with autism have with imitation (Jones & Prior, 1985) may have related to poor performance on this subtest. Furthermore, the Imitating Hand Position Subtest requires close inspection of the examiner's hand as it is held in position for the child to imitate. When the hand is in position, however, the examiner's face is in the child's field of vision, and this may have an adverse effect on performance because children with autism avoid eye contact. Additionally, difficulty with motor programming (Manual Motor Sequencing, $p < .03$) may be related to poor performance on Imitating Hand Positions. The HFA group performance was also poorer than that of the NCs on a task that required drawing lines quickly through progressively narrower and more convoluted tracks without going outside the tracks (VP, $p < .008$). Bilateral differences in tactile perception were observed between the HFA clinical group and the NC group (Finger Discrimination-preferred, $p < .014$; Finger Discrimination-nonpreferred, $p < .004$), suggesting the presence of sensory deficits in children with Autistic Disorder.

Although the Visuospatial Core Domain Score ($p < .149$), did not differ for the HFA and the NC groups, there was significant intersubtest scatter. Therefore, it did not reflect visuospatial functioning overall for the children with HFA. The two groups displayed differences in performance on a subtest requiring judgment of line orientation (Arrows, $p < .003$). Executive dysfunction evident in the HFA group on Tower and Design Fluency may have influenced poor performance on Arrows. Attending to multiple stimuli (eight arrows) requires response inhibition and monitoring in order to consider each of the arrows carefully before making a choice. While the HFA and NC groups demonstrated no difference in visual-motor integration skills for two-dimensional construction (DC, $p < .537$), they performed poorly on an Expanded Subtest, Block Construction ($p < .015$). Block Construction assesses three-dimensional construction with time bonuses on the most difficult items. A lack of time bonuses earned on Block Construction due to slower performance may have affected the HFA group scores on Block Construction as compared to scores of the NC group. The children with HFA appeared to be able to copy geometric two-dimensional geometric figures with paper and pencil but not to imitate three-dimensional figures in an interpersonal task. Differences in performance between the two groups also occurred on Route Finding ($p < .001$), a schematic map-reading task that requires understanding of symbolic representations of space, as well as directionality and orientation. Children with autism have difficulty understanding symbolic representations (Fay & Schuler, 1980), which may have affected performance on Route Finding adversely. Thus, it would appear that, as a group, children with HFA can perform visual-spatial analysis when the task does not require a significant contribution from executive functions, rapid performance, or the use of symbolic representations.

Performance of the two groups on the Memory and Learning Core Domain Score differed ($p < .016$) but showed significant subtest scatter. The groups did not differ in performance on the Memory for Names subtest ($p < .419$), which is consistent for their performance on SN. Although the HFA group had no difficulty with the line drawings of children's faces on the Memory for Names subtest, they recognized fewer faces ($p < .004$) than the NC group when actual photographs of children's faces were used on the Memory for Faces subtest. These results are consistent with the view that social, perceptual deficits occur in children with autism. They also displayed poor performance on another Core subtest, Narrative Memory ($p < .010$). Performance may have been affected by receptive language deficits in listening to and encoding details from a large quantity of oral language. In contrast, the two groups did not differ ($p < .317$) on the Expanded Subtest, Sentence Repetition, a rote task of auditory short-term memory on which the child recalls single sentences. The children with HFA performed poorly, as compared to NCs, on List Learning, which involves learning a list of 15 items over five trials (.033). This subtest requires executive functions to inhibit extraneous intrusions and intrusions from one list to another and to employ strategies such as clustering the items efficiently.

Although individual children in this clinical group may show much heterogeneity, as a group, children with HFA displayed a profile on NEPSY that include the following characteristics:

Although NEPSY was not designed specifically to assign *DSM-IV* (American Psychiatric Association, 1994) diagnoses, it can be used to determine the presence of deficits that are associated with Autistic Disorder, as shown in Rapid Reference 6.8. Such assessment can also provide the opportunity to observe numerous other behaviors associated with autism. Of course, any such diagnosis must only be made within the context of the child's developmental, medical, social, and educational history, as well as the manner in which he or she functions in every day life.

≣ Rapid Reference 6.8

••

The Profile of the HFA Group in NEPSY Validity Studies

Individually, children with Autistic Disorder show much heterogeneity. As a group, however, when compared to NCs, they displayed the following profile:

Executive dysfunction

• Poor ability to plan, strategize, and monitor performance on problem-solving tasks (Tower; Design Fluency)

• Difficulty inhibiting responses

• Difficulty with symbolic representations (Route-Finding)

• Problems predicting an event from information presented (Arrows)

Receptive and expressive language deficits

• Difficulty understanding oral instructions (CI)

• Deficit in rapid production of words in categories (Verbal Fluency)

Secondary verbal memory deficits

• Difficulty learning a long list over five trials (List Learning)

• Problems encoding large quantities of detail-laden language for later recall (Narrative Memory)

Sensorimotor deficits

• Poor tactile perception bilaterally, suggesting sensory deficits (Finger Discrimination)

• Poor integration of motor programming, visual-spatial analysis, and kinesthetic feedback to reproduce a static hand position (Imitating Hand Positions)

• Poor visuomotor precision when both speed and accuracy are required (Visuomotor Precision)

• Difficulty with three-dimensional constructions (Block Construction)

Social imperception

• Difficulty with interpersonal aspects of tasks (Imitating Hand Positions)

• Poor facial recognition (Memory for Faces)

No deficits seen in

• Visuospatial analysis for two-dimensional construction without time constraints (Design Copying)

• Rote learning of single names; rote repetition of single sentences (Memory for Names, Sentence Repetition)

• Phonological processing (Phonological Processing)

• Oromotor programming (Oromotor Sequences)

• Simple and complex auditory and visual attention; but due to executive dysfunction and difficulty understanding language, these children may appear inattentive (AARS, AA, RS; VA)

Rapid Reference 6.9

Selective Assessment for Diagnosis of Autistic Disorder Based on NEPSY Validity Studies

You should administer a **NEPSY Core Assessment** plus the following Expanded subtests across domains which showed differences in performance between the HFA and NC groups.

Attention/Executive Domain
- Design Fluency

Language Domain
- Verbal Fluency

Sensorimotor Domain
- Manual Motor Sequences
- Finger Discrimination

Visuospatial Domain
- Route Finding
- Block Construction

Memory and Learning Domain
- List Learning

With this diagnosis, in particular, but with many diagnoses of developmental disorders in general, it is wise to observe the child in a peer group setting in order to observe social interaction. Diagnoses of the more complex developmental disorders may require that even a Core assessment be administered over time, performing a few subtests in multiple 30 to 60 min sessions, rather than attempting to assess the child in one long session with dubious results. If the clinician knows in advance that the referral question is to rule out Autistic Disorder, he or she should take the time for preparation, as noted in Chapter 2 (pp. 40–41) and as outlined in Rapid Reference 6.9. This may make the difference between a successful and an unsuccessful evaluation.

Occasionally, a child is untestable in the first session. In these cases, the clinician should gather as much information as possible from parents, teachers, medical personnel and caregivers, have adaptive behavior scales filled out, use the time to attempt interactive play with the child, and perform an in-depth observation of the child's behaviors. The clinician should discuss with the parents all aspects of the initial observation and interaction with the child and make recommendations for therapies. The clinician should schedule an appointment to see the child in about two to three months, after intensive therapies have been initiated, and attempt the evaluation again. Due to characteristic language deficits in these children, the clinician should always include a nonverbal cognitive assessment in the evaluation of a child with autism.

APPLICATION OF THE NEPSY IN ASSESSING NEUROLOGICAL AND TERATOLOGICAL DISORDERS

Very low birthweight and severe perinatal asphyxia may have negative long-term sequelae, which a clinician must assess over time in order to track any change in cognitive functioning (Robertson & Finer, 1993). Children with certain types of epilepsy may show fluctuations in or deterioration of cognitive abilities which require on-going follow-up (Aicardi, 1994). Recovery of function in children with acquired brain damage, such as traumatic brain injury (TBI), also needs to be tracked over time in order to identify improvements and persistent deficits in functioning, as well as to adapt interventions to changing needs (Korkman, Kirk, & Kemp, 1998). NEPSY assessment of children with TBI reveals performance that falls more than two standard deviations below the mean of the standardization sample on most subtests. The lowest Core Domain Scores occurred in the Attention/Executive Functions, Language, and Sensorimotor Domains (Korkman, Kirk, & Kemp, 1998).

Previous studies with the Finnish NEPSY have shown that early left-sided damage in children with hemiplegia did not result in a significant verbal disadvantage as compared to nonverbal performance (Korkman & von Wendt, 1995). Other studies employing different instruments show similar findings (Aram & Ekelman, 1988; Varga-Khadem & Polkey, 1992). Thus, due to plasticity, the brain appears to adapt to focal damage.

A second study examined children who were subject to three types of perinatal risks. Their performance differed in degree, but not in type of impairment, and there was no characteristic pattern of strengths and weaknesses by group. The study excluded children who were moderately and severely disabled. Children who had a very low birth weight (< 1500 g) and were small for gestational age (VLBW-SGA) had the poorest results. Children who had VLBW but were appropriate size for gestational age (VLBW-AGA) were somewhat less impaired, and, as a group, the full-term children with acute birth asphyxia performed at a control group level. Selective differences were observed on subtests of different types: one subtest of visual-motor integration, one attention task, one phonological processing task, one body part naming task, and one tactile discrimination task. No child displayed a specific learning disability or attentional disorder (Korkman, Liikanen & Fellman, 1996).

Korkman and her Finnish colleagues (Korkman, Autti-Rämö, Koivulehto, and Granström, 1998) also studied three groups of children, aged 5 to 9, exposed to alcohol in utero during the first trimester only, during the first two trimesters, and throughout pregnancy. The group exposed to alcohol throughout pregnancy was significantly impaired on composite NEPSY scores of naming, receptive language, and attention. To a lesser degree, they also showed problems with manual motor and visual-motor performance. The group exposed during the first two trimesters had the same pattern of findings as those exposed throughout pregnancy; the naming score only was significantly different from that of NCs. There were no differences on subtests of visual and verbal memory or manual motor precision.

These three Finnish studies demonstrate that the performance of children with different types of neurological impairments on NEPSY may be associated with characteristic neuropsychological effects: Children with Fetal Alcohol Syndrome had particularly pronounced verbal and attentional problems; children with hemiplegia tended to have more visuoconstructive than verbal impairments, irrespective of side of lesion; and VLBW children tended to have diffuse impairment.

Fetal Alcohol Syndrome (FAS) is an example of a teratological disorder. It is caused by prenatal exposure to alcohol and is characterized by craniofacial abnormalities, dysplasias, growth deficiencies, and neurocognitive deficits (Stratton, Howe, & Battaglia, 1996) as well as behavioral deficits (Nanson & Hiscock, 1990). The severity of these deficits depends on the amount of alcohol ingested, in which trimester exposure took place, the number of trimesters exposed, and other concomitant risk factors (Coles, 1994; Korkman, Autti-Rämö, Koivulehto, & Granström, 1998; Stratton et al., 1996). A milder form of this teratological disorder is Fetal Alcohol Effects, which may be more prevalent than the 0.2 to 4 of every 1,000 births for FAS (Stratton et al.) A very small ($N = 10$) validity group of children diagnosed with FAS was evaluated with NEPSY.

With the exception of performance on the Sensorimotor Domain ($p < .114$), the FAS group performed significantly below the matched NCs on all other NEPSY Core Domains ($p < .001$ in each case). On the Attention/Executive Domain subtest performance, the two groups differed on the simple and complex auditory attention (AARS, $p < .001$) and visual (VA, $p < .03$) attention tasks, but not on executive function subtests on which they had to plan and strategize for problem-solving (Tower, $p < .08$) or generate unique designs fluently according to rules (Design Fluency, $p < .375$). Performance also did not differ between the two groups on the "go-no-go" task of motor inhibition (Knock and Tap, $p < .073$), but it did differ on another motor task (Statue, $p < .028$) in which noise distracters are meant to elicit a motor response when the child is standing quietly with eyes closed. The greater attentional requirements of Statue may have adversely affected performance, because inattention is characteristic of children with FAS (Korkman, Autti-Rämö, Koivulehto, & Granström, 1998). It is important to note that this was a very small sample of children with FAS ($N = 10$), that their performance

≡*Rapid Reference 6. 10*

The Profile of the FAS Group on NEPSY Validity Studies

In relation to the NC group performance, the small sample (n = 10) of children with FAS displayed the following profile as a group:

Attention deficits
- poor auditory and visual attention (AARS, VA)

Mild executive dysfunction
- Poor ability to inhibit motor response to noise distracters (Statue; Knock and tap, a go-no-go task approached significance and might also have differed with a larger sample)

Language deficits
- poor phonological processing—difficulty recognizing word segments, conceptualizing speech-sound patterns and manipulating the patterns to produce new ones; difficulty repeating novel speech-sound patterns (Phonological Processing & Repetition of Nonsense Words)
- poor lexical access (SN)
- inability to understand oral language of increasing linguistic complexity (Comprehension of Instructions)

Secondary verbal memory deficits
- poor ability to learn and recall names (Memory for Names)
- inability to recall a long detail-laden story (Narrative Memory)
- weak auditory short-term memory for the recall of isolated sentences (Sentence Repetition)
- poor ability to learn a long list of isolated words (List Learning)

Motor deficits
- poor motor programming—inability to reproduce articulatory or hand movement sequences (Oromotor Sequences; Manual Motor Sequences)

Pervasive visuospatial deficits
- poor visuomotor integration for reproducing two- and 3-dimensional constructions (DC and Block Design)
- weak ability to judge line and angle orientation (Arrows)
- poor visuospatial analysis and directionality for map-reading (Route-Finding)

No deficits in
- one-word expressive verbal fluency (Verbal Fluency)
- fine motor coordination (Fingertip Tapping)
- ability to imitate a static hand position (Imitating Hand Positions)
- ability to plan, strategize and monitor performance for problem solution (Tower) approached significance, however, and might have differed if the sample were larger

(Tower, Knock and Tap) approached significance. With a larger sample, both of these executive function tasks might have reached significance.

The only Language Domain subtest on which performance did not differ between the FAS and NC groups was Verbal Fluency (p < .188). On this expressive language task, the FAS group and the NC group did not differ in producing words in categories rapidly. The two groups differed in the phonological ability to conceptualize speech-sound patterns and to manipulate them to create new words or to repeat novel speech-sound patterns (Phonological Processing p < .014; Repetition of Names p < .004), in rapid lexical access (SN, p < .001), in the ability to understand linguistically complex sentences (Comprehension of Instructions, p < .019), and in the production of oromotor sequences (Oromotor Sequences, p < .045). These results suggest that children with FAS have more difficulty with receptive than expressive language and may have problems with reading acquisition due to significant phonological processing deficits. Furthermore, motor programming deficits were observed in these children with FAS on both Oromotor Sequences and Manual Motor Sequences.

The latter subtest, which required the production of motor sequences with the hands, was the only Sensorimotor subtest on which performance differed (p < .036) between the two groups.

Performance differed for the FAS group as compared to the NC group on all visuospatial subtests. The children with FAS were not able to integrate visuospatial analysis with motor output to complete two-dimensional constructions on DC (p < .021) or three-dimensional constructions on Block Construction (p < .007). As compared to the NC group, the FAS group displayed poor judgement of line orientation (Arrows, p < .001) and difficulty with visuospatial analysis and directionality on a schematic map-reading task (Route Finding, p < .032). These results suggest that children with FAS have pervasive visuospatial deficits.

Performance differed between the NC and FAS groups on all verbal memory subtests, as might be expected due to the language deficits of children with FAS. As a group, the children with FAS were not able to learn and recall names (Memory for Names, p < .001), encode and recall story details spontaneously or with cueing (Narrative Memory, p < .007), utilize auditory short-term memory to repeat rote sentences (Sentence Repetition, p < .001), or learn a long list over five trials, recalling the list after an interference trial and 30 min later (List Learning, p < .001). Despite their pervasive visuospatial deficits, the performance of the two groups did not differ on Memory for Faces (p < .213).

In summary, although children in the FAS group may show individual differences, as a group, the children with FAS displayed the profile seen on p. 217:

RELIABILITIES ON NEPSY

The NEPSY *Manual* provides reliability coefficients (Korkman et al., 1998) for all subtests, both Core and Expanded, for Core Domain Scores on NEPSY, and for Scaled Supplemental Scores. They were calculated for each age level separately and then averaged across ages in two groups: ages 3 to 4 and ages 5 to 12. This was done because different patterns of tests make up the domains for the two different age groups.

The internal consistency reliability of the Core Domain Scores was determined based on the reliability of composite variables procedures described by Nunnally (1978). Average internal consistency reliabilities for Core Domain Scores for ages 3 to 4 vary between .70 for the Attention/Executive Function Core Domain Score and .91 for Memory and Learning. The developmental variability of the 3- to 4-year-olds in the attentional area may well have contributed to the lower reliability coefficient for the Attention/Executive Domain. For ages 5 to 12 internal consistency reliabilities for Core Domain Scores range from .79 (Sensorimotor) to .87 (Language; Memory and Learning).

Split-half reliabilities were derived on those subtests that could be divided into two halves that were equal in length and best-approximated the qualities of parallel forms. The derived correlation coefficient was then corrected for length using the Spearman-Brown formula (Crocker & Algina, 1986). Split-half reliabilities for Core and Expanded subtests for ages 3 to 4 vary between .74 (Body Part Naming) and .91 (Sentence Repetition). The Core and Expanded Subtest split-half reliabilities for ages 5 to 12 range from .72 (Block Construction) to .91 (List Learning).

Test-retest stability is reported on those subtests for which parallel forms could not be created because the scores are based on item-level scores that are not strictly independent. The lack of independence was due to the time allowed for a response in order to receive full or partial credit (e.g., AARS) or in order to use speed of performance as a scoring criterion (e.g., Fingertip Tapping). These subtests showed some of the lowest reliabilities, so the clinician should use caution in interpreting results in follow-up administration. This type of task yields higher performance on re-test because children have learned the task and the clinician may see practice effects. The average (across age levels) reliabilities based on test-retest correlation for ages 5 to 12 vary on the Core and Expanded subtests from .71 (Tower) to .81 (AARS).

For ages 3 to 4 test-retest correlations were used for two subtests, Statue and Verbal Fluency. On Statue (.50) in the second administration, the child knew the "secret" of the subtest (the presence of noise distracters when the child's eyes are closed). Verbal Fluency (.59) also showed a low reliability, possibly due to practice effects or to the fact that even normally developing children at this very young age

CAUTION

Use Caution Interpreting These Subtests in Follow-up

Split-half reliability procedures were used for NEPSY subtests to establish internal consistency coefficients, except in two cases:

- If item-level scores were not strictly independent due to allowed latency time for response and the child could receive full or partial credit, or speed of performance was used as a scoring criterion, test-retest reliability had to be used.
- If subtests had a speed and accuracy component, multiple sources of error were present, so a generalizability coefficient was used to account for these.

The subtests below have the lowest reliabilities, so use caution when interpreting them in follow-up.

Ages 3–4	Ages 5–12
Statue (.50)	Design Fluency (.59)
Verbal Fluency (.59)	Fingertip Tapping (.71)
	VP (.68)
	VA (.71)
	SN (.74)

may produce words well one day and may not perform the next. Even a normally developing preschooler, for instance, may start talking about a favorite animal in the middle of the subtest, so the task is forgotten.

For three subtests, VA, SN, and VP, a generalizability coefficient had to be calculated. (See Rapid Reference 6.11.) This was done to account for multiple sources of error that are present due to the multidimensional nature of the tasks. They all have a Total Score based on both speed and accuracy. The generalizability coefficients range from .68 (VP) to .74 (SN). Inter-rater agreement for QOs varies from kappa coefficients of .42 (fair agreement) on Misarticulations to .100 (perfect agreement) on Visual Guidance, Incorrect Position, and Body Movement. A kappa of .50 is generally considered an acceptable level of rater agreement (Fleiss, 1981). With a few exceptions, reliability measures were adequate to good, considering their highly subjective nature. As outlined in Rapid Reference 6.12, the high reliability of a number of these QOs makes them valuable adjuncts to test results in arriving at a diagnosis.

Having reviewed the types of developmental and acquired disorders for which a *NEPSY Developmental Neuropsychological Assessment* (Korkman, Kirk, & Kemp, 1998) is appropriate and having discussed patterns observed in representative disorders in the NEPSY validity studies that can guide the clinician in selecting additional subtests beyond the NEPSY Core to aid diagnosis, we discuss in Chapter 7, the end product of the assessment process, the reporting of test results.

≡Rapid Reference 6.11

Reliabilities of Core Domain Scores And Core Subtest Scores

Core Domains and Subtests	Average Ages 3–4	5–12
Attention/Executive Function	**.70**	**.82**
Tower		.82
AARS		.81
VA	.76	.71
Statue	.50	
Design Fluency		.59
Language	**.90**	**.87**
Body Part Naming	.74	
Phonological Processing	.83	.91
SN		.74
Comprehension of Instructions	.89	.73
Repetition of Nonsense Words		.80
Verbal Fluency	.59	.74
Sensorimotor	**.88**	**.79**
Fingertip Tapping		.71
Imitating Hand Positions	.89	.82
VP	.81	.68
Visuospatial	**.88**	**.83**
DC	.86	.79
Arrows		.78
Block Construction	.80	.72
Memory and Learning	**.91**	**.87**
Memory for Faces		.76
Memory for Names		.89
Narrative Memory	.85	.77
Sentence Repetition	.91	.81
List Learning		.91
Scaled Supplemental Scores		
Auditory Attention		.75
Auditory Response Set		.78
Immediate Memory for Faces		.58
Delayed Memory for Faces		.65
Immediate Memory for Names		.80
Delayed Memory for Names		.68

Note: Reliability coefficients for NEPSY were calculated separately for each age. Split-half, test-retest, and generalizability procedures were employed, depending on the nature of the subtest.

Rapid Reference 6.12

Interrater agreement for Qualitative Observations by Domain and Subtest

Attention/Executive Behaviors

Domain	Subtest	Behavior	kappa
Attention/ Executive	Tower	Rule Violations	0.79
	AARS	Off-Task Behavior	0.82
	VA	Off-Task Behavior	0.50
Language	Phonological Processing	Asks for Repetition	0.65
	Comprehension of Instruct.	Asks for Repetition	0.58
Memory/Learning	Sentence Repetition	Asks for Repetition	0.89

Oral/Verbal Behaviors

Domain	Subtest	Behavior	kappa
Language	SN	Reversed Sequences	0.77
		Voice Volume	0.83
	Repetition of Nonsense Words	Misarticulation	0.42
	Verbal Fluency		0.86

Motor Behaviors

Domain	Subtest	Behavior	kappa
Attention/ Executive	Tower	Motor Difficulty	1.00
Language	SN	Body Movement	0.74
	Verbal Fluency	Body Movement	0.74
	Oromotor Sequences	Oromotor Hypotonia	0.50
Sensorimotor	Fingertip Tapping	Visual Guidance	1.00
		Incorrect Position	1.00
		Posturing	0.89
		Mirroring	0.34
		Overflow	0.85
	Imitating Hand Positions	Other Hand Helps	0.89
	Manual Motor Sequences	Overflow	0.69
		Loss of Asymmetry	0.69
		Body Movement	1.00
		Forceful Tapping	0.63

Rate Change

Domain	Subtest	Behavior	kappa
Sensorimotor	Fingertip Tapping	Rate Change	0.45
	Manual Motor Sequences	Rate Change	0.64
Language	Oromotor Sequences	Rate Change	0.61

Pencil Grip

Domain	Subtest	Behavior	kappa
Sensorimotor	VP	Pencil Grip	0.35
Visuospatial	DC	Pencil Grip	0.64

🐾 TEST YOURSELF 🐾

True-False:

1. **The SS for Auditory Attention showed a significant difference between children with ADHD and NCs in the Huckeba and colleagues (submitted for publication) study.** True or False?

2. **Children with ADHD showed significantly more motor deficits than NCs in the ADHD validity study.** True or False?

3. **Children with ADHD had difficulty with motor control.** True or False?

4. **The clinical sample of children with reading disabilities (RD) in the NEPSY validity studies showed significant differences on both subtests of phonological processing.** True or False?

5. **The results of the validity studies suggest that children with RD are more apt to have articulation problems than are children without RD.** True or False?

6. **Validity studies showed memory deficits across modalities for children with RD.** True or False?

7. **The RD sample differed from the NCs on Narrative Memory Free Recall, but not on Cued Recall.** True or False?

8. **The validity studies of children with autism suggested more executive dysfunction than attentional deficits.** True or False?

9. **The sample of children with autism in the NEPSY validity studies were high-functioning (IQ greater than or equal to 100).** True or False?

10. **The social and imitative aspects of Imitating Hand Positions may affect performance in children with autism.** True or False?

Matching:

Match the letter of the correct answer with the corresponding number.

11. _____ **Only this validity group showed impaired facial recognition in NEPSY validity studies.**

(a) **VLBW-SGA**

(b) **TBI**

12. _____ **An example of a disorder caused by exposure to a teratogen.**

(c) **FAS**

(d) **plasticity**

13. _____ **In this group most results on NEPSY fall more than –2 SD from the mean.**

(e) **Lead exposure**

14. _____ **This American validity group showed deficits on all subtests in the Visuospatial Domain.**

(f) **HFA**

15. _____ **Due to this, brain development in children appears to adapt to focal damage.**

16. _____ **When compared to other perinatal risks in the Finnish study, children in this group fared the worst.**

Answers: 1. False; 2. True; 3. True; 4. False; 5. True; 6. False; 7. True; 8. True; 9. False; 10. True; 11. f; 12. e; 13. b; 14. c; 15. d; 16. a

Seven

ILLUSTRATIVE CASE REPORTS

This chapter synthesizes the principles and concepts presented in the first six chapters of this book and guides you through the process of presenting the wealth of data available from a NEPSY evaluation in a clear, understandable manner. Hypotheses should be validated through results on NEPSY Core or Expanded subtests, Supplemental Scores, Qualitative Observations, the Comprehensive History, school records, and results of other assessments. The chapter includes the case studies of two children referred for neuropsychological evaluation. One is a brief neuropsychological screening with the NEPSY Core only. The second case involves a comprehensive neuropsychological evaluation integrating a Full NEPSY with other assessments. These are actual case histories, but the names and identifying information have been changed to protect client confidentiality.

CASE REPORT #1

The first case study presents the interpretation and discussion of NEPSY results only, illustrating the principle of drawing inferences about a primary deficit and its secondary deficits.

April McCoy, 9.2 years of age

Referral Question: Why is April's written work of such poor quality, both in content and appearance in relation to her good cognitive ability?

April McCoy, a girl 9.2 years of age, was brought for evaluation by her parents because they had concerns following a parent conference with her teacher. The teacher stated that April had "such creative ideas." When she turned in her work, which was based on the ideas discussed with the teacher, however, the quality was far below the level expected given April's excellent verbal skills. The teacher felt that April did not spend enough time on her homework and noted that it was "messy and difficult to read." April's parents were also distressed by her very messy handwriting and made her recopy assignments. Nonetheless, they also knew that April spent a great deal of time on her homework, more than they felt a 9-year-old child should. Time spent on homework had increased markedly during the spring when the teacher began emphasizing creative writing. April's parents were concerned because she was attending a suburban public school with very high college preparatory standards, and they were not sure that she would be able to handle the pressure.

Just six months before, a WISC-III had been administered to April for placement in a gifted class. Although she did not make the cut-off (97th percentile) for inclusion in the gifted program, April showed good cognitive ability. Both her teacher and her parents felt that April should be able to handle the school's academic demands. April's WISC-III IQ levels were in the superior range and there was no discrepancy between the Verbal and Performance Scales. April's performance on the Coding Subtest suggested a relative weakness in terms of her excellent cognitive ability, but it was within the low-average range for age. She did well in all other areas. The results of the Iowa Tests of Achievement for the current school year showed April's achievement scores in the 89 to 98th percentiles overall. Prior to the evaluation, the teacher submitted a summary to the clinician at the mother's request that stated April was "bright but seemed lazy and careless about completing her homework." Because April had so recently completed an evaluation, including a WISC-III, only a NEPSY Core was administered.

Neuropsychological Screening

Name: April Louise McCoy
Date of Birth: 12-18-1992
CHART #:   1397
Date Of Evaluation: 02-19-2000

Referral Statement

April McCoy is a 9.2-year-old female and is the only child of Joan and Sam McCoy, 40 and 42 years of age, respectively. Ms. McCoy holds an MBA, was employed as bank officer until April's birth, and now works in the home as a full-time wife and mother. Dr. McCoy is a family physician. April was referred for evaluation by her pediatrician, Joseph Brown, MD after April's parents expressed concerns about the teacher's comments concerning her school work. They reported April's lengthy homework periods, underachievement in written language areas, and messy and careless work. April's parents and Dr. Brown wished to know whether a learning disability might be contributing to her underachievement. (See Rapid Reference 7.1.)

Rapid Reference 7.1

Information to Include in the Referral Section

The Referral Statement should
- Identify the child by full name (with nickname in quotation marks if there is one), age, and gender.
  —Include race only if it is pertinent to the condition (e.g., Sickle Cell Anemia).
- Present a very brief description of the child's family including
  —Parents—their respective ages, whether divorced, with whom the child has principal residence, brief description of highest school level obtained (i.e., high school diploma, college degree), and present occupation *as the parent reported it* (e.g., "stay-at-home mom").
  —Siblings by gender and age.
- Give the referral source.
  —If the child was referred by a professional, including area of specialty and when the child was treated.
- State clearly the presenting or identified problem.
  —This focuses the report immediately on answering the presenting questions.
  —Provide a brief description of supporting evidence for the problem.

Relevant Background Information

According to her parents, April was the product of a full-term pregnancy and normal delivery with no prenatal or perinatal complications. April was an "easy" infant who was breast-fed and slept well. She attained developmental landmarks within normal limits. April's general health is excellent. She has some seasonal allergies for which she takes over-the-counter medications. At 5 years of age, April had a tonsillectomy and adenoidectomy. She has never had any serious illnesses, accidents or surgeries, nor has she ever been unconscious.

April began preschool three days a week at 3 years of age and attended five days a week at 4 years of age. When April began preschool, she experienced a little separation anxiety, but soon adjusted well. She made friends easily. During preschool, April had difficulty with cutting and coloring activities. At 5 years of age, April entered kindergarten at her present school, Kingsclere Elementary. She made the transition between schools successfully. Academically, April achieved well but continued to have difficulty with cutting and coloring. Learning to write was a bit difficult for April until her teacher added a gripper to April's pencil, after which her handwriting improved somewhat.

First and second grades went well for April. She acquired excellent reading skills and her math performance was good. In third grade, she began to have a few problems copying from the board in a timely manner and written work was messy. Academics were excellent, nonetheless, but April was very slow in completing written work. In the spring, the children began keeping journals daily. April had to stay in at recess a number of times because she needed extra time to finish her entry.

April's present fourth grade teacher emphasizes creative writing. According to April's parents, the teacher was "thrilled" with April's creative ideas when the children initially developed ideas as a class and the teacher wrote them on the blackboard in a cooperative story. When the children began composing their own stories, the teacher felt that April's finished product reflected her original ideas in a very superficial manner. Further, her work was "messy," according to the teacher, and was difficult to read. April sometimes needed extra time to finish a story. Although she stayed in at recess, she would have to take home a longer story to finish it. April's parents reported that she had become increasingly resistant to homework, and sometimes became tearful about having to do homework when her friends did not. April began having trouble completing math in class and had to bring it home, too. The homework sessions became increasingly problematic for April and her parents. She seemed to understand the work, so it was hard for April's parents to see why she was so resistant to it and why it took so long to complete.

In November 1999, before she began experiencing so much difficulty, April was evaluated for the Gifted and Talented Program, because her teacher felt she was unusually creative and might benefit from the increased stimulus in that class. April did not qualify for placement, but her WISC-III Verbal IQ was 121, Performance IQ was 123, and Full Scale IQ was 121, all in the superior range. April's parents had noticed that she was having more difficulty getting to sleep during the month before the evaluation. She tried to prolong the evening ritual to delay bedtime, and she awakened several times with nightmares during this period.

Socially, April has always related well to her peers, according to her parents and to teacher report. Because April was an only child, when she was 4 years of age Mr. and Ms. McCoy moved to a neighborhood with many children, so April would have playmates. April also loved Girl Scouts and her ballet lessons. Mr. and Ms. McCoy endorsed the following words on the history form to describe April: friendly; moody; sensitive; independent at times, but dependent during homework time; affectionate; and cooperative most of the time.

A review of history in the extended family revealed no neurological, psychological, learning, or behavioral problems. April has a maternal male first cousin with ADHD, Predominately Inattentive Type, which is treated successfully with counseling and medication. He has no learning problems. (See Rapid Reference 7.2.)

Rapid Reference 7.2

Information to Include in the Relevant Background Information Section

The Relevant Background Information should be focused toward the presenting problem with more discussion given to salient points possibly related to it. This section should include the following:

History of pregnancy, delivery, and perinatal history

• Length of pregnancy, any complications described, drug use—substance, stressors

• Type of delivery, reasons given for any emergency procedure, perinatal complications, NICU care, any complications and procedures

• Bonding—secure, anxious, disturbed due to parental depression, illness, death, removal from home

Developmental milestones and early childhood behaviors

• Precocious, within normal limits, delayed, mixed (specify areas that were delayed)

• Sleeping and eating patterns

• Sensory sensitivities to textures, touch, sounds, visual stimulus—increased/same/declined with time

• Activity level—increased/same/declined with time

• Repetitive behaviors—describe; increased/same/declined

Medical history

• Significant illnesses or surgeries—outpatient/hospitalization, treatment, asthma, allergies, recurrent ear infections—duration, how treated

• Head injuries, loss of consciousness, coma—duration, results of CAT scan, MRI, EEG, other studies

• Vision/hearing tested—most recent date, correction

Psychosocial history

• Parent's description of the child's temperament (can endorse list of descriptive words)

• Social interaction—eye contact, interactive play, conversational with others, shy, bossy

• Peer/family relationships—different/same

• Behavioral problems—description of behavior, frequency, worse with one parent or the other, at home or school, unprovoked or in response to "no," destructive, trouble with the law

• Emotional status—any apparent depressive behavior, suicidal gestures or remarks, violent behavior toward others/self (e.g., cutting arms or legs), anxiety, panic attacks

- Significant trauma
  - physical/sexual abuse—type, age at time, duration, perpetrator; removed from home—age, in foster care, number of placements, with or without siblings
  - significant illness or death of parent—age at time, caregiver, in home/out of home, saw/did not see parent at time of death or severe illness; reaction seen—withdrawn, acting out, tearful
  - severe or chronic health problems for child—duration, reaction to treatment, family members stayed with child if hospitalized, awareness of changes in life, aware of terminal condition
- Unusual behaviors—describe
- Counseling—by whom, duration, improvement seen

School history

- Brief history of academic strengths or weaknesses; behavior, any problems observed salient to referral question, problem progressively worse or improvement seen, teacher's comments and opinions
- Homework—resistant to particular type, protracted process, child unfocused, parent/child struggles
- Salient details only for each school level

Family history

- Any developmental, neurological, psychological, or genetic factors; learning disabilities in nuclear or extended family; maternal/paternal side; treatment; outcome

Discussion of previous testing

- Tests administered, where/by whom, when, summary of findings

Test Administered

NEPSY Developmental Neuropsychological Evaluation

Test Observations and Interview

April is a young girl with red, curly hair, freckles, and green eyes. She greeted this psychologist appropriately. Affect was bright, and eye contact was good. April's speech was not pressured, and prosody was appropriate. She had no difficulty separating from her mother. April conversed easily with this examiner. There was no apparent restricted movement, wide-based gait or ataxia present. During her interview, April stated that she likes reading and seeing friends at school, and she doesn't like math or "Writing Workshop" time. April stated that she often had to stay in at recess to finish her math or creative writing, and she disliked missing time to play with her friends. She reported that she had no trouble with math until the teacher quit giving printed worksheets, and she had to start copying all the problems. Given the opportunity to make three wishes, April wished "to have a big house, a swimming pool, and to be able to finish her work faster." When asked what changes she might like to make in herself, April noted that she would like to "get rid of her freckles and be faster in school." Given the opportunity to make changes in her family, April replied that she liked it just as it is. Then she added, "I'd like Mom not to get mad at me when I do my homework." She stated that her mother got upset with her when she took too long to start her homework. April acknowledged, "I just don't like to do it." April reported that she is happy when she gets to play with friends and sad when she has to stay in at recess.

April performed well on verbal tasks, but sometimes she became fidgety when listening to oral language without any visual materials to anchor her attention. This was especially true on the Response Set section of the auditory attention task. She seemed to enjoy the one-to-one interaction with the examiner. On paper/pencil tasks, however, she frequently sighed and whined a bit. April used a right-handed, thumb-over awkward pencil grip with very heavy pencil pressure. After completing the VP Subtest, April flapped her hand and stated that it hurt. She commented, "My hand hurts in school a lot when I have to write a bunch." On the Fingertip Tapping Subtest, she lacked fluid fine motor movement, frequently lapsing into a flat-fingered, pincer position rather than being able to hold her fingertip against her thumb forming a circle. April applied herself to the assessment; therefore, results should reflect the level of April's neuropsychological functioning. (See Rapid Reference 7.3.)

Test Results and Interpretation

April is a 9-year-old girl who, on a previously administered WISC-III (Kingsclere Public Schools, 11-10-99), displayed a Verbal IQ of 121, Performance IQ of 123, and Full Scale IQ of 121, all in the superior range of cognitive functioning. A NEPSY Core Assessment was administered in the present evaluation, followed by a NEPSY Selective Assessment comprising Expanded subtests across domains to further probe problematic areas. April's performance on the NEPSY Core revealed a significant discrepancy between the Sensorimotor Core Domain Score (77) and the Core Domain Scores obtained on the Attention and Executive (109), Language (119), Visuospatial (115), and Memory and Learning (114) Domains.

April's performance on the Language Core subtests revealed well-developed receptive language skills (Comprehension of Instructions; SS = 14), needed to understand linguistically complex oral directions and excellent phonological processing skills needed for reading decoding and spelling (Phonological Processing = 14). Both were *Above Expected Level*. Lexical access was *At Expected Level* (SN, SS = 10), with naming accuracy *Above Expected Level* (>75th percentile) and speed *At Expected Level*

Information to Include in the Test Observations and Interview Section

This section should allow your reader, either parent or professional, to get to know the child. Here is the child's perspective on the problems, as well as the "how" of his or her performance.

Initial impression

• Physical description of child and grooming, stature appropriate for age, obese or emaciated

• Affect—flat/bright/sad; body language—distancing, appropriate, provocative

• Voice and speech—rate is pressured/slow, prosody—appropriate rhythm and expression or monotone (flat without expression), volume—loud or too soft, does not modulate, articulation problem

• Ability to separate—ignores parent as leaves, hangs on, cries, tantrum

• Emotional status—overly anxious, angry or resentful, cooperative and interactive

• Compliance—does as asked, resistant to settling in

Child interview

• Why are you here? (Reassure—no grades; some very easy, when the questions are hard, you can guess or say you do not know)

• Favorite thing at school (not limited to subjects)/Don't like at school

• Hardest/easiest subjects; other things that are hard—finishing tests, copying from board, etc.

• Three wishes (anything, not just school)

• Changes in self, in family

• What makes you happiest/saddest

• Anything else you would like to tell me about home or school that will help me understand how things are going?

Test behaviors

• What tasks seem hardest/easiest for the child?

• How does child perform various tasks—verbal mediation, "writing" on table, cueing on fingers, etc.

• Does he or she give up easily? On which types of tasks?

• Is she or he motivated/persistent, resistant/argumentative, lethargic/sleepy, active/distractible? Briefly describe what the child does (i.e., "Johnny worked standing and leaning across the table. Whenever the blower came on, he stopped his work and looked up," or "Whenever a paper/pencil task was presented, Chris became resistant and wanted to stop.")

• Speed—works very slowly; is fast and impulsive; makes many errors, works quickly, but is accurate

• Motor vs. nonmotor; verbal vs. nonverbal—which is better?

• Error recognition—monitors, so catches errors and corrects spontaneously; doesn't check for or notice errors

(26–75th percentile) on SS. Speed was somewhat slow for April, in the light of her good cognitive abilities, but still within normal limits in terms of the norm for her age.

On the Memory and Learning Core Domain subtests, April displayed very balanced abilities for learning and recalling names (Memory for Names, SS = 12), recognizing faces (Memory for Faces, SS = 12), and recalling story details (Narrative Memory, SS = 12).

April had difficulty on all the Sensorimotor Core subtests: She demonstrated poor fine motor coordination and motor programming on a finger-tapping and finger sequencing task (Fingertip Tapping, SS = 6). She demonstrated borderline ability to integrate visuospatial information, motor programming, and kinesthetic feedback in order to reproduce a static hand position (Imitating Hand Positions, SS = 7). When April had to draw lines quickly through winding tracks without going outside the tracks, her graphomotor control was low average (VP, SS = 8). Nonetheless, this performance reflected a relative weakness in terms of April's personal core subtest mean (11) on NEPSY.

A review of SS in the Sensorimotor Domain indicated that April's performance on Fingertip Tapping was *Below Expected Level* (3–10% of standardization population her age) for Repetitions and *Borderline* or *Slightly Below Expected Level* (11–25%) for Sequences. Her performance across tasks (fingertip tapping and sequences of movement) was *Borderline* (11–25%) with the Preferred hand, and it was *Below Expected Level* (3–10%) with the Nonpreferred hand. She had no difficulty with either hand on Finger Discrimination (Preferred Hand SS = 10; Nonpreferred SS = 9), an Expanded Subtest assessing perception of light touch. Thus, the reception of sensory input was within normal limits, but the production of rapid, coordinated finger movements was not. April worked more slowly than expected for 9-year-olds (*Borderline* for speed) on the simple and difficult VP tasks. She made few errors *(At Expected Levels)*, because she worked slowly. It appeared that she also consciously slowed her rate of production as a way to compensate for poor motor coordination. These results could explain her problems with written assignments at home and in school. She appears to know that if she does her written work quickly, it will be messy, and she will make errors. Frequently, however, it appears that she just gets tired of having to work so laboriously in order to be neat, and she rushes through her work impulsively, producing a poor quality of work.

April's fine performance on Arrows (SS = 16), which assesses nonmotor, visuospatial judgement of line orientation, was above expected level. It stood in sharp contrast to her borderline performance on Imitating Hand Positions (SS = 7), which was a relative weakness for April. The latter subtest requires visuospatial analysis, but it also requires motor programming and kinesthetic feedback from positions so that the child can tell when the hand is in the correct position. Her performance was average on two subtests that require varying degrees of visuospatial and visuomotor coordination, DC (SS = 9) and on an Expanded subtest Block Construction (SS = 10). Both were significantly below (>–2 *SD*) her nonmotor visuospatial judgment performance on Arrows. Though Design Copying required paper/pencil copying, the task was untimed and April could perform at expected level. She received no time bonuses on her block constructions, however. Taken together, April's performance on these subtests provided additional evidence of a primary deficit in fine motor coordination contributing to a secondary visuomotor coordination and integration problem.

Because visuomotor deficits frequently co-occur with attention and executive problems, April's performance in the Attention/Executive Domain was reviewed. She performed well on Tower (SS = 13), a nonverbal problem-solving task that makes minimal demands on motor skills. This performance was consistent with her cognitive abilities. In contrast, however, she had significant difficulty on the structured and random arrays of Design Fluency (ss = 5), an executive function, an expanded subtest assessing nonverbal fluency and creativity. This task also requires graphomotor speed and precision. April did not make many errors, but she produced few designs within the time limit. April monitored for errors, and her designs were unique indicating good executive functions. Her slow graphomotor speed and, in a couple of instances, her lack of visuomotor precision when she did not actually join the line to the dot, adversely affected April's results. This is a case where error analysis of performance made clear the primary deficit: fine motor coordination, which adversely affected visuomotor performance (secondary deficit). Executive dysfunction could be ruled out, because there was no other evidence of such in April's NEPSY performance, and she attended to the task well. She is also considered to be creative by her teacher, so this should not have impeded performance. April's performance was *Above Expected Level* for 9-year-olds on Knock and Tap (ss = 13), an Expanded executive function subtest that requires the ability to develop, maintain, and change sets but makes minimal demands on motor dexterity. Therefore, it appears April's primary deficit is fine motor coordination, which secondarily affected performance on Design Fluency due to its visuomotor constraints.

April's performance was *At Expected Level* on the VA Subtest (ss = 10) and the AARS Total Score (ss = 11), as well as on both the AA and RS sections. These subtests require selective and sustained attention, and the RS section also requires set-maintenance and set-shifting executive functions. The QOs for Off-Task Behavior on AARS occurred more frequently than would be expected at age 9, however. She became distracted several times during this test, fiddling with her necklace and reaching for pencils and materials to play with. Only 3 to 10% of the standardization group of April's age displayed this level of Off-Task Behavior on AARS. VA Off-Task Behaviors were *At Expected Level* for 9-year-olds. These results suggest that, though April can attend to visual stimuli that "anchors" her attentions, she may be coping also with mild or fluctuating levels of auditory attention (Kemp, Kirk, & Korkman, 1998).

Summary

April's performance on NEPSY revealed that, despite good cognitive ability, as measured by the WISC-III, her Sensorimotor Domain Score differed significantly from the Attention/Executive, Language, Visuospatial, and Memory and Learning Domain Scores. April displayed well-developed language and memory skills, but she displayed primary deficits in fine motor coordination and motor programming, with a secondary deficit in visuomotor integration. Therefore, this clinician administered a Selective Assessment using Expanded subtests across domains. April's performance on these Expanded subtests further supported the presence of a visuomotor deficit that secondarily affected April's performance on subtests in the Attention/Executive Functions (Design Fluency) and Visuospatial Domains (Block Construction) where she received no time bonuses. On SN her naming skills were very accurate, but speed was a relative weakness in relation to her naming ability. Design Fluency was also affected by inefficient graphomotor performance. The NEPSY Core and Selective Assessment results were consistent with parental and teacher reports of problems with written work at home and in school. They suggested, however, that April's problems are due to primary fine motor dyscoordination and secondary visuomotor problems rather than to carelessness, not spending enough time, or lack of effort. The QOs, which revealed a significant number of Off-Task Behaviors on AARS, suggest the possibility of a mild or fluctuating auditory attention problem. Here a relative weakness in speed of processing seems to support the hypothesis of a mild attentional problem, as well, because slowed processing often underlies attentional deficits. This possibility could be further evaluated through classroom observation, parent and teacher rating scales, and the administration of auditory and visual continuous performance tests. (See Rapid Reference 7.4.)

The second case presents NEPSY as a part of a full neuropsychological evaluation. It illustrates the type of assessment that might be undertaken to elucidate fully the profile of a child with the type of disorder that could be identified without a NEPSY assessment (e.g., cerebral palsy, Asperger's Syndrome, hydrocephalus, etc.), but it provides a detailed description of neurocognitive strengths

≣Rapid Reference 7.4

Information to Include in the Test Results and Interpretation Section of a Brief Report

In a brief report, it is permissible to combine test results and interpretation in one section

- Interpret results for each Core Domain Score, including the actual score in the text. Provide the mean in parentheses after the first Core Domain Score reported.
- Discuss any discrepancies among the Domain Scores and the implications of these discrepancies.
- Interpret the subtests, including the scores in parentheses. Use the "ss" abbreviation for scaled score (Name of Subtest: ss = score). Provide the mean with the first subtest results (e.g., Tower, SS = 10; mean = 10±3).
- Integrate the results clinically across subtests and domains.
- Specify the primary deficit and any secondary deficits.
- Verify the interpretation with scores and observations which converge on the same deficit.
- Briefly summarize, discussing the implications of primary and secondary deficits for the child's learning.

and weaknesses. In this child's case, the NEPSY provided a wealth of data that contributed significantly to identifying the condition, and to developing recommendations for addressing his deficits. Even if the diagnosis had been made previously, however, the NEPSY would have been valuable for providing in-depth information about the child's capacities. The comprehensive detailing of neurocognitive strengths and weaknesses on NEPSY performance, integrated with other test results, gives parents and professionals a fuller understanding of the child's neuropsychological functioning. This makes possible the development of a comprehensive treatment plan with focused and targeted intervention techniques. Because the report to follow involves a differential diagnosis, a discussion of the disorders to be ruled out and the process of arriving at a differential diagnosis will be presented prior to the report in order to facilitate understanding.

Differential Diagnosis: Obsessive-Compulsive Disorder vs. Autistic Disorder vs. Asperger's Syndrome vs. Nonverbal Learning Disability

The first step in reaching a differential diagnosis is to consider disorders about which there are significant concerns or to which diagnostic clusters of symptoms appear to point. Because Garry's parents have concerns about whether or not he is subject to Attention Deficit Hyperactivity Disorder or Obsessive-Compulsive Disorder (OCD), these disorders should be included in the process of arriving at a differential diagnosis. They should be discussed thoroughly with Garry's parents so they understand why they are or are not appropriate diagnoses. Although Garry was very distractible, it appeared to be a part of a much more complex disorder than ADHD. Therefore, this disorder was discarded early in the differential diagnosis process.

Children who are subject to OCD may have obsessions or compulsions or both. Obsessions are "recurrent and persistent thoughts, impulses, or images that are experienced . . . as intrusive and inappropriate and that may cause marked anxiety or distress." They are "not simply excessive worries about real-life problems," and the child may attempt to "ignore or suppress" them. The child may recognize that the obsessions "are a product of his or her own mind," though this latter insight may not be true of the young child. Compulsions are "repetitive behaviors (e.g. hand washing, ordering . . .) or mental acts (. . . counting, repeating words silently) that the person feels driven to perform in response to an obsession or according to rules that must be applied rigidly." Compulsions are "aimed at preventing or reducing distress or some dreaded event . . . ; however, they are not connected in a realistic way with what they are designed to neutralize or prevent." (American Psychiatric Association, 1994). Rapid Reference 7.5 outlines DSM-IV criteria for OCD.

Observations of and interactions with Garry were characterized by his extremely hyperverbal behavior on very restrictive, stereotypical topics and his lack of perception of social cues. Initially, Garry appeared quite precocious, and his expressive vocabulary left the impression of an older child's language skills due to the advanced topics that he discussed using appropriate terms and names. For instance, Garry discussed mythology in a seemingly erudite manner, presenting all sorts of facts, referring to the mythological characters and gods by their Greek names, and relating their stories. The clinician realized shortly, however, that he was very concrete and full of strings of rote facts concerning his stereotypical areas of interest. Although children with OCD become fixated on certain topics, these usually revolve around compulsive washing, counting or checking; obsessive fears of contamination or illness of self or family; or of dire happenings, such as tornadoes, and so forth. Garry's parents did not report any of these types of obsessions or compulsions. They did report his need for sameness, which is typical of a number of developmental disorders. Some separation anxiety was also reported but the Whites had not observed any anxiety that appeared to be relieved by compulsive behavior. His stereotypical interests appeared to be more of the re-

≡Rapid Reference 7.5

DSM-IV Criteria for Diagnosis of OCD

A. Children who are subject to OCD may have obsessions, compulsions, or both.

Obsessions

- "Recurrent and persistent thoughts, impulses, or images that are experienced ... as intrusive and inappropriate and that may cause marked anxiety or distress."
- They are "not simply excessive worries about real-life problems."
- The child may attempt to "ignore or suppress" them.
- The child may recognize that the obsessions "are a product of his or her own mind," though this latter insight may not be true of the young child.

Compulsions

- "Repetitive behaviors (e.g., hand washing, ordering ...) or mental acts (... counting, repeating words silently) that the person feels driven to perform in response to an obsession or according to rules that must be applied rigidly."
- The behaviors or mental acts (compulsions) are "aimed at preventing or reducing distress or some dreaded event ... however, they are not connected in a realistic way with what they are designed to neutralize or prevent or are clearly excessive."

B. At some point the client recognizes that the obsessions and compulsions are excessive and unreasonable. NOTE: This does not apply to children.

C. The obsessions and compulsions cause marked distress, are time-consuming, or significantly interfere with the person's normal routine, occupational or academic functioning, or usual social activities or relationships.

(American Psychiatric Association, 1994)

---

stricted type seen in children with Autistic Disorder, Asperger's Syndrome, or Nonverbal Learning Disability. Therefore, Garry's symptoms would not appear to meet the criteria for OCD (American Psychiatric Association, 1994), so it would be ruled out. Therefore, the remaining three disorders for consideration in the differential diagnosis would then be considered.

Because of Garry's facile use of language, albeit with some subtle language difficulties, Autistic Disorder would not be high on the list of diagnostic alternatives. Garry did not display, nor had he displayed in the past, the general language delay, jargoning or echolalia characteristic of the idiosyncratic language in Autistic Disorder. Also, Garry was reported to be a little more socially interactive than a child with autism, and this was observed by this clinician during the evaluation. He actually interacted fairly well with an adult, once his initial reticence was overcome, but he was completely oblivious of social reciprocity. Because of the level of his language and the course of its development, as well as the higher level of social relatedness than is usually seen in a child with autism, Garry did not meet the criteria for Autistic Disorder, which is outlined in Rapid Reference 7.6.

There is quite a bit of disagreement over whether or not Asperger's Syndrome and High Functioning Autism (HFA) are actually separate entities. Of fourteen eminent authorities surveyed by Schopler (1996), two maintained that AS and HFA are distinct disorders; six felt that the distinction is ambiguous, and six maintained that they are not distinct developmental disorders. In order to avoid confusion in terminology and to help the reader understand the diagnostic considerations being hypothesized, two further disorders will be discussed before the report of Garry's evaluation is presented: AS, or Asperger's Disorder as it is termed in the DSM-IV, and Nonverbal Learning Disability (NLD). AS was first described in 1944 by Dr. Asperger in a German journal of psychiatry and neurology. Unfortunately, it did not receive much attention until Wing (1981) published a paper on the clinical features of Asperger's Syndrome. Slowly recognition of this disorder grew, and in 1994, it was first included in the Diagnostic and Statistical Manual of Mental Disorders—4th Ed. (American Psychiatric Association, 1994).

According to the diagnostic criteria in the DSM-IV, AS is a "qualitative impairment in social interaction . . . manifested by two of the following: a) marked impairment in the use of multiple nonverbal behaviors, such as eye-to-eye gaze, facial expression, body postures, and gestures to regulate social interaction; b) failure to develop peer relationships appropriate to developmental level, c) lack of spontaneous seeking to share enjoyment, interests, or achievements with other people . . . , and d) lack of social or emotional reciprocity." Other characteristics of AS include, "restricted, repetitive and stereotyped patterns of behavior, interests, and activities, as manifested by at least one of the following: (a) . . . stereotyped and restricted pattern of interest that is abnormal in intensity or focus; (b) apparently inflexible adherence to specific, nonfunctional routines or rituals; (c) stereotyped and repetitive motor mannerisms (e.g. hand or finger flapping or twisting . . .); and (d) persistent preoccupations with parts of objects." The disturbance causes "clinically significant impairment in social, occupational, or other important areas of functioning." Finally, there is "no general delay in language" and "no clinically significant delay in cognitive development, age-appropriate self-help skills, adaptive behavior (other than in social interaction) and curiosity about the environment." (American Psychiatric Association, 1994). Garry appears to meet many of these

≡ Rapid Reference 7.6

DSM-IV Criteria for Diagnosis of Autistic Disorder

Children who are subject to Autistic Disorder meet the following DSM-IV criteria.

I. A total of six (or more) items from (A), (B), and (C) with at least two from (A) and one each from (B) and (C)

    A. Qualitative impairment in social interaction, as manifested by at least two of the following

        1. Marked impairment in multiple nonverbal behaviors to regulate social interaction—(eye contact, facial expression, body postures, gestures).

        2. Failure to develop peer relationships appropriate to developmental level.

        3. Lack of spontaneous seeking to share interests or achievements.

        4. Lack of social or emotional reciprocity.

    B. Qualitative impairments in communication as manifested by at least one of the following

        • Delay in, or total lack of, the development of spoken language.

        • If adequate speech, marked impairment in the ability to initiate or sustain a conversation with others.

        • Stereotyped and repetitive use of language or idiosyncratic language.

        • Lack of varied, spontaneous make-believe play or social imitative play appropriate to developmental level.

    C. Restricted repetitive and stereotyped patterns of behavior, interests, and activities, as manifested by at least one of the following

        1. Preoccupation with one or more stereotyped and restricted patterns of interests that is abnormal either in intensity or focus.

        2. Apparently inflexible adherence to specific, nonfunctional routines or rituals.

        3. Stereotyped and repetitive motor mannerisms (hand/finger flapping, complex whole body movements).

        4. Persistent preoccupation with parts of objects.

II. Delays or abnormal functioning in at least one of the following areas with onset prior to 3 years of age

    1. Social interaction.

    2. Language as used social communication.

    3. Symbolic or imaginative play.

III. Clear evidence of clinically significant impairment in social, academic, or occupational functioning.

IV. The disturbance is not better accounted for by Rett's Disorder or Childhood Integrative Disorder.

(American Psychiatric Association, 1994)

DSM-IV Criteria for Diagnosis of Asperger's Disorder

Children who are subject to Asperger's Disorder meet the following *DSM-IV* criteria:

A. Qualitative impairment in social interaction, as manifested by at least two of the following:

- Marked impairment in multiple nonverbal behaviors to regulate social interaction—(eye contact, facial expression, body postures, gestures).
- Failure to develop peer relationships appropriate to developmental level.
- Lack of spontaneous seeking to share interests or achievements.
- Lack of social or emotional reciprocity.

B. Restricted repetitive and stereotyped patterns of behavior, interests, and activities, as manifested by at least one of the following:

- Preoccupation with one or more stereotyped and restricted patterns of interests that is abnormal either in intensity or focus.
- Apparently inflexible adherence to specific, nonfunctional routines or rituals.
- Stereotyped and repetitive motor mannerisms (hand/finger flapping, complex whole body movements).
- Persistent preoccupation with parts of objects.

C. The disturbance causes clinically significant impairment in social, occupational, or other important areas of functioning.

D. There is no clinically significant general delay in language (e.g., single words used by 2 years of age, communicative phrases used by 3 years of age).

E. There is no clinically significant delay in cognitive development or in the development of self-help skills, adaptive behaviors (other than in social interaction), and curiosity about the environment in childhood.

F. Criteria are not met for another specific Pervasive Developmental Disorder or Schizophrenia.

(American Psychiatric Association, 1994)

---

criteria, so it will be retained in the differential diagnosis and discussed in the light of Garry's test results and behavioral characteristics. (See Rapid Reference 7.7.)

After ruling out OCD and Autistic Disorder and retaining Asperger's Disorder in the differential diagnosis, the next disorder to be considered is Nonverbal Learning Disability (NLD). It comes from the tradition of neuropsychology, whereas Asperger's Syndrome comes from psychiatry. The NLD model was first described in 1971 by Johnson & Mylkebust, and a similar model, Social-Emotional

Learning Disability, has also been described by Denckla (1983) and Weintraub & Mesulam (1983). According to Rourke, (1989), who derived the NLD model psychometrically, not neurologically, symptoms of NLD are: bilateral tactile-perceptual deficits, usually more marked on the left, bilateral psychomotor coordination deficiencies, often marked on the left; significant deficiencies in visual-spatial abilities; marked relative deficiencies in mechanical arithmetic as compared to proficiencies in word recognition and spelling; significant deficits in nonverbal problem-solving, concept formation, hypothesis testing, and the capacity to benefit from feedback in novel or complex situations, problems understanding cause-effect relationships, and marked deficiencies in the appreciation of incongruities (age-appropriate sense of humor). Children with NLD, according to Rourke (1995) have well-developed rote verbal capacities, including rote verbal memory skills, but extreme difficulty in adapting to novel and otherwise complex situations. Further, they display much verbosity of a repetitive, straightforward nature and little prosody. There are problems with pragmatics (slightly formal, "cocktail party" speech with lack of awareness of the "give and take" of conversation). Such children tend to rely on language as the principal means of social relatedness, information gathering, and relief from anxiety. Most notably the child with NLD shows significant deficits in social perception, social judgement, and interaction with a marked tendency to social withdrawal as age increases (Rourke, 1994).

Rourke (1995) postulates that developmentally NLD (see Rapid Reference 7.8) is due to right hemisphere dysfunction, especially in neuronal white matter, the long myelinated fibers, which facilitate intermodal integration in the adult (Goldberg and Costa, 1981). NLD would be expected to develop under any circumstance that significantly interferes with the functioning of the right hemisphere or with access to those systems (e.g. agenesis of the corpus callosum). Functionally, symptoms of NLD should be observable by 7–9 years of age, and they implicate neuropsychological, academic, and social-emotional/adaptive domains in a fashion similar to the emergent learning characteristics seen in children with AS (Rourke, Young, & Leenaars, 1989).

Increasingly, NLD is being considered as a neuropsychological model of Asperger's Syndrome (AS) (Volkmar & Klin, 1998). In other words, it appears that AS is marked by a cluster of neuropsychological strengths and weaknesses that are captured by the NLD profile. A stringent 1995 study (Klin, Volkmar et al., 1995) demonstrated a high degree of correspondence between the NLD profile and AS cases (21/21), whereas, only 1 of 19 individuals with HFA appeared to exhibit the NLD profile. Six areas of deficits were associated with AS: fine and gross

Rapid Reference 7.8

Characteristics of Nonverbal Learning Disability (NLD)

The model of NLD is generally described (Rourke, 1989) as including

* Bilateral psychomotor deficits (may be greater on left due to right-hemisphere dysfunction).
* Significant deficiencies in visual-spatial abilities
* Marked relative deficiencies in mechanical arithmetic in comparison to word recognition and spelling
* Significant deficits in
  —Nonverbal problem-solving
  —Concept formation
  —Hypothesis testing
* Impaired ability to benefit from feedback and to adapt to novel or complex situations
* Problems understanding cause-effect relationships
* Deficiencies in the appreciation of incongruities (age-appropriate sense of humor)
* Well-developed rote verbal abilities,
  —Good rote, verbal memory
* Subtle language problems
  —Poor pragmatics (little give and take of conversation; cocktail party speech)
  —Repetitive verbosity
  —Little prosody
* Rely on language for
  —Social relatedness.
  —Information gathering.
  —Relief from anxiety.
* Marked social deficits include
  —Social perception
  —Social judgment
  —Increasing social withdrawal with age

These deficits should be observable by 7 to 9 years of age.

They implicate neuropsychological, academic, and social emotional/adaptive domains in a fashion similar to emergent learning characteristics seen with Asperger's Syndrome (Rourke, Young, & Leenaars, 1989).

These deficits are postulated to be caused by right hemisphere dysfunction, especially in neuronal white matter (Rourke, 1995).

≡Rapid Reference 7.9

Making a Differential Diagnosis

In making a differential diagnosis,

1. Include any specific condition which the parents questioned in their history or your interview. If a disorder is not appropriate to be included, explain why in your discussion.

2. Include any disorders that seem to be logical possibilities. These would include disorders that share primary and secondary deficits with or show the diagnostic behavioral cluster for a particular disorder and symptoms of the disorder are observed in the child's test results or your observations.

3. In the summarizing findings, discuss why or why not a finding fits the disorders being considered. Narrow the field by excluding those disorders that are not logical, appear in only one result, or in which there are key symptoms missing. Support your conclusions with results across assessments, as much as possible.

4. Finally, narrow the field to the disorder that is most appropriate diagnosis, is logical in the light of the child's functioning, and can be verified with two or more results from the testing, family report, developmental, medical, psychological, and school history. If a diagnosis does not fit fully, but you want to watch how the symptoms develop, you can make a provisional diagnosis and explain why.

motor skills, visual-motor integration, visual-spatial perception, nonverbal concept formation, and visual memory. Both HFA and AS individuals showed deficits in verbal concept formation, verbal content, prosody, social competence, emotional responses, and in the academic areas of reading comprehension and arithmetic. A "not-AS" group could be predicted by deficits in articulation, verbal output, auditory perception, vocabulary, and verbal memory. This study indicated marked overlap of NLD with AS, but not with HFA. Many consider NLD to be synonymous with AS or a variant of it (Volkmar & Klin, 1998). Therefore, for the purposes of this report and the discussion of Garry's performance, NLD and AS will be considered as one disorder with NLD as a variant. We then need to consider whether Garry's pattern of neurocognitive strengths and weaknesses corresponds to the diagnostic behavioral cluster associated with Asperger's Disorder or NLD. (See Rapid Reference 7.9.)

The report that follows presents the results of the Full NEPSY and the other assessments added to the neuropsychological evaluation. Recommendations are included. It also includes printouts produced by the *NEPSY Scoring Assistant* (The Psychological Corporation, 2000). These were imported into the text of the report, and modified to present the data for Garry's parents.

CASE REPORT #2

Garry White, 7.10 years of age

Referral Question: Why does Garry appear so bright and know so much factual information yet does not seem to perform at that level in his schoolwork?

Neuropsychological Evaluation

Name:	Garry K. White
Date of Birth:	10-13-1991
Chart#:	459
Date Of Evaluation:	08-19-1999

Referral Statement

Garry is the 7.10 year-old son of Kirk and Jillian White, who also have one daughter, 5-year-old Leslie, for whom no learning or behavioral problems were reported. Ms. White holds a BA in Accounting and is currently a homemaker, and Mr. White holds an Associate of Arts degree in psychology and is employed in sales. Garry was referred for testing by his parents due to concerns regarding his inability to sustain attention, his inappropriate social behavior, discipline problems, a tendency to extreme nervousness in some circumstances, separation anxiety and inability to control his temper. The parents wished to rule out Attention Deficit Hyperactivity Disorder (ADHD) and/or Obsessive Compulsive Disorder. They seek strategies by which they "may help Garry cope with his problems, improve his pronunciation of /s/, and learn social interaction techniques."

Relevant Background Information

Garry was the product of a 36-week, uncomplicated pregnancy and normal delivery. A nuchal cord was present, but was removed from the neck prior to delivery, and there were no perinatal complications. Parents noted that Garry attained developmental landmarks at a normal rate with language landmarks being somewhat precocious. He spoke in two or more word sentences by 19 mos. of age. He was breastfed for 11 months. Ms. White stated, "As an infant, Garry was happy, cuddly, quiet and content, ate and slept well, and was sweet and healthy." As a toddler, however, Garry was subject to tantrums. His parents characterize him now as moody, fearful, talkative, a follower, dependent, sensitive, friendly, happy, cooperative, but hard to discipline. Furthermore, his parents describe Garry as "not very well coordinated." For example, Garry cannot catch a ball, run fluidly, or balance enough to play Hopscotch. He still cannot balance on a bicycle with training wheels. Parents also reported that eye contact is not good, and he does not interact with his peers, though he relates better to adults. One area of particular concern is Garry's inability to control his temper.

Garry's medical history revealed few problems, other than recurrent otitis media in the first five years of life. These episodes were treated with antibiotics, no ventilating tubes were placed. Present allergies are treated occasionally with Claritin. Hearing was tested as normal (5-15-99; Middlebrook Health Department). Visual evaluation (6-10-99; G. Douglas, MD) described Garry as "borderline myopic," but glasses were not prescribed. Garry's mother reported that his general health is excellent.

A review of family history revealed that Ms. White has no history of learning or behavioral difficulties. In first through third grades, the father needed remedial reading and had speech and language therapy for an articulation problem (pronunciation of the letter "s," a trait Garry shared). The father suffers from migraine headaches. In the extended family, the paternal grandmother had migraine headaches and was diagnosed late in life with Obsessive Compulsive Disorder (OCD). A maternal uncle has dyslexia and suffered a stroke at 27 years of age, apparently brought on by a staphylococcal heart infection, according to Ms. White. Two male cousins on the paternal side have ADHD and take Ritalin.

Garry attended preschool two mornings a week from 2 to 4 years of age. He also had bible study once a week from 2 to 6 years of age. Initially, he performed very well and seemed interested in reading at a very early age. At three, he read signs and some words in books, according to his mother, who is also his teacher. He is presently home-schooled, and is now reading at the 2nd grade level. Ms. White stated, however, that he is "nearly one year behind in math for his age." Garry has great difficulty in sustaining attention on anything which is not of great interest to him. He is hard to motivate, easily distracted, and is given to grumbling, according to his mother.

Ms. White reported that Garry is very sensitive to certain stimuli. For example, he becomes upset if there are lumps in Cream of Wheat or in the meat sauce on spaghetti; he doesn't like sticky substances on his hands, and he refuses to be seen with wet hair. His parents have observed that he can imitate characters in television commercials and produce the dialogue almost verbatim. He watches certain videos repetitively, and he displays intense interest in pirates, Egypt, China, mythology, and several other areas. He is likely to talk about them at great length and in minute detail.

His parents report that Garry's separation anxiety can be almost paralyzing at times, and he feels he must keep track of his mother constantly. According to his parents, Garry is also lacking in certain social skills. He seems unable to grasp the need for give and take in conversation and, irrespective of who may be talking already, he is liable to interrupt. Despite numerous reminders, Garry does not seem to understand that he should not interrupt. He is upset by chaos and disorder, and is very sensitive to being embarrassed, even in situations that do not seem to warrant a sense of embarrassment, such as someone seeing him with a wet head. Garry is not, however, without a few close friends in the neighborhood who are younger than he is. Nonetheless, according to the Whites, he relates best to adults.

Tests Administered

- Differential Ability Scales
- Peabody Picture Vocabulary Test—3rd Ed.
- Expressive Vocabulary Test
- Rey-Osterreith Complex Figure (Scoring according to Bernstein & Weber)
- Vineland Adaptive Rating Scales
- Childhood Autism Rating Scale
- NEPSY Developmental Neuropsychological Assessment
- Wechsler Individual Achievement Test

Test Observations*

Garry was in the playroom with his mother and father when this clinician greeted them. He looked around when she spoke his name, but his eye contact was fleeting. When prompted by his parents, Garry looked around and said, "Hi," but did not make direct eye contact. When this psychologist sat down on the floor a moderate distance from Garry, he then moved closer to his mother. When this clinician began talking to him, however, he relaxed and began talking about the Egyptian pharaohs, using correct names. From that point on, he was hyperverbal. After hearing all about Egypt for about 10 min and playing with Garry (which consisted of running a car in and out of the car elevator of a toy garage repetitively), this clinician then walked with Garry and his parents to the testing room. When Ms. White explained to Garry that he was going to play some games and do "school-things," he separated easily from his parents and entered the testing session cooperatively. He warmed to the tasks quickly. Eye contact improved, but it was still fleeting at times. He was frequently distracted by his own hyperverbal behavior.

*Note to Essentials reader: This section is much longer than it would be for some children, because behavioral observations are key to this child's diagnosis.

Garry displayed a mild articulation problem. He was somewhat impulsive, reaching for materials before all of the directions had been completed. He talked constantly, guiding himself through tasks or speaking of tangential topics. He frequently came back to the Egyptian pharaoh topic or talked about films on the Disney channel. He stated that he especially likes to watch *Hercules*. Garry knew many facts about mythology, named numerous characters from Greek mythology correctly (Perseus, Theseus, etc.) and told their stories. He also talked about the internet, produced specific internet addresses from memory that he recommended, and described his computer chess game play-by-play. The child interview had to be discontinued, because it seemed only to provide more opportunity for Garry to talk about his stereotypical interests. Garry did report that it is hard to write when doing his schoolwork and that he would rather just tell his mother the answer.

When drawing the designs on the Differential Ability Scales (DAS) Recall of Designs, Garry talked about how the designs looked like "ancient Chinese" and then began a monologue on China. When he was discussing one of his favorite topics, he could become quite animated, but at other times, his affect was somewhat flat, and his voice lacked prosody. Occasionally, however, he would smile appropriately. It appeared that if he were not redirected Garry would talk indefinitely. He did not seem to detect any nonverbal social cues that might indicate boredom or fatigue on the part of his listener. He redirected easily, however, and was not at all oppositional. After each redirection, he applied himself to the task at hand and worked diligently for a short period. He soon became distracted, however and began talking again without realizing it. Garry did not seem aware of cues about the necessity of completing a task first before talking, unless he was explicitly told. When he was urged to get his tasks done so he could have his prizes, Garry immediately launched into a discussion of the difference between "prizes" and "surprises."

Garry was subject to off-task behavior during the VA Subtest. He stopped to talk about how he needed to look at every line of pictures on the stimulus page, about the target picture of a cat having a big tail, other animals, and so forth. He also distracted himself markedly on Repetition of Nonsense Words when he attempted to "outdo" the nonsense words on the tape by using Chinese, Egyptian, and Russian words in response. Subsequently he forgot the original nonsense word that he was to imitate. Although the tape was stopped, and Garry was redirected several times, he did not seem to be able to inhibit his need to use foreign words. He displayed stable misarticulation errors on Repetition of Nonsense Words, but these did not adversely affect performance, because Garry's monologue about ancient languages and their words distracted him so completely that he reproduced few of the subtest target words. He also had difficulty accessing words for size, color, and shape on SN, even though he named them on the Teaching Trial.

Despite Garry's seemingly facile language when discussing his "peak" interests, he made some phonological errors in pronouncing words (e.g., "surpob" for syrup), and his language did not always make complete sense, because he seemed to mix two thoughts. For instance, just before the break, Garry stated, "I'm thirsty, I wish you had some 7-up, because I like Sprite." He also appeared to understand the gist of a message, but missed the subtleties. Although he wanted to be funny, he appeared not to understand humor. For instance, he tried to tell a joke and stated, "Why did the lady put lipstick on her head?" Without waiting for a reply, he went on, "She wanted her hair to be red."

For the most part, Garry used a right-handed, thumb-over, intermediate pencil grip, but periodically, he used his left hand. He also slipped into an immature, tight, low pincer grasp on the VP Subtest of NEPSY, apparently to help himself draw lines quickly. Nonetheless, he frequently strayed outside the lines, consequently making errors. He verbally mediated most tasks. On the VP Subtest, for instance, Garry "talked" his way through the tracks as he drew his lines, "I go around here and then up. Oops, I bumped into the wall." When performing fine motor tasks, finger tapping and sequential finger movements, Garry displayed a number of associated movements: overflow in the tongue and mouth, and mirroring on the right when the left hand was moving. As he performed movement sequences with each hand, Garry recruited his whole body into the task, bouncing awkwardly forward and backward from the waist. He had difficulty choosing the correct fingers when attempting to imitate the examiner's hand positions. Garry showed tactile defensiveness when his hands were first touched lightly on the Finger Discrimination subtest. Garry's marked tangential verbosity and distractibility adversely affected his performance, so these test results may not reflect his full potential. His test behaviors, however, provided an excellent opportunity to observe Garry's lack of social perception, subtle language deficits, and the extent to which his stereotypical interests interfere with learning and social interaction.

TEST RESULTS

COGNITIVE

Differential Ability Scales—School Age

General Cognitive Ability: 86 **(95% Confidence Interval: 80–92)** **Percentile: 18**

Low Average (Mean = 100+15)

Subtest	Assesses	Subtest T-score (Mean = 50+10)	Cluster Standard Score (Mean = 100+15)
Word Definitions	Expressive vocabulary	59	**Verbal Cluster: 109**
Similarities	Verbal abstract reasoning	53	**73rd percentile**
			Average
Matrices	Nonverbal reasoning (Visual analogies)	47	**Nonverbal Cluster: 85**
			16th percentile
Sequential and Quantitative reasoning	Visual-sequential & Quantitative-relation-ships	36	**Average**
Recall of Designs	Spatial memory & Visual-motor inte-gration.	27	**Spatial Cluster: 70**
			2nd percentile
Pattern Construction	Visuospatial analysis & Reproduction of design	37	**Borderline**
	All Nonverbal Cluster & Spatial Cluster subtests taken together		**Special Nonverbal Cluster:75**
			5th percentile
			Borderline

RECEPTIVE & EXPRESSIVE PICTURE VOCABULARY

Peabody Picture Vocabulary Test—3rd Ed. (Form IIIa) (PPVT-IIIa)

Standard Score: 100 (95% confidence. interval: 92–108) Percentile: 50 Age Score: 7.11 (Mean = 100+15)

Garry displayed average receptive one-word picture vocabulary (understanding of language at the one-word level).

Expressive Vocabulary Test (EVT)

Standard Score: 108 (95% confidence interval: 100–116) Percentile: 70 Age Score: 8.5 (Mean = 100+15)

Garry performed within the average range on this assessment of one-word expressive vocabulary

NEPSY Developmental Neuropsychological Assessment
Core Domain Score mean = 100±15; Scaled Score mean = 10±3;
Cumulative percentages/percentiles based on standardization sample for age:
>75%—above expected level (EL); 26–75%—at EL 11–25%—slightly below EL or borderline;
3–10% below EL; <2%—well below EL

NEPSY Developmental Neuropsychological Assessment (continued)
Attention/Executive Core Domain Score: 77 (Borderline)

Confidence Interval: 71–91   Percentile: 6

Subtest	Assesses	Scaled Score	Percentile (Cum %)	Classification	Strength/ Weakness*
Tower	Planning, strategizing, self-monitoring, problem-solving	8		Slightly below expected level (Borderline)	—
Auditory Attention & Response Set	Simple and complex auditory attention and inhibition	7		Slightly below expected level (Borderline)	—
Auditory Attn	Simple auditory attention Maintaining a set**	8		Slightly below expected level (Borderline)	—
Omission errors	attention**		11–25%	Slightly below (Borderline)	
Commission errors	inhibition of response**		11–25%	Slightly below (Borderline)	
Response set	Complex auditory attention Maintenance & shift of set**	7		Slightly below expected level (Borderline)	—
Omission errors	attention**		11–25%	Slightly below (Borderline)	
Commission errors	inhibition of response*		11–25%	Slightly below (Borderline)	
Visual Attention	Simple visual search and complex visual attention to multiple targets**	6		Below expected level	—
Cats	Time to completion		3–10%	Below expected level	
Omissions	attention**		>75%	Above expected level	
Commissions	inhibition of response**		3–10%	Below expected level	
Faces	Time to completion		>75%	Above expected level	
Omissions	attention**		26–75%	At expected level	
Commissions	inhibition of response**		3–10%	Below expected level	

NEPSY Developmental Neuropsychological Assessment (continued)

Expanded Subtests (Not included in Core Domain Score)

Subtest	Assesses	Scaled Score	Percentile (Cum %)	Classification	Strength/ Weakness*
Statue	Inhibition of motor response to noise		3–10%	Below expected level	—
Design Fluency	Planning, strategizing* Monitoring to generate unique designs	1		Well below expected level	**W**
Structured Array			<2%	Well below expected level	
Random Array			<2%	Well below expected level	
Knock and Tap	Inhibition of motor response		<2%	Well below expected level	**W**

*Table B.4 (Compared to Core and Expanded within domains).

**Additional notations added to printout. Copyright 1999

Language Core Domain Score: 85   Low Average—strength compared to Visuospatial

Confidence Interval: 78–96   Percentile: 16

Subtest	Assesses	Scaled Score	Percentile (Cum %)	Classification	Strength/ Weakness*
Phonological Processing	Conceptualization of changing speech-sound patterns. Underlies decoding & spelling	9		At expected level	—
Speeded Naming	Speeded access to language labels (names)**	8		Slightly below expected level (Borderline)	—
Time	Speed of access**		11–25%	Slightly below expected level (Borderline)	—
Accuracy	Accessing the correct name**		>75%	Above expected level	

NEPSY *Developmental Neuropsychological Assessment* (continued)

Subtest	Assesses	Scaled Score	Percentile (Cum %)	Classification	Strength/ Weakness*
Comprehension of Instructions	Receptive language understanding of complex linguistic cues in oral directions	6		Below expected level	—

Expanded subtests (not included in Core Domain Score)

Subtest	Assesses	Scaled Score	Percentile (Cum %)	Classification	Strength/ Weakness*
Repetition of Nonsense Words	Processing of novel phonological sound patterns (**negatively affected by distractibility**)**	1		Well below expected level	**W#**
Verbal Fluency	Rapid production of words in categories	11		At expected level	S
Semantic items	Animals; things to eat/drink**		>75%	Above expected level	
Phonemic items	Words beginning with /f/ & /s/		26–75%	At expected level	
Oromotor Sequences	Oral-motor programming to produce speech		11–25%	Slightly below expected level (Borderline)	—

*(Compared to Core & Expanded within domains).

**notations added to printout.

#invalid performance

Sensorimotor Core Domain Score: 68 (Deficient)—weakness compared to Memory Core

Confidence Interval: 64–84   Percentile: 2

Subtest	Assesses	Scaled Score	Percentile (Cum %)	Classification	Strength/ Weakness*
Fingertip Tapping	Simple and complex fine motor movements**	6		Below expected level	—
Preferred hand	Repetitions & sequences**		11–25%	Slightly below expected level (Borderline)	
Nonpreferred hand	Repetitions & sequences**		3–10%	Below expected level	

NEPSY Developmental Neuropsychological Assessment (continued)

Expanded Subtests (Not included in Core Domain Score)

Subtest	Assesses	Scaled Score	Percentile (Cum %)	Classification	Strength/ Weakness*
Repetitions	Finger tapping against the thumb**		11–25%	Slightly below expected level (Borderline)	
Sequences	Sequential finger tapping**		3–10%	Below expected level	
Imitating Hand Positions	Integration of visuo-spatial info. with kines-thetic feedback/motor prog.	5		Below expected level	—
Preferred hand	static hand position-pref.		3–10%	Below expected level	
Non-preferred hand	static hand position–pref.		3–10%	Below expected level	
Visuomotor Precision	Graphomotor speed/ accuracy	6		Below expected level	—
Car					
Time	speed		>75%	Above expected level	
Errors	accuracy		3–10%	Below expected level	
Motorcycle					
Time	speed		>75%	Above expected level	
Errors	accuracy		3–10%	Below expected level	

Expanded Subtests (Not included in Core Domain Scores)

Manual Motor Sequences	Fluid hand movements in sequence; motor programming		<2%	Well below expected level	—
Finger Discrimination	Tactile discrimination/differentiation				
Preferred Hand	preferred hand tactile discrim		<2%	Well below expected level	—
Nonpreferred Hand	nonpreferred hand tactile discrim		<2%	Well below expected level	—

*Table B.4 (Compared to Core and Expanded within domains)

**Additional notations added to printout. Copyright 1999.

Visuospatial Core Domain Score: 66 (Deficient)—weakness compared to Language/Memory

Memory Confidence Interval: 56–76   Percentile: 0.3

Subtest	Assesses	Scaled Score	Percentile (Cum %)	Classification	Strength/ Weakness*
Design Copy	Visuomotor integration and two-dimensional construction**	2		Well below expected level	—
Arrows	Judgement of orientation of lines and angles	6		Below expected level	—

Expanded Subtests (Not included in the Core Domain Score)

Subtest	Assesses	Scaled Score	Percentile (Cum %)	Classification	Strength/ Weakness*
Block Construction	Reproduction of three-dimensional constructions**	5		Below expected level	—
Route Finding	Visuospatial analysis for map reading		3–10%	Below expected level	—

*Table B.4 (Core and Expanded within domains).

**Additional notations added to printout.

Copyright 1999; Portions of this report are protected by copyright by The Psychological Corporation, a Harcourt Assessment Company.

Normative data copyright 1998 by The Psychological Corporation.

Memory Core Domain Score: 86   Low Average—a strength compared to Sensorimotor Visuospatial

Confidence Interval: 79–97   Percentile: 18

Subtest	Assesses	Scaled Score	Percentile (Cum %)	Classification	Strength/ Weakness*
Faces	Immediate and delayed memory for faces	5		Below expected level	**W**
Immediate	Immed. recognition**	6		Below expected level	
Delayed	30 min. delay**	4		Below expected level	
Names	Name learning and delayed recall	10		At expected level	—
Immediate	After 3 Learning Trials**	9		At expected level	
Delayed	30 min. delay**	12		At expected level	

NEPSY Developmental Neuropsychological Assessment (continued)

Subtest	Assesses	Scaled Score	Percentile (Cum %)	Classification	Strength/ Weakness**
Narrative Memory	Story memory	9		At expected level	—
Free Recall	Spontaneous recall**		>75%	Above expected level	
Cued Recall	Questioning for recall**		>75%	Above expected level	

Expanded Subtests (Not included in Core Domain Score)

Subtest	Assesses	Scaled Score	Percentile (Cum %)	Classification	Strength/ Weakness**
Sentence Repetition	Auditory short-term memory for language	11		At expected level	—
List Learning	Supraspan memory; learning over trials (Total words learned Trial 1–5)**	7		Slightly below expected level (Borderline)	—
Learning**	Words added to the initial recall over 5 trials (Trial 1: 5 words; Trial 5: 6 words)		12%	Slightly below expected level (Borderline)	
Interference**	Effect of an interference list on retention (Trial 7 recall after interference: 7 words; 1 more word than Trial 5 recall: 6 words)		>66%	At expected level	
Delay Score**	Delay vs. Consolidation of memory after 30 minutes (Delayed Recall: 7; 1 more word after 30 min. than Trial 5: 6 words)**		>62%	At expected level	

*Table B.4 (Core and Expanded within domains).

**Additional notations added to the printout.

Qualitative Observations Across Subtests

Qualitative Observations below will be interpreted in the Interpretation section to follow.

Attention/Executive Behaviors	Raw Score	Cum %	Classification
Off-Task Behavior			
Auditory Attn/Set	2	11–25%	Slightly below expected level (Borderline)
Visual Attention	2	3–10%	Below expected level
Sentence Repetition	1	11–25%	Slightly below expected level (Borderline)
Miscellaneous Attn/Exec Behaviors			
Rule Violations (Tower)	9	<2%	Well below expected level
Novel Intrusions (LL Trials 1 to 7)	8	11–25%	Slightly below expected level (Borderline)
Interference (Trial 5>6; Trial 6>7)	0	>75%	Above expected level
Repetitions (LL Trials 1 to 7)	2	26–75%	At expected level
Rate Change			
Fingertip Tapping	7	3–10%	Below expected level

Pencil Grip**

Garry's pencil grip was *Intermediate* on the Design Copying. This level of grip was demonstrated by 21% of children aged 7 in the standardization sample, a result of borderline frequency. Garry's pencil grip was *Immature* on the Visuomotor Precision. This level of grip seen in 1% of children aged 7 in the standardization sample, a significant problem when Garry was required graphomotor skills under time pressure.

The following Oral/Verbal Behavior was present:

Reverse Sequencing (Speeded Naming)
This behavior was evident in 25% of children aged 7 in the standardization sample, a result which occurs with enough frequency in 7-year-olds not to be of particular concern. A watch should be kept on this area, however, to see if the gap widens or narrows.**

The following Motor Behaviors were present:

Visual Guidance (Fingertip Tapping)   Overflow (Fingertip Tapping)
Incorrect Position (Fingertip Tapping)   Mirroring (Fingertip Tapping)
Other Hand Helps (Imitating Hand Positions)   Overflow (Manual Motor Sequences)
Body Movement (Speeded Naming)   Body Movement (Manual Motor Sequences)
Motor Difficulty (Tower) This number of motor behaviors was evident in 1% of children aged 7 in the standardization sample, a significant result suggesting a neurologically-based motor deficit.**

**Change in text of scoring printout

VISUOSPATIAL SKILLS/VISUOMOTOR INTEGRATION AND VISUOSPATIAL MEMORY

Rey–Osterreith Complex Figure (Scoring system: Bernstein & Waber)

	(Scores presented in percentiles)		
	Copy	Immed. Recall	Delayed Recall
Organization	10	75	75–90
Style	Intermediate	Intermediate	Intermediate
Accuracy			
Structural Elements	<10	25	10–25
Incidental Elements	<10	<10	<10
Errors	<2	<4	<4
	Below Normal Limits	Below NL	Below NL

Garry copied a complex figure and then drew it from memory immediately afterwards and 30 min. later.

ACADEMIC

Wechsler Individual Achievement Test (WIAT)
(Standard Score Mean = 100+15)

Subtests	Standard Score	95% Confidence Interval	Percentile	Age	Grade Equivalent
Basic Reading	122	115–129	93	9.9	4:5**
Math Reasoning	76	67–85	5	6.0	K:4*
Spelling	128	120–136	97	10.0	4:8**
Reading Comprehension	100	92–108	50	8.0	2:6
Numerical Operations	79	68–90	8	6.9	1:2*
Listening Comprehension	80	69–91	9	5.9	K:2*
Oral Expression	111	102–120	77	9.9	4:0

*Relative weakness (Discrepancy of –20 or more points between achievement standard score and Garry's DAS Verbal Cluster of 109, the best measure of his cognitive ability)

**Relative strength (Discrepancy of +20 or more) in terms of Garry's ability.

Composites	Standard Score	95% Confidence Interval	Percentile	Age	Grade Equivalent
Reading	112	107–117	79	8.9	3:4
Mathematics	73	65–81	4	6.3	1:3*
Language	95	87–103	37	7.3	1:9
Total	103	99–107	58	7.9	2:4

Differences Between Composite Scores

	Difference	Significance	Frequency
Reading/Mathematics	39	.05	0.2%
Reading/Language	17	.05	23.2%
Mathematics/Language	22	.05	13.4%

ADAPTIVE BEHAVIOR

Vineland Adaptive Behavior Rating Scales—Interview Edition (Expanded Form)

(Standard Score Mean = 100+15)   Informant: Ms. White, mother
Adaptive Behavior Composite of 52+5 (low adaptive level) **Age Equivalent: 4.0.**

Motor Skills Domain (97)—Adequate

Communication (66)—Low

   Receptive Communication—moderately low (AE: 3.1)

   Expressive Communication—adequate (AE: 8.9).

Daily Living Skills (50)—Low

Socialization (55)—Low

Childhood Autism Rating Scale (CARS)

The CARS is a rating scale of autistic symptoms in 14 different areas of functioning. A rating of <30 is seen as non-autistic; 30–36 is associated with mild/moderate autism, and >37 yields a rating of severe autism. Garry was rated by his father, his mother, who is also his teacher, and his maternal grandparents who spend a great deal of time with him.

Informant	Rating	Classification
Father	20	Non-autistic
Mother (teacher)	25	Non-autistic
Grandmother	28	Non-autistic
Grandfather	30	Mild/moderate autism

INTERPRETATION

Garry is a 7.10 year-old boy who is in the second grade program of his home-schooling curriculum, but who is achieving more than one grade level below that in math. Furthermore, he is not progressing in other areas as quickly as his father and mother, who is his home-schooling teacher, had thought he would with his apparently excellent verbal skills. Garry's parents also have additional concerns about his poor ability to sustain attention, his apparent inability to pick up social cues and to relate to his peers, his constant talking, his marked interest in a narrow group of topics that seem "too advanced" for a 7-year-old, his lagging math skills, his extreme "nervousness" in certain situations, some separation anxiety (though this was improving of late), and an inability to control his temper. His parents would like to rule out or rule in ADHD and/or OCD. Additionally, they seek strategies to help Garry with his mild articulation problem in pronouncing /s/ and to teach him skills for social interaction.

Cognitive: Verbal vs. Nonverbal Skills

Garry displayed a *Differential Ability Scale (DAS)* General Cognitive Ability (GCA) standard score of 86 in the low average range (18th percentile). Given the standard error of measurement on the DAS, there is a 95% probability that his GCA would fall in the range of 80–96. Certainly, when one initially talks to Garry, the impression could be that of a gifted child due to his apparently advanced verbal skills. Thus, overall low average functioning might not be anticipated. Garry's Verbal Cluster Score of 109, however, was average, just one point below the high average level. This cluster was derived from his high average expressive vocabulary as demonstrated by defining words, and his average verbal abstract reasoning. The latter was assessed through Garry's ability to state similarities between two words that seemed divergent but were associated on an increasingly abstract level. Children with Asperger's or NLD tend to be very concrete, but this aspect often does not become apparent in the early years because children of 7 are just beginning to reason in the abstract. Therefore, concrete answers would be more appropriate for a child of 7 than for a child of 12, because abstract reasoning skills in the normally-developing child evolve by approximately 12 years of age. The child with Asperger's Syndrome (AS) or Nonverbal Learning Disability (NLD) does not make that cognitive shift from concrete to abstract thinking very well, so the gap between expressive language skills and verbal abstract reasoning begins to widen. This may become more apparent when the curriculum begins to require much more abstract reasoning in approximately sixth to seventh grade.

Garry's low average Nonverbal Cluster Score (85) was based on his average ability to solve purely visual analogies and his Borderline ability to generate a rule needed to continue a sequential or numerical pattern. There was a significant discrepancy between the average Verbal Cluster (109) and the Nonverbal Cluster (85) of −24 points, indicating significantly better verbal than nonverbal skills for Garry. Garry's Spatial Cluster Score (70) was Borderline based on his poor spatial memory and his ability to reproduce 2-D designs with paper and pencil, as well as his Borderline visuospatial analysis and visual-motor integration in reproducing 3-D block designs. There was a significant difference between Garry's Spatial Cluster Score and his Verbal Cluster of −39 points. Thus, Garry displayed a significant deficit in visual-spatial analysis. On the DAS, Garry's verbal abilities were significantly better developed than his abilities in visual memory, visuospatial analysis, visual-motor integration, and reproduction of concrete designs taken together. Furthermore, the Borderline Special Nonverbal Composite (75) composed of all subtests in the Nonverbal Cluster and the Spatial Cluster, showed a significant discrepancy with the Verbal Cluster of −34 points. Thus, on the DAS, Garry's verbal skills were significantly better developed than all nonverbal skills, a pattern characterizing children with AS/NLD.

Garry's low average NEPSY Language Core Domain Score (85) revealed more problematical language areas for Garry than did the average Verbal Cluster of the DAS (109). The DAS Verbal Cluster was derived from expressive vocabulary and verbal abstract reasoning, whereas the NEPSY assessed receptive language and language subprocesses. When the low average NEPSY Language Core Domain Score (85) was compared to the deficient NEPSY Visuospatial Core Domain Score (66), however, a significant discrepancy between higher language/lower visuospatial skills was observed. This difference in verbal/nonverbal skills was also seen on the DAS between the Verbal Cluster and the Borderline Spatial Cluster (70). Thus, Garry displayed the typical pattern of the child with AS/NLD who has better verbal than nonverbal/visuospatial skills.

Language Skills

Receptive and Expressive Language
At the one-word picture vocabulary level, Garry's performance was average for receptive one-word vocabulary on the *Peabody Picture Vocabulary Test—3rd Ed.* (Form IIIa) and for expressive one-word vocabulary on the *Expressive Vocabulary Test* (EVT). Despite Garry's apparently well-developed language as observed in discourse and his high average expressive vocabulary on the *DAS*, Garry scored in the average range on these assessments at the one-word level. He could name pictures on the EVT, but when synonyms were required, Garry often did not know another word that meant the same thing as the word presented. Understanding that several different words can mean the same thing is a more abstract language skill than simply naming. Naming was not a problem for Garry on the EVT, the Speeded

Naming (SN) subtest or Memory for Names from the NEPSY. There was no significant difference between the two standard scores on the *PPVT-IIIa* and the *EVT,* indicating that at the one-word level on these tasks, Garry displayed no differences in receptive or expressive picture vocabulary.

Also at the one-word level, when Garry had to produce as many words in a category as possible within 1 min, he showed an average performance on the NEPSY Verbal Fluency (VF). The Supplemental Scores (SS) for the VF subtest revealed that performance on the Semantic Fluency section of VF was *Above Expected Level* when Garry had to produce words rapidly in the categories of animals and food/drink. He had many single words in his lexicon that he could produce fluently within these categories. This was a concrete, expressive language fluency task, however. Garry's performance was *At Expected Level* on the Phonemic Fluency section of VF on which he was required to produce rapidly as many words as possible that began with *F* and with *S* in 1 min each.

The clearest evidence of Garry's subtle language deficits was observed through his performance on the NEPSY Comprehension of Instruction (CI) Subtest that assesses understanding of connected speech, rather than understanding at the one-word level. He performed *Below Expected Level* for age in listening to oral instructions of increasing linguistic complexity on CI. The good vocabulary, excellent reading decoding skills, and verbosity evident in many AS/NLD children can lead to an overestimation of their receptive language abilities. Research has shown that the ability of these children to understand complex language is impaired (Klin et al., 1995). Garry had marked difficulty understanding oral directions on CI despite adequate attention and the fact that there was a visual stimulus sheet in front of him as the oral directions were being read. He began having difficulty on the third item, rather than on much later items in which working memory might have been a factor. Negatives appeared to be a significant problem for Garry on several CI items. For instance, he evidently thought that "Point to one that is not a cross and not blue or yellow" necessitated two responses, so he pointed to a red circle ("not a cross") and to a black circle ("not blue or yellow"). When asked to "Point to a shape that is not a cross, but is yellow or black," Garry pointed to a yellow cross. He did not understand the linguistic message of "that is not a—, but is—. . ." He was also confused by language for visuospatial concepts ("Point to a shape which is above a circle and between two crosses"). Furthermore, Garry did not perceive temporal order words that override word order, such as "Point to a blue circle last and a black cross first." For this item, Garry pointed to the blue circle and then the black cross, suggesting that he did not understand the linguistic cues in the sentence. Thus, when receptive language requirements exceeded the one-word level, Garry had difficulty comprehending. Because he is so verbose, those around Garry may not realize that he does not always understand oral language.

Garry's parents were aware of his difficulty processing incoming language, because their ratings on the *Vineland Adaptive Behavior Scales* revealed a moderately low Receptive Communication score (Age Equivalent: 3.1) and an adequate Expressive Communication score (Age Equivalent: 8.9). This is the same pattern Garry displayed on his performance on the Listening Comprehension subtest of the WIAT (bottom of the low average range, 80), and his performance on the Oral Expression subtest (high average range, 111). The latter performance was consistent with his Verbal Cluster on the DAS, which is derived from expressive language measures. Garry's Listening Comprehension performance on the WIAT was consistent with his below average Comprehension of Instructions performance on the NEPSY. These results illustrate how easily one could assume that Garry is understanding oral language, because the apparently well-developed level of his expressive language masks a significant deficit in verbal comprehension.

In addition, Garry appeared to have subtle expressive language deficits. AS/NLD children have subtle language problems related to pragmatics. They use slightly formal "cocktail party" speech and do not understand the reciprocity of conversation. They also have difficulty with the abstract aspects of language, such as inference, innuendo, and figurative language. Initially, Garry's apparently effortless ability to discuss advanced topics could lead one to believe that an assessment of his language abilities would reveal very superior, or at the least, superior verbal skills. In fact, he achieved an average Verbal Cluster Score on the *DAS* and showed a deficit in verbal comprehension of complex oral instructions on the *NEPSY*. When an initial attempt was made to engage Garry in conversation, however, it was clear that he was not aware of the "give and take of conversation." He discerned none of the nonverbal cues his listener gave him about a desire to contribute to the discussion or of boredom because his monologue had lasted so long. When he was asked direct questions, Garry's responses were frequently off target, or he attempted to direct the conversation back to mythology, ancient Egypt, Greece, or China, his areas of interest. He also displayed poor understanding of humor when he attempted to tell a joke. Therefore, Garry displayed a primary deficit in language with receptive language weaker than expressive. The latter initially appeared, on the surface, to be well-developed, but Garry soon displayed poor pragmatic skills.

Lexical Access
Slowed lexical access was evident in Garry's performance on the SN Subtest of the NEPSY Language Domain, which was slightly *Below Expected Level* (Total Score).

Garry knew all of the concept labels individually and could even access two labels in sequence on the Teaching Trials, but he had difficulty accessing three labels for the same shape (Big, red, circle) quickly and shifting fluidly from one shape to the next. He hesitated frequently and made spontaneous corrections as he struggled to access the labels quickly. The SSs for SN revealed that accuracy was *Above Expected Level* in naming but that speed of access was *Borderline*. Slowed processing and difficulty integrating three labels for one shape rapidly and shifting from one shape to the next (executive functions) appeared to contribute to Garry's accessing problem. His performance in naming on the EVT was within normal limits, as it was on SN and Memory for Names. Thus, a naming deficit can be ruled out. Qualitative Observations (QOs) (p. ***) on NEPSY revealed the presence of two or more Reversed Sequences on SN. Inspection of frequencies, however, revealed that 25% of children aged 7 in the standardization sample also reversed sequences on SN. Therefore, the presence of the reversal phenomenon at age 7 is not considered significant.

Phonological Processing, Hyperlexia, and Reading

Children with AS/NLD generally display strong word recognition and spelling skills. Garry's performance was *At Expected Level* on the NEPSY Phonological Processing (PP) Subtest, which assesses the ability to recognize word segments, conceptualize speech-sound patterns, and manipulate those patterns to produce new ones. Phonological processing is essential to successful reading decoding and spelling. Garry performed *At Expected Level* on the Phonemic section of the PP subtest and displayed superior reading decoding and spelling results on the WIAT. He performed poorly on another phonological processing subtest when he was required to repeat taped nonsense words. His poor performance on Repetition of Nonsense Words was not due to a problem with phonological processing, but rather to the fact that Garry could not inhibit the need to produce his own Russian or Chinese words between each item. As a result, he did not hear the next taped word or forgot the nonsense word he was supposed to repeat. Despite redirection, he did not inhibit the need to say foreign words. This was an excellent example of how Garry's stereotypical interests can distract him and affect performance on a task adversely. The Repetition of Nonsense Words Subtest results from NEPSY should not be considered valid for Garry.

The ability to read many words at a young age but with limited or no understanding of meaning is known as hyperlexia. It is a characteristic frequently observed in children with developmental disorders such as Autistic Disorder (AD), AS, and NLD. It is sometimes known as "word-calling." Garry appears by history to have been hyperlexic, having "taught himself to read" at about 3.5 years of age, according to his parents. Because of this, he was, quite naturally, considered gifted. Unfortunately, reading comprehension over time does not stay abreast of reading decoding and spelling. In the present evaluation, Garry's performance on the WIAT Reading Comprehension Subtest was average (100), but this standard score was significantly discrepant from both the WIAT Basic Reading (–22 points) and Spelling (–28 points) standard scores. These results suggest that Garry can decode and spell many more words than he can understand in context. This gap may well widen in the next year or so as comprehension questions become more abstract, and Garry is required to comprehend the underlying abstract themes of stories. At present, however, Garry's reading comprehension achievement is within the range of his DAS Verbal Cluster: 109.

Articulation

Garry's performance on the Oromotor Sequences subtest was *Borderline,* due to a lack of fluid movement in the musculature of the mouth and tongue. He appeared to have mild oromotor dyspraxia that produced his mild articulation problems. A referral to a speech/language therapist to confirm this finding would be appropriate. His mild difficulty with the oromotor programming needed for speech is a part of a broader motor deficit to be discussed in the Motor section of this report.

Verbal Memory

Garry learned 8 names of children from line drawings *At Expected Level* on the NEPSY Memory for Names Subtest. He recalled more on the Delay Trial than on the Learning Trials, possibly due to slow consolidation of the names in memory. Again, Garry showed no problems with the basic expressive language function of naming. It is also of interest that he had no difficulty remembering the drawings of children's faces when he could attach a language label to each, but on Memory for Faces, he did not recall faces he had just seen but had not labeled. Garry's performance on Sentence Repetition, a subtest of auditory short term memory for isolated sentences, was also *At Expected Level.* On Narrative Memory, a task of logical learning, his recall of a detail-laden story was *At Expected Level,* because he understood the simple words and content, and it had a coherent structure. The fact that Garry could recall all the details of the story but could not carry out the oral instructions correctly on CI supports the hypothesis of a receptive language deficit for understanding linguistic complexities that affected CI performance. He performed poorly because he was unable to understand the linguistic complexity of the instructions, rather than being unable to remember them.

The one verbal memory test from NEPSY on which Garry had some difficulty was List Learning (LL). The influence of executive dysfunction on learning, as opposed to a verbal memory problem *per se,* could be observed clearly in Garry's Borderline performance (total words recalled over 5 learning trials) on the LL subtest. LL is a supraspan verbal memory task in the Memory and Learning Domain. The list of 15 items is too long to learn by rote, something Garry can do well. Therefore, he needed to be able to employ executive functions in order to organize the activity, create strategies, monitor performance, and sustain effort. Garry failed to inhibit response so he could reflect, plan ahead, and develop a strategy for recall, such as clustering objects semantically (pupil, teacher, pencil) or phonemically (window, water, winter). Consequently, Garry's SS for Learning revealed that over 5 trials, he had learned only one more word than he recalled after his first learning trial, a result seen only in the lowest 12% of the standardization sample for age. He recalled the words randomly after each learning trial, so words previously recalled were forgotten, and new words were recalled but not retained. The QO for Novel Intrusions on LL (Borderline performance) revealed 8 intrusions of words that were not on any list during the learning trials. He apparently was not able to inhibit extraneous words from intruding on his recall of list words. On the other hand, Garry did not make Interference errors by recalling words incorrectly from List A (the first list he learned) into List B (the Interference Trial list). Similarly, he did not then incorrectly recall List B words into List A when asked to repeat List A. Even though he was not able to learn many words over the 5 trials, the ones he learned, he then maintained in a rote manner, allowing him to inhibit Interference errors from one list to another. His Interference Errors were *At Expected Level* for age. He also did not perseverate on the same word during recall. After 30 minutes, Garry continued to retain 7 items, the number he had learned by Trial 5 (SS for Delay).

One of the concerns Garry's parents voiced was why he does not learn as well as would be expected, given the level of his knowledge and ability to express himself. The LL subtest sheds light on this problem by demonstrating that Garry's executive dysfunction does not allow him to plan and develop strategies to learn the amount of information expected for his age, thereby limiting the amount he can learn to rote facts. It would appear that his learning is subject to constant intrusions of extraneous information which are not inhibited. The information Garry learns in a rote manner appears to be retained in separate modules without association with the information in any other module. For instance, while Garry provided facts on ancient China and facts on ancient Egypt, he did not relate either civilization to the other in his monologues. The above results support the hypothesis that Garry has a primary executive function deficit. Further, his executive dysfunction has marked effects on learning, a secondary deficit.

Attention/Executive Function

Garry displayed overall Borderline functioning on the NEPSY A/E Domain. Results on the NEPSY subtests implicated executive dysfunction causing a lack of response inhibition, more than a lack of attention. Attention was *Above Expected Level* on the simple visual search task of the Visual Attention (VA) Subtest of NEPSY and *At Expected Level* on the complex visual attention section. On the other hand, the ability to inhibit a response, an executive function, was *Below Expected Level* on both the simple and complex VA Subtest sections as observed in the high number of Commission Errors (CEs). This level of functioning appeared to be true regardless of speed. Garry showed Borderline inattention and impulsivity on both the simple and complex sections of the Auditory Attention and Response Subtest (AARS) of NEPSY. On the QOs for NEPSY (see p. 2**) Garry displayed Borderline ability to inhibit Off-Task Behaviors during simple and complex sustained auditory attention tasks (AARS) and on Sentence Repetition, a task of auditory short-term memory. His ability to inhibit Off-task Behaviors was *Below Expected Level* for age on VA. Although Garry was off-task to the extent he needed to be redirected (the criteria for endorsing this QO), he did not make omission errors (OEs), suggesting that he remained attentive to the task, despite his impulsivity and hyperactivity.

Response inhibition is an important frontal executive function, according to Barkley's model of ADHD (1997). A lack of response inhibition permits impulsive responding, which was a significant problem for Garry. His mother, who is also his home-schooling teacher, complains of distractibility and impulsivity during school time and within the family. The question that remains is whether he is subject to ADHD only or whether his distractibility and impulsivity are a part of another developmental disorder. Most neurologically-based developmental disorders also include attention problems, distractibility, hyperactivity, and/or impulsivity.

Executive functions include inhibiting impulses, planning and strategizing for problem-solving, and monitoring performance. They are essential to efficient cognitive functioning and are closely related to attention. On Tower, a NEPSY task of nonverbal reasoning, Garry's ability to plan and strategize on a nonverbal problem-solving task was Borderline and his ability to adhere to the rules was *Well Below Expected Level* for age. On another executive function task, Design Fluency, Garry's performance was *Well Below Expected Level*. He did not adhere to the rules and duplicated his original design several times because he did not monitor his performance. He also made curved instead of straight lines and failed to connect dots. Garry had difficulty inhibiting motor response on both Statue and

Knock and Tap (*Below* and *Well Below Expected Level* performance, respectively). On the Statue Subtest, he had to stand quietly with his eyes closed and try not to respond to noise distracters. Knock and Tap required Garry to inhibit the same movement the examiner was performing in order to do an alternative movement.

Garry's poor inhibition of impulses was seen across the evaluation. For instance, in the Language Domain, on the SN Subtest, Garry's executive functions should have helped him organize and integrate rapidly into one response the three labels *(big, red, circle)* that he knew individually and then help him shift to the next shape to be named. Poor performance on Repetition of Nonsense Words was due to inability to inhibit the impulse to say words which were a part of his stereotypical interest in ancient cultures. These interests frequently distracted him from the task at hand. He also displayed lack of impulse control over his stereotypical interests on one item of the DAS Recall of Designs subtest. He was shown a design that reminded him of an ancient Chinese sign for "sun." He then attempted to launch into a discussion of other Chinese characters and their meanings. Garry was redirected immediately to the task at hand, but he did not remember the design he was supposed to draw. Instead, he drew the Chinese character. From that point forward on this DAS subtest, however, his inhibition of impulses and monitoring skills improved. Unfortunately, this was not true for other subtests. The above results suggest that Garry's executive dysfunction is a primary deficit with broad secondary effects.

Visuospatial Analysis

Children with NLD have all the characteristics of children with AS, but have been purported to show more significant visuospatial deficits. On Garry's DAS, there was a significant −15 point discrepancy between the Nonverbal Cluster Score and the Spatial Cluster Score, suggesting that the visuospatial/visuomotor abilities were the most impaired of Garry's nonverbal skills. There was a significant −11 point difference on the DAS at the subtest level between the two subtests of Garry's Nonverbal Cluster: Matrices and Sequential and Quantitative Reasoning. On the former task, he displayed average nonverbal ability to solve purely visual analogies, which at Garry's level were very simple patterns and required little visuospatial analysis. On the latter task, he demonstrated a *Borderline* level of the nonverbal reasoning required to generate a rule in order to continue a sequential or numerical pattern. His *Borderline* score on Sequential and Quantitative Reasoning in the Nonverbal Cluster was more consistent with his *Borderline* score on the Pattern Construction subtest of the Spatial Cluster than with his average score on the

Matrices subtest. Pattern Construction requires visuospatial analysis of a design and integration of that design with motor output in order to reproduce it in design blocks. Thus, Garry's problem areas on the DAS appear to be both visuospatial and sequential/numerical reasoning areas appear to be problematical for Garry on the DAS.

On the NEPSY, Garry displayed a deficient Visuospatial Core Domain Score (66) which was a weakness in terms of the average child of his age in the standardization population (NEPSY Core Domain Mean = 100±15). It was also a relative weakness for Garry in terms of his performance on the Language Core Domain and the Memory and Learning Core Domain, on which his score was largely derived from good verbal memory performance. Analysis of those NEPSY visuospatial subtests that involved no motor output revealed poor judgement of line and angle orientation on Arrows when Garry had to judge which 2 of 8 arrows clustered around a target would hit the center. Garry's also showed poor visuospatial analysis for route-finding skills using orientation and directionality.

Visuospatial deficits were not only apparent on Garry's DAS performance, but in his performance on other instruments as well. On the Rey-Osterreith Complex Figure that Garry was asked to copy, he showed poor performance initially in organizing the visuospatial elements, but organization improved over time, suggesting that he consolidates visuospatial information slowly. Garry's accuracy in copying the Structural Elements and Incidental Elements of the complex figure was poor (<2nd percentile for age). In other words, a copy of the Rey Figure with this many visuospatial errors was executed by fewer than 2 out of 100 children Garry's age in the standardization sample for the Bernstein & Waber (1999) scoring system. Garry initially was not able to organize the visuospatial elements, and his piecemeal approach to copying the structural elements accurately increased the likelihood of errors in recall. It appears that he never encoded the Incidental Elements. His visuospatial deficits caused numerous errors from the outset. Executive dysfunction, visuospatial deficits in perceiving the figure and difficulty integrating visuospatial information with motor output appear to have adversely affected Garry's ability to copy this complex figure.

In other domains of NEPSY, Garry had difficulty understanding visuospatial words and concepts in oral directions on Comprehension of Instructions. Memory for faces is theorized to rest on visuospatial analytic skills, and Garry displayed a poor performance in facial recognition. The latter is purported to contribute to social perceptual deficits. An analysis of Garry's visuospatial abilities suggests that he is subject to a pervasive visuospatial deficit, a primary deficit that affects facial recognition and understanding of visuospatial language concepts (secondary deficits). Further secondary deficits stemming from Garry's visuospatial deficits are discussed later in this report.

Visual Memory

Although Garry's List Learning performance on NEPSY was *Borderline,* the one NEPSY memory subtest on which Garry showed a significant deficit was Memory for Faces. His performance was impaired and fell at the 5th percentile overall. He was required to sort 16 photos of real children's faces into boys and girls so that he would look at each for 5 sec. He had to indicate which faces he had seen before from arrays with 2 distracter faces and the target face. Garry's performance was poor on both the Immediate and Delayed Recall Trials. Rather than continuing to consolidate information as he did on the Memory for Names Delayed Trial, Garry lost information in the 30 min between the two trials, even though performance on both Immediate and Delayed Memory for Faces Trials was *Below Expected Level* for age. These results suggest that Garry encodes facial information poorly. This deficit could adversely affect Garry's social perception and his ability to pick up nonverbal social cues from the faces of others. Facial recognition skills are purported to be dependent on visuospatial analysis, which is subserved by right hemisphere. Children with NLD are theorized to have right hemisphere dysfunction in white matter that is responsible for communication and integration of information across modalities in the adult (Goldberg & Costa, 1981). It is not yet fully understood if the same purpose is served in children.

Sensorimotor

Because visuospatial functioning must often be integrated with motor output in the real world, it was important to assess Garry's fine motor skills. Furthermore, children with developmental disorders, including AS and NLD often have sensory hypersensitivity and/or hyposensitivity, as well as motor deficits. Garry's sensorimotor functions were, therefore, assessed with NEPSY. Garry's Sensorimotor Core Domain Score on NEPSY reflected deficient functioning (68) overall. Fine motor coordination and programming were *Below Expected Level* on the Fingertip Tapping Subtest of NEPSY. Preferred hand performance across finger tapping and finger sequences was *Borderline;* Nonpreferred hand performance was *Below Expected Level.*

Garry's performance on the Expanded Subtest Manual Motor Sequences, which assesses motor programming of the hands, was very poor, *Well Below Expected Level* for age. Not only did he have difficulty executing the motor sequences fluidly and without hesitations, he also missequenced them and seemed to have difficulty holding sequences of three different hand movements in working memory (executive dysfunction). This is similar to the executive dysfunction he displayed in accessing three labels for each shape on SN. Children with AS/NLD have difficulty with complex tasks across modalities. Garry's difficulty with motor programming and coordinated movements may contribute to awkwardness in carrying out motor tasks, especially those requiring a sequential pattern, such as writing, playing the piano, keyboarding, assembling crafts, and so forth. In the Language Domain of NEPSY, Garry's performance on the Oromotor Sequences subtest was *Borderline,* reflecting an apparent oromotor dyspraxia producing his mild articulation problems. His mild difficulty with the oromotor programming needed for speech should be confirmed by a speech/language therapist. It appears to be a part of a larger motor programming deficit.

The NEPSY QOs for Motor Behaviors revealed Motor Difficulty in placing the balls on the pegs during the Tower Subtest and the need for the other hand to help place the fingers into a hand position on the Imitating Hand Positions subtest. Associated movements observed during the Fingertip Tapping subtest included Mirroring in the contralateral hand when either hand was moving and Overflow, involuntary movements of the mouth and of the tongue. These associated movements suggest that Garry is not getting a discrete neural message to that area of the motor strip subserving the body part he wishes to move. Rather, the message is diffuse, "overflowing" to other areas on the motor strip. Since the areas dedicated to the mouth and tongue are adjacent to those for the hands, subtle involuntary, associated movements can be seen in the contralateral hand or around the mouth and tongue, in addition to the correct hand movement. QOs for the Fingertip Tapping Subtest also revealed Visual Guidance in order to provide visual feedback for finger movement, due, perhaps, to a need to compensate for poor kinesthetic feedback from the muscles. The Fingertip Tapping Subtest performance also demonstrated Incorrect Position (using a pincer position) and Rate Change during the production of finger movements. Garry also demonstrated Overflow movements of the mouth and tongue on Manual Motor Sequences and body movements were recruited during the production of the sequence. Recruitment of other systems into a task was also observed on SN. Garry bent forward and back from the waist with each effort to access the labels for the next figure. The large number of motor behaviors observed in Garry across subtests was evident in the lowest 1% of children aged 7 in the standardization sample. This reflects how difficult it was for Garry to produce discrete movements.

On the Vineland Adaptive Behavior Rating Scales, Garry's mother rated his motor skills overall as average. This would appear to be somewhat of an over-estimate. Garry is the White's oldest child, and Ms. White states herself that she doesn't "have much of a yardstick to measure Garry's development against." Actually, poor fine motor coordination and motor programming appear to be parts of a primary deficit in fine motor function. Garry should have an occupational therapy evaluation to further delineate this fine motor deficit and should have a physical therapy evaluation, as well, to see if his motor deficit is generalized to gross motor functions.

Garry's performance on the Finger Discrimination Subtest of NEPSY was also *Well Below Expected Level* for age when he was required to perceive tactile input and differentiate which finger or fingers had been touched. Initially, on the Finger Discrimination subtests for Preferred and Nonpreferred hand, light touch appeared aversive to Garry. When the task was first attempted, he pulled his hand away, demonstrating tactile defensiveness. After talking with Garry, reassuring him, and, addressing sensory integration issues, by using deep pressure to rub his hands, which he enjoyed, he then agreed to try again and cooperated well, but he appeared mildly anxious during the remainder of the subtest. Though he attended to the Finger Discrimination task, Garry frequently misidentified fingers that had been touched and twice did not perceive double simultaneous touch, suggesting that one signal was suppressed. Finger Discrimination performance for each hand was *Well Below Expected Level*. These results support the hypothesis of sensory perception deficits reported in Garry's history, such as a dislike of any lumps in his food, especially Cream of Wheat and an aversion to certain textures and stickiness. These sensory issues point to the primary sensory deficit usually seen in AS and NLD.

Garry's performance on Imitating Hand Positions, a more integrative motor task on NEPSY, was *Below Expected Level* on both hands. Integration of visuospatial information with motor programming and kinesthetic feedback from the muscles was required to reproduce the examiner's static hand position. Performance with each hand was *Below Expected Level*. Garry often used the wrong fingers to form the position, suggesting difficulty with visuospatial analysis, and he had difficulty programming his fingers into position, using the other hand to assist. Garry may also have received poor kinesthetic feedback from his muscles to give him information about the correctness of his hand position. Therefore, it appears that problems integrating poor motor programming, kinesthetic feedback, and visuospatial abilities influenced Garry's Imitating Hand Performance. It is likely that he shows secondary deficits on integrative tasks which require these three types of functions or a combination of them.

Visuomotor Integration

Garry's graphomotor control on paper/pencil task was assessed for speed and accuracy on the NEPSY VP Subtest. His performance was *Below Expected Level* for age. SS for Time showed unusually fast performance for a 7-year-old *(Above Expected Level)* for both the wider and narrower tracks. This ability to be precise and stay within the lines was *Below Expected Level* for age. These results suggest that he did not keep both constraints of the task in mind: work quickly without making mistakes. Instead, he sacrificed accuracy for speed. Children who have graphomotor problems often think that they can mask their imprecision by being very fast. It is also possible that drawing a line feels more stable and less jerky with a swift movement than with a slow one.

From the NEPSY developmental data, it is known that normally developing 7-year-olds work more slowly than younger or older children in order to be accurate. Prior to age 7 they are fast and inaccurate, and after age 7 they become increasingly fast and accurate (Kirk, McAuliffe, Kemp, and Korkman, 2000). Garry's inability to inhibit his impulsivity may have adversely affected his performance.

Garry used an Intermediate pencil grip (See QOs, p. 306) on the DC Subtest of the Visuospatial Domain, which was untimed. This level of grip was demonstrated by the bottom 21% of children aged 7 in the standardization sample, so it is not uncommon for a child of this age. His grip was Immature on the VP Subtest when he was required to draw lines quickly. This awkward, fisted grip was demonstrated by the lowest 1% of children aged 7 in the standardization sample. These results suggest that under time constraints Garry grasped the pencil in a primitive manner in order to stabilize it for speed. Garry's handwriting was observed to be large, messy, and poorly controlled on his WIAT Spelling Subtest. Taken together, these results suggest secondary dysgraphia which will make it difficult for him to complete written work quickly and neatly.

In the real world, visuospatial analysis often needs to be integrated with motor output. Garry's difficulties with visuomotor integration were evident across tests. Garry's DAS Recall of Designs performance was poor and his DAS Pattern Construction Subtest performance was borderline. Both of these tasks require visuomotor integration; the former requires graphomotor performance in drawing the designs recalled, and the latter requires the handling of three-dimensional blocks. While visuospatial analysis is the key component on these subtests, motor output influences performance as well. On NEPSY there is a three-dimensional constructional task (Block Construction) and a two-dimensional constructional task (Design Copying) on which Garry's performances were *Below Expected Level* and *Well Below Expected Level,* respectively. On Block Construction, Garry could not transition from copying a three-dimensional model to copying a two-dimensional picture of the three-dimensional construction. The latter requires more sophisticated visuospatial skills. He did not always seem to perceive the configuration well, and in one case, he did not allow for spaces in his reproduction. On DC, Garry's designs showed difficulties with directionality, closure, and orientation. This was an untimed task, so speed was not an issue. Although Garry showed poor performance on both the NEPSY two-dimensional and three-dimensional constructions, the significant difference (-1 SD) between the subtests may have been due to the graphomotor skills required for DC.

Impaired motor output can contribute significantly to adverse performance on a task requiring visuomotor integration. In Garry's case this is especially true when a task requires graphomotor performance. In the classroom he can be expected to have difficulty copying from the board or from a book to a paper. His visuospatial deficits can adversely affect his ability to read maps and graphs, but it can affect especially his achievement in mathematics, which has a visuospatial substrate. Coupled with his primary sensorimotor deficit, Garry's primary visuospatial deficits can be expected to cause him a significant secondary deficit in visuomotor skills.

Mathematics

A child who meets the criteria for AS, and has a very significant visuospatial deficit, may have a significant math disability as well. This constellation of symptoms is associated more with NLD than AS. Therefore, Garry's math performance needs to be considered in relation to other children his age, his cognitive ability, and other academic achievement. Garry displayed a borderline performance on the DAS Sequential and Numerical Reasoning Subtest, which contrasted significantly with his average verbal and nonverbal performances on Similarities and Matrix Reasoning. His performance on the Mathematics Reasoning and Numerical Operations subtests of the *Wechsler Individual Achievement Test (WIAT)* was borderline. These results differed very significantly from the best measure of Garry's cognitive ability (DAS Verbal Cluster, 109). His borderline Mathematics Composite on the WIAT was significantly discrepant from his high-average Reading Composite. Further significant discrepancies were evident between each of the math subtests and all other subtests except Listening Comprehension, including Basic Reading (decoding), Spelling, Reading Comprehension, and Oral Expression. Garry's Mathematics Disorder appears very robust on the WIAT and DAS. When children first begin math instruction, it is often very concrete, so sometimes a math disability of a child with NLD does not become apparent until mid-elementary school. Garry's Mathematics Disorder is already apparent, a deficit secondary to his poor visuospatial abilities. Many math concepts such as place value, temporal order, estimation, and so forth rest on visuospatial understanding, as does graphing of any type. Additionally, as math becomes more abstract, children with NLD tend to have more difficulty because of their concrete thinking. Often children with NLD must use a calculator for mathematical operations, because they do not understand the numerical operations. Garry meets the criteria for AS with better verbal than nonverbal skills, social perceptual deficits, restricted interests, and stereotypical behaviors; however, his math disability coupled with his visuospatial deficit thus far makes the diagnosis of NLD more appropriate for Garry than AS. A very important characteristic of AS/NLD, adaptive behavior, including social skills and social perception still has not been discussed thoroughly.

Adaptive Behavior

Garry's Vineland Adaptive Behavior Scales indicated deficient adaptive behavior overall with deficient Daily Living Skills and Socialization Domains (communication and Motor Skills have already been discussed). The Childhood Autism Rating Scales (CARS) showed nonautistic ratings for Garry by his father, mother, and grandmother, although his grandmother's approached significance. His grandfather's ratings were significant for mild autism. AS is a developmental disorder with stronger language skills than nonverbal skills, but causing subtle language problems with pragmatics, complex linguistics, receptive language for connected speech, and abstract language. These children also display motor deficits and share some milder traits of Autistic Disorder: social imperception, stereotypical interests, sensory issues, and poor pragmatics. In addition, as noted previously, children with NLD display all of the above symptoms, but have significant visuospatial deficits and a math disability. The comments on Garry's CARS record forms, the comprehensive history filled out by his parents, and his parental interview revealed that Garry relates better to adults than to children, and his relationships with children are only with a few much younger children, not with his peers. He does not understand the give and take of conversation; Garry "just talks over others." He is sensitive to noises, lumps in his food, and stickiness on his hands. He bounces on his trampoline for hours (seeking vestibular stimulation). His play is imitative of his Magic School Bus, Pinocchio videos, and videos about pirates, Egypt, and China, all of which he watches repetitively. He uses dialogue from them and from TV commercials during play. Little or no truly imaginary play is observed. Garry likes routine and order. He does not like changes in his schedule and is apt to have a tantrum when they occur. He does not transition well from one activity to the next. He loves to amass facts about mythology, ancient China, Egypt, and Russia, and he will talk on these topics for hours unless he is stopped. Redirecting him from them is difficult. Eye contact is fleeting to poor. It took Garry "forever" to learn to ride his bicycle, and he does not like coloring or cutting activities. He writes "awkwardly" and his handwriting is "a mess." He could read very early (approximately 3 years of age) and could recite "The Night Before Christmas" in its entirety just before he was 4 years of age.

Summary and Diagnosis

Key to the consideration of Asperger's Syndrome versus Autistic Disorder is the fact that language emerged early, and Garry used two or more word sentences by 15 months of age. A diagnostic criterion for Autistic Disorder is significant language delay. Therefore, AS, but not Autistic Disorder, would be a diagnostic consideration for Garry. There are additional aspects to Garry's profile, however, that make NLD the more appropriate diagnostic choice in this psychologist's clinical judgement, and these are the primary deficit of a significant visuospatial weakness and the secondary deficit stemming from it, a math learning disability. Garry's standard scores for Mathematical Reasoning and Numerical Operations on the WIAT both showed a highly significant discrepancy with his ability level. As he progresses in school and math becomes more abstract, without intensive intervention, the gap between ability and math achievement may well widen also. Coupled with his significantly deficient visuospatial skills observed on NEPSY, the DAS, and the Rey-Osterreith Complex Figure, these results suggest the visuospatial deficits underlying the significant math problems experienced a child with NLD.

Additional aspects of this disorder were observed in the significant difference between Garry's Verbal and Spatial Clusters on the DAS. Further, he displayed a significant discrepancy between his Verbal and Nonverbal Clusters, as well as the Nonverbal and Spatial Clusters, implicating the latter nonverbal area as showing the most dysfunction. Visuospatial and Sensorimotor Domains on NEPSY were deficient, while Language and Memory Domains were in the low-average range. Language and rote verbal memory are two strengths for children with NLD, but children with NLD also display subtle language deficits. Expressive language was much better developed than receptive language, but Garry displayed no knowledge of the social implications of pragmatics. Verbal memory was within normal limits, for the most part, but a secondary deficit of Garry's primary executive dysfunction was observed in his problems learning large quantities of information that required organization and monitoring of the material. Visuospatial deficits were observed in judgement of line and angle orientation, visuospatial analysis, directionality, and visuomotor integration for two- and three-dimensional constructions. Garry also displayed the primary motor deficits seen in AS/NLD: fine motor dyscoordination, poor programming, and graphomotor problems. Executive dysfunction was present. Garry displayed significant lack of response inhibition, producing impulsivity across many domains. It is this secondary impulsivity and distractibility, as a result of his primary deficit in response inhibition, that appears to be an attentional problem. Indeed, attention is secondarily affected by the impulsivity and distractibility. These deficits are a part of Garry's neurologically based developmental disorder. A medical evaluation to consider psychopharmacological intervention to allow better inhibition of responses and, thus, less impulsivity, distractibility, and inattention would be very helpful, along with the behavioral recommendations. Finally, academic achievement testing revealed the secondary deficit of the primary visuospatial weakness is a significant math learning disability, observed in the diagnostic behavioral cluster of NLD as Figure 7.1 shows. Based on the present assessment, the comprehensive history, school performance, parent interview, and adaptive behavior rating scales, the diagnostic behavioral cluster that appears to define this disorder best, in this psychologist's clinical judgement, is a Nonverbal Learning Disability as a variant of Asperger's Disorder.

The Recommendations included in this report are far more numerous than those in a standard report, which usually number from 10–20, depending on the complexity of the child. Many more recommendations are included here than are needed, but they are meant to serve as a guide to the types of recommendations that may be helpful. Recommendations should be made for treatment, for home, for school, and for social and behavioral needs. They are not necessarily meant to be carried out simultaneously, but you should attempt to provide an array of recommendations, which can be carried out over an extended period of time and in many different settings. After you have given feedback to the parents, if they are agree-able, it is very helpful to have a meeting with school personnel and therapists to review each person's role in helping the child. In this way, everyone can plan together for the greater good of the child, and the parents and child will feel supported.

Recommendations

Treatment

1. Garry's parents may wish to consult a developmental pediatrician, pediatric neurologist, or general pediatrician concerning Garry's attentional problems, which appear to be a part of his neurologically based developmental disorder.
2. Garry should have a speech and language evaluation and follow-up therapy to address his mild articulation problem, pragmatics, and linguistic understanding in language, and any other deficit areas.

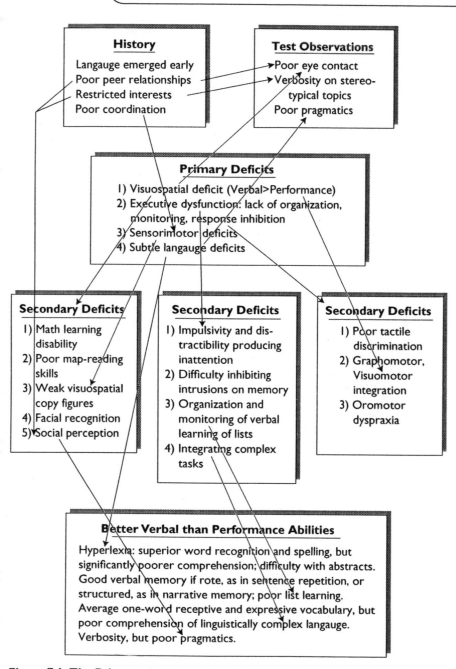

Figure 7.1 The Primary and Secondary Deficits from Garry's Test Profile Pointing to a Diagnostic Behavioral Cluster for NLD

3. Garry should have an occupational therapy evaluation, including evaluation of sensory sensitivities. If indicated by the evaluation, follow-up therapy should be undertaken to address fine motor and visuomotor deficits as well as to desensitize Garry to a variety of sensory input.

4. Garry should have a physical therapy evaluation to evaluate gross motor functions. Follow-up therapy should be undertaken, if indicated from Garry's evaluation.

5. Garry may need very concrete, cognitive, behavioral therapy to help him with the development of social skills, some flexibility, and so forth. His parents should receive parenting guidance through this process.

6. If Garry's mother continues to home-school, his parents should seek therapies through the school system, and she may wish to avail herself of special education techniques available to Garry through the school resource room. Because of Garry's need for social interaction, if home-schooling is the option they choose, Garry needs to take part in a home-school cooperative, so that he can participate in socialization, music, art, PE, and field trips.

7. A social skills group would be helpful for Garry.

8. If Garry returns to public school, his test results should be submitted to the school placement team for consideration for learning disability services. In this psychologist's clinical judgement, Garry's least restrictive educational placement would include placement in the mainstream classroom with resource room assistance in math 45 min daily in addition to his therapies listed previously.

School and Instructional Methods

9. If Garry is to attend public school, Garry's parents should begin talking to him about going to a new school and should drive several times, even walking around the building and playing on the playground. He should visit the classroom before the first day of school, meet his new teacher, and learn where everything is in the classroom.

10. A communication notebook can be set up between home and school so that parents can stay abreast of Garry's progress in school and therapies. The teacher or therapist can just provide a short synopsis of what was done that day and Garry's part in it. His parents can then write a brief synopsis that will help the teacher know how Garry is doing at home. It would be helpful if parents, teachers, and therapists

meet periodically to be sure that they are using consistent methods and language with Garry.

11. Garry's instruction should be very language-based in all subject areas. Parents and teachers should be careful, however, not to speak too quickly. He needs to be able to "talk" his way through tasks. Math processes should be taught as a sequence of steps in language. He will need to be assisted in developing a method of subvocalization to assist himself. This could be a focus in language therapy.

12. It is important for Garry's teacher to realize that an increase in unusual or difficult behaviors probably signals an increase in stress. Garry may be having difficulty comprehending something, may be having difficulty with sound sensitivity or some other sensory issue, may feel uncomfortable because another child is too close, and so forth. Taking the time to talk with Garry and analyze what is going on may avoid an emotional "melt-down."

13. Garry should be given very concrete examples for all new concepts. Presenting material via both written and verbal instructions will be helpful.

14. Instruction should also be active, rather than passive, allowing a language interchange between the teacher and child as much as possible.

15. Garry needs as predictable a schedule as possible. A written schedule taped to his desk should be helpful. If schedule changes are unavoidable, structure should be provided for him. Some examples might be a new schedule for the day, a note taped to his desk, a map to the different location in the school building taped on the inside of his notebook, or walking buddies to accompany him from the classroom to the new location.

16. The teacher should allow extra time to complete assignments or respond to oral questions in order to compensate for slowed processing.

17. Teachers and parents should guide learning with role-playing, direct with cues ("Tell me more. How many did you see?"), written models, and leading questions.

Organization and Study Skills

18. For poor organizational skills, directions should be written in numbered steps rather than paragraph form. The teacher should use short, simple sentences emphasizing key points with voice variations and intonations. The teacher should specify the topic and write it on the board as he or she talks.

19. The teacher can give Garry a short written list of tasks to be completed before recess, before lunch, and so forth.
20. Garry should study at the kitchen or family room table with radio and television off. He will accomplish more in several short work sessions than he will in one long one. Study should be divided into short-term goals with a break when each goal is accomplished. He can wear headphones playing music with no lyrics. This will cut out distracting noises in the house.
21. Later, when Garry begins changing classes, his books and materials for each subject should be color-coded (i.e., his English book is covered in red with a red spiral notebook and a red folder to coordinate). Each subject has its own color, and a color key should be on a card inside the door of his locker. In this way, he will be able to reach for all the red materials on his way to English class, and he is more apt to get to class with all of his materials.

Impulsivity, Distractibility, and Secondary Inattention

22. Garry should sit at the front of the classroom.
23. Garry's parents should not give him more than two items to remember at a time, or they should supply a short list.
24. If Garry is making comments that are tangential, his parents and teachers establish a nonverbal cue to stop him when he deviates from the topic; they should teach Garry to recognize nonverbal cues (e.g., lack of interest, desire to make a comment); they should stop him, refocus, and restate the question.
25. When giving him oral directions, the teacher should present material after the directions have been completed once and then repeat the instructions. If material is given prior to directions, he may impulsively begin without knowing what to do.
26. Materials should be presented one at a time. For example, the teacher should only give the first page of a two-page task. He or she should give the second after the first is turned in. It is also important to keep his work area very clear of extra visual stimulus.
27. Because Garry has poor auditory memory, he should get in the habit of carrying a small notebook with him at all times. He should jot down important information immediately when he hears it. At home, small, wipe-off "white boards" can display reminders. A large wipe-off calendar in his bedroom will be good for planning out long-term assignments, such as book reports.

Language and Reading

28. Although he is very verbal, Garry may not always understand complex oral directions. When complex oral directions are given, the teacher should check back with Garry to be sure he understands. Written directions would be preferable.

29. Garry best handles only one direction given at a time with a period of a few seconds to process the information. If directions are more than single commands or repeated several times quickly with no processing time given, he may have difficulty and may not be able to respond appropriately.

30. Garry will need language therapy for the pragmatics and subtleties of language, but parent and teachers should foster pragmatics by having short conversations with him. They should use social stories (*Social Stories* by Carol Gray) to give him a context for a new situation and practice some of the things he can say. They should practice interchanges that might take place in that context (e.g., for a baseball game, practicing questions such as, "What's the score?" "Whose up?", responses he might make, and the context in which he would ask them).

31. Parents should not allow Garry to watch the same videotapes or read the same books on his peak interests repetitively. They should keep a variety of materials about different topics and allow a certain period of time each day when he can discuss his area of interest.

32. Parents should allow certain short periods of 10 to 15 min when the topic of discussion can be one of Garry's stereotypical interests (Egypt, mythology, etc.). When that period is over, parents should have a verbal cue for the end of the topic.

33. As other children develop more abstract reasoning, Garry may have difficulty in this area. Garry should be taught common phrases used for satire, idioms, puns, and these styles should not be used when speaking with him (teaching or correcting behavior). Parents and teachers should avoid using figurative or abstract language with Garry.

34. For delayed responses, parents and teachers should allow extra time and avoid too many questions one after another.

35. Using Aesop's Fables or other fables, parents should begin to work with Garry on the meaning "under" the story. After reading the story to Garry or having him read it aloud, he can fold a sheet of paper in half horizontally and put the title of the story at the top. Parents should have him retell the story for them and, above the middle fold, write down the important details (Parents can serve as secretary and

write them). Then discuss what the story means and write down the moral or theme "under" the story below the middle fold. This will illustrate for him, in a concrete way, how we look for subtle meanings or themes in stories.

Mathematical and Sequencing Skills

36. For sequencing problems; parents should teach sequencing skills, practicing with 3- and 4-step sequences to sort and organize. They should not allow Garry to skip steps even if he claims to know what to do.

37. The teacher could let Garry use a computer program which covers the same math processes as the class is doing on paper.

38. Parents should use numbers in practical ways around the house. ("Bring me three forks, five nails," etc.)

39. Garry may need to use a calculator in class if he cannot master numerical operations.

40. Parents should play board games with Garry that use dice or spinning to teach sequential math.

41. Parents should play games or activities that require keeping score. They should teach him how to tally, using four upright lines, with a fifth running diagonally and counting by fives.

42. Parents should play games such as blackjack that require practicing mental addition and rehearsing higher and lower number facts.

43. Parents should play space estimation games. (How long is the table in hands, ruler lengths, or books?)

44. Parents should make a master card with letters, having point values (a = 1, b = 2, c = 3, etc.) and then have Garry do math with words (Dad + Garry = ?, Mother × Leslie = ?).

45. Parents should have a measuring wall for family growth or plant height.

46. Parents should make calendars (reinforces multiplying by sevens).

47. Parents should engage in practical multiplication and division such as dividing cookies. For example, parents can give Garry 21 cookies to put on three plates. They can demonstrate that three times seven is 21. They can do this again with seven plates.

48. Parents should use recipes that require sequencing, measuring, and fractions.

49. Computer drills and practice in math for 10 min. two to three times a day should be very beneficial.

50. Parents should play informal number games that include number

word concepts such as "more" and "each." (i.e., "Which pile has more M&Ms? Put the same number of M&Ms on each plate.")

Visuospatial

51. Parents should use directions in conversation and ask which it is. ("We're going left at the end of this aisle; which way is that?")
52. Parents should give commands with directions. ("Put the plant to the left of the window")
53. For visuospatial concepts and directions, teachers should use external memory aid in the classroom (i.e., written explanation taped to desk with explanation of the concept; laminated card to use). For instance, when learning to set up an addition or subtraction problem, teachers should write out the process with an illustration.
54. Parents should play directional games, such as Simon Says. ("Show me your right leg, lift your left arm.") Parents should hide an object and give directions to find it. ("Turn right, go three steps, turn left go two.") They should reverse these so Garry has to give the directions in addition to following.
55. Parents should fold a sheet of paper in half lengthwise and then in thirds horizontally. Unfolding it creates six "boxes" into which a math problem can be placed. This separates each problem into its own "space" and prevents errors from math problems being crowded onto one another.
56. Garry should begin to work on simple block designs, tangrams, puzzles, constructions, and so forth in order to help spatial understanding. Feuerstein methods of strategic, analytical problem-solving may be helpful. He should only work on these activities for short periods of time, but frequently.
57. Parents should walk a short route at home or school, having Garry note whether he turned left or right. They should then help him draw a very simple schematic map of it and use visuospatial words in walking the route and drawing the map (left/right, diagonal to, angle, circular, over, beside, etc.). They should work on a simple schematic map to locate a target house. Using a simple schematic map with a few houses and shops depicted, parents should have Garry tell them how to find the shortest way from a certain shop to a specific house.
58. Parents should play tracing games using Garry's hand. With his eyes closed, parents should trace a shape (or letter), have him guess what it is, or draw on his back and have him guess.

59. He should learn to read very basic bar graphs and charts. Again, parents should write out the process.
60. Garry should use computer software with simple visuospatial games.

Handwriting/Fine Motor Coordination

61. Garry should do activities which develop hand and finger strength to improve pencil grip, such as hanging on the jungle gym or squeezing (little rubber balls, clothespins).
62. Garry should pick up small objects with thumb, index, and middle fingers. Then he should place them on a surface one at a time. This works on separation between the two sides of the hand, as well as distal (fingertip) refinement. This can be combined with math work. Using small candies as a reward may help motivate Garry.
63. Garry can "write" letters on a wall with a squirt gun to improve his fine motor coordination.
64. Garry needs to develop word-processing skills early. The use of an Alpha-Smart in class would be helpful for written work. Garry should compose creative or expository writing directly into the computer, and then go back and edit. This will allow his ideas to be unimpeded by motor output. Let him start by keeping a journal. On the computer, he writes one sentence about his day. The fine motor coordination needed for typing is less refined than that needed for graphomotor control, but by starting early, he will be ready to do his work on the computer by fourth grade, when the writing demands increase greatly.
65. Parents should help Garry make signs or posters for his room.
66. Parents should have Garry be the family scribe and help make lists.
67. Garry may have difficulty copying from the board, and it would be helpful if he could work from preprinted sheets. Later, when he is not using a workbook, it might also be possible just to photocopy the math book page, and he could work problems directly on the copied sheet.
68. Garry should use a thick-barreled pencil and pen, or he should have a gripper on his pencil.
69. Desk and chair height are important. Feet and heels should be resting on the floor and table or desk height should be no higher than two inches above bent elbow.

Sensory

70. Parents and teachers should be aware that Garry does not always perceive well through touch. The kinesthetic approach is not a good one for him.

71. Parents should introduce a variety of textures in foods slowly. He only needs to have one small bite.

72. Parents should not get annoyed at Garry if Garry becomes upset by sticky substances on his hands, has to sit on a chair with a texture he cannot tolerate, and so forth. They should simply let him wash his hands or change chairs because these are sensory issues, and until he begins to benefit from his sensory integration therapy, he will be so anxious if he is made to "tough it out" that he will not be able to learn or attend. Parents should teach him what to say to an adult or friend when he needs relief from sensory irritation.

73. If certain textures of clothing or tags at the back of the neck bother him, parents should let him wear the textures he likes for school and cut the tags out, so he can concentrate when he is there. Work on wearing the problematic garment very brief periods on the weekend.

74. Parents should cut a hand-sized opening into a box and play a game in which Garry reaches in and feels an object until he can identify it. Parents should start with larger objects with little detail and work up to small objects which need to be identified by detail (e.g., coins).

Social Problems and Behavior

75. For poor social interaction and poor reading of nonverbal cues, parents should develop a pre-established and practiced nonverbal cue to alert Garry that his behavior is inappropriate, take time to explain what was wrong with the behavior, and what would have been appropriate.

76. When Garry has an altercation or gets in trouble because he did not pick up a social cue, parents should ask him to think back about what the other individual's face looked like just before he or she got upset with Garry. What did the voice sound like? Did it sound deeper? How did the individual use his or her body? Were the hands on the hips? Was the foot tapping?

77. The teacher (and any other adult) must be sure that Garry is looking at her or him when he or the adult is talking. Parents should remind him of the importance of this with his friends and work out a nonverbal cue with him that will serve as a reminder. Parents should role-play eye contact in social situations, talking Garry through the process and why it is so important.

78. Garry will benefit from involvement in a small group activity such as

Cub Scouts, where he can learn to function with a group cooperatively, practice social skills, and build self-esteem.

79. It will be helpful for building social skills if a peer is invited over for a sandwich and to play for about an hour. Parents can facilitate the interactive play by taking part in a game of catch, block building, a board game, and so forth.

80. Garry probably will not read social cues well, therefore it is important for the teacher to say as concretely as possible what he or she needs to convey. "I did not like the way you pushed your paper aside, please put it back."

81. Using magazine pictures, parents can help Garry make cards demonstrating various emotions. They can help Garry recognize various emotions when he sees them. They can play with the cards, discuss them, and act out different emotions. They can help Garry recognize when a face looks happy and when a face looks sad, and he can group them according to feelings. This will help him begin to identify feelings in himself.

82. An adult can videotape Garry when he is with a parent and is presenting a monologue on his interest. Parents can talk about the video with him, stopping the tape, so he can see that his parent cannot get a word in. They should discuss this and role-play how it might be handled differently.

83. More difficult behavior problems should be dealt with through counseling, and a behavior modification plan should be designed to maximize learning and eliminate harmful or disruptive behaviors.

84. Garry would benefit from being involved in an extracurricular area of success that would help him build his self-esteem.

85. Garry's parents should be aware that he is less mature than his chronological age. Responsible independence should be fostered whenever possible. If he is able to do something for himself, they should let him take care of it. If he has not yet mastered a task they should assist him, but do not do it for him. He needs to be held accountable for chores on a daily basis. Parents should keep a chore chart or let him pull a chore from a "Job Jar."

86. Family rules need to be simple and clear-cut. When Garry breaks a family rule, the consequences should be employed immediately, but in a nonjudgmental, nonthreatening manner. He needs much positive reinforcement for positive actions.

Follow-up

87. Handouts and a bibliography on Asperger's and NLD will be given to Garry's parents. If they have any questions after the parent conference, they should feel free to consult with this psychologist. The name of a support group and referrals for therapists will be supplied.

88. Garry should have a brief reevaluation to assess progress in one year.

🐦 TEST YOURSELF 🐦

True-False

1. **The NEPSY Core can be used as a brief neuropsychological screener.** True or False?

2. **It is important to include any history of substance abuse during pregnancy, but history of stress need not be included, because keeping calm during pregnancy is "an old wives' tale."** True or False?

3. **If the child has a nickname that is used all the time, the first reference to the child in the text should be the child's full name with the nickname in quotation marks. From then on, use the nickname.** True or False?

4. **Comprehensive medical information should be included in the health history even if it clearly is not related to the presenting problem.** True or False?

5. **Bonding information should be included in the child's history.** True or False?

6. **Any disorders in the extended family of a stepparent are important to include in family history.** True or False?

7. **The child interview includes three wishes about school.** True or False?

8. **A difference in the *DSM-IV* criteria for Asperger's versus Autistic Disorder is the lack of language delay in Asperger's that is present in Autism.** True or False?

9. **Including Test Observations and Qualitative Observations in the report helps explain the "why" of the child's approach to a task.** True or False?

10. **Use the abbreviation *SS* for *scaled score* when reporting scores in the text of a report for a brief evaluation.** True or False?

Fill in the blank(s):

The Referral Statement should do the following:

11. Identify the child by _____, _____, and _____.

12. Present a very brief description of the child's _____.

13. Give the referral source, including area of _____ and period of _____.

14. State clearly the _____ or _____ problem.

(continued)

The Relevant Background Information

15. History of pregnancy should include _____ and _____ .

16. The discussion of developmental milestones and early childhood behaviors should include sensory sensitivities to _____, _____, and _____, for instance.

17. Medical history should include illnesses or (a) _____, head injury and especially the duration of (b) _____, results of (c) _____, (d) _____, (e) _____, and other studies, as well as dates of most recent (f) _____ and (g) _____ tests.

18. Among the important questions in the School History of the report is one concerning homework. It has to do with resistance to a particular _____.

19. Psychosocial history should include the parent's description of the child's (a) _____; (they can endorse a list of descriptive words); social (b) _____ with peers/family; (c) _____ problems; (d) and a description of when and with whom they are most apt to occur. The presence of any significant trauma would be included in the discussion of (e) _____ status.

Interpretation

20. As results are interpreted, you will attempt to define the (a) _____ and (b) _____ pointing to a diagnostic behavioral cluster(s) that may ultimately define the disorder.

21. A secondary deficit of Garry's primary deficit, _____, was observed in his problem with learning large quantities of verbal information that required organization and monitoring of the material.

22. In a report of a brief assessment, it is permissible to interpret results for each Core Domain Score, including the _____ _____ in the text. Provide the _____ in parentheses after the first Core Domain Score reported.

23. Verify the interpretation with _____ and _____ that converge on the same deficit.

24. In summarizing findings, discuss _____ or _____ a finding fits the disorders being considered for a differential diagnosis.

25. Support your conclusions with results across _____, as much as possible.

Answers: 1. True; 2. False; 3. True; 4. False; 5. True; 6. False; 7. True; 8. True; 9. True; 10. False; 11.(a) full name, (b) age, (c) gender; 12. Family; 13.(a) specialty, (b) treatment; 14.(a) presenting, (b) identifying; 15.(a) delivery, (b) perinatal course; 16.(a) tactile (texture/touch), (b) auditory (sounds), (c) visual (sights); 17.(a) surgeries, (b) coma, (c) CAT scan, (d) MRI, (e) EEG, (f) vision, (g) hearing; 18. type/subject; 19. temperament; 20.(a) primary deficits and secondary deficits, (b) interaction/relationships, (c) behavioral, (d) emotional; 21. executive dysfunction; 22.(a) standard scores, (b) mean; 23.(a) scores, (b) observations; 24.(a) why, (b) why not; 25. assessments

ppendix A

IEPSY Data Worksheet

Iame _____ DOB _____ CA _____

able A.I Step I & 2: Enter Data and Find Differences

Attention/Executive Functions Domain

:ore ubtests	SS (x=10±15)	%ile	Perf. Level	*$\frac{-}{x}$	Diff.	Req. for Sig.	Freq. of Diff.	S/W Within Domain
:atue[(3–4)]								
:ower[(5–12)]								
ARS[(5–12)]								
'A[(3–12)]								

Iomain core X=100±15)		%ile	Confiden. Interval	Performance Level		Interpretable? Yes? No?		
xpanded ubtest	SS	%ile	Perf. Level	**$\frac{-}{x}$	Diff.	Req. for Sig.	Freq. of Diff.	S/W Within Domain
IF[(5–12)]								
:T[(5–12)]								
:atue[(5–12)]								

To determine Core Domain Score interpretability use personal core subtest mean comparison able B.3 in Manual); or pair-wise subtest comparison (Table B.7).

Core and Expanded Subtest mean can be computed to look at total domain performance across ore and Expanded subtests (Table B.6) but not domain interpretability.

Table A.1 Continued

Language Functions Domain

Core Subtests	SS (x=10±15)	%ile	Perf. Level	$\overset{*}{x}$	Diff.	Req. for Sig.	Freq. of Diff.	S/W Within Domain
BPN[(3–4)]								
PP[(5–12)]								
SN[(5–12)]								
CI[(3–12)]								

Domain Score (X=100±15)		%ile	Confiden. Interval	Performance Level		Interpretable? Yes? No?		
Expanded Subtest	SS	%ile	Perf. Level	$\overset{**}{x}$	Diff.	Req. for Sig.	Freq. of Diff.	S/W Within Domain
RNW[(5–12)]								
VF[(5–12)]								
OMS[(5–12)]								

*To determine Core Domain Score interpretability use personal core subtest mean comparison (Table B.3 in Manual); or pair-wise subtest comparison (Table B.7).

**Core and Expanded Subtest mean can be computed to look at total domain performance across Core and Expanded subtests (Table B.6) but not domain interpretability.

able A.I Continued

Sensorimotor Domain

Core ubtests	SS (x=10±15)	%ile	Perf. Level	$\frac{*}{x}$	Diff.	Req. for Sig.	Freq. of Diff.	S/W Within Domain
TT(5–12)								
HP(3–12)								
MP(3–12)								

Domain core X=100±15)		%ile	Confiden. Interval	Performance Level		Interpretable? Yes? No?		
xpanded ubtest	SS	%ile	Perf. Level	$\frac{**}{x}$	Diff.	Req. for Sig.	Freq. of Diff.	S/W Within Domain
IMS(3–12)								
D-PII(5–12)								
D-NPII(5–12)								

To determine Core Domain Score interpretability use personal core subtest mean comparison able B.3 in Manual); or pair-wise subtest comparison (Table B.7).

*Core and Expanded Subtest mean can be computed to look at total domain performance across ore and Expanded subtests (Table B.6) but not domain interpretability.

Table A.I Continued

Visuospatial Domain

Core Subtests	SS (x=10±15)	%ile	Perf. Level	$\frac{*}{x}$	Diff.	Req. for Sig.	Freq. of Diff.	S/W Within Domain
DC$^{(3-12)}$								
ARROWS$^{(5-12)}$								
BC$^{(3-4)}$								

Domain Score (X=100±15)		%ile	Confiden. Interval	Performance Level		Interpretable? Yes? No?		
Expanded Subtest	SS	%ile	Perf. Level	$\frac{**}{x}$	Diff.	Req. for Sig.	Freq. of Diff.	S/W Within Domain
BC$^{(5-12)}$								
RF$^{(5-12)}$								

*To determine Core Domain Score interpretability use personal core subtest mean comparison (Table B.3 in Manual); or pair-wise subtest comparison (Table B.7).

**Core and Expanded Subtest mean can be computed to look at total domain performance across Core and Expanded subtests (Table B.6) but not domain interpretability.

Table A.1 Continued

Memory/Language Functions Domain

Core Subtests	SS (x=10±15)	%ile	Perf. Level	$\frac{*}{x}$	Diff.	Req. for Sig.	Freq. of Diff.	S/W Within Domain
MF(5–12)								
MN(5–12)								
MM(5–12)								
R(3–4)								

Domain Score (X=100±15)		%ile	Confiden. Interval	Performance Level		Interpretable? Yes? No?		

Expanded Subtest	SS	%ile	Perf. Level	$\frac{**}{x}$	Diff.	Req. for Sig.	Freq. of Diff.	S/W Within Domain
R(5–12)								
L(7–12)								

To determine Core Domain Score interpretability use personal core subtest mean comparison (Table B.3 in Manual); or pair-wise subtest comparison (Table B.7).

*Core and Expanded Subtest mean can be computed to look at total domain performance across core and Expanded subtests (Table B.6) but not domain interpretability.

Table A.2 Step 3. Interpretation of Domain Scores and Overview of Test Profile

Domain Score X=100±15	A/E Diff.	Freq. of Diff.	L Diff.	Freq. of Diff.	S Diff.	Freq. of Diff.	V Diff.	Freq. of Diff.	M/L Diff.	Freq. of Diff.
A/E										
L										
S										
V										
M/L										

Consult Table B.1 (Manual, p. 305) for differences required for significance and Table B.2 (pp. 306–309) for cumulative percentages of standardization sample showing these differences.

References

Achenbach, T. M., & Edelbrock, C. (1991). *Manual for the child behavior checklist–Revised*. Burlington: University of Vermont.

Aicardi, J. (1994). *Epilepsy in children* (2nd ed.) *International Review of Child Neurology Series*. New York: Raven Press.

American Psychiatric Association. (1994). *Diagnostic and statistical manual of mental disorders* (4th ed.). Washington, DC: Author.

Aram, D. M., & Ekelman, B. L. (1988). Scholastic aptitude and achievement among children with unilateral brain lesions. *Neuropsychologia, 26,* 903–916.

Aram, D. M., Ekelman, B. L., & Nation, J. E. (1984). Preschoolers with language disorders: 10 years later. *Journal of Speech and Hearing Research, 27,* 232–244.

Baddeley, A. (1991). *Human memory: Theory and practice*. Hove, UK: Erlbaum.

Baddeley, A. (1992). Working memory. *Science, 255,* 556–559.

Barkley, R. A. (1988). Attention. In M. G. Tramontana & S. R. Hooper (Eds.), *Assessment issues in child neuropsychology* (pp. 145–176). New York: Plenum Press.

Barkley, R. A. (1991). The ecological validity of laboratory and analogous assessment methods of ADHD symptoms. *Journal of Abnormal Child Psychology, 19,* 149–178.

Barkley, R. A. (1996). Critical issues in research on attention. In G. R. Lyon & N. A. Krasnegor (Eds.), *Attention, memory, and executive function* (pp. 45–56). Baltimore: Brookes.

Barkley, R. A. (1997). Attention deficit hyperactivity disorder: The nature of self-control. New York: Guilford Press.

Barkley, R. A., Grodzinsky, G., & DuPaul, C. J. (1992). Frontal lobe functions in attention deficit disorder with and without hyperactivity: A review and research report. *Journal of Abnormal Child Psychology, 20*(2), 163–188.

Baron, I. S., Fennel, E., & Voellner, K. (1995). *Pediatric neuropsychology in the medical setting*. Oxford, England: Oxford University Press.

Bassett, S. S., & Slater, E. J. (1990). Neuropsychological function in adolescents sustaining mild closed head injury. *Journal of Pediatric Psychology, 15,* 225–236.

Bawden, H. N., Knights, R. M., & Winogron, H. W. (1985). Speeded performance following head injury in children. *Journal of Clinical and Experimental Neuropsychology, 7*(1), 39–54.

Beardsworth, E. D., & Zaidel, D. W. (1994). Memory for faces in epileptic children before and after brain surgery. *Journal of Clinical and Experimental Neuropsychology, 16*(4), 589–596.

Beery, K. E. (1982). *Developmental Test of Visual-Motor Integration*. Cleveland, OH: Modern Curriculum Press.

Bellugi, U., Sabo, H., & Vaid, J. (1988). Spatial deficits in children with Williams syndrome. In J. Stiles-Davis, M. Kritchevsky, & U. Bellugi (Eds.), *Spatial cognition: Brain bases and development* (pp. 273–298). Hillsdale, NJ: Erlbaum.

Benasich, A. (1998). Temporal integration as an early predictor of speech and language development. In C. von Euler, I. Lundberg, & R. Llinás, (Eds.), *Basic mechanisms in cognition and language* (pp. 123–142). Oxford, England: Elsevier Science.

Bennetto, L., Pennington, B. F., & Rogers, S. I. (1996). Intact and impaired memory functions in autism. *Child Development, 67,* 1816–1835.

Benson, D. F., & Geschwind, N. (1970). Developmental Gerstmann syndrome. *Neurology, 20,* 293–298.

Bentin, S., Hammer, R., & Cahan, S. (1991). The effects of aging and first grade schooling on the development of phonological awareness. *Psychological Science, 2,* 271–274.

Benton, A. L., Hamsher, K de S., Varney, N. R., & Spreen, O. (1983). *Contributions to neuropsychological assessment.* New York: Oxford University Press.

Berninger, V. W. (1996). *Reading and writing acquisition: A developmental neuropsychological perspective.* Boulder, CO: Westview Press.

Berninger, V. W., Mizokawa, D. T., & Bragg, R. (1991). Theory-based diagnosis and remediation of writing disabilities. *Journal of School Psychology, 29,* 57–79.

Bernstein, J. H., & Waber, D. P. (1990). Developmental neuropsychological assessment: The systemic approach. In A. A. Boulton, G. B. Baker, & M. Hiscock (Eds.), *Neuromethods: Vol. 17. Neuropsychology* (pp. 311–371). Clifton, NJ: Humana Press.

Biederman, J., Faroane, S. V., Keenan, K., & Tsuang, M. T. (1991). Evidence of familial association between attention deficit disorder and major affective disorders. *Archives of General Psychiatry, 48,* 633–642.

Biederman, J., Newcorn, J., & Sprich, S. (1991). Comorbidity of attention deficit hyperactivity disorder with conduct, depressive, anxiety, and other disorders. *American Journal of Psychiatry, 148*(5), 564–577.

Bishop, D. V. M. (1992). The underlying nature of specific language impairment. *Journal of Child Psychology and Psychiatry, 33,* 3–66.

Bishop, D. V. M., & Rosenbloom, L. (1987). Classification of childhood language disorders. *Developmental Medicine, 101–102,* 16–41.

Blachman, B. A. (1984). Relationship of rapid naming ability and language analysis skills to kindergarten and first-grade reading achievement. *Journal of Educational Psychology 76*(4), 610–622.

Boehm, A. E. (1986). *Boehm Test of Basic Concepts–Revised.* San Antonio, TX: Psychological Corp.

Bornstein, R. A., Carroll, A., & King, G. (1986). Relationship of age to neuropsychological deficits in Tourette's Syndrome. *Journal of Neuropsychiatry and Clinical Neurosciences, 3,* 157–62.

Bos, C. S., & Van Reusen, A. K. (1991). Academic interventions with learning-disabled students: A cognitive/neurocognitive approach. In J. Obrzut & G. W. Hynd (Eds.), *Neuropsychological foundations of learning disabilities* (pp. 659–684). Orlando, FL: Academic Press.

Bradley, L. (1989). Predicting learning disabilities. In I. J. Dumont & H. Nakken (Eds.), *Learning disabilities: Vol. 2. Cognitive, social and remedial aspects* (pp. 1–17). Amsterdam: Swets & Zeitlinger.

Bradley, L., & Bryant, P. E. (1978). Difficulties in auditory organisation as a possible cause of reading backwardness. *Nature, 271,* 746–747.

Brookshire, B., Butler, I., Ewing-Cobbs, L., & Fletcher, J. (1994). Neuropsychological characteristics of children with Tourette Syndrome: Evidence for a nonverbal learning disability? *Journal of Clinical and Experimental Neuropsychology, 2,* 289–302.

Brown, A. L., & DeLoache, J. S. (1978). Skills, plans, and self-regulation. In R. S. Siegler (Ed.), *Children's thinking: What develops?* (pp. 3–35). Hillsdale, NJ: Erlbaum.

Bryan, T., & Lee, J. (1990). Social skills training with learning disabled children and adolescents: The state of the art. In T. E. Scruggs & B. Y. L. Wong (Eds.), *Intervention research in learning disabilities* (pp. 263–278). Berlin: Springer.

Byrne, B., & Fielding-Barnsley, R. (1993). Evaluation of a program to teach phonemic awareness to young children: A 1 year follow-up. *Journal of Educational Psychology, 85,* 104–111.

Camfield, P. R., Gates, R., Ronen, G., Camfield, C., Ferguson, A., & MacDonald, C. W. (1984). Comparison of cognitive ability, personality profile, and school success in epileptic children with pure right versus left temporal lobe EEG foci. *Annals of Neurology 15*(2), 122–126.

Cantwell, D. P., & Baker, L. (1987). *Developmental speech and language disorders.* New York: Guilford Press.

Carmichael-Olson, H., Sampson, P. D., Barr, H., Streissguth, A. P., & Bookstein, F. L. (1992). Prenatal exposure to alcohol and school problems in late childhood: A longitudinal prospective study. *Development and Psychopathology, 4,* 341–359.

Carpentieri, S. C., & Mulhern, R. K. (1993). Patterns of memory dysfunction among children surviving temporal lobe tumors. *Archives of Clinical Neuropsychology, 8,* 345–357.

Casey, J. E., Rourke, B. P., & Picard, E. M. (1991). Syndrome of nonverbal learning disabilities: Age differences in neuropsychological, academic, and socioemotional functioning. *Development and Psychopathology, 3,* 329–345.

Cermak, S. A., & Murray, E. A. (1991). The validity of the constructional subtests of the sensory integration and praxis tests. *American Journal of Occupational Therapy 45*(6).

Chandlee, L., Tuesday-Heathfield, L., & Radcliffe, J. (1999). NEPSY findings among 4-year-old children with low to moderate lead toxicity. *Journal of the International Neuropsychological Society, 5,* 147.

Christensen, A.-L. (1975). *Luria's neuropsychological investigation.* Copenhagen: Munksgaard.

Christensen, A.-L. (1984). The Luria method of examination of the brain-impaired patient. In P. E. Logue & J. M. Scheat (Eds.), *Clinical neuropsychology: A multidisciplinary approach* (pp. 5–28). Springfield, IL: Thomas.

Colarusso, P., and Hamill, D. (1972). *Motor Free Visual Perception Test.* Novato, CA: Academic Therapy Publications.

Coles, C. (1994). Critical periods for prenatal alcohol exposure: Evidence from animal and human studies. *Alcohol Health & Research World, 18*(1), 22–29.

Conners, C. K. (1989). *Conners' Rating Scales.* Toronto, Canada: Multi-Health Systems.

Conners, C. K. (1994). *Conners' Continuous Performance Test* (Version 3.0) [Computer software]. Toronto, Canada: Multi-Health Systems.

Conry, J. (1990). Neuropsychological deficits in fetal alcohol syndrome and fetal alcohol effects of alcoholism. *Clinical and Experimental Research, 14,* 650–655.

Cooley, E. L., & Morris, R. D. (1990). Attention in children: A neuropsychologically based model for assessment. *Developmental Neuropsychology, 6,* 239–274.

Copeland, L. R., Pfefferbaum, B., Fletcher, J., Jaffee, N., & Culbert, S. (1982, April). Neuropsychological assessment of long-term survivors of leukemia. Paper presented at the American Society of Clinical Oncology, St. Louis, MO.

Copeland, D. R. (1992). Neuropsychological and psychosocial effects of childhood leukemia and its treatment. *Cancer Journal for Clinicians, 42*(5), 283–295.

Cowan, W. W. (1979, September). The development of the brain. *Scientific American,* 107–117.

Critchley, M. (1966). *The parietal lobes.* New York: Hafner.

Crocker, L., & Algina, J. (1986). *Introduction to classical and modern test theory.* Fort Worth, TX: Harcourt Brace Jovanovich.

Davenport, L., Yingling, C. D., Fein, G., Galin, D., & Johnstone, J. (1986). Narrative speech deficits in dyslexics. *Journal of Clinical and Experimental Neuropsychology, 8*(4), 347–361.

Davies, S., Bishop, D., Manstead, A. R., & Tantam, D. (1994). Face perception in children with autism and Asperger's syndrome. *Journal of Child Psychology and Psychiatry and Allied Disciplines, 35,* 1033–1057.

DeBruyn, I., Smith, R., & Berninger, V. W. (1985). *Visual and linguistic correlates of beginning skills.* Las Vegas, NV: National Association of School Psychologists.

Delis, D. C. (1989). Neuropsychological assessment of learning and memory. In F. Boller & J. Grafman (Series Eds.), *Handbook of neuropsychology* (Vol. 3, pp. 3–33). Amsterdam: Elsevier.

Denckla, M. (1973). Development of speed in repetitive and successive finger-movements in normal children. *Developmental Medicine and Child Neurology, 15,* 635–645.

Denckla, M. B. (1983). The neuropsychology of social-emotional learning disabilities. *Archive of Neurology, 40,* 461–462.

Denckla, M. B. (1985). Development of motor coordination in dyslexic children. In F. H. Duffy & N. Geschwind (Eds.), *Dyslexia: A neuroscientific approach to clinical evaluation.* Boston: Little, Brown.

Denckla, M. B. (1996). A theory and model of executive function: A neuropsychological perspective. In G. R. Lyon & N. A. Krasnegor (Eds.), *Attention, memory, and executive function* (pp. 263–278). Baltimore: Brookes.

Denckla, M. B., & Rudel, R. G. (1976a). Naming of object-drawings by dyslexic and other learning disabled children. *Brain and Language, 3,* 1–15.

Denckla, M. B., & Rudel, R. G. (1976b). Rapid "automatized" naming (RAN): Dyslexia differentiated from other learning disabilities. *Neuropsychologia, 14,* 471–479.

Denckla, M. B., & Rudel, R. G. (1978). Anomalies of motor development in hyperactive boys. *Annals of Neurology, 3,* 231–233.

De Renzi, E., & Faglioni, P. (1978). Normative data and screening power of a shortened version of the Token Test. *Cortex, 14,* 41–49.

Doehring, D. G. (1985). Reading disability subtypes: Interaction of reading and nonreading deficits. In B. P. Rourke (Ed.), *Neuropsychology of learning disabilities* (pp. 133–146). New York: Guilford Press.

Done, A., & Rourke, B. P. (1995). Fetal alcohol syndrome. In B. P. Rourke (Ed.), *Syndrome of nonverbal learning disabilities: Neurodevelopmental manifestations* (pp. 372–406). New York: Guilford Press.

Douglas, V. I. (1984). Attentional and cognitive problems. In M. Rutter (Ed.), *Developmental neuropsychiatry* (pp. 280–329). Edinburgh, UK: Churchill Livingstone.

Douglas, V. I., & Benezra, E. (1990). Supraspan verbal memory in attention deficit disorder with hyperactivity, normal, and reading disabled boys. *Journal of Abnormal Child Psychology, 18,* 617–638.

Drake, W. (1968). Clinical and pathological findings in a child with a developmental learning disability. *Journal of Learning Disabilities, 1,* 468–475.

Duane, D. D. (1991). Dyslexia: Neurobiological and behavioral correlates. *Psychiatric Annals, 21*(12), 703–708.

Dunn, L. M., & Dunn, L. M. (1997). *Peabody Picture Vocabulary Test* (3rd ed.). Circle Pines, MN: American Guidance Service.

Dykman, R. A., & Ackerman, P. T. (1991). Attention deficit disorder and specific reading disability: Separate but often overlapping disorders. *Journal of Learning Disabilities, 24,* 96–103.

Eden, G. F., VanMeter, J. W., Rumsey, J. M., Maisog, J. M., Woods, R. P., & Zaffiro, T. A. (1996). Abnormal processing of visual motion in dyslexia revealed by functional brain imaging. *Nature, 382,* 66–69.

Ehlers, S., & Gilberg, C. (1993). The epidemiology of Asperger's Syndrome: A total population study. *Journal of Child Psychology and Psychiatry, 34,* 1327–1350.

Elliot, C. (1983). *Differential Ability Scales (DAS).* U.S. Adaptation (1990). San Antonio, TX: Psychological Corp.

Ellis, E. S., & Lenz, B. K. (1991). *The development of learning strategy interventions.* Lawrence, KS: Edge Enterprise.

Ewing-Cobbs, L., & Fletcher, J. (1991). Developmental changes in performance on tests of purported frontal lobe functioning. *Developmental Neuropsychology, 7,* 377–395.

Ewing-Cobbs, L., Levin, H. S., Eisenberg, H. M., & Fletcher, J. M. (1987). Language functions following closed head injury in children and adolescents. *Journal of Clinical and Experimental Neuropsychology, 9,* 593–621.

Fay, G. C., Jaffe, K. M., Polissar, N. L., Liao, S., Rivara, J. B., & Martin, K. M. (1994). Outcome of pediatric traumatic brain injury at three years: A cohort study. *Archives of Physical and Medical Rehabilitation, 75,* 733–741.

Fay, W. H., & Schuler, A. L. (1980). *Emerging language in autistic children.* Baltimore: University Park Press.

Fein, D., Pennington, B., Markowitz, P., Braverman, M., & Waterhouse, L. (1986). Toward a neuropsychological model of infantile autism: Are the social deficits primary? *Journal of the American Academy of Child Psychiatry 25*(2), 198–212.

Felton, R. H. (1992). Early identification of children at risk for reading disabilities. *Topics in Early Childhood Special Education, 12*(2), 212–229.

Felton, R. H., & Brown, I. S. (1991). Neuropsychological prediction of reading disabilities. In J. E. Obrzut & G. W. Hynd (Eds.), *Neuropsychological foundations of learning disabilities: A handbook of issues, methods, and practice* (pp. 387–410). San Diego, CA: Academic Press.

Fischer, K. W., & Rose, S. P. (1994). Dynamic development of coordination of components in brain and behavior: A framework for theory and research. In G. Dawson & K. W. Fischer (Eds.), *Human behavior and the developing brain* (pp. 3–66). New York: Guilford Press.

Fleiss, J. L. (1981). Statistical methods for rates and proportions (2nd ed.). New York: Wiley.

Fletcher, J. M. (1985). Memory for verbal and nonverbal stimuli in learning disability subgroups: Analysis by selective reminding. *Journal of Experimental Psychology, 40,* 224–259.

Fletcher, J. M., Bohan, T. P., Brandt, M. E., Brookshire, B. L., Beaver, S. R., Francis, D. J., Davidson, K. C., Thompson, N. M., & Miner, M. E. (1992). Cerebral white matter and cognition in hydrocephalic children. *Archives of Neurology, 49,* 818–824.

Fletcher, J. M., & Levin, H. (1988). Neurobehavioral effects of brain injury in children. In D. K. Routh (Ed.), *Handbook of pediatric psychology* (pp. 258–295). New York: Guilford Press.

Fletcher, J. M., Shaywitz, S., Shankweiler, D., Katz, L., Liberman, I., Stuebing, K., Francis, D., Fowler, A., & Shaywitz, B. (1994). Cognitive profiles of reading disability: Comparisons of discrepancy and low achievement definitions. *Journal of Educational Psychology, 86*(1), 6–23.

Galaburda, A. M., & Eidelberg, D. (1982). Symmetry and asymmetry in the human posterior thalmus; II, Thalamic lesions in a case of developmental dyslexia. *Archives of Neurology, 39,* 333–336.

Galaburda, A. M., & Kemper, T. L. (1979). Cytoarchitectonic abnormalities in developmental dyslexia: A case study. *Annals of Neurology, 6,* 94–100.

Galaburda, A. M., & Livingstone, M. (1993). Evidence for magnocellular defect in developmental dyslexia. In P. Tallal, A. M. Galaburda, R. Liinas, & von Euler, K. (Eds.), Temporal processing in the nervous system, *Annals of the New York Academy of Sciences, 682,* 71–82.

Galaburda, A. M., Sherman, G. F., Rosen, G. D., Aboitiz, E., & Geschwind, N. (1985). Developmental dyslexia: Four consecutive patients with cortical anomalies. *Annals of Neurology, 18*(2), 222–233.

Gathercole, S. E., & Baddeley, A. D. (1990). Phonological memory deficits in language disordered children: Is there a causal connection? *Journal of Memory and Language, 29,* 336–360.

Gaskins, I., Downer, M., Anderson, R., Cunningham, P., Gaskins, R., Schommer, M., & teachers of the Benchmark School. (1988). A metacognitive approach to phonics: Using what we know to decode what you don't. *Remedial and Special Education, 9,* 36–66.

Geschwind, N. (1975). The apraxias: Neural mechanisms of disorders of learned movement. *American Scientist, 63,* 188–195.

Geschwind, N., & Strub, R. (1975). Gerstmann syndrome without aphasia: A reply to Poeck and Orgass. *Cortex, 11,* 296–98.

Goldberg, E., & Costa, L. D. (1981). Hemisphere differences in the acquisition and use of descriptive systems. *Brain and Language, 14,* 144–173.

Goldman-Rakic, P. S. (1992). Working memory and the mind. *Scientific American, 267*(3), 111–117.

Goodyear, P., & Hynd, G. W. (1992). Attention-deficit disorder with (ADD/H) and without (ADD/WO) hyperactivity: Behavioral and neuropsychological differentiation. *Journal of Clinical Child Psychology, 21*(3), 273–305.

Gray, J. W., & Dean, R. S. (1989). Approaches to the cognitive rehabilitation of children with neuropsychological impairments. In C. R. Reynolds & E. Fletcher-Janzen (Eds.), *Handbook of clinical neuropsychology* (pp. 397–408). New York: Plenum Press.

Hall, P. K., & Tomblin, J. B. (1978). A follow-up study of children with articulation and language disorders. *Journal of Speech and Hearing Disorders, 43*, 227–241.

Halperin, J. M. (1996). Conceptualizing, describing, and measuring components of attention: A summary. In G. R. Lyon & N. A. Krasnegor (Eds.), *Attention, memory, and executive function* (pp. 119–136). Baltimore: Brookes.

Halperin, J. M., Gittleman, R., Klein, D. F., & Rudel, R. (1984). Reading disabled-hyperactive children: A distinct subgroup of attention deficit disorder with hyperactivity? *Journal of Abnormal Child Psychology, 21*, 1–14.

Hamsher, K. de S., Levin, H. S., & Benton, A. L. (1979). Facial recognition in patients with focal brain lesions. *Archives of Neurology, 36*, 837–839.

Head, D., Bolton, D., & Hymas, N. (1989). Deficit in cognitive shifting ability in patients with obsessive-compulsive disorder. *Biological Psychiatry, 25*, 929–937.

Hécaen, H. (1983). Acquired aphasia in children: Revisited. *Neuropsychologia, 21*(6), 581–587.

Huckeba, W., Kreiman, C., Korkman, M., Kirk, U., & Kemp, S. (1998, August). *Qualitative observations in ADHD children.* Poster session presented at the annual meeting of the American Psychological Association, San Francisco, CA.

Hurford, D. P., Schauf, J. D., Bunce, L., Blaich, T., & Moore, K. (1994). Early identification of children at risk for reading disabilities. *Journal of Learning Disabilities, 27*(6), 371–382.

Hynd, G., & Hynd, C. (1984). Dyslexia: Neuroanatomical/neurolinguistic perspectives. *Reading Research Quarterly, 4*, 482–498.

Hynd, G. W., & Willis, W. G. (1987). *Pediatric Neuropsychology.* Orlando, FL: Grune & Stratton.

Iversen, S., & Tummer, W. E. (1993). Phonological processing skills and the reading recovery program. *Journal of Educational Psychology, 85*, 112–126.

James, E. M., & Selz, M. (1997). Neuropsychological bases of common learning and behavior problems in children. In C. R. Reynolds & A. Puente (Series Eds.) & C. R. Reynolds & E. Fletcher-Janzen (Vol. Eds.). *Handbook of clinical child psychology: Vol. 4. Critical issues in neuropsychology* (2nd ed., pp. 157–179). New York: Plenum.

Jeeves, M. A., Silver, P. H., & Milne, A. B. (1988). Role of the corpus callosum in the development of a bimanual motor skill. *Developmental Neuropsychology, 4*, 305–323.

Johnson, D. J., & Myklebust, H. R. (1971). *Learning disabilities.* New York: Grune & Stratton.

Jones, V., & Prior, M. (1985). Motor imitation abilities and neurological signs in autistic children. *Journal of Autism and Developmental Disorders, 15*, 37–46.

Kaplan, E. (1988). A process approach to neuropsychological assessment. In T. Boll & B. K. Bryant (Eds.), *Clinical neuropsychology and brain function: Research, measurement, and practice* (pp. 129–137). Washington, DC: American Psychological Association.

Kaplan, E. (1998). Foreword. In *Manual of NEPSY Developmental Neuropsychological Assessment* (pp. iii–iv). San Antonio, TX: Psychological Corp.

Kaufman, A., & Lichtenberger, E. (1999). *The essentials of WAIS-III assessment.* New York: Wiley.

Kemp, S. L., & Kirk, U. (1993). An investigation of frontal executive dysfunction in attention deficit disorder subgroups. In P. Tallal, A. M. Galaburda, R. R. Llinás, & C. von Euler (Eds.), *Annals of the New York Academy of Sciences: Vol. 682. Temporal information processing in the nervous system: Special reference to dyslexia and dysphasia* (pp. 363–365). New York: New York Academy of Sciences.

Kemp, S. L., Kirk, U., Korkman, M., Huckeba, W., Harrington, K., & Matson, M. (2000). *The effects of methylphenidate on the auditory processing and auditory and visual attention of children diagnosed with ADHD.* Manuscript in preparation.

Kinsbourne, M. (1990). Testing models for attention deficit hyperactivity disorder in the behavioral laboratory. In K. Conners & M. Kinsbourne (Eds.), *ADHD: Attention deficit hyperactivity disorder* (pp. 51–69). Munich, Germany: MMV Medizin.

Kinsbourne, M., & Warrington, E. K. (1963). Developmental factors in reading and writing backwardness. *British Journal of Psychology, 54,* 145–146.

Kirk, U. (1981). The development and use of rules in the acquisition of perceptual motor skill. *Child Development, 52,* 299–305.

Kirk, U. (1983). Language and the brain: Implications for education. In U. Kirk (Ed.), *Neuropsychology of language, reading, and spelling* (pp. 257–272). New York: Academic Press.

Kirk, U. (1985). Hemispheric contributions to the development of graphic skill. In C. T. Best (Ed.), *Hemispheric function and collaboration in the child* (pp. 193–228). Orlando, FL: Academic Press.

Kirk, U. (1992). Evidence for early acquisition of visual organization ability: A developmental study. *The Clinical Neuropsychologist, 6*(2), 171–177.

Kirk, U., & Kelly, M. S. (1986). Children's differential performance on selected dorsolateral prefrontal and posterior cortical functions: A developmental perspective. *Journal of Clinical and Experimental Neuropsychology, 7,* 604.

Kirk, U., & Kemp, S. (1999, February). The role of age and gender in the development of semantic and phonemic fluency in children between the ages of 3 and 12. Poster session presented at the annual meeting of the International Neuropsychological Society, Boston, MA.

Kirk, U., Kemp, S., & Korkman, M. (2000). *Phonemic analysis.* Manuscript in preparation.

Kirk, U., Kemp, S., Korkman, M., & McAuliffe, P. (2000). The role of executive function in visuomotor precision. Manuscript in preparation.

Klenberg, L., & Korkman, M. *Development of attention and executive functions: Two separate developmental trends.* Manuscript submitted for publication.

Klin, A., Volkmar, J. F. R., Sparrow, S. S., Cicchetti, D. V., & Rourke, B. P. (1995). Validity and neuropsychological characterization of Asperger's syndrome: Convergence with nonverbal learning disabilities syndrome. *Journal of Child Psychology and Psychiatry, 36,* 1127–1140.

Korhonen, T. T. (1991). Neuropsychological stability and prognosis of subgroups of children with learning disabilities. *Journal of Learning Disabilities, 24,* 48–57.

Korkman, M. (1980). *NEPS. Lasten neuropsykologinen tutkimus. Kasikirja* [NEPS Neuropsychological Assessment of Children: Manual]. Helsinki, Finland: Psykologien kustannus.

Korkman, M. (1988a). NEPS-U. Lasten neuropsykologinen tutkimus. Uudisstettu laitos. [NEPSY: Neuropsychological Assessment of Children (Rev. ed.)]. Helsinki, Finland: Psykologien kustannus.

Korkman, M. (1988c). NEPSY—An adaptation of Luria's investigation for young children. *The Clinical Neuropsychologist, 2,* 375–392.

Korkman, M. (1990). *NEPSY Neuropsykologisk undersokning: 4–7 ar. Svensk version* [NEPSY Neuropsychological Assessment: 4–7 years (Swedish version)]. Stockholm, Sweden: Psykologiforlaget.

Korkman, M. (1993). *Neuropsykologisk undersogelse 4–7 ar. Dansk vejleding* [NEPSY Neuropsychological Assessment 4–7 years (Danish Manual)]. (K. Holm, K. Fransden, J. Jordal, & A. Trillingsgaard, Trans.). Denmark: Dansk psykologisk Forlag.

Korkman, M. (1995). A test-profile approach in analyzing cognitive disorders in children: Experiences of the NEPSY. In M. G. Tramontana & S. R. Hooper (Eds.), *Advances in child neuropsychology* (Vol. 3, pp. 84–116). New York: Springer-Verlag.

Korkman, M. (1999). Applying Luria's diagnostic principles in the neuropsychological assessment of children. *Neuropsychology Review, 9*, 89–105.

Korkman, M. (2000, in press). NEPSY Handbok: Bakgrund, konstruktion och diagnostika anvisningar. Stockholm, Sweden: Psykologiforlaget.

Korkman, M., Autti-Rämö, I., Koivulehto, H., & Granström, M.-L. (1998). Neuropsychological effects at early school-age of fetal alcohol exposure of varying duration. *Journal of Child Neuropsychology, 3*, 199–212.

Korkman, M., Barron-Linnankoski, S., & Lahti-Nuuttila, P. (1999). Effects of age and duration of reading instruction on the development of phonological awareness, speeded naming, and verbal memory span. *Developmental Neuropsychology, 16*, 415–431.

Korkman, M., & Hakkinen-Rihu, P. (1994). A new classification of developmental language disorders (DLD). *Brain and Language, 47*, 96–116.

Korkman, M., Kemp, S. L., & Kirk, U. (in press). Developmental assessment of neuropsychological function with the aid of NEPSY. In A. Kaufman & N. Kaufman (Eds.), *Specific learning disabilities: Psychological assessment and evaluation*. Boston, MA: Cambridge University Press.

Korkman, M., Kirk, U., & Kemp, S. L. (1997). NEPSY Lasten neuropsykologinen tutkimus [NEPSY: A developmental neuropsychological assessment]. Helsinki, Finland: Psykologien kustannus.

Korkman, M., Kirk, U., & Kemp, S. L. (1998). *NEPSY: A developmental neuropsychological assessment*. San Antonio, TX: Psychological Corp.

Korkman, M., Kirk, U., & Kemp, S. L. (2000). *Neurocognitive development in the age range 5–12 years: Differences between age levels and functions*. Manuscript submitted for publication.

Korkman, M., Kirk, U., & Kemp, S. L. (2000, in press). NEPSY. Neuropsykologisk bedömning: 3–12 år Stockholm, Sweden: Psykologiförlaget.

Korkman, M., Liikanen, A., & Fellman, V. (1996). Neuropsychological consequences of very low birth weight and asphyxia at term: Follow-up until school age. *Journal of Clinical and Experimental Neuropsychology, 18*, 220–233.

Korkman, M., & Peltomaa, K. (1991). A pattern of test-findings predicting attention problems at school. *Journal of Abnormal Child Psychology, 19*, 451–467.

Korkman, M., & Peltomaa, K. (1993). Preventive treatment of dyslexia by a preschool training program for children with language impairments. *Journal of Clinical Child Psychology, 22*, 277–287.

Korkman, M., & Pesonen, A. E. (1994). A comparison of neuropsychological test profiles of children with attention deficit hyperactivity disorder and/or learning disorder. *Journal of Learning Disabilities, 27*, 383–392.

Korkman, M., & von Wendt, L. (1995). Evidence of altered dominance in children with congenital spastic hemiplegia. *Journal of the International Neuropsychological Society, 1*, 251–270.

Korkman, M., Autti-Rämö, I., Koivulehto, H., & Granström, M.-L. (1998). Neuropsychological effects at early school age of fetal alcohol exposure of varying duration. *Child Neuropsychology, 3*, 199–212.

Koziol, L. F., & Stout, C. E. (1992). Use of a verbal fluency measure in understanding and evaluating ADHD as an executive function disorder. *Perceptual and Motor Skills, 75*, 1187–1192.

Kracke, I. (1994). Developmental prosopagnosia in Asperger's syndrome: Presentation and discussion of an individual case. *Developmental Medicine and Child Neurology, 36*, 873–886.

Langus, M. L., & Miller, D. C. (1992). Luria's theory of brain functioning: A model for research in cognitive psychophysiology. *Educational Psychologist, 27*(4), 493–511.

Levin, H. S., Culhane, K. A., Hartmann, J., Evankovich, K., Mattson, A. J., Harward, H., Ringholz, G., Ewing-Cobbs, L., & Fletcher, J. (1991). Developmental changes in performance on tests of purported frontal lobe functioning. *Developmental Neuropsychology, 7*, 377–395.

Levin, H. S., Mendelsohn, D., Lilly, M. A., Fletcher, J. M., Culhane, K. A., Chapman, S. B., Harward, H., Kusnerik, L., Bruce, D., & Eisenberg, H. M. (1994). Tower of London performance in relation to magnetic resonance imaging following closed head injury in children. *Neuropsychology, 8*(2), 171–179.

Levine, M. D. (1987). Developmental variation and learning disorders. Cambridge, MA: Educators.

Liberman, I. Y., Shankweiler, D., Fisher, F. W., & Carter, B. (1974). Reading and the awareness of linguistic segments. *Journal of Experimental Child Psychology, 18*, 201–212.

Lincoln, A. J., Dickstein, P., Courchesne, E., Elmasian, R., & Tallal, P. (1992). Auditory processing abilities in non-retarded adolescents and young adults with developmental receptive language disorder and autism. *Brain and Language, 43*, 613–622.

Loring, D. (Ed.). (1999). *INS dictionary of neuropsychology.* New York: Oxford University Press.

Lovegrove, W. (1994). Visual deficits in dyslexia: Evidence and implications. In A. Fawcett & R. Nicolson (Eds.), *Dyslexia in children: Multidisciplinary perspectives* (pp. 113–135). New York: Harvester Wheatsheaf.

Luria, A. R. (1963). *Restoration of function after brain injury.* Oxford: Pergamon Press.

Luria, A. R. (1973). *The working brain: An introduction to neuropsychology* (B. Haigh, Trans.). London: Penguin Press.

Luria, A. R. (1980). *Higher cortical functions in man* (2nd ed.; B. Haigh, Trans.). New York: Basic Books. (Original work published 1962)

Mannuzza, S., Klein, R. G., Bessler, A., Malloy, P., & LaPadula, M. (1993). Adult outcome of hyperactive boys: Educational achievement, occupational rank, and psychiatric status. *Archives of General Psychiatry, 50*, 565–576.

Martin, R. C., Jerger, S., & Breedin, S. (1987). Syntactic processing of auditory and visual sentences in a learning-disabled child: Relation to short-term memory. *Developmental Neuropsychology, 3*(2), 129–152.

Matier-Sharma, K., Perachio, N., Newcom, J. H., Sharma, V., & Halperin, J. M. (1995). Differential diagnosis of ADHD: Are objective measures of attention, impulsivity, and activity level helpful? *Child Neuropsychology, 1*, 118–127.

Mattis, S. (1992). Neuropsychological assessment of school-aged children. In I. Rapin & S. J. Segalowitz (Vol. Eds.) & F. Boller & J. Grafman (Series Eds.), *Handbook of neuropsychology* (pp. 395–415). Amsterdam: Elsevier.

McCarthy, R. A., & Warrington, E. K. (1990). *Cognitive neuropsychology: A clinical introduction.* New York: Academic Press.

McFie, J. (1961). Intellectual impairment in children with localized post-infantile cerebral lesions. *Journal of Neurology, Neurosurgery, and Psychiatry, 24*, 361–365.

Miller, M. W. (1986). Effects of alcohol on the generation and migration of cerebral cortical neurons. *Science, 233*, 1308–1311.

Milner, B. (1975). Psychological aspects of focal epilepsy and its neurosurgical management. In D. P. Purpura, J. K. Penny, & R. D. Walter (Eds.), *Advances in neuropsychology* (Vol. 8, pp. 299–321). New York: Raven Press.

Minshew, N. J., & Goldstein, G. (1993). Is autism an amnesic disorder? Evidence from the California Verbal Learning Test. *Neuropsychology, 7*(2), 209–216.

Minshew, N. J., Goldstein, G., Muenz, L. R., & Payton, J. B. (1992). Neuropsychological functioning in non-mentally retarded autistic individuals. *Journal of Clinical and Experimental Neuropsychology, 14*(5), 749–761.

Mirsky, A. F. (1989). The neuropsychology of attention elements of complex behavior. In E. Perecman (Ed.), *Integrating theory and practice in clinical neuropsychology* (pp. 75–91). Hillsdale, NJ: Erlbaum.

Mirsky, A. F. (1996). Disorders of attention: A neuropsychological perspective. In G. R. Lyon

& N. A. Krasnegor (Eds.), *Attention, memory, and executive function* (pp. 71–95). Baltimore: Brookes.

Mirsky, A. F., Anthony, B. I., Duncan, C. C., Ahearn, M. B., & Kellam, S. G. (1991). Analysis of the elements of attention: A neuropsychological approach. *Neuropsychological Review, 2*(2), 109–145.

Morris, R., Blashfield, R., & Satz, P. (1996). Developmental classification of reading-disabled children. *Journal of Clinical and Experimental Neuropsychology, 8*(4), 371–392.

Morrison, F. J., Smith, L., & Dow-Ehrensberger, M. (1995). Education and cognitive development: A natural experiment. *Developmental Psychology, 31,* 789–799.

Nanson, J. L., & Hiscock, M. (1990). Attention deficits in children exposed to alcohol prenatally. *Alcoholism: Clinical and Experimental Research, 14*(5), 656–661.

Nash, D. L. (1995). *Interrater reliability of behavioral observations on NEPSY.* Unpublished master's thesis, Trinity University, San Antonio, TX.

Neisser, U. (1967). *Cognitive psychology.* New York: Appleton-Century-Crofts.

Nunnally, J. C. (1978). *Psychometric theory* (2nd ed.) New York: McGraw-Hill.

Nass, R., & Gutman, R. (1998). Boys with Asperger's disorder, exceptional verbal intelligence, tics, and clumsiness. *Developmental Medicine and Child Neurology, 148,* 691–695.

Olson, H. C., Sampson, P. D., Barr, H., Streissguth, A. P., & Bookstein, F. L. (1992). Prenatal exposure to alcohol and school problems in late childhood: A longitudinal prospective study. *Development and Psychopathology, 4,* 341–359.

Olson, R., Folz, G., & Wise, B. (1986). Reading instruction and remediation with the aid of computer speech. *Behavior Research Methods, Instruments, and Computers, 18,* 93–99.

Osterrieth, P. A. (1944). Le test de copie une figure complexe. *Archives de Psychologie, 30,* 206–356.

Pennington, B. F. (1991). *Diagnosing learning disorders: A neuropsychological framework.* New York: Guilford Press.

Pennington, B. F., Groisser, D. M., & Welsh, M. C. (1993). Contrasting cognitive deficits inattention deficit hyperactivity disorder versus reading disability. *Developmental Psychology, 29,* 511–523.

Pirozzolo, F. J., & Rayner, K. (1978). Cerebral organization and reading disability. *Neuropsychologia, 17,* 485–491.

Preilowski, B. F. B. (1972). Possible contributions of the anterior forebrain commissures to bilateral motor coordination. *Neuropsychologia, 10,* 267–277.

Psychological Corporation. (2000). *NEPSY scoring assistant.* San Antonio, TX: Author.

Psychological Corporation. (1992). *Wechsler Individual Achievement Test (WIAT).* San Antonio, TX: Author.

Rack, J. P., & Olson, R. K. (1993). Phonological deficits, IQ and individual differences in reading disability: Genetic and environmental influences. *Developmental Review, 13*(3), 269–278.

Rapin, I., & Allen, D. A. (1988). Syndromes in developmental dysphasia and adult aphasia. In F. Plum (Ed.), *Language, communication and the brain* (pp. 57–74). New York: Raven Press.

Rapin, I., Allen, D. A., & Dunn, M. A. (1992). Developmental language disorders. In F. Boiler & J. Grafman (Series Eds.) & S. J. Segalowitz & I. Rapin (Section Eds.), *Handbook of neuropsychology: Vol. 7. Child neuropsychology* (pp. 111–137). Amsterdam: Elsevier.

Rapin, I., Mattis, S., Rowan, A. J., & Golden, G. G. (1977). Verbal auditory agnosia in children. *Developmental Medicine and Child Neurology, 19,* 192–207.

Regard, M., Strauss, E., & Knapp, P. (1982). Children's production on verbal and nonverbal fluency tasks. *Perceptual Motor Skills, 55,* 839–844.

Reitan, R. M. (1979). *Manual for administration of neuropsychological batteries for adults and children.* Tucson, AZ: Reitan Neuropsychological Laboratory.

Reynolds, C. R. (1997). Measurement and statistical problems in neuropsychological assessment of children. In C. R. Reynolds & A. Puente (Series Eds.) & C. R. Reynolds & E. Fletcher-Janzen (Vol. Eds.). *Critical issues in neuropsychology: Vol. 4. Handbook of clinical child psychology* (2nd ed., pp. 180–203). New York: Plenum.

Rezai, Andreasen, Alliger, Cohen, Swayze, O'Leary, 1993 (Tower)

Robertson, C. M. T., & Finer, N. N. (1993). Long-term follow-up of term neonates with prenatal asphyxia. *Clinics of Perinatology, 20,* 483–497.

Rourke, B. P. (1975). Brain behavior relationships in children with learning disabilities: A research program. *American Psychologist, 30,* 911–920.

Rourke, B. P. (1987). Syndrome of nonverbal learning disabilities: The final common pathway of white matter disease/dysfunction? *Clinical Neuropsychologist, 1,* 209–234.

Rourke, B. P. (1988). The syndrome of non-verbal learning disabilities: Developmental manifestations in neurological disease, disorder and dysfunction. *Clinical Neuropsychologist, 2,* 293–330.

Rourke, B. P. (1989). *Nonverbal learning disabilities: The syndrome and the model.* New York: Guilford Press.

Rourke, B. P. (1993). Arithmetic disabilities, specific and otherwise: A neuropsychological perspective. *Journal of learning disabilities, 26,* 214–226.

Rourke, B. P. (1994). Neuropsychological assessment of children with learning disabilities: Measurement issues. In C. R. Lyons (Eds.), *Frames of reference for the assessment of learning disabilities: New views on measurement issues* (pp. 475–514). Baltimore: Brookes.

Rourke, B. P. (1995). *Syndrome of nonverbal learning disabilities: Neurodevelopmental manifestations.* New York: Guilford Press.

Rourke, B. P., & Finlayson, M. A. J. (1978). Neuropsychological significance of variations in patterns of academic performance: Verbal and visual-spatial abilities. *Journal of Abnormal Psychology, 6,* 121–133.

Rourke, B., Fisk, J. L., & Strang, J. D. (1986). *Neuropsychological assessment of children: A treatment oriented approach.* New York: Guilford Press.

Rourke, B. P., Young, G. C., & Leenaars, A. A. (1989). A childhood learning disability that predisposes those afflicted to adolescent and adult depression and suicide risk. *Journal of Learning Disabilities, 22,* 169–185.

Rovet, J., & Alvarez, M. (1996). Attention and thyroid hormone in school-age children with congenital hypothyroidism. *Journal of Child Psychology and Psychiatry, 37,* 579–585.

Russell, E. W. (1986). The psychometric foundation of clinical neuropsychology. In S. Filskov, & T. J. Boll (Eds.), *Handbook of clinical neuropsychology* (pp. 45–80) New York: Wiley.

Scarborough, H. S. (1990). Very early language deficits in dyslexic children. *Child Development, 61,* 1728–1743.

Scheuffgen, K. (1998). Domain-general and domain-specific deficits in autism and dyslexia. Unpublished doctoral dissertation, University of London.

Schopler, E. (1996). Are autism and Asperger's syndrome different labels or different disabilities? *Journal of Autism and Developmental Disorders, 26,* 109–110.

Semrud-Clikeman, M., & Hynd, G. (1991). Specific nonverbal and social skills deficits in children with learning disabilities. In J. E. Obrzut & G. W. Hynd (Eds.), *Neuropsychological foundations of learning disabilities: A handbook of issues, methods, and practice* (pp. 603–630). Orlando, FL.: Academic Press.

Shallice, T. (1982). Specific impairments of planning. In D. E. Broadbent & L. Weiskranz (Eds.), *Neuropsychological functions* (pp. 199–209). London: Royal Society.

Shapiro, E. S. (1989). *Academic skills problems: Direct assessment and intervention.* New York: Guilford Press.

Shaywitz, B. A., & Shaywitz, S. E. (1987). Attention deficit disorder: Current perspectives. *Pediatric Neurology, 3,* 129–135.

Shaywitz, B. A., & Shaywitz, S. E. (1998). Dyslexia. *New England Journal of Medicine, 338,* 307–312.

Siegel, L. S., & Ryan, E. B. (1989). The development of working memory in normally achieving and subtypes of learning disabled children. *Child Development, 60,* 973–980.

Sparrow, S. S., Balla, D., & Cicchetti, D. (1984). *Vineland Adaptive Behavior Scales (Expanded Form).* Circle Pines, MN: American Guidance Service.

Spellacy, F., & Peter, B. (1978). Dyscalculia and elements of the developmental Gerstmann syndrome in school children. *Cortex, 14,* 197–206.

Spreen, O., Risser, A. H., & Edgell, D. (1995). *Developmental neuropsychology.* New York: Oxford University Press.

Spohr, H.-L., & Steinhausen, H.-C. (1987). Follow-up studies of children with fetal alcohol syndrome. *Neuropediatrics, 18,* 13–17.

Stanford, L. D., & Hynd, G. W. (1994). Congruence of behavioral symptomatology in children with ADD/ADDHD, and learning disabilities. *Journal of Learning Disabilities, 27,* 243–254.

Stanovich, K. E. (1981). Relationships between word decoding speed, general name-retrieval ability and reading progress in first-grade children. *Journal of Educational Psychology, 73*(6), 809–815.

Stanovich, K. E., & Siegel, L. S. (1994). Phenotypic performance profile of children with reading disabilities: A regression-based test of the phonological-core variable-difference model. *Journal of Educational Psychology, 86,* 24–53.

Stein, J. (1994). A visual defect in dyslexics. In A. Fawcett & R. Nicolson (Eds.), *Dyslexia in children: Multidisciplinary perspectives* (pp. 137–156). New York: Harvester Wheatsheaf.

Strang, J. D., & Rourke, B. P. (1985). Adaptive behavior of children with specific arithmetic disabilities and associated neuropsychological abilities and deficits. In B. Rourke (Ed.), *Neuropsychology of learning disabilities: Essentials of subtype analysis* (pp. 302–328). New York: Plenum Press.

Stratton, K., Howe, C., & Battaglia, F. (Eds.). (1996). *Fetal alcohol syndrome: Diagnosis, epidemiology, prevention, and treatment.* Washington, DC: National Academy Press.

Strauss, E., Satz, P., & Wada, J. (1990). Note: An examination of the crowding hypothesis in epileptic patients who have under gone the carotid amytal test. *Neuropsychologia, 28,* 1221–1227.

Streissguth, A. P., Barr, H. M., Sampson, P. D., Parrish-Johnson, J. C., Kirchner, G. L., & Martin, D. C. (1986). Attention, distraction and reaction time at age 7 years and prenatal alcohol exposure. *Neurobehavioral Toxicology and Teratology, 8,* 717–725.

Szatmari, P., Saigal, S., Rosenbaum, P., Campbell, D., & King, S. (1990). Psychiatric disorders at five years among children with birthweights <1000 g: A regional perspective. *Developmental Medicine and Child Neurology, 32,* 954–962.

Tallal, P., Miller, S. L., Bedi, G., Byma, G., Wang, X., Nagarajan, S. S., Schreiner, C., Jenkins, W. M., & Merzenich, M. M. (1996). Language comprehension in language-learning impaired children improved with acoustically modified speech. *Science, 271,* 81–84.

Tallal, P., Miller, S. L., & Fitch, R. (1993). Neurobiological basis of speech: A case for the preeminence of temporal processing. In P. Tallal, A. M. Galaburda, R. Liinas, & K. von Euler (Eds.), *Temporal information processing in the nervous system: Special reference to dyslexia and dysplasia* (pp. 27–47). New York: New York Academy of Science.

Taylor, H. G., & Fletcher, J. M. (1983). Biological foundations of "specific learning disabilities": Methods, findings, and future directions. *Journal of Clinical Child Psychology, 12,* 46–65.

Taylor, H. G., & Fletcher, J. M. (1990). Neuropsychological assessments of children. In G. Goldenstein & M. Hersen (Eds.), *Handbook of Psychological Assessment* (pp. 228–255). New York: Pergamon Press.

Teeter, P. A. (1989). Neuropsychological approaches to the remediation of educational deficits. In C. R. Reynolds & E. Fletcher-Janzen (Eds.), *Handbook of clinical child neuropsychology* (pp. 357–376). New York: Plenum Press.

Teeter, P. A., & Semrud-Clikeman, M. (1998). Child clinical neuropsychology: Assessment and intervention for neuropsychiatric and neurodevelopmental disorders of childhood. Boston: Allyn & Bacon.

Torgesen, I. K., Wagner, R. K., & Rashotte, C. A. (1994). Longitudinal studies of phonological processing and reading. *Journal of Learning Disabilities, 27*(5), 276–286.

Truwit, C. L., Barkovich, A. J., Koch, K., & Ferreiro, D. M. (1992). Cerebral palsy: MR findings in 40 patients. *American Journal of Neuroradiology, 13,* 67–78.

Tzavaras, A., Hécaen, H., & LeBras, H. (1970). Le problème de la spécificité du déficit de la reconnaissance du visage humain lors des lésions hémispheriques unilaterales. *Neuropsychologia, 8,* 403–416.

Udwin, O., & Yerle, W. (1991). A cognitive and behavioral phenotype in William Syndrome. *Journal of Clinical and Experimental Neuropsychology, 13,* 232–244.

Udwin, O., Yule, W., & Martin, N. (1987). Cognitive abilities and behavioural characteristics of children with idiopathic infantile hypercalcaemia. *Journal of Child Psychology and Psychiatry, 28,* 297–309.

Vargha-Khadem, F., & Polkey, C. E. (1992). A review of cognitive outcome after hemidecortication in humans. In F. D. Rose & D. A. Johnson (Eds.), *Recovery from brain damage: Reflections and directions* (pp. 137–151). New York: Plenum Press.

Venger, L. A., & Holmomskaya, V. V. (Eds.). (1978). *Diagnostika umst vernogo nazvitja doskolnekov* [Diagnosing the cognitive development of preschool children]. Moscow: Pedagogika.

Vellutino, F. R., & Scanlon, D. M. (1989). Auditory information processing in poor and normal readers. In J. J. Dumont & H. Nakken (Eds.), *Learning disabilities: Vol. 2. Cognitive, social and remedial aspects* (pp. 19–46). Amsterdam: Swets & Zeitlinger.

Volkmar, F. R., & Klin, A. (1998). Asperger syndrome and nonverbal learning disabilities. In E. Schopler, G. Mesibov, & L. Kunce (Vol. Eds.) & E. Schopler & G. Mesibov (Series Ed.). *Asperger Syndrome or High Functioning Autism?* New York: Plenum Press.

Waber, D. P., & Bernstein, J. H. (1985). Assessing children's copy productions of the rey-osterrieth complex figure. *Journal of Clinical and Experimental Neuropsychology, 8,* 563–580.

Waber, D. P., & Bernstein, J. H. (1994). Repetitive graphomotor output in learning-disabled and nonlearning-disabled children: The repeated patterns test. *Developmental Neuropsychology, 10*(1), 51–65.

Walker, H. M., Holmes, D., Todis, B., & Horton, G. (1988). *The Walker Social Skills Curriculum: The ACCESS Program: Adolescent curriculum for communication and effective social skills.* Austin, TX: Pro-Ed.

Walker, H. M., McConnell, S., Holmes, D., Todis, B., Walker, J., & Golden, N. (1988). *The Walker Social-Skills Curriculum: The ACCEPTS Program.* Austin, TX: Pro-Ed.

Wang, P. P., & Bellugi, U. (1994). Evidence from two genetic syndromes for a dissociation between verbal and visual–spatial short-term memory. *Journal of Clinical and Experimental Neuropsychology, 16*(2), 317–322.

Wechsler, D. (1984). *Wechsler Preschool and Primary Scale–Revised.* San Antonio, TX: Psychological Corp.

Wechsler, D. (1997). *Wechsler Intelligence Scale for Children–Third Edition (WISC-III).* San Antonio, TX: Psychological Corp.

Weintraub, S., & Mesulam, M. M. (1983). Developmental learning disabilities of the right hemisphere. *Archives of neurology, 40,* 463–468.

Welsh, M. C., Pennington, B. F., & Groisser, D. B. (1991). A normative-developmental study of executive function: A window on prefrontal function in children. *Developmental Neuropsychology, 7*(2), 131–149.

West, J. R., & Pierce, D. R. (1986). Perinatal alcohol exposure and neuronal damage. In J. R. West (Ed.), *Alcohol and brain development* (pp. 120–157). New York: Oxford University Press.

Williams, K. (1997). *Expressive Vocabulary Test (EVT)*. Circle Pines, MN: American Guidance Service.

Wilson, B. C. (1992). The neuropsychological assessment of the preschool child: A branching model. In F. Boller & J. Grafman (Series Eds.) & I. Rapin & S. J. Segalowitz (Section Eds.), *Handbook of neuropsychology: Vol. 6. Child neuropsychology* (pp. 377–394). Amsterdam: Elsevier.

Wilson, B. C., & Risucci, D. A. (1986). A model for clinical-quantitative classification. Generation I: Application to language-disordered preschool children. *Brain and Language, 27,* 281–309.

Wimmer, H., & Frith, U. (1997). Reading difficulties among English and German children same cause-different manifestation. In C. Pontecorvo (Ed.), *Writing Development: An Interdisciplinary View* (pp. 259–271). Amsterdam: Benjamins.

Wimmer, H., Landerl, K., Linortner, R., & Hummer, P. (1991). The relationship of phonemic awareness to reading acquisition: More consequence than precondition but still important. *Cognition, 40,* 219–249.

Wing, L. (1981). Asperger's syndrome: A clinical account. *Psychological Medicine, 11,* 115–129.

Winogron, H. W., Knights, R. M., & Bawden, H. N. (1984). Neuropsychological deficits following head injury in children. *Journal of Clinical Neuropsychology, 6*(3), 269–286.

Wise, B. W., & Olson, R. K. (1991). Remediating reading disabilities. In J. E. Obrzut & G. W. Hynd (Eds.), *Neuropsychological foundations of learning disabilities: A handbook of issues, methods, and practice* (pp. 631–658). Orlando, FL: Academic Press.

Wise, B. W., Olson, R. K., Anstett, M., Andrews, L., Terjak, M., Schneider, V., Kostuch, J., & Kriho, L. (1989). Implementing a long-term remedial reading study in the public schools: Hardware, software, and real world issues. *Behavior Research Methods and Instrumentation, 21,* 173–180.

Wolf, M. (1986). Rapid alternating stimulus naming in the developmental dyslexias. *Brain and Language, 27,* 360–379.

Wolf, M., & Obregon, M. (1992). Early naming deficits, developmental dyslexias and a specific deficit hypothesis. *Brain and Language, 42,* 219–247.

Yeates, K. O., & Grey, (1998). In Goldstein, Nussbaum, & Beers, (Eds.) *Neuropsychology.* New York: Plenum.

Yeates, K. O., & Taylor, H. G. (1997). Predicting premorbid neuropsychological functioning following pediatric traumatic brain injury. *Journal of Clinical and Experimental Neuropsychology, 19,* 825–837.

Yeates, K. O., Blumenstein, E., Patterson, C. M., & Delis, D. C. (1995). Verbal learning and memory following pediatric closed-head injury. *Journal of the International Neuropsychological Society, 1,* 78–87.

Index

Accessing language, 161–162, 164, 168, 200–201. *See also* Subtests: SN; BPN; MN

ADHD, 153–156, 167, 169–171, 183, 186. *See also* Subtests, A/E Domain

Learning disabilities, co-occurring, 200–201

Validity studies, 192–200

Administration, 10, 22, 32–85

Breaks, to avoid spoiling delayed tests, 32–34

Complex for certain subtests, 22, 45

Ease of, 10

Item repetition, 47–48

Modified administration, 36–37, 39–40, 42

Prompting, querying, 47

Recording responses, 45–46

Self-correction, 47

Start/Discontinue, rules for, 45

Subtest administration, *see* Subtests

Subtest-by-subtest rules for, 48–85

Teaching tasks, 48

Timing, 46

Age, computation of, 88

Appendices of the NEPSY Manual, 99

Appendix A, 92, 96

Appendix B, 120

Appendix C, 99

Appendix D, 102

Appendix F, 93

Arithmetic disorder, 175, 179, 181. *See also* Gerstmann's Syndrome

Arrows, *see* Subtests

Asperger's Disorder, 181–183, 237–243

Assessment:

Core Assessment, 8, 14, 34, 36

Dissociation of subcomponents, 16, 18

Expanded Assessment, 8, 14, 34, 36

Flexibility, 13–14, Fig. 1.1, 15, 34

Full Assessment, 8, 14, 35–36

Purposes in children, 7

Selective Assessment, 34, 36

Special Needs, of, 35–44

Attentional Problems (ADHD), 44, 197–199

Autistic Disorder, 40–41

Blind child, 37–38

Hearing-impaired, 39–40

Language Impairment, 43–44

Motor Deficits, 41–43

Associated movements, 171, 174

Attention, 5, 155–156

Deficits in, 155–156, 165, 185, 192–200

Modulation of, 5

Attention/Executive Functions Domain, *see* Subtests

Auditory acuity, 161

Auditory Attention and Response Set, *see* Subtests

Autistic Disorder, 159, 165, 167, 171, 175, 181–184. *See also* Clinical applications
  High-functioning Autistic Disorder, 237–239
  Validity studies of, 209–214

Basic physiological functions, 5
Blind child, assessment of, *see* Assessment
Block Construction, *see* Subtests
Body Part Naming, *see* Subtests
Brain, 5–6, 7–8, 13
  Blocks I-III, 5
  Damage, 7–8, 115
    Age at time of event, 8
    Focal and diffuse, 8, 115
    Lateralized or localized, 8
    Neural plasticity, 8, 115
    Recovery of function, 8, 115
    Pathology, inferences about, 13
Breaks, *see* Administration

Case reports, 224–286
  ADHD case, 224–234
  NLD case, 244–286
Clinical Applications, 191–218
  Assessing the child with FAS, 215–218
  Diagnosis of ADHD, 192–199. *See also* ADHD
  Diagnosis of Autistic Disorder, 172, 209–214. *See also* Autistic Disorder
  Diagnosis of reading disability, 200–209. *See also* Dyslexia
Commission errors, 156–157
Comparisons at the subtest level, 119
Complex cognitive functions, 5–7, 115
Comprehension of Instructions, *see* Subtests

Computer Scoring, 123
  Print-out of, 250–256
Confidence interval, *see* Interpretation; Scoring
Constructional apraxia, 176, 179. *See also* Gerstmann Syndrome
Convergence insufficiency, 157, 172, 176
Core Analyses, 88
Core Domain, *see* Scores; Scoring; Subtests
Core Subtests, *see* Scores; Scoring; Subtests
Core Subtest Scaled Scores, *see* Scores
Corpus Callosum, anterior, 171

Data worksheet, Appendix A, 289–293
Design Copying, 49–50
Design Fluency, *see* Subtests
Developmental trends, 13
Diagnostic Behavioral Cluster, *see* Interpretation
Differential diagnosis, 235–243
Discontinue rules, *see* Administration
Domain Analyses page, 88–89, 96–97
Down Syndrome, 186
Dyslexia, 34–35, 161, 164, 166, 176
  Neural signature, 166
  Predictors of, 201
  Selective Assessment for, 34–35
  Validity studies, 200–209
Dyspraxia, *see* Motor programming

Epilepsy, left temporal lobe, 186
Error analysis, 46
Executive dysfunction, 154–160, 163, 172–174, 181, 184, 186–187, 192–200, 213
Executive functions, 5, 153–154, 158

Expanded subtests, *see* Scores; Scoring; Subtests

Fetal Alcohol Effects, 216
Fetal Alcohol Syndrome (FAS), 153–159, 176, 179, 183, 215–216. *See also* Assessment
Fine motor coordination, 171–172, 179–180
Finger agnosia, 175. *See also* Gerstmann Syndrome
Finger Discrimination, *see* Subtests
Fingertip Tapping, *see* Subtests
Follow-up evaluation, 220
Frequencies, 121, 129–130
Frontal cortex, 153–154, 156
Frontal lobe damage, 154, 167. *See also* Executive dysfunction

Gerstmann Syndrome, 169, 175
Graphomotor problems, 176

Hearing-impairment, 39–40, 167, 171
Hemiplegia, 41–42, 215
High-functioning autism, *see* Autistic Disorder
History of NEPSY, 1–4
Hydrocephalus, 178

Imitating Hand Positions, *see* Subtests
Information processing, 5
Interference, 187–188
Interpretation of NEPSY, 104–152
    Child vs. adult tests, differences in, 114–115
    Clinical Level, 106–114
        Diagnostic behavioral clusters, 111–113, 277

Primary and secondary deficits, 107–113
    Analyzing & specifying, 111–112, 140–142, Fig. 4.1, 140–142, Fig. 7.1, 277
    Identifying, 107–109
Core Domain interpretability, 116
Goals, 104, 117
Integration of all information, 115–117, 145–151
Neuroanatomic axes, by, 113–114
Neurocognitive development, 138–140
Psychometric Level, interpretation at, 105–106
    Cumulative percentages, 135–136
    Differences, within and across domains, 118–128
    Differences between domains, 129–134
    Pairwise comparison, 125
    Significance levels, 121–124, 133–134
    Smoothed percentile ranks, 135
Step-by-step process, 117–151
Verification of interpretation, 145–147

Judgement of line orientation, 178

Kinesthetic processing, 171–172
Knock and Tap, *see* Subtests

Language disorders, 161–162, 204, 210
    Expressive, 162, 184–185
    Dysnomia, 20, 160–162, 164, 183–184

Language disorders (*continued*)
  Specific Verbal Dyspraxia, *see*
    Oromotor Dyspraxia
  Global subtype, 161, 164–165, 167–
    168, 171, 184–186
  Reading disabilities, in, 201
  Receptive, 161, 165, 184–185
  Specific Comprehension sub-
    type, 161, 165–167, 184–186
Language Domain, *see* Subtests
Learning disabilities, 183, 200–202
List Learning, *see* Subtests
Localizing, cautions against, 8–9
Lurian Theory, *see* Theoretical Foun-
  dations
Lymphocytic leukemia, 176

Manual Motor Sequences, *see* Subtests
Materials:
  Child-friendly, 19
  Placement of, 30
Mathematics disability, 201–202
Memory for Faces, *see* Subtests
Memory for Names, *see* Subtests
Memory span, 184–186
Misarticulation, 169, 204
Model of NEPSY, 9–10
Modified Administration, *see* Adminis-
  tration
Monitoring, 153–155
Motor persistence, 158
Motor programming, 170–174, 196,
  200–201, 205

Naming, *see* Accessing language; Language Disorders: Dysnomia
Narrative Memory, *see* Subtests
Neural networks, 115. *See also* Complex
  cognitive functions

Neurocognitive development, *see* Interpretation
Neuropsychological assessment, purposes of, 7
Nonverbal Learning Disability, 169,
  172, 175, 179, 240–243. *See also*
  Case Reports

Observations as a part of evaluation, 30
Obsessive-Compulsive Disorder
  (OCD), 181, 235–237
Omission errors (OE), 156–157
Oromotor dyspraxia, 160–161, 163,
  167–168
Oromotor Sequences, *see* Subtests

Parietal lobe, 175. *See also* Gerstmann
  Syndrome
Patterns of deficiencies, 7–8
Percentages, cumulative, 22
Percentile ranks, 22
Phonological Processing, *see* Subtests
  Deficit in, 167–168, 200–201, 204–
    205
Planning, 153–155, 158
Plasticity, 215
Primacy effect, 188
Primary deficits, *see* Interpretation
Processing speed, 164, 171
PTSD, 158
Publisher, 24
Purposes of NEPSY, 9–10

Qualitative Observations, *see* Scores

Rapport, establishing/maintaining,
  31–32
Reading disability, 200–209. *See also*
  Dyslexia

Recency effect, 188
Recommendations
  Follow-up, 287
  Handwriting/fine motor coordination, 284
  Impulsivity, distractibility, and secondary attention, 280
  Language and reading, 281–282
  Mathematical and sequencing skills, 282–283
  Organizational and study skills, 279–280
  School and instructional methods, 278–279
  Sensory, 284–285
  Social problems and behavior, 285–286
  Treatment, 276–278
  Visuospatial, 283–284
Recording responses, see Administration
Recruitment, 165
References, 294–307
Reliabilities, 16–17, 219–222
Repetition of Nonsense Words, see Subtests
Reports:
  Referral Information, 226
  Relevant Background Information, 228–229
  Test Observations and Interview, 231
  Test Results and Interpretation, 235
Response inhibition, 153–155, 158, 160
Route-Finding, see Subtests

Scores, 7, 14, 18, 22
  Classification levels of, 100
  Complex scores, 22

Core Domain Scores
  Mean, 15
  Reliabilities of, 16, 223
Core Subtest score mean, 16
Performance levels, 106. See also Classification levels
Qualitative Observations (QO), 7, 18, 47, 137
  ADHD, in, 193
Standard Scores, 14
Supplemental Scores (SS), 18, 90, 136
Types of scores, 22
Scoring, 22, 87–103
  Complex scoring, subtests with, 89–96
  Computer scoring, 123
  Computing Core and Expanded Subtest scores, 96–97
  Computing Core Domain Scores, 97–99
  Computing raw scores, 88–89
  Confidence interval, 98
  Qualitative Observations, 99–102
  Raw score conversions, 92
  Subtests, scoring of specific, see Subtests
  Supplemental Scores (SS), 99–100
Search strategy, 156–157
Secondary deficits, see Impairments
Set, maintaining, shifting, 155, 160
Significance levels, 124
Small for gestational age (SGA), 170, 215
Social-perceptual deficit, 172, 182–184, 213
Sound discrimination, 163
Special Needs, assessment of, see Assessment

Speech-sound patterns, conceptualiza-
tion of, 163
Speed and fluency factor, 154, 159,
164
Speeded Naming, *see* Subtests
Standardization, 3–12
Bias Review, 10
Over-sampling of minority groups,
10–11
Sample, 3, 10–12
Standard Scores, *see* Scores
Start rules, *see* Administration
Statue, *See* Subtests
Strengths of NEPSY, 10–20
Subtests, comprehensive information
by domain:
Attention/Executive Domain, in,
153–154, 193–194, 203, 209–
210, 216–217
Auditory Attention and Re-
sponse Set:
Administration, 56–58
Analysis, 155–156
Recording, 94–95, Fig. 3.2,
95
Scoring, 93–96
Design Fluency:
Administration, 75–76
Analysis, 158–159
Knock and Tap:
Administration, 83–84
Analysis, 160
Statue:
Administration, 72–73
Analysis, 158
Tower:
Administration, 54–56
Analysis, 154–155

Visual Attention:
Administration, 63–64
Analysis, 156–158
Scoring, 90–91
Language Domain, in, 160–162,
194, 204, 210, 216–218
Body Part Naming:
Administration, 48–49
Analysis, 162
Comprehension of Instruc-
tions:
Administration, 65–66
Analysis, 165–166
Oromotor Sequences:
Administration, 81–82
Analysis, 168–169
Phonological Processing:
Administration, 50–51
Analysis, 163–164
Repetition of Nonsense Words:
Administration, 76–77
Analysis, 166–167
Speeded Naming:
Administration, 58–59
Analysis, 164–165
Scoring, 91–92
Verbal Fluency:
Administration, 78–79
Analysis, 167–168
Memory/Learning Domain, in,
182–183, 196–197, 206–207,
212–213, 216–217
List Learning:
Administration, 74–75
Analysis, 186–188
Memory for Faces:
Administration, 52–54
Analysis, 182–183

Memory for Names:
  Administration, 60–61
  Analysis, 183–184
Narrative Memory:
  Administration, 69–70
  Analysis, 184–185
Sentence Repetition:
  Administration, 71–72
  Analysis, 185–186
Sensorimotor Domain, in, 169–171,
  195–196, 205, 210–211, 216–
  217
  Finger Discrimination:
    Administration, 82–83
    Analysis, 174–175
  Fingertip Tapping:
    Administration, 61–62
    Analysis, 171
  Imitating Hand Positions:
    Administration, 66–67
    Analysis, 171–172
  Manual Motor Sequences:
    Administration, 79–81
    Analysis, 173–174
  Visuomotor Precision:
    Administration, 67–68
    Analysis, 172–173
    Scoring, 89–90, Fig. 3.1, 91
Visuospatial Domain, in, 175–176,
  196, 205–206, 211–212, 216–218
  Arrows:
    Administration, 59–60
    Analysis, 178–179
  Block Construction:
    Administration, 70–71
    Analysis, 179–180
  Design Copying:
    Administration, 49–50

  Analysis, 176–177
  Scoring, 92–93
  Route-Finding:
    Administration, 77–78
    Analysis, 180–182
Subtests, general concepts:
  Core, 8
  Correlation with Core Domain
    Scores, 22
  Expanded, 8
  Normed on same sample, 12–13
  Rules for administration of, see Ad-
    ministration
  Supplemental Score page, 89
  Supplemental Scores (SS), 90. See also
    Scores

Tactile perception, 169, 171, 174
Test Conditions, 29–34
Test Considerations, 34–35
Test Yourself, 25–27, 85–86, 103,
  151–152, 223, 287–288
Theoretical foundations of NEPSY,
  3–7
  Luria, A. R., 3
    Brain regions, see Brain, Blocks
      I–III
    Primary deficit, 6–7
    Secondary deficit, 6–7
    Working brain, 8
Tourette's Disorder, 170, 175, 181
Tower, see Subtests
Traumatic Brain Injury (TBI), 185,
  187, 215

Verbal Fluency, 205. See also Subtests
Verbal memory deficit, 196–197, 206–
  207

Very low birth weight (VLBW), 170, 215
Visual Attention, *see* Subtests
Visual field cut, 178–179
Visual memory test, lack of, 23
Visual-spatial deficit, 175–176, 178–179, 180–181. *See also* Parietal lobes

Visuomotor deficit, 172, 176, 179
Visuomotor Precision, *see* Subtests

Weaknesses of NEPSY, 20–24
Williams Syndrome, 175, 178, 182
Working memory, 154–155, 157, 163, 165–166
Written language disability, 202–203

Acknowledgments

The authors would like to thank Alan Kaufman, Series Editor of the *Essentials* books, for conceptualizing the idea of a series of clear, simple guides for the administration and interpretation of specific tests. We are honored to have NEPSY included. We thank him also for his patience. Thanks also go to Tracey Belmont, our editor at John Wiley & Sons, who worked with us in a kind, patient, and caring manner, even though our contact was only through the technological magic of e-mail. Her guidance was very helpful.

Sally Kemp would like to thank her co-authors for their help and insight. Thanks also go to her daughters, all grown now, but supportive of NEPSY through so many years, and, most especially, her husband, Garry, who proofread, looked up citations, cooked, cleaned, and was generally the most wonderful of helpmates over the extended period of time it took to compose this guide. A special note of gratitude to Per Udden, M.D., whose insatiable thirst to find out what lies beneath children's learning disorders first inspired Dr. Kemp to pursue a Ph.D., and whose support often made it possible. That same thirst for answers fathered the Rodin Remediation Academy, an international multi-disciplinary research body whose biannual symposia have been an inspiration to me and to outstanding investigators from around the world. Through their careful research answers are beginning to emerge. Thank you also to Dr. Kemp's colleagues at Tulsa Developmental Pediatrics and Center for Family Psychology from whom she has learned so much. Finally, thanks to the children with whom it is the privilege of all pediatric neuropsychologists to work. Daily, we are amazed by their coping skills and tenaciousness in trying to overcome their problems. They are our inspiration.

About the Authors

Sally Kemp is a developmental psychologist with a subspecialty in neuropsychology. She is a partner at Tulsa Developmental Pediatrics and Center for Family Psychology, a multidisciplinary practice in Tulsa, Oklahoma. She is also an adjunct Associate Professor in Pediatrics at the University of Oklahoma Medical College—Tulsa and a practicum supervisor in the Clinical Psychology program at the University of Tulsa. Dr. Kemp began her vocational career in nursing; later returned to the university to train as a teacher, and for 20 years taught middle school, worked with LD children and was a school psychometrist in several settings, both public and private, across the country. Always, she had concerns about the children who were not learning for reasons that appeared to be beyond their ability to change. Her medical background caused her to question the neurological bases of such difficulties. Her pursuit to find some answers for these children finally took her to Teachers College, Columbia University for doctoral study with Ursula Kirk, a pioneer in addressing the neurological underpinnings of learning and developmental disorders. She has been privileged to collaborate with Dr. Kirk since those days, and since 1987 with Marit Korkman, who, at that time, first brought her Finnish NEPSY to Columbia for Dr. Kirk's review. Dr. Kemp is co-author with Drs. Korkman and Kirk of the present NEPSY (Korkman, Kirk, & Kemp, 1998). She is a frequent presenter at workshops and conferences, as well as a scientist-practitioner, continuing research and clinical work. Areas of particular interest for Dr. Kemp are dyslexia, ADHD, autism, and Asperger's syndrome.

Ursula Kirk is the author of the *Neuropsychology of Language, Reading, and Spelling* (Kirk, 1983) and numerous studies in aspects of children's learning difficulties. After many years as a teacher and administrator, she pursued doctoral study at Teachers College, Columbia University and subsequently postdoctoral study in pediatric neuropsychology in Boston. During this time of ferment in neuropsychology, she was privileged to learn from pioneers in adult and developmental neuropsychology: Edith Kaplan, Martha Denckla, and Jane Holmes Bernstein. Dr. Kirk brought back to her beloved New York the insight, empathy, and sensitivity of these early pioneers and sought to develop a program at Teacher's College, Columbia, which would apply the emerging principles of neuropsychology to children's developmental disorders and learning disabilities. Ultimately, the Program in Neuroscience and Education emerged, which she has headed for 15 years. Currently, it is one of the Applied Educational Psychology programs in the Department of Health and Behavior Studies at Teachers College, Columbia University. As well as being a co-author of NEPSY, Dr. Kirk's research interests include the role of executive functions in emerging cognitive competencies, and developmental processes that underlie typical and atypical language, graphomotor, visuospatial, learning and memory skills.

Marit Korkman is also a pioneer in the field of child neuropsychology, having developed the first neuropsychological assessment designed specifically for children and based on Lurian principles. The original NEPSY was her doctoral dissertation, but she continued to hone and develop it, publishing it in her native Finland, as well as Denmark and Sweden. The senior author of the present NEPSY, Dr. Korkman was for many years a pediatric neuropsychologist at the Children's Castle Hospital in Helsinki, as well as a highly-respected researcher. A prolific and internationally productive investigator in a wide-ranging array of acquired and developmental disorders, Dr. Korkman has also taught pediatric neuropsychology for the post-doctoral specialization in neuropsychology in Finland and at the University of Maastricht (Netherlands). She is presently a Professor of Child Neuropsychology at Abo Academy University in Finland and a senior neuropsychologist at Helsinki University Central Hospital, Hospital for Children and Adolescents, Helsinki, Finland. Dr. Korkman divides her time between Brussels, where her husband is with the European Union, and Finland, where she continues to carry out research and teach. Particular research interests have been language and reading disorders, epilepsy, the effects of low birth weight and Fetal Alcohol Syndrome. She is a frequent presenter at conferences and workshops all over the world.

Printed in the United States
48466LVS00002B/177